PAGE 36 **ON THE ROAD**

YOUR COMPLETE DESTINATION GUIDE
In-depth reviews, detailed listings
and insider tips

Accommodation p208

La Palma
p173

Lanzarote
p92

Fuerteventura
p70

La Gomera
p157

Tenerife
p115

El Hierro
p194

**Gran
Canaria**
p38

D0973245

PAGE 251 **SURVIVAL GUIDE**

VITAL PRACTICAL INFORMATION TO
HELP YOU HAVE A SMOOTH TRIP

Language

THIS EDITION WRITTEN AND RESEARCHED BY

Josephine Quintero
Stuart Butler

welcome to the Canary Islands

A Dramatic Landscape

The Canary Islands boast near-perfect year-round temperatures, which means whether it's summer or winter you can enjoy the dramatic and varied landscape here that you usually have to cross continents to experience. Marvel at the subtropical greenery of La Gomera's national park, the pine-forested peaks in Gran Canaria's mountainous interior, or the tumbling waterfalls of La Palma. Then contrast all this lushness with the extraordinary barren flatlands flanking Tenerife's El Teide, the surreal play of colours of Lanzarote's lava fields and Fuerteventura's endless plains, punctuated by cacti, scrub and lots (and lots) of goats.

Be a Good Sport

It is this very diversity of landscape, coupled with those predictable sunny days, that makes outdoor activities so accessible and varied here. Hike the signposted footpaths that criss-cross the islands, ranging from meandering trails to trudging up mountains and across volcanic fields; scuba dive in enticing warm waters, marvelling at more than 350 species of fish (and the odd shipwreck or two); kick back with a glass of sparkling wine on the deck of a catamaran cruiser; or pump up that adrenalin by catching the wind and the waves on a kiteboard or windsurf board. For the slightly less energetic, there are camel rides, rounds of golf, horse treks and boat rides.

Looming volcanoes, prehistoric sites, lush pine forests, lunar landscapes, camel rides, and miles of pristine Sahara-style sand dunes. Yes, there is another world beyond the Canary Islands' seafront resorts.

(left) Endemic plants in the Malpais de Güimar, Tenerife
(below) Children on La Gomera

Or Just Relax...

If your idea of a perfect holiday is that enticing combo of R&R, you've come to the right place. The most obvious place to relax here is on a beach, and there are plenty to choose from, ranging from the soft rolling dunes in Fuerteventura to the wide arcs of golden sand in Tenerife. Others may like to gloss up the self-pampering stakes by visiting a spa. Thalassotherapy centres are spouting forth throughout the islands and offer a tempting range of treatments and massages. There's also a tidal wave of ocean-front bars where you can enjoy a cocktail at sunset contemplating nothing more challenging than the gently lapping sea.

Superb Art & Architecture

While the Canary Islands may not boast the grand-slam museums of Spain's big mainland cities, there is plenty to compel art an-dculture aficionados here. Surrealist fans should check out world-acclaimed painter Óscar Domínguez' spectacular canvases in his Santa Cruz de Tenerife home town, while the huge abstract sculptures of local lads Martín Chirino and César Manrique are near impossible to miss on Gran Canaria and Lanzarote. If buildings are your thing, look for the emblematic wooden balconies, leafy internal patios and brightly painted facades that typify vernacular Canarian architecture.

18°W   17°W   16°W

30°N

Parque Nacional de la Caldera de Taburiente
Walk stunning trails (p187)

San Sebastián de la Gomera
Buy the delicious local palm honey (p162)

La Laguna
Visit a superbly preserved historical town (p126)

El Teide
Hike around this unique landscape (p140)

29°N

Roque de los Muchachos
(2426m)

Los Llanos de Aridane

Santa Cruz de la Palma

La Laguna

Santa Cruz de Tenerife

Volcán San Antonio
(657m)

Los Canarios de Fuencaliente

LA PALMA

Puerto de la Cruz

TENERIFE

La Orotava

Puerto de Santiago

Pico del Teide
(3718m)

Alto de Garajonay
Trek up to the peak (p165)

Alto de Garajonay
(1487m)

San Sebastián de la Gomera

Playa de las Américas

Valle Gran Rey

LA GOMERA

Playa Santiago

Los Cristianos

28°N

EL HIERRO

Valverde

Tamaduste

Puerto de la Estaca

Malpaso
(1501m)

La Restinga

Playa de las Américas
It's time for dawn-to-dusk partying (p149)

Santa Cruz de Tenerife
Party hard – it's Carnaval time (p125)

La Restinga
Dive the watery depths (p203)

ATLANTIC OCEAN

27°N

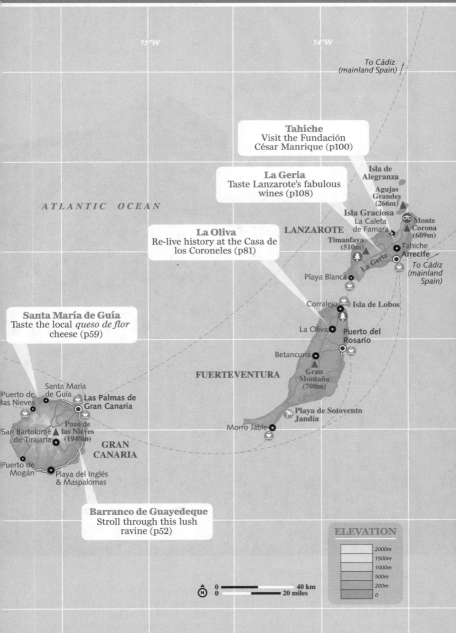

ATLANTIC OCEAN

To Cádiz
(mainland Spain)

Tahiche
Visit the Fundación
César Manrique (p100)

La Geria
Taste Lanzarote's fabulous
wines (p108)

Isla de
Alegranza

Agujas
Grandes
(266m)

La Oliva
Re-live history at the Casa de
los Coroneles (p81)

Isla Graciosa
La Caleta
de Famara

LANZAROTE

Monte
Corona
(609m)

Timanfaya
(510m)

Tahiche
Arrecife

To Cádiz
(mainland
Spain)

Santa María de Guía
Taste the local *queso de flor*
cheese (p59)

Playa Blanca

Corralejo   Isla de Lobos

La Oliva   Puerto del
Rosario

Betancuria

FUERTEVENTURA

Gran
Montaña
(708m)

Santa María
de Guía

Puerto de
las Nieves

Las Palmas de
Gran Canaria

Pozo de
las Nieves
(1949m)

San Bartolomé
de Tirajana

**GRAN
CANARIA**

Playa de Sotovento
Jandía

Morro Jable

Puerto de
Mogán

Playa del Inglés
& Maspalomas

Barranco de Guayedeque
Stroll through this lush
ravine (p52)

ELEVATION

	2000m
	1500m
	1000m
	500m
	200m
	0

Ⓝ 0 ——————— 40 km
    0 ——————— 20 miles

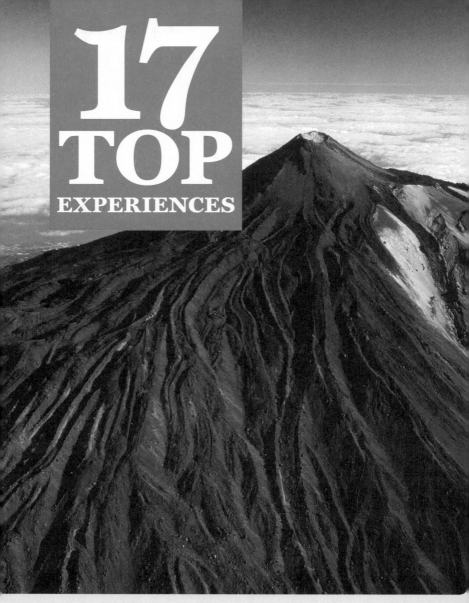

El Teide Magnificence

1 Start off gradually with a gentle hike around the base of Tenerife's El Teide (p140), kidding yourself that you are enjoying a stroll around the surface of the moon; it really *is* that extra-ordinary. The trails take you deep into an alien landscape with red, yellow and brown craters resembling giant prehistoric molehills, bizarre volcanic rock formations and pebble-like lapilli. Top it off by taking the cable car to the summit for the ultimate heady experience. Wrap up warm, though; it can get pretty chilly up there in the clouds.

Carnaval!

2 The Canarians love a good party and, in Santa Cruz de Tenerife, the fiesta spirit reaches its sequin-bedecked crescendo during the annual carnival. Festivities generally high-kick off with a flourish in early February and last for around three weeks, featuring gala performances, fancy-dress competitions, fireworks and Rio-style parades. All the islands celebrate Carnaval with dawn-to-dusk frivolity and distinctive customs, so book your accommodation way ahead (if you intend to go to bed, that is).

Fuerteventura's Stunning Beaches

3 Some of the Canary Islands' most glorious beaches are located in Fuerteventura. If you want to escape the rows of sunbeds topped by slowly roasting tourists, head for the northwest of the island and the wild beaches and thundering surf around El Cotillo. Windsurfers can catch the waves at Playa de Sotovento de Jandía, while more watersports are on offer at Morro Jable's spectacular arc of a beach. For paddling tots and kids' activities, check out family-friendly beaches like Costa Calma and Caleta de Fuste.

Barranco de Guayadeque

5 The best time to visit this lush ravine in Gran Canaria (p52) is springtime, when the almond blossom is in brilliant pink-and-white bloom. Year-round, however, it is leafy and lovely, flanked by steep mountains where caves have been dug out for restaurants, bars and even a chapel. Time your visit for a mealtime, when you can dine deep inside the rock. Walk off your lunch by following one of the trails, which will reward you with stunning views stretching right to the sea.

Wrinkly Potatoes

4 They may not sound like the most appetising dish in the world, but the ubiquitous *papas arrugadas* (wrinkly potatoes) are a lot tastier in the flesh (skins and all). Called *papas*, the Native American name, these small new potatoes are boiled and coated with coarse sea salt. The main treat here is the accompaniment: a choice of up to three sauces – *mojo picón*, *mojo verde* and *mojo de coriander* (laced with chilli, parsley and coriander respectively). Washed down with an ice-cold *cerveza* (beer), they sure beat a bag of potato chips...

La Laguna's Historic Old Quarter

6 Visit Tenerife's La Laguna (p126) for a stroll around one of the best-preserved historical quarters on the island: all cobbled alleys, spruced-up merchants' houses and pine-balconied mansions. The unique vernacular architecture and layout was originally provided as a model for many colonial towns in the Americas. La Laguna may have an air of old-fashioned history about it, but it is far from dull. There is a tangible youthful energy about the place. It has a vigorous nightlife, and plenty of terrace bars and cafes where you can kick back with a coffee or beer.

Street Markets

7 Glossy blue-black aubergines, blood-red tomatoes, plump purple figs, bunches of fragrant mint and parsley, gigantic garlic bulbs, long shiny green peppers... Who can resist a street market? Throughout the islands, weekly street markets concentrate on local produce, with farmers selling fresh fruit, vegetables, meats and cheeses. Look for specialities of the area such as the creamy *queso de flor* from Gran Canaria, or Fuerteventura's famous Majorero goat's cheese – ask for a taste.

Wine Tasting in Lanzarote

8 La Geria (p108) is not your standard bucolic viticulture scenario of lush green vineyards, scenic rows of vines and verdant rolling hills. On Lanzarote, wine cultivation is, well, extraordinary, with vines grown in dimpled craters within volcanic stone semicircles called *zocos*. Wine tasting is made really easy here: you can visit most of the main bodegas on the same stretch of bumpy road in La Geria, facilitating an easy sampling tour, including a taste of the famous *malvasía* sweet wine, once the tipple of the European aristocracy. Swot up first at the nearby wine museum.

CAROLA KOSEROWSKY/PHOTOLIBRARY ©

César Manrique Art & Architecture

9 A native of Lanzarote, the late César Manrique's lingering influence on the art and architecture of the island is very special. That rich forest green you see is the specified colour of door and window frames everywhere here. Then there are those huge, zany steel sculptures decorating so many roundabouts. Visit Manrique's former home, built around a cave and housing fabulous works by masters like Picasso and Klee, plus his other top sights: the Cueva de los Verdes and Jameos del Agua (p104), which combine magical natural phenomena with Manrique's flair for architectural wizardry.

MARC DOZIER/PHOTOLIBRARY ©

Casa de los Coroneles

10 Even if you are not an art buff, this 17th-century fortified manor house in Fuerteventura's La Oliva (p81) is a real show-stopper, located like an oasis overlooked by a cookie-cutter volcano shaped in a perfect geometric triangle. Wander around the building, taking in the magnificent carved wooden balconies made of canary pine and the cool inner courtyard studded with lofty palms. Then get into smock-and-beret mode and dip in and out of the galleries on the 1st floor, which are used for temporary exhibitions by local painters and sculptors.

JUERGEN RICHTER/PHOTOLIBRARY ©

DAMIEN SIMONIS/LONELY PLANET IMAGES ©

Hiking the Caldera de Taburiente

11 Put your best foot forward and discover the spectacular Parque Nacional de la Caldera de Taburiente (p187) by hiking one of the national park's numerous trails. For many, the pine forests and curtains of clouds slipping over the side of the sheer caldera walls add up to what is quite simply the finest walking experience in the archipelago. Walks here range from simple hour-long strolls to demanding day-long feats of endurance. Don't forget to check out the informative displays at the park visitor centre beforehand!

Surfing El Quemao

12 Known to surfers as the 'Hawaii of the Atlantic', the Canary Islands are full of world-class surf spots, but none comes with a bigger rep than Lanzarote's radical left reef break, El Quemao (p106). For expert surfers able to snag a wave off the locals, these huge barrels promise the ultimate rush. For those not quite up to El Quemao standards, nearby La Caleta de Famara offers ideal conditions for learners to get on a board and get wet.

Alto de Garajonay

13 Peeking above the clouds that lie across La Gomera for much of the year, Alto de Garajonay (p165) is La Gomera's highest peak (1487m). Ascending to its summit offers the chance to get to know the fascinating *laurisilva* (laurel) forests that sit like a bright green wig atop this small circular island. The walk is easy but the views from the summit, which take in these forests and (on clear days) snow-dusted El Teide on Tenerife, are anything but ordinary.

CARLOS VILLOCH – MAGICSEA.COM/ALAMY ©

Diving El Hierro

14 Get in a tangled embrace with an octopus, blow kisses to a wrasse or two and strike a pose with a crabby crab. Under the waves of southern El Hierro (p203) is a hidden wonderland of weird and wonderful aquatic creatures, which combined with warm waters and reliable diving conditions, make this one of the most exciting diving locations in all the North Atlantic. Getting underwater is also easy here with several dive schools offering anything from 'try dives' to full courses.

Tenerife Nightlife

15 Let your hair down in the mega resort of Las Américas (p149), where you can drink yourself silly in a British pub, dance to pounding beats in a state-of-the-art nightclub, relax to gentle jazz in a late-night haunt or pop from starlit bar to starlit bar along the beachfront. But there's much more to Tenerife nightlife than the excess of the resorts. From La Laguna's student-fuelled *marcha* (nightlife; p129) to a highbrow opera in the stunning Auditorio de Tenerife in Santa Cruz (p119), Tenerife knows how to party.

Searching For Moby Dick

16 Human tourists aren't the only ones who like swimming in the seas off the Canary Islands. Pods of whales and schools of dolphins also love a good splash about in these warm waters. The channel between Tenerife and La Gomera is their favourite holiday destination, and if you're staying on either of these islands a whale- and dolphin-watching boat tour is an absolute must.

Gourmet San Sebastián

17 The western isles are renowned for having the best food in the archipelago and little La Gomera seems to have an excess of local delicacies. Get to know some of them by buzzing around San Sebastián's market (p162) in search of the island's wonderfully tangy palm honey, made, as you might guess, from the sap of palm trees. Another local Gomeran speciality worth sniffing out is *almogrote*, a spicy cheese pâté made with hard cheese, pepper and tomato, and spread on bread.

need to know

Currency
» Euro (€)

Language
» Spanish

When to Go

La Palma
GO Mar–Apr

Tenerife
GO Jan–Apr

La Gomera
GO Feb–Apr

El Hierro
GO Feb–Apr

Gran Canaria
GO Feb–Apr

Lanzarote
GO Feb–Mar

Fuerteventura
GO Mar–May

Arid desert, hot climate
Arid desert, moderate climate

High Season
(Dec–Apr & Jul–Aug)

» Coincides with Christmas, carnival season and Easter celebrations

» Accommodation prices are highest in January and February

» Mid-summer is holiday time on the Spanish mainland, so expect more tourists

» July and August are the hottest months of the year, but temperatures rarely hit higher than 38°C

Shoulder Season
(May–Jun & Sep–Nov)

» Temperature does not differ hugely from summer, although nights are cooler

» Fewer tourists visit in the autumn overall

» Higher altitudes, particularly in Gran Canaria and Tenerife, can be far cooler with some fog

Your Daily Budget

Budget less than
€60

» Budget hotel room (with shared bathroom): €25–35

» Excellent markets and supermarkets for self-caterers

» Check out museums with free entry, parks, churches and walks

Midrange
€60– 120

» Double room in midrange hotel: €55–75

» Three-course meal in midrange restaurant: €25, plus wine

» Top museums, galleries and sights: average €6

Top End over
€120

» Four-star hotel room: €110

» Fine dining for lunch and dinner

» Car rental from €35 per day

Money

» ATMs are widely available. Credit cards are accepted in most hotels, restaurants and shops.

Visas

» Generally not required for stays of up to 90 days; some nationalities will need a Schengen visa.

Mobile Phones

» Buy a pay-as-you-go mobile with credit from €25. Local SIM cards are widely available and can be used in European and Australian mobile phones.

Accommodation

» If you are looking for a place to stay, refer to the Accommodation chapter (p208).

Websites

» **Lonely Planet** (www.lonelyplanet .com/canary -islands) Destination information.

» **Canary Islands Government** (www .gobiernodecanarias .org, in Spanish) Local government information.

» **Official Tourism Office** (www.turismode canarias.com) Region-wide and island-specific information.

» **Rural Tourism** (www .turismoruralcanarias .com) Rural accommodation.

» **Daily English-language news** (www .islandconnections.eu) Daily news.

Exchange Rates

Australia	A$1	€0.75
Canada	C$1	€0.74
Japan	¥100	€0.90
UK	£1	€1.14
New Zealand	NZ$1	€0.51
US	US$1	€0.71

For current exchange rates see www.xe.com.

Important Numbers

If you are calling within the Canaries, all numbers will have a total of nine digits beginning with 9.

country code	✆34
directory enquiries	✆11818
international access code	✆00
ambulance	✆61
police	✆112

Arriving

» **Aeropuerto de Gran Canaria**
Regular buses to Las Palmas. Taxis – €28; around 25 minutes (p51)

» **Aeropuerto de Lanzarote**
Regular buses to Arrecife. Taxis – €11; around 15 minutes (p99)

» **Aeropuerto Tenerife Sur**
Regular buses to Los Cristianos. Taxis – €18; around 30 minutes (p155)

» **Aeropuerto de Fuerteventura**
Regular buses to Puerto del Rosario. Taxis – €7; around 15 minutes (p75)

Driving in the Canary Islands

Driving in the Canary Islands is a pleasure – honest. Larger islands have motorways (auto-pistas) that connect with the airport and to major resorts, while secondary roads are, over-all, well surfaced with a minimum of potholes. Aside from those predictable Sunday drivers, they are also generally light on traffic. If you are exploring the more mountainous interior of La Palma or Gran Canaria, consider a car with at least a 1600cc engine for smooth handling of those steep winding roads; they are generally among the islands' most scenic, as well. See the boxed text 'Pack a Picnic' (p69) for one suggested route. Aside from the main coastal resorts, street parking is usually easy to find and often free; blue zones are metered with a limit of up to four hours. If you're planning to rent a car on the smaller islands of La Gomera and El Hierro, book well in advance, especially in peak season.

if you like...

Beaches

Deciding on a beach (and there are many) depends on what you want from your sand-between-the-toes experience. The southern resorts have magnificent beaches, but the sand is barely visible beyond the columns of sunbeds. Fuerteventura has quieter swathes of sand, while Lanzarote, La Palma and La Gomera all have their black-sand gems. The golden dunes of Maspalomas and the capital's Canteras beach are striking landscape features on Gran Canaria, while Tenerife has imported golden sand to enhance its *playa* resorts.

Playa de las Canteras This magnificent city beach is flanked by a wide promenade (p47)

Playa de las Teresitas Head here for powder-soft sand, good seafood restaurants and a reassuringly Spanish vibe (p129)

Endless dunes Go the full Sahara and visit the extraordinary dunes in Fuerteventura (p82) and Gran Canaria (p63)

Playas Mujeres Drive along a dirt track to this rare pale-sand beach in a picturesque cove (p114)

Culture

Away from the main resorts, Canarian culture thrives. Archaeology aside, there are world-class contemporary art museums, while more traditional craftwork includes superb embroidery, Guanche-style pottery, handmade silk and intricate basketry. For living culture, hit the festivals, in particular carnival, with its theatrical costumes and street-stage setting.

Embroidery centres Be wary of Chinese imports. Instead, head for the source: La Orotava (Tenerife), Mazo (La Palma) and Ingenio (Gran Canaria) are famed for their needle skills tradition

Tenerife Espacio de las Artes An exciting new contemporary art centre with an emphasis on photography, modern art and edgy, socially conscious exhibits (p120)

Latin American influences There's a tangible sense of South American influences here; La Orotava Iberoamericana museum explores the connection (p137)

Santa Cruz cultural highs Combine Prado exhibits and contemporary masterpieces with the annual classical music festival and carnival street culture (p119)

Theme Parks

If you like, or rather your children like, theme parks then you've come to the right place. Just be selective. Some of the themed entertainment here is, frankly, a rip-off and you would be far better plonking your kiddies on the beach with a bucket and spade. There are exceptions, however, and even one or two that may appeal to adult kids-at-heart.

Water parks Probably the best overall value. Good ones in Tenerife, Fuerteventura, Gran Canaria and Lanzarote. Alternatively, seek out the natural saltwater pools, particularly in La Palma (p193) and El Hierro (p199)

Tropical parks Tenerife's Loro Parque is well respected (and well advertised!). It is also huge, with exhibits that include a dolphinarium and a penguin house (p133)

Science themed Okay, not theme parks as such, but there are a handful of exceptional science and natural history museums here that are seriously kiddie-geared. In Gran Canaria, check out the Museo Elder de la Ciencia y La Tecnología (p47); and in Tenerife, the Museo de la Ciencia y el Cosmos (p128) and the exceptional Museo de la Naturaleza y el Hombre (p119)

» Carnaval performers, Gran Canaria (p47)

Watersports

Don that colour-coordinated lycra, grab your windsurf board or kiteboard and head for the waves. Fuerteventura is a watersports wonderland with some spectacular wild beaches, particularly on the northwest coast. A short splash away, Lanzarote is also famed for its superb windsurfing and kiteboarding conditions. All the islands have wind and wave potential, with courses and gear rental available.

El Cotillo At the heart of Fuerteventura's surfing scene, surrounded by unspoiled windswept beaches (p85)

La Caleta de Famara Lanzarote's hottest west-coast surf spot for kiteboards, windsurf boards or that original Malibu favourite: the bodyboard (p106)

Southern resorts More commercial and crowded on the shore but once out at sea, the ocean is, well, the ocean. In Tenerife, check out the watersports in Los Cristianos (p149); and in Gran Canaria, Taurito (p67)

Clean Ocean Project Contribute towards clean beaches by buying your ecofriendly surf garb here (p87)

Scenic Landscapes

The Canaries' diversity of landscape is not just a holiday-brochure cliché, it really does have an extraordinary range of big-time, big-sky scenery. Consider hiring a car to really maximise your photo-snapping potential. Thankfully, the local authorities have thoughtfully built miradors throughout the archipelago so you don't have to do too much neck-craning while negotiating those cliff-hugging hairpin bends.

Gran Canaria Inland here it's fabulous and a bit like the Rockies, especially around the Cruz de Tejeda (p53) and Artenara (p62)

Tenerife No car necessary to reach the Pico del Teide, accessible by cable car and the highest place in Spain, with suitably heady views (p141)

Lanzarote For a moonscape of extraordinary rock formations, colours and atmosphere, head to the Parque Nacional de Timanfaya (p109)

La Gomera One of the finest lookout spots here is the Alto de Garajonay, although the whole island is photographic heaven (p163)

Hiking

All the right conditions are here for lacing up those hiking boots and striding out. Aside from July and August, when the weather is at its hottest, the climate is sufficiently mild to enjoy some spectacular walking routes throughout the islands, with landscapes that vary from dramatic ravines to rocky coastal paths and dense pine forests. Increasingly, local authorities are clearing and signposting often historic paths, with maps available at tourist offices. There are also guided walking tours available (particularly in German!). Again, check at the tourist office for lists of reputable organisations.

Lanzarote The local *cabildo* publishes a booklet of signposted walks including level of difficulty and distance (p97)

Tenerife Hike around magnificent Mount Teide (p142); park rangers organise guided walks

Gran Canaria Walk barefoot along the capital's 3km-long Playa de las Canteras or get serious and explore the mountainous interior (p55)

And the rest... All the islands have terrific scope for walking. For more information see p24

» Oak barrels in Bodega La Geria, Lanzarote (p108)

Nightlife

You don't have to be a Lady Gaga wannabe to enjoy the nightlife here, although karaoke bars still reign supreme in the islands' southern resorts. Island capitals like Las Palmas de Gran Canaria and Santa Cruz de Tenerife have an infinitely more authentic Spanish-style nightlife with late-night music bars, nightclubs and, yes, even theatres and concert halls, if you're feeling a bout of highbrow coming on.

Santa Cruz de Tenerife For capital nightlife and a party-loving crowd check out the area around Plaza España (p124)

Las Palmas de Gran Canaria Head for the bars and nightspots in the cobbled backstreets of the Vegueta barrio (p49)

Lanzarote Puerto del Rosario has some moving-and-shaking clubs on Calle José Antonio, while Puerto del Carmen's El Varadero area is home to inviting harbour-front bars (p112)

Opera, ballet, jazz...? Try Tenerife's Auditorio de Tenerife or Teatro Guimerá (p124), Gran Canaria's Auditorio Alfredo Kraus (p49), and the Centro Insular de Cultura El Almacén in Lanzarote (p97)

Being Pampered

Having your partner rub sunscreen on your back is a start but not quite in the same indulgence league as having an essential oils wrap or chocolate massage. There are some superb spas here where you can check in for individual treatments or wallow in a day of self-pampering pleasure. If lounging on the deck of a yacht being plied with cocktails is more your thing, consider yacht charter (www.yachtbooker.com); expect to pay from €800 for a week, not counting crew (or champagne).

Tenerife Spas Tenerife is the Canaries spa capital, with choices from north to south, including Hotel Botánico, Puerto de la Cruz; Mare Nostrom, Playa de las Américas; and Aqua Club Termal, Costa Adeje (p153)

Balneario Thalasso Visit Fuerteventura's impressive glass cube of a beachside thalassotherapy centre at Caleta de Fuste (p80)

San Agustín Europe's reputedly largest thalassotherapy centre is in Gran Canaria (p63)

Wine & Cheese

By happy coincidence wine and its favourite accompaniment are both Canary Island specialities. Fuerteventura is the big cheese when it comes to queso, with the most famous being majoreno. Pick up a wheel then hop on the 15-minute ferry to neighbouring Lanzarote, which has some of the most famous wines in the archipelago – although La Palma and Tenerife also have plenty of locally produced vintages to get sniffy about.

La Geria Lanzarote's most famous vine-growing region, with several bodegas for tasting and buying (p108)

Queso Majoreno Try and buy your Fuerteventura cheese at a local queseria where you can taste it first (p75)

Malvasía wine The malvasía grape produces a sweet red dessert wine, which you can taste at bodegas in Tenerife and La Palma (p190)

Tacoronte Acentejo More than 50 vineyards in the northeast of Tenerife produce this robust red wine, which was the first to earn the DO (denominación de origen) grade in the Canaries (p139)

month by month

1 **Carnaval**, February–March

2 **San Juan**, June

3 **Festival de Música de Canarias**, January–February

4 **International Jazz Festival**, July

5 **Gay Pride**, May

January

A popular month to visit the Canaries as, overall, the southern coastal resorts are still warm enough for beach days. Northern regions and inland are cooler and Tenerife's El Teide can be snow-capped.

✨ Festival de Música de Canarias

This month sees the launch of the annual classical music festival (www.festivalde-canarias.com), which has been waving the baton here for over 25 years.

February

A great time to visit. Southern resorts are generally sunny, while cooler weather in the islands' interiors creates ideal conditions for walking. This is also carnival month, so book your bed early!

✨ Carnaval

Second only to Rio in terms of sheer exuberance and party spirit, carnival here is at its biggest and best in Las Palmas de Gran Canaria (p47) and Santa Cruz in Tenerife (p125). Expect carafe-loads of fiesta spirit in the streets.

March

Enjoy springtime flowers, particularly on the hillsides of El Hierro, La Palma, La Gomera and Gran Canaria. During Easter week, expect tourist crowds.

✨ Opera Season

March sees the middle of the opera festival (www.operalaspalmas.org) in Las Palmas de Gran Canaria, attracting world-class virtuosos from around the world.

✨ Easter Parades

Easter bunnies and chocolate eggs take a back basket here during Easter week, when there are evocative parades with religious floats throughout the islands' towns and villages.

🍴 Canarian Food Fair

Held mid-month for one week in Tenerife's Los Cristianos; taste and buy traditional goodies from all the islands here.

April

The sun still shines brightest on the southern beaches, although evenings are cooler and there can be showers, particularly on Tenerife.

✨ International Film Festival

The annual Las Palmas de Gran Canaria film festival is a great place to get the lowdown on up-and-coming film-makers. See what's screening on www.lpafilm festival.com.

May

Another good month with plenty of towel space on the sand, plus warmer evenings, which make dining al fresco a delight.

⭐ Gay Pride

Spain's second-largest gay pride event (after Madrid). Held mid-month in Maspalomas, Gran Canaria (www.gaymaspalomas.com).

Deliciously Cheesy

Celebrate the delicious Gran Canaria *queso de flor* at its source – in Santa María de Guía at the annual cheese festival (www.santamaria deguia.es).

June

You're still just ahead of the tourist onslaught, and the weather is perfect with an average of 10 hours of daily sunshine.

For Folk-Music Fans

Get foot-tapping to traditional folk music and dancing by local and visiting groups during this month's annual folk music festival in Las Palmas (www.grancanaria.com).

Bonfire Night

Barbecues and dusk-to-dawn partying on the beach, plus big-bang fireworks and concerts. An annual tradition on San Juan (23–24 June), celebrated throughout the islands, but with particular gusto in Lanzarote and Las Palmas (Gran Canaria).

July

The mercury level is rising but the average temperature in the southern resorts is still a tolerable 35°C. Tourism numbers are up with the summer holiday crowd.

Cool Jazz for Hot Days

The Festival Internacional Canarias Jazz & Más Heineken attracts big names from the international jazz world. Check out www.canariasjazz.com for names and venues.

Music, Dance & Theatre

Another world-class festival: Gran Canaria's Festival Internacional de Teatro, Musica y Danza (www.teatro ydanzalaspalmas.com) – recent performers include the New York City Ballet.

August

This is the month you use your umbrella – as a sunshade: the weather is at its hottest. But it still rarely hits the 40°C norm of the southern Spain costas.

Saint's Day

The Dia San Ginés on the 25th of the month is a mega-celebration in Lanzarote, with week-long celebrations that include concerts, football matches and beauty contests.

Windsurfing World Championship

Like flocks of colourful butterflies, kiteboarders and windsurfers descend on Fuerteventura's Playa de Sotovento de Jandía early in the month to compete in this world-class competition.

September

There are still around seven hours of daily sunshine this month, while nights are growing a tad cooler, particularly at higher altitudes.

Canarian Wrestling (and more)

The Fiesta del Santísmo Cristo in La Laguna (Tenerife) is held throughout the month, and includes tournaments of *lucha canaria,* vintage car rallies and big-bang firework displays.

October

The average monthly temperature is 23°C, with cooler nights. It's perfect weather for hiking in the islands – or sitting on the beach.

Rollerblade on Land

Or walk, or run or even spin those wheelchair wheels. The annual Music Marathon Festival (www.music marathonfestival.com) in Puerto del Carmen, Lanzarote (22 October), is open to all, including four-year-old tots (½-mile race). Live music lines the route.

December

Christmas sees more tourists, particularly from northern Europe seeking some winter sun. Temperatures drop considerably at night and the northernmost island resorts can be cloudy, though seldom wet.

Street Party

El Hierro's Fiesta de la Virgen de la Concepción on the 8th is full of religious revelry while, on the previous evening, Valverde's streets are packed with jolly locals, eating, drinking and making merry.

itineraries

Whether you've got three days or 30, these itineraries provide a starting point for the trip of a lifetime. Want more inspiration? Head online to lonelyplanet.com /thorntree to chat with other travellers.

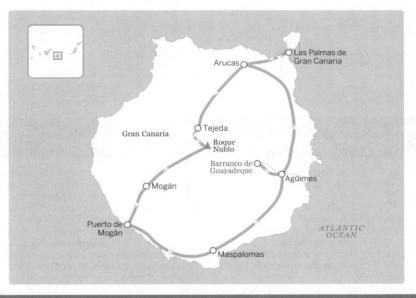

One Week
Gran Canaria Round Trip

> Immerse yourself in the capital: **Las Palmas de Gran Canaria**. Start off scuffing sand with a gentle stroll on Playa de las Canteras, flanked by bars, restaurants and buskers. Spend the afternoon being a kid at heart twiddling knobs at the science museum. Pass the second day wandering the cobbles of historic Vegueta with its youthful energy and inspiring sights. Day three head for the ancient **Roque Nublo** volcano. Consider hiking the circuit then reward yourself sweetly with **Tejeda's** famous almond treats. Next day, head south to **Mogán**, via the spectacularly scenic GC-605 road. After lunch in this picturesque town, take a short hop south to the **Puerto de Mogán**, with its quintessential Med-style yachting harbour, plus beach, boat rides and bars. Day five, swing southeast to the shimmering sands of **Maspalomas** for a camel ride, followed by a swim and snooze on the sand. Continue northeast to the lush ravine of the **Barranco de Guayadeque** for a late lunch in a cave setting. Stay overnight in nearby **Agüimes** with its lovely pastel painted buildings and historic charm. Next continue north, via lovely **Arucas**, and return to Las Palmas.

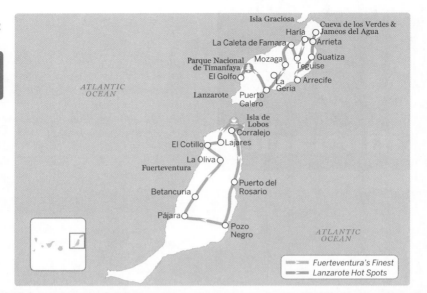

Isla Graciosa

Cueva de los Verdes &
Jameos del Agua

Haría

La Caleta de Famara

Arrieta

Parque Nacional
de Timanfaya

Mozaga

Guatiza

El Golfo

Teguise

La
Geria

Arrecife

Lanzarote

Puerto
Calero

ATLANTIC
OCEAN

Isla de
Lobos

Corralejo

El Cotillo

Lajares

La Oliva

Fuerteventura

Betancuria

Puerto del
Rosario

Pájara

Pozo
Negro

ATLANTIC
OCEAN

Fuerteventura's Finest
Lanzarote Hot Spots

Six Days
Fuerteventura's Finest

Start at **Corralejo's** pretty harbour for a relaxing stroll or a little beach time. Continuing in seaside mode, head southeast, past the endless shifting dunes on the FV-1 road. Wind up the day by enjoying a city stroll and dinner at one of capital **Puerto del Rosario's** fine restaurants. Day two, continue south, stopping at pint-sized **Pozo Negro**, where the simple *chiringuitos* (seafood restaurants) serve freshly caught seafood and overlook the surf. It's time for a break from all those blues, so wend your way inland to the pretty, small **Pájara**. Pop into the extraordinary church here and pray for a free room at the town's lovely *casa rural*. Day three stop at **Betancuria**, where there is plenty going on to pass the time. Stop by the eye-catching church, visit quirky museums and dine in style at Casa Santa María – one of the island's serious culinary stars. Next day, continue north via the rural gem of **La Oliva** to the low-key beachside town of **El Cotillo**. Day five return to Corralejo via the hip, young surfing village of **Lajares**, with its eclectic retail and cafe choices. Stay overnight then hop on a ferry to unspoilt **Isla de Lobos** for a relaxing day of island strolls and sands.

Six Days
Lanzarote Hot Spots

Arrecife deserves a full day: have a dip at the white sandy beach of Playa del Reducto before exploring the sights (and the shops). Eat like a king at MIAC Restaurant, with its castle setting, and stay in town overnight. Next day head north for the **cactus garden** near **Guatiza** before the tour buses roll up. Carry on to the famous **Cueva de los Verdes** and **Jameos del Agua** caves, then backtrack and take the rest of the day off in simple seaside **Arrieta**. Day three head for postcard-pretty **Haría** with its traditional architecture and lofty palms. Then head south to **Teguise**, a great little town with innovative restaurants and original shops. The next day it's the seaside, and the beautiful beach resort of **La Caleta de Famara** to watch the surfers and enjoy a fresh fish lunch. Stay overnight in nearby **Mozaga's** *casa rural*. Day five visit the wineries in **La Geria**, ending up in the yacht harbour of **Puerto Calero** for cocktails at sunset. Day six explore the lava fields of the **Parque Nacional de Timanfaya**, joining the bus tour through the dramatic Ruta de los Volcanes. Spend the night in the unspoiled small fishing community of **El Golfo** and enjoy more good seafood overlooking the waves.

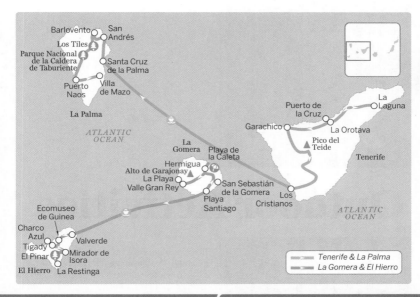

10 Days
Tenerife & La Palma

One Week
La Gomera & El Hierro

On Tenerife, stay two nights in **Puerto de la Cruz**, enjoying the shops, bars and beaches. Day three visit **La Orotava**, with its grand 17th-century mansions. Still in historical mode, continue on to **La Laguna's** superbly preserved traditional quarter for an overnight stay. Next day, retrace your steps and head on to contrasting **Garachico** and its simple fishermen's cottages, plus nearby hiking trails. Day five head for the extraordinary **El Teide** for a day of walking, gawping and camera snapping. Day six hightail it to **Los Cristianos** and catch the daily ferry to **La Palma**.

Spend a couple of nights in and around the capital **Santa Cruz**, exploring the old town, kicking back on Los Cancajos beach and taking a mini-pilgrimage to the Santuario de la Virgen de las Nieves (you're really here for the views). Continue north to explore the hilly, cobbled streets of **San Andrés**. Day eight visit the lush rainforest of **Los Tiles** before cooling off at the salt-water pools near **Barlovento**. Day nine hike through the stunning **Parque Nacional de la Caldera de Taburiente**. Continue south for a night at lively **Puerto Naos** before stuffing your hand-luggage with handicrafts from laid-back **Villa de Mazo**.

Spend the first day on La Gomera exploring the backstreets, big streets and everything in between in weeny **San Sebastián**. The next day recover from all that urban exhaustion with a dip (and a doze) at **Playa Santiago**. Day three head to the verdant north, stopping at traditional **Hermigua** and postcard-pretty **Playa de la Caleta**. Next day continue south for a trek through a fern-filled rainforest up to the lofty peaks (and views) of the **Alto de Garajonay**. Drive beside the stunning **Valle Gran Rey** gorge until it reaches the sea. Stay overnight at **La Playa**, before returning to San Sebastián to catch the ferry to **El Hierro**.

Check out the low-key capital of **Valverde**, before heading south to the **Ecomuseo de Guinea**, a nature-cum-cultural treat. Dine on superb Canarian food at down-to-earth **Tigady** and stay overnight. Next day head for the natural pools at **Charco Azul**, before heading cross-country to the incredible **Mirador de Isora**, the lush pines of **El Pinar** and the famous off-shore scuba-diving sites at **La Restinga**.

Outdoor Activities

Best Island for...

» Hiking A question guaranteed to cause heated discussions among the walking fraternity. We say Tenerife and La Palma, but fans of La Gomera, please present your case now!

» Kiteboarding & Windsurfing The Canary Islands have some of the best kiteboarding and windsurfing conditions in the world, but it's Fuerteventura that really gets the wind up people's sails.

» Surfing The Canaries aren't called the 'Hawaii of the Atlantic' for nothing. Most of the islands have great surf, but it's Lanzarote that's the centre of the scene.

» Scuba Diving & Snorkelling If you think tiny El Hierro looks good from dry land, just wait until you dip yourself under its waters.

Being outdoors is what the Canary Islands are all about. With average temperatures around 18°C in winter and 24°C in summer, and an average rainfall hovering around 250mm, you're almost guaranteed the perfect weather for whatever activity suits your fancy. And the astonishing variety of landscapes here – from La Gomera's humid and verdant Parque Nacional de Garajonay to the vast lunarscapes of Lanzarote – means that the same pursuit will be different on each island.

Most trekkers and adventure-seekers gravitate toward the smaller islands, especially La Gomera, La Palma and, for watersports, Lanzarote and Fuerteventura, but it's possible to get away from the crowds and test your adventurous spirit on any of the seven islands. Most boast excellent hiking trails and the abundance of watersports is obvious. Countless outfitters offer guidance (details are provided in the individual island chapters) in your activity of choice or the experienced can set out alone.

Hiking

Hundreds of trails, many of them historic paths used before the days of cars and highways, criss-cross the islands. A good place to start is the national parks – the Parque Nacional del Teide (p140) on Tenerife, the Parque Nacional de Garajonay (p163) on La Gomera and the Parque Nacional de la Caldera de Taburiente (p187) on La Palma all have excellent hiking. Each of these parks offers a variety of walks and hikes, ranging from easy strolls

HIKING GUIDES

There are loads of dedicated hiking guides to the Canary Islands speak Spanish) that are easily available in all main bookshops ac English the best books for the general walker are those produce(ing Guides, which publishes guidebooks and accompanying map Palma, La Gomera and Tenerife, and Sunflower Books, which has to all the islands.

ending at lookout points to multi-day treks across mountains and gorges.

When to Go

You can walk in the Canary Islands any time of year, but some trails become dangerous or impossible in rainy weather, and others (like the trek up to the peak of El Teide) are harder to do in winter, when parts of the trail are covered in snow. Be aware that while along the coast and in the lowlands it's normally warm and sunny, as you head into higher altitudes, the wind, fog and air temperature can change drastically, so always carry warm and waterproof clothing. Don't forget to take water along with you, as there are few water sources or vendors out along the trails.

Best Hikes

» **Pico Viejo to El Teide** (p142) The most challenging – and easily the most stunning – trek in the Canary Islands is this mammoth hike that takes in not just Spain's highest peak but its little climbed, little brother.

» **Ruta de los Volcanes** (p187) Skip along the summits of a whole ridge of volcanoes on this long and challenging trek.

» **La Laguna Grande to Alto de Garajonay** (p165) Saunter through the mist-drenched forests at the summit of La Gomera on this moderately easy walk.

» **Camino de Jinama** (p201) Hike through history, and through the best of delightful El Hierro.

» **Isla de Lobos** (p83) Loop the loop around this desert island.

Hiking on...

» **Tenerife** The Parque Nacional del Teide is one of the finest walking areas in all of Spain. But there's more to Tenerife hiking than El Teide. The forested Anaga mountains (p129) in the northeast offer hikes through a mist-drenched forest filled with birdsong, and in the far northwest, the hamlet of

Masca (p144) is the gateway to some stunning, and very challenging, hikes.

» **La Gomera** Thanks to a near-permanent mist (called horizontal rain), the green forest of Parque Nacional de Garajonay (p163) is dripping with life and moss. From the park's highest point, the Alto de Garajonay, you can see Tenerife and El Teide – if the clouds don't interrupt the view. There's excellent walking in and around this park for all levels of hiker.

» **La Palma** Regarded by many as the finest island of all to walk on, La Palma's Parque Nacional de la Caldera de Tauriente (p187) offers a landscape somewhere between the verdant Garajonay and the stark Teide. You can hike along the rock walls of the park's interior or meander among the pine forests on the outer slopes of the park. Numerous other trails spin off across the island and walking these can see you slipping in and out of rain forests or clambering up parched volcanic slopes.

» **El Hierro** The newbie on the walking scene, tiny El Hierro offers a real bonanza of trails, from family-friendly coastal hikes such as the easy walk between Las Puntas and La Maceta (p204) to shady ambles around the pine forests of El Pinar (p202) or the much longer Camino de Jinama (p201).

» **Gran Canaria** Much less hiked than the western islands, Gran Canaria nevertheless offers superlative walking opportunities. The best trails are to be found radiating away from the Cruz de Tejeda (p55), which sits close to the highest point of Gran Canaria.

Watersports

Surfing, windsurfing and kiteboarding are popular watersports on most of the islands, and who can resist the temptation of a swim off any of the gorgeous beaches? Schools offering classes and equipment rental are scattered around the windier coasts and there are a variety of spots to choose from, ranging from the beginner-friendly sandy beaches

..I as the big-ticket walks mentioned here there are plenty of off-the-beaten-
..I hikes throughout the Canary Islands. Among our favourites are the walks
.Iround the Unesco-protected Los Tiles biosphere reserve (p192) on La Palma and
the dunes of Maspalomas (p63) on Gran Canaria. For a truly spectacular walk, sign
up for the Tremesana guided hike (p109) in the Parque Nacional de Timanfaya; you'll
have to plan in advance, but the effort will be well rewarded.

of Fuerteventura to the heavy reef breaks of Lanzarote and Gran Canaria.

Surfing

There's a wide variety of waves in the islands, from heart-in-the-mouth barrels breaking over super-shallow reef ledges to gentle sandbanks ideal for learners. The best season for surfing in the Canaries is from October through to April. At this time of year you will need a full 3mm wetsuit.

At many of the better-known spots there is a very high degree of sometimes violent localism and you should never leave a car or valuables unattended around any of these spots.

For more on surfing in the Canaries get hold of a copy of the excellent *Stormrider Guide: Atlantic Islands* published by Low Pressure. And if going solo on a surf trip sounds a little daunting, **Errant Surf Holidays** (www.errantsurf.com) is a UK-based surf travel company that offers a number of surf holidays to the Canaries. Trips are suitable for learners.

Best Surf Breaks

SURF SPOT	WAVE TYPE
El Quemao, Lanzarote	Very heavy and scary left barrel
San Juan, Lanzarote	Long, challenging left
Los Lobos, Fuerteventura	Long, hollow right-point break
El Fronton, Gran Canaria	One of the world's heaviest waves
Confital, Gran Canaria	Radical reef break offering huge tubes
Spanish Left, Tenerife	Long left with plenty of tube sections

Top Beginner Surf Spots

» **La Caleta de Famara, Lanzarote** (p106) With its endless stretch of sand and plenty of surf schools, it's perfect for learners.

» **El Cotillo, Fuerteventura** (p85) Offers equally perfect learner conditions.

» **Playa de las Américas, Tenerife** (p149) Has a few mellow, learner-friendly waves and several surf schools.

Windsurfing & Kiteboarding

With constant winds, good waves and a perfect climate, the Canary Islands offer some of the best conditions in the world for windsurfing and kiteboarding.

International competitions are held here every year, and enthusiasts from all over the globe converge on the long, sandy beaches to test the waters. If you're new to the game, beginners' courses are easy to come by at all the main spots. Courses last between two days and a week and prices vary widely according to how much you're aiming to learn.

The Kite & Windsurfing Guide Europe by Stoked Publications is a superb glossy guide to the continent's best kite and windsurf spots. It includes chapters on the Canary Islands.

For more on kiteboarding in the Canaries, see our interview with a champ who first fell in love with the sport on Lanzarote, p107.

Best Windsurfing & Kiteboarding Spots

ISLAND	BEACH
Fuerteventura	Playa de Sotavento de Jandía
Fuerteventura	Playa de Barlovento de Jandía
Gran Canaria	Pozo Izquierdo
Lanzarote	Costa Teguise
Tenerife	Las Galletas
Tenerife	El Médano

Swimming

Year-round sun and warm water (18°C to 26°C) makes swimming an obvious activity in the Canary Islands. From the golden beaches of the eastern islands to the volcanic pools of the western islands, there are plenty of splashing opportunities.

Beaches come in every shape and size – long and golden, intimate and calm, family-friendly and action-packed, rocky and picturesque, solitary and lonely, windy and wavy. We have highlighted our favourite beaches throughout the text.

You do need to be cautious, especially when swimming in the ocean. The first rule is never, ever swim alone. There can be very strong currents and undertows in the Atlantic, and rip currents can be so strong that they can carry you far from shore before you can react. If you're caught in a current, swim parallel to the shore (don't try to get to the beach) until you're released. Then make your way to shore.

The water quality around the Canary Islands is generally excellent. The only place you may find pollution is near ports (the occasional small oil spill is not unheard of) and on overcrowded tourist beaches. Smokers seem to think of some beaches as a huge ashtray, so you may need to watch out for butts.

Scuba Diving & Snorkelling

The variety of marine life and the warm, relatively calm waters of the Canary Islands make them a great place for scuba diving or snorkelling. You won't experience the wild colours of Caribbean coral, but the volcanic coast is made up of beautiful rock formations and caves. As far as life underwater goes, you can spot around 350 species of fish and 600 different kinds of algae.

Scuba schools and outfitters are scattered across the islands, so you won't have trouble finding someone willing to take you out. A standard dive, with equipment rental included, costs around €25 to €30, but a 'try dive' (a first-timer diving with an instructor) can be double that. Certification classes start at €270 and generally last between three days and a week. Many scuba outfitters also offer snorkelling excursions

BEST BEACHES

The Canary Islands have more than their fair share of beaches and trying to pick the best is likely to lead to heated arguments, but in the cause of good arguments everywhere here's our list of the best of the best.

» **Playa de las Canteras** (Gran Canaria; p47) This has to rate as one of the most enticing capital-city beaches in Europe; its 3km arc of golden sand fronted by a wide promenade is ideal for sunset strolls.

» **Grandes Playas** (Fuerteventura; p82) Backed by Sahara-style sand dunes with powder-soft sand, these pristine natural beaches are among the island's best.

» **La Caleta de Famara** (Lanzarote; p106) A wonderful wild beach popular with kiteboarders and windsurfers, sporting a laid-back vibe and plenty of towel space on the sand.

» **Puerto de la Cruz** (Tenerife; p134) The old dame of Tenerife tourism has the lot – stunning location, lots going on, safe swimming, all sorts of watersports and a wealth of places to stay and eat.

» **Playa Santiago** (La Gomera; p169) OK, so it might be hard pebbles rather than soft sand, but with its shelter from the wind and cloud that can plague other beaches on the island, chilled-out hippy vibe, some good accommodation and great places to eat we think you'll like this one.

» **Puerto Naos** (La Palma; p190) It might be a purpose built resort but it's low-key and easy on the eye. With soft black sand and generally safe bathing it's perfect for all the family.

» **Playa de las Arenas Blancas** (El Hierro; p206) On the wild island of El Hierro this white-washed gem of a beach is utterly pristine but often wind and wave lashed (so swimming can be dangerous). Some great coastal walks fan out from it as well.

for nondivers; prices tend to be about half the cost of a regular dive.

Best Diving Spots

» **La Restinga** (p203) A wealth of marine life and plenty of diving operators to show you the underwater wonders.

» **Puerto Calero** (p112) Visibility up to 20m and especially warm waters. You'll find marlin, barracuda and a host of other fish.

» **Los Gigantes & Puerto de Santiago** (p145) Wreck dives, cave dives and old-fashioned boat dives. Marine life ranges from eels to angel sharks and stingrays.

» **Puerto de Mogán** (p67) Dive in and around the caves and wrecks that lie not far offshore.

Whale Watching & Boating

Sticking a mask on your face and peering underwater at a few blennies and wrasse is cool, but the waters surrounding the Canaries are home to much bigger creatures than that. Around 30 species of whales and dolphins pass through Canarian seas; the most commonly seen are pilot whales and bottle-nosed and common dolphins.

The best area to see such creatures is in the waters between Tenerife and La Gomera and a number of different operators run dolphin- and whale-spotting boat trips departing from the harbour at Los Cristianos (p151).

Other whale-watching ports:

» **Los Gigantes & Puerto de Santiago** (Tenerife)

» **Valle Gran Rey** (La Gomera)

» **Puerto Rico** (Gran Canaria)

Whichever operator you choose it's worth taking note of their environmental credentials (we have tried to include only responsible operators) as it's not unknown for some boat operators to take their clients too close to the whales, which causes them undue distress and can eventually cause the whales and dolphins to completely change their behaviour or even leave an area altogether.

Away from whales and dolphins, virtually every tourist beach town in the archipelago offers some form of boat trip, but maybe the most impressive boat cruises on the islands are those running from Valle Gran Rey (p170) in La Gomera. The cruise boats float past kilometre after kilometre of impene-

trable rock cliffs before arriving at one of the island's most unique sites, Los Órganos (The Organs), a rock formation seen only from the water that does indeed look just like an enormous pipe organ carved into the rock.

Golf

In the past decade, southern Tenerife has become the Canary Islands' golf hot spot. Golfers who love the balmy temperatures that let them play year-round have spawned the creation of a half-dozen courses in and around the Playa de las Américas alone. The courses are aimed at holiday golfers and are not known for being particularly challenging.

You'll also find a few courses around Las Palmas de Gran Canaria, and a course or two dotted around Lanzarote and Fuerteventura.

The lack of water on the islands makes golf rather environmentally unfriendly and a difficult sport to sustain. Golf course owners say the water for those lush greens comes from runoff and local water-purification plants, but environmental groups say the golf courses take water from agriculture. The truth is in there somewhere, and local politicians, golfers, environmentalists and farmers are still arguing about where.

In winter, green fees hover around €85, but in midsummer they could be half that.

For an overview of golfing on Tenerife, see www.tenerifegolf.es.

Cycling

If you've got strong legs, cycling may be the perfect way to see the Canary Islands. The price of renting a bike depends largely on what kind of bike you get – suspension and other extras will cost more. In general, a day's rental starts at about €20, and a guided excursion will be around €45.

Best Cycling Areas

ROUTE	LEVEL
El Teide (Tenerife)	Advanced
Alto de Garajonay (La Gomera)	Advanced
Valle Gran Rey (La Gomera)	Moderate
Los Llanos de Aridane (La Palma)	Moderate
Maspalomas (Gran Canaria)	Easy

» (above) Parque Nacional del Teide,
   Tenerife
» (left) Kiteboarding near Costa Calma,
   Fuerteventura

Travel with Children

Best Regions for Kids

Tenerife

Parents may balk, but the theme parks around Los Cristianos have undeniable appeal for children, while go-karting, whale-watching, beaches and boat rides should have the whole family smiling.

Fuerteventura

The sandy choice at Corralejo is superb. Older kids will love striding out on the dunes south of town, while tiny tots may prefer the small sheltered coves by the harbour. Splashier options include the massive Baku Water Park, plus boat rides and children's snorkelling courses.

Lanzarote

Parque Nacional de Timanfaya is something to impress the most blasé whippersnapper, with natural geysers, moonscape terrain, audiovisual presentations and camel rides. The restaurant's volcano-powered BBQ is pretty cool as well.

Gran Canaria

Las Palmas is not the most obvious region, but the city beach is magnificent, the Casa Museo de Colón's model galleon is awesome and the science museum should blow their little socks off.

The Canary Islands has to be one of the most family-friendly destinations this side of Disneyland. Stripped back to basics, the beaches and virtual year-round sunshine are pretty good raw ingredients, and then there are the theme parks, camel rides, museums, parks and watersports. To get the most of what is on offer, plan ahead.

Canary Islands for Kids

While there are plenty of attractions designed specifically with children in mind, including theme parks and zoos, public spaces, such as town and village plazas, also morph into informal playgrounds with children kicking a ball around, riding bikes and playing, while parents enjoy a drink and tapa in one of the surrounding terrace bars. Local children also stay up late and at fiestas it's commonplace to see even tiny ones toddling the streets at 2am. Visiting children invariably warm to this idea, but can't always cope with it quite so readily.

Discounts

Discounts are available for children (usually under 12) on public transport and for admission to sights. Those under four generally go free.

Eating & Drinking

Whole families, often including several generations, sitting around a restaurant or bar table eating and chatting is a fundamental element of the lifestyle here and it is rare to find a restaurant where children are not made welcome. Even if restaurants do not advertise children's menus (and few do), they will still normally be willing to prepare a small portion for your child or suggest a suitable tapa or two.

Aside from the normal selection of soft drinks on offer, the island is well known for its *zumerias* (juice bars), which whizz up a healthy variety of fresh fruit juices, including strawberry, mango and banana. In bars, a popular choice for children is *Cola Cao* (chocolate drink) served hot or cold with milk.

Resources

Always make a point of asking staff at tourist offices for a list of family activities, including traditional fiestas, plus suggestions on hotels that cater for kids.

For further general information about travelling with children, see Lonely Planet's *Travel with Children* or visit the websites www.travelwithyourkids.com, www.oddizzi .com and www.familytravelnetwork.com.

Children's Highlights
Theme Parks

» **Palmitos Park**, Maspalomas, Gran Canaria. An excellent combination of botanical garden, aquarium, aviary and zoo with daily shows, including dolphins and birds of prey, plus a superb butterfly and orchid house.

» **Aqualand Maspalomas**, Gran Canaria. Touted as the largest water park in Europe with all the standard watery slides, including the vertiginous kamikaze.

» **Loro Parque**, Puerto de la Cruz, Tenerife. A spacious 13.5-hectare (33-acre) zoo, including a shark tunnel, dolphin show, parrots, penguin exhibition and the largest Thai village outside Thailand.

» **Pardelas Park**, Orzola, Lanzarote. A children's petting farm and playground with donkey rides, clay modelling and playground, plus a tapas bar and restaurant.

» **Guinate Tropical Park**, Guinate, Lanzarote. Some 1300 exotic birds with aviaries, landscaped gardens and paths.

» **Camel Park**, Arona, Tenerife. Camel-breeding and riding centre, plus a modest petting farm.

» **Siam Park**, Costa Adeje, Tenerife. Owned by the same folks as Loro Parque, this massive water park has the works, including raft rides (on

rapids), an artificial wave pool and even a white sandy stretch of beach.

» **Maroparque**, Breña Alta, La Palma. A small zoo with some 300 species of animals.

Watersports & Boat Rides

» **Dive Academy**, Arguineguín, Gran Canaria (www.diveacademy-grancanaria.com). One-day bubble-maker course for children from eight to 10 years old.

» **Diving Center Sun-Sub**, Hotel Buenaventura, Playa del Inglés, Gran Canaria (www.sunsub.com). Several children's courses, including Flipper 1 (eight to 10 years), Flipper 2 (10 to 12 years), Basic Diver (over 12 years), and Open Water Dive (over 14 years).

» **Aquatis Diving Center**, Playa de las Cucharas, Lanzarote (www.aquatis-lanzarote.eu). One-day bubble-maker course for children up to eight years old; Discover Scuba Diving (eight to 10 years).

» **Submarine Safaris**, Tenerife and Lanzarote (www.submarinesafaris.com). Underwater boat trips with diving opportunities for older, experienced children.

» **Nashíra Uno**, Los Gigantes, Tenerife (www .maritimaacantilados.com). Daily two-hour whale- and dolphin-spotting boat trips.

» **Flag Beach**, Calle General Linares 31, Corralejo, Fuerteventura (www.flagbeach.com). Children's courses in surfing (over 10 years); windsurfing (over 12 years) and kiteboarding (over 14 years).

» **Kayak Tours**, El Cotillo and Corralejo, Fuerteventura (www.kayakisland.com). One-hour kayaking tours (over 10 years).

» **Charter María**, Tazacorte, La Palma (www .fancy2.com). Boat excursions, including dolphin-spotting and sunset cruises.

» **Tina**, Valle Gran Rey, La Gomera (www .excursiones-tina.com). Four-hour whale-watching excursions, including lunch.

Beaches

All the following beaches have shallow waters, fine sand (for sandcastles), various activities (pedalos, boat rides, volleyball or similar), plus family-friendly restaurants and ice-cream vendors within tottering distance of the sand.

» **Fuerteventura**: Corralero Viejo, Muelle Chico (Corralero), Caleta de Fuste, Costa Calma, Playa del Matorral (Morro Jable)

» **Lanzarote**: Playa Grande, (Puerto del Carmen), Playa Blanca

» **Gran Canaria**: Playa de las Canteras, Playa del Inglés, Playa de Puerto Rico, Playa Mogán

» **Tenerife**: Los Cristianos, Playa de las Américas, Costa Adeje, Las Teresitas

La Palma, La Gomera and El Hierro have mainly black beaches with, overall, fewer activities for children, aside from whale-watching cruises and the ubiquitous glass-bottom boat trips.

» **La Palma**: Puerto Naos, Puerto de Tazacorte, Charco Azul (natural pools cut out of the rock)

» **La Gomera**: Playa de las Vueltas, Playa de Valle Gran Rey, Playa Santiago

» **El Hierro**: La Restinga

Museums

» **Museo de la Piratería**, Teguise, Lanzarote. A swashbuckling museum about the history of piracy on the island.

» **Museo de Cetáceos**, Puerto Calero, Lanzarote. Natural history museum primarily devoted to whales.

» **Museo Artesania**, Betancuria, Fuerteventura. Folklore and crafts, plus excellent underwater 3D film.

» **Ecomuseo La Alcogida**, Tefía, Fuerteventura. Restored agricultural hamlet with plenty of outbuildings to explore (or play hide and seek).

» **Museo Elder de la Ciencia y la Tecnología**, Las Palmas de Gran Canaria. Fascinating science and technology museum with lots of hands-on exhibits for kids.

» **Casa-Museo de Colón**, Las Palmas de Gran Canaria. Museum recounting Columbus' voyages with an impressive replica galleon.

» **Museo de la Naturaleza y El Hombre**, Santa Cruz de Tenerife. Natural science and archaeology, including Guanche mummies.

» **Museo de la Ciencia y El Cosmos**, La Laguna, Tenerife. Great science museum for children, includes a planetarium.

Other Sights & Activities

» **Castillo de Tostón**, El Cotillo, Fuerteventura. Display of arsenal and sight-and-sound exhibition should impress the youngsters.

» **Isla de Lobos**, Fuerteventura. Children should enjoy the ferry ride and Robinson Crusoe–style novelty of landing on a tiny, virtually uninhabited island.

» **Lanzarote Aquarium**, Costa Teguise, Lanzarote. Includes plenty of colourful fish, plus a touch pool.

» **Cueva de los Verdes & Jameos del Agua**, Malpaís de la Corona, Lanzarote. Intriguing caves and caverns.

» **Parque Nacional de Timanfaya**, Lanzarote. Fascinating volcanic park with geyser displays and camel rides.

» **Lanzarote a Caballo**, Puerto del Carmen, Lanzarote. Horse riding and short treks.

» **Pueblo Canario**, Las Palmas de Gran Canaria. Mock Canarian village with playground and folk-music displays.

» **Troglodyte caves**, Artenara, Gran Canaria. Fascinating Flintstone-style prehistoric caves.

» **Lago Martiánez**, Puerto de la Cruz, Tenerife. A fabulous watery playground.

» **La Caldera del Rey**, Los Cristianos, Tenerife. Horse riding, plus petting farm, climbing wall and low rope course for kiddies.

Planning

This is an easy-going, child-friendly destination with precious little advance planning necessary. July and August can be very busy with Spanish families from the mainland, and hotels in the main tourist resorts are often block booked by tour companies. Early spring is a good time to travel with young children as the weather is still warm enough for beach days, without being too hot, and the theme parks and attractions are not too crowded – until the Easter holidays, that is.

You can buy baby formula in powder or liquid form, as well as sterilising solutions such as Milton, at *farmacias* (pharmacies). Disposable nappies (diapers) are widely available at supermarkets and *farmacias*.

Before You Go

☐ You can hire car seats for infants and children from most car-rental firms, but you should always book them in advance.

☐ Most hotels have cots for small children, but numbers may be limited so reserve one when booking your room.

☐ When selecting a hotel, check whether your hotel has a kids club, activities geared for youngsters and/or babysitting facilities.

☐ No particular health precautions are necessary, but don't forget the sun protection essentials, including sun block and sun hat, although they can also be purchased here.

☐ Avoid tears and tantrums by planning which activities, theme parks, museums and leisure pursuits you want to opt for and, more importantly, can afford early on in the holiday.

regions at a glance

The Canary Islands may share the same archipelago, but in every other way they are truly diverse. If you love the outdoors there are some stunning natural landscapes and scope for scenic strolls or more arduous hikes, particularly in Gran Canaria, La Palma, El Hierro and La Gomera. Beaches are on every island but Fuerteventura has, arguably, the best of the bunch, and is a hot and happening destination for watersports as well. Something darkly different? That has to be Lanzarote: its black volcanic lava fields forming the ideal backdrop for some dramatic sculpture and architecture. History buffs have plenty to ponder here as well, particularly in Gran Canaria, which digs deep into its past with some truly extraordinary archaeological sites.

Gran Canaria

Mountains ✓✓✓
Archaeology ✓✓
Beaches ✓✓

Mountains
The mountainous interior is ruggedly beautiful and fabulous to explore, either by car or by taking one of the hiking trails. Laurel and pine forests, volcanic craters and cool mountain reservoirs all contribute to this spectacular scenery, especially during the springtime when the almond trees create a blush of pink-and-white blossom on the landscape.

Archaeology
The ancient Guanche history of the island is vividly brought to life at the excellent Cueva Pintada (painted cave) museum in Gáldar, the nearby Cenobio de Valerón 350-plus small caves and several fascinating museums.

Beaches
Superb stretches of sand range from the cityside strip at Las Palmas to the pristine desert-like landscape of Maspalomas. Add to this windswept black-stone beaches, rocky, surf-lashed coves and tourist strips with sunbeds and pedalos.

p38

Fuerteventura

Beaches ✓✓✓
Surfing ✓✓✓
Food ✓✓

Beaches

Fuerteventura's beaches are its major draw and justifiably so. They are magnificent and sufficiently varied to suit everyone's sandy choice, including secluded golden-sand coves, wild surf-thrashing beaches or darkly volcanic pebbles with a backdrop of cliffs.

Surfing

Going hand-in-hand with the beautiful beaches are watersports. Surfing, windsurfing and kiteboarding are immensely popular throughout the island, particularly on the northwest coast. And, no need to fret, you can rent all the equipment necessary if your board doesn't fit in your hand baggage.

Food

There are some great traditional dishes from here, many deriving from the island's most prodigious natural inhabitant: the goat. Try *cabrito frito* (fried baby goat) and don't miss the world-renowned *queso Majorero* (goat's cheese).

p70

Lanzarote

Volcanic Landscape ✓✓✓
Art ✓✓
Beaches ✓✓

Volcanic Landscape

Love it or not, the dark brooding volcanic landscape here has real drama, particularly at the Timanfaya core where a national park unfolds in undulating peaks, chasms and shifting colours. Driving through the interior of the island is an extraordinary experience with more than 300 volcanic cones. Start counting...

Art

The whole island is like a giant piece of art, mainly thanks to César Manrique's influence. Open-air sculptures, art museums and some exceptional architecture and galleries contribute to the island's art lovers' appeal.

Beaches

Although it is the black-pebble beaches that are so emblematic of the island, there are plenty of golden sands here as well, such as the beautiful and remote beaches on Punta del Papagayo and tiny Isla Graciosa's sandy strips.

p92

Tenerife

Volcanic Landscape ✓✓✓
Festivals ✓✓✓
Traditional Villages ✓✓

Volcanic Landscape

Be impressed by the soaring peak of Mount Teide, the world's third-largest volcano. The surrounding natural park is fabulous for walking. Or you can stride out (or take the cable car) to the dizzy heights of the summit.

Festivals

The Canarios love to party and scarcely a month passes without some festival here. The annual Carnaval is on the Rio-scale in terms of vivacity and fiesta spirit, while annual music festivals, food fairs and one of the largest gay pride celebrations outside San Francisco can be equally memorable.

Traditional Villages

Traditional villages and towns with cobbled streets and typical architecture provide a low-key antithesis to the busy resorts. La Laguna and La Orotava provide a suitable taster, but explore further and you'll discover some real rural gems.

p115

La Gomera

Nature ✓✓✓
Food ✓✓
Walking ✓✓✓

Nature
It's hard to find a road that doesn't pass through stunning scenery. From vast banana plantations to huge boulders, extraordinary rock formations, deep ravines, laurel forests and over 100,000 date palms, let's just say there are plenty of Kodak moments.

Food
Traditional culinary highlights include the delicious *miel de palma* honey made from the sap of palm trees, *sopa de berros* (watercress soup) or *sopa ranchero* (with vegetables), smoked goat's cheese and *almogrote* (pate of goat's cheese, oil and garlic). Enjoy a fresh papaya juice on the side.

Walking
It is only common sense that where there is wonderful natural scenery, there is going to be a real temptation to lace up those walking shoes and stride out. Fortunately, La Gomera has plenty of trails, particularly around the national park.

p157

La Palma

Nature ✓✓✓
Adventure Sports ✓
Walking ✓✓✓

Nature
Dense tropical forests, pine-clad mountains, rolling hills and rocky cliffs: La Palma has some truly sensational scenery, plus some real contrast with a starker, more arid south. There are no golden beaches, however – something has to give.

Adventure Sports
Pump up that adrenalin and try something new. Paragliding, tandem glides, caving, sea kayaking and canoeing are all popular here, plus guided mountain biking, scuba diving and strenuous treks.

Walking
The scenery certainly lends itself to walking and hiking and, appropriately enough, there are many kilometres of signposted trails, particularly around the pristine nature reserve of Taburiente. Walking trails criss-cross most of the island, giving you a chance to explore landscapes that vary from a lushly beautiful rainforest in the north to the lunar-like volcanic scenery in the south.

p173

El Hierro

Nature ✓✓✓
Hiking ✓
Diving ✓

Nature
The landscape here has a wonderfully remote feel with vast big-sky views, windswept groves of juniper trees, wild pine-tree-clad terrain (often shrouded in mist), historic paths and, well, very few people: only around 11,000 folk live here year-round.

Hiking
Signposted, well-maintained trails criss-cross the island, including the famous *Camino de la Virgen* (26km) historic trail stretching from Nuestra Señora de los Reyes to Valverde, and paths that pass through the cool pine forests of the south.

Diving
There are some thrilling dive sites around the island. Head for La Restinga, where several outfits offer equipment hire and courses, and the surrounding waters have been officially designated a marine reserve. Water temperatures are a tad higher than other islands, which means some different fish species, as well.

p194

Look out for these icons:

 Our author's recommendation

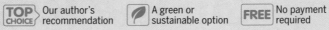 A green or sustainable option

FREE No payment required

See the Index for a full list of destinations covered in this book.

On the Road

Gran Canaria

928 / POP 805.000

Best Places to Eat

» Deliciosa Marta (p48)

» El Salsete (p65)

» Jack El Negro (p68)

Best Places to Stay

» La Hacienda del Molino (p211)

» Fonda de la Tea (p211)

» Casa Rural Doña Margarita (p211)

Why Go?

Gran Canaria is the third-largest island in the Canaries' archipelago but accounts for almost half the population. It lives up to its cliché as a continent in miniature, with a dramatic variation of terrain, ranging from the green and leafy north to the mountainous interior and desert south. To glean a sense of this impenetrable quality, head to the centre, where the sheer drama of the mountains more resembles the Tibetan highlands than a relatively small island.

The flip side to these unspoiled peaks and valleys is a rugged coastline interspersed with white sandy beaches and, more famously (and depressingly), a garish tiara of purpose-built holiday resorts.

Beyond the sands, though, Gran Canaria can keep the adrenalin pumping, with scope for hiking, horse trekking and watersports, while culture-vultures can be similarly satiated, particularly in the historic cosmopolitan capital of Las Palmas.

When to Go

Peak season here is the springtime: February through to Easter, when the weather is warm, rain is sporadic and the island's stunning interior is green and verdant with the occasional visual blast of almond trees in blossom. It is also party season, with the February Carnaval followed by other festivities, culminating with the ceremonial passion of Semana Santa (Holy Week). Autumn is also a good time of year for visitors, but avoid crowded July and August, when Spaniards from the mainland take their annual hols.

Getting Around

Global (www.globalsu.net) provides the island with a network of bus routes.

Car hire is highly recommended to explore the interior; **Cicar** (www.cicar.com) is a good local choice with representation throughout the island.

Taxis are plentiful, especially in Las Palmas and tourist resorts.

THREE PERFECT DAYS

Day One

Head for Vegueta, Las Palmas' exquisite colonial-style neighbourhood and home to its top cultural treasures. Get the lowdown on your surroundings from the high-point of the **cathedral tower**, before exploring **Columbus' House** (Casa-Museo de Colón). Staying in history mode, stop by the splendid **Museo Canario**, then pull up a chair at atmospheric **El Herreño** for a coffee, tapa or benchtime slumber in leafy relaxing surrounds.

Day Two

Head for the **Cruz de Tejeda** to contemplate the surrounding sacred mountains and towering peaks. Stride out on a half-hour walk to the mystic **Roque Nublo** landmark, before rewarding the exertion with a visit to Tejeda's famous **bakery**. Next stop is **Artenara**, with its cave dwellings and panoramic views, especially from the terrace of **Bar La Esquina**, a handy refuelling spot. Spend the afternoon exploring the backroads of the island's magnificent interior.

Day Three

Take a walk on the fabulous **Maspalomas dunes**, a peaceful haven from the clamour of the coast. Next, stop by the **Fedac** store at the Playa del Inglés tourist office to stock up on quality handicrafts. Head down the coast to picturesque **Puerto de Mogán** and a late seafood lunch at **Patio Canario**, overlooking the bobbing boats. After lunch, collapse on a sunbed on the beach before heading up to **Mogán** itself for a stroll around one of the most delightful small towns on the island.

Getting Away from It All

» **Hike in the mountains** Pick up a tourist-office brochure of mapped walks around Tejeda (p54).

» **Pack a picnic** Head for the lush and green Barranco de Guayadeque (p52) or the lakeside picnic tables at Presa de las Cuevas de las Niñas (p69).

» **Visit a farmers market** Teror is one of the interior's most stunning small towns. Come here on a Saturday morning to join the locals at the weekly produce market (p57).

DON'T MISS

Exploring the interior of the island with its dramatic scenery, including pine-clad massive mountain ranges stretching for as far as the eye can see.

Best Archaeological Sites

» **Troglodyte caves** (p62) Fascinating prehistoric caves; some are still inhabited.

» **Cueva Pintada** (p60) Intriguing geometric paintings in a cave once occupied by the Guanches.

» **Cenobio de Valerón** (p59) Over 350 ancient silos and caves historically used for storing grain.

Best Beaches

» **Playa de las Canteras** (p47) A truly capital-city beach with calm waters and a 3km-long arc of golden sand.

» **Maspalomas** (p62) Fabulous golden sand dunes in the south of the island.

» **Puerto de Mogán** (p67) A crescent of pale sand fronts this delightful small harbour resort.

Resources

» Official tourism site: www.grancanaria.com

» Rural tourism and accommodation: www.ecoturismocanarias.com

» Gay website with info on bars and nightlife: www.gay-grancanaria.com

» Online magazine www.islandconnections.eu

History

For many, one of the attractions of Gran Canaria is the intriguing mix of nationality and ethnic cultures, particularly in the capital, Las Palmas. This is nothing new. The island has historically been home to waves of settlers who have all had a lingering impact.

First on the scene, around 500 BC, were north Africans (better known as the Guanches), who named the island Tamarán after the date palms *(tamar)*. In 1478, despite their plucky resistance, the Guanches' culture was largely obliterated by the Spanish. Gran Canaria was soon colonised by a ragtag assortment of adventurers and landless hopefuls from as far away as Galicia, Andalucía, Portugal, Italy, France, the Low Countries and even Britain and Ireland.

Las Palmas subsequently became the seat of the Canary Islands' bishopric and royal court, as well as a way station en route to the Americas. The economy was further boosted by sugar exports and transatlantic trade. But, as the demand for Canary Islands' sugar fell, and the fortunes of wine grew, the island declined before its main rival and superior wine-grower, Tenerife.

Many Canarians emigrated to South America, initiating a strong affinity between the two cultures that is still in evidence today. It was not until the late 19th century, however, that Gran Canaria recovered its position; and the importance of the island as a refuelling port for steamships resulted in investment from foreign merchants, including the British.

It's an investment that continues to this day, only now in the form of tourism. The package-holiday boom of the mid-20th century has brought lasting prosperity to the island although, inevitably, there has been an environmental price to pay.

❶ Getting There & Away

AIR

Major operators from other Canary Islands include **Air Europa** (www.aireuropa.com), **Spanair** (www.spanair.com), **Vueling** (www.vueling.com), **Binter** (www.binternet.com) and **Islas Airways** (www.islasairways.com).

BOAT

Acciona Trasmediterránea (Map p44; ☎902 45 46 45, www.trasmediterranea.com) runs a weekly ferry at 2pm on Thursday that makes the following stops:

» Santa Cruz de Tenerife, Tenerife (€30, four hours)

ROAD DISTANCES (KM)

	Arucas	Maspalomas	Puerto de Mogán	Las Palmas de Gran Canaria
Maspalomas	68			
Puerto de Mogán	95	29		
Las Palmas de Gran Canaria	14	56	104	
Teror	13	66	35	21

Approximate distances only

» Puerto del Rosario, Fuerteventura (€33, six hours)

» Arrecife, Lanzarote (€33, 9½ hours)

Naviera Armas (Map p44; www.navieraarmas.com) runs the following direct ferry services:

» Santa Cruz de Tenerife, Tenerife (€31, 2½ hours, two or three times daily Monday to Friday)

» Morro Jable, Fuertenventura (€43, three hours, 7.10am daily)

» Arrecife, Lanzarote (€43, eight hours, 11.50pm Monday to Friday)

There are also twice-weekly services to Santa Cruz de la Palma, La Palma, via Santa Cruz de Tenerife.

LAS PALMAS DE GRAN CANARIA

POP 377,000

Las Palmas has a mainland-Spain feel, spiced up with an eclectic mix of other cultures, including African, Chinese and Indian, plus the presence of container-ship crews, and the flotsam and jetsam that tend to drift around port cities. It's an intriguing place, with the sunny languor and energy you would normally associate with the Mediterranean or north Africa. The hooting taxis, bustling shopping districts, chatty bars and thriving port all give off the energy of a city: Spain's seventh-largest.

Vegueta, the oldest quarter and declared a Unesco World Heritage site in 1990, is both atmospheric and fashionable; many of the best bars and restaurants are here. At the other end of town, the sweeping arc of Playa de las Canteras provides you with the tantalising possibility of having a plunge in between your sightseeing and shopping. Above all, Las Palmas is an

To Santa Cruz de Tenerife; Santa Cruz de la Palma

To Cádiz (Spain)

To Santa Cruz de Tenerife

Punta Sardina

Faro de Sardina
Sardina
Gáldar

Santa María de Guía
GC-2

Playa de las Canteras

Punta de la Vieja
Isleta (239m)
La Isleta
Roque Negro

Bahía del Confital

Vegueta
5 Las Palmas de Gran Canaria

Pico del Viento (837m)
GC-330
La Montaña de Arucas
Moya
Arucas
GC-23

San Fernando
GC-305
Firgas
GC-21

Jardín Botánico Canario Viera y Clavijo
Playa de la Laja

Puerto de las Nieves
Agaete

Barranco de Agaete

Los Berrazales
GC-75

Teror
Tafira
GC-110
Bandama
To Puerto del Rosario (Fuerteventura); Arrecife (Lanzarote); Morro Jable (Fuereventura)

Tamadaba (1444m)
GC-200
Valleseco

Santa Brígida

Caldera de Bandama
GC-140

Artenara 7
Cruz de Tejeda
La Atalaya
GC-42

Telde
GC-130
GC-140
GC-1

Puerto de la Aldea

Aldea de San Nicolás
Roque Bentayga (1404m)
2 Tejeda
GC-15
Vega de San Mateo
GC-41

Artejévez

GC-210
Roque Nublo (1803m)
Ayacata
Pozo de las Nieves (1949m)

Montaña de las Monjas (1471m)

Barranco de Guayadeque
GC-100

Los Azulejos

Presa de las Cuevas
GC-605
San Bartolomé de Tirajana
Taidia
Airport

Mogarenes (892m)

Santa Lucía de Tirajana
Temisas
Ingenio
Agüimes
Las Rosas

Mogán
Guirre (932m)
Fataga
GC-551
GC-1

Amurga (1131m)
GC-65
GC-500
Arinaga

Puerto de Mogán
Taurito
Palmitos Park
GC-60
Vecindario

Playa del Cura
Playa del Tauro
Puerto Rico
Mundo Aborigen
El Doctoral
Juan Grande
Playa de Tarajalillo (Bahía Feliz)

Arguineguín
GC-500
GC-1
San Agustín
Maspalomas
Playa Aguila
Playa de las Burras

Playa de Triana
Costa Meloneras
Playa de Carpinteras
Pasito Bea
Playa del Inglés
Dunas de Maspalomas

Playa de Maspalomas

ATLANTIC OCEAN

Barranco de Tirajana

Gran Canaria Highlights

1 Ponder the pastel-painted buildings in lovely **Agüimes** (p52), an aesthetically restored 15th-century village

2 Drink in the incredible views at **Cruz de Tejeda** (p55), positioned at the very centre of the island

3 Dig into lunch at a cave restaurant in the dramatic

Barranco de Guayadeque (p52)

4 Hop on a boat at **Puerto de Mogán** (p67), with its bridges, waterways and picturesque harbour

5 Wander the ancient streets of **Vegueta** (p48), a fascinating capital-city *barrio*

6 Wonder at the ancient cave paintings at Gáldar's fascinating **Cueva Pintada Museum & Archaeological Park** (p60)

7 Explore the cave houses in stuck-in-a-time-warp **Artenara** (p62)

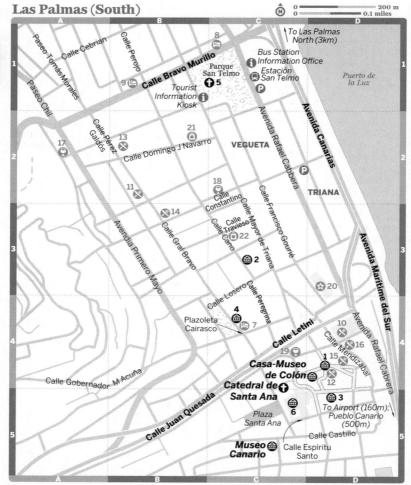

authentic Spanish working city that doesn't warrant its somewhat seedy image. Sure, like any port, there are areas where you wouldn't walk at night with an expensive camera slung round your neck but, overall, you should feel perfectly safe here and the city is well-deserving of at least a couple of days of exploration.

History

By the time Christopher Columbus passed by on his way to the Americas in 1492, the busy little historic centre had already been traced out by the Spanish. The city benefited greatly from the Spanish conquest of Latin America and subsequent transatlantic trade but, inevitably, became a favourite target for pirates and buccaneers. In 1595 Sir Francis Drake raided Las Palmas with particular gusto.

In 1821 Santa Cruz de Tenerife was declared capital of the single new Spanish province of Las Islas Canarias, which left the great and good of Las Palmas seriously disgruntled; redress didn't arrive until 1927, when Las Palmas became capital of Gran Canaria, Fuerteventura and Lanzarote.

GRAN CANARIA LAS PALMAS DE GRAN CANARIA

The fortunes of the port city continued to fluctuate until the end of the 19th century, when prosperity arrived thanks to the growing British presence in the city. In early 1936 General Franco was appointed General Commander of the Canaries and, on 18 July, the city gained dubious fame when the Spanish dictator stayed at the Hostal Madrid, from where he planned and launched the coup that sparked the Spanish Civil War; he also sparked small-time fury at the hotel for reputedly leaving without paying for his room.

Since the 1960s tourism boom, Las Palmas has grown from a middling port city of 70,000 to a bustling metropolis of close to 400,000 people. And, while it shares the status of regional capital evenly with Santa Cruz de Tenerife, there is no doubt that Las Palmas packs the bigger punch in terms of influence and size.

PLAIN SAILING

In the 1880s, when Puerto de la Luz (Las Palmas) was developing as a port, merchant and passenger ships had to moor some way from the docks. A quasi-rowing boat–cum-yacht was developed to ferry people and goods from ship to shore.

Like any business, these little *botes* (boats) suffered both busy and slack times. During the latter, their captains and crews organised regattas in the port area. This idea, born to ease the boredom of long days before Facebook, eventually developed into a regular competition, and the tradition continues.

Eighteen of these curious craft remain today and regularly gather for an afternoon's racing on Saturday (usually from 5pm) and Sunday (around noon) from April to October. Crewed by eight to 12 people, each boat represents a district of Las Palmas.

Apart from the odd appearance of the participating vessels, the race itself is delightfully eccentric in that competitors race only *en bolina* (against the wind), but in such a way as to get maximum power from it. The fact that the prevailing wind remains pretty much the same off the east coast of Gran Canaria makes it the ideal spot for such races. The *botes* start at Playa de la Laja, a few kilometres south of the southern suburbs of Las Palmas, and finish at Playa de Alcaravaneras.

◉ Sights

The most interesting sights, as well as most of the hotels, are concentrated in Vegueta, while the heavier, more international action is around Santa Catalina. The 3km-long golden sands of Playa de las Canteras is one of the loveliest city beaches in Europe. Ensure you make the time to have a leisurely stroll along the promenade during your visit.

VEGUETA & TRIANA

This is the most historic and architecturally rich city district with traditional colonial buildings and enticing hidden courtyards. Take the time to stroll the streets, ducking into the atmospheric bars and restaurants along the way.

TOP
CHOICE **Casa-Museo de Colón**   MUSEUM
(Map p42; www.casadecolon.com; Calle Colón 1; admission free; ⊙9am-7pm Mon-Fri, to 6pm Sat, to 3pm Sun; 🖝) A superb example of Canarian architecture, the museum is built around two balconied patios, complete with fountains, palm trees and parrots. The exterior is a work of art itself, with some showy *plateresque* (silversmith-like) elements, combined with traditional heavy wooden balconies.

Las Palmas (North)

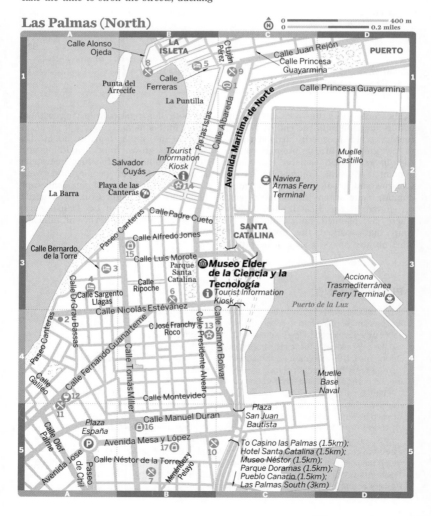

Although called Columbus' House (it's possible he stopped here in 1492), most of what you see dates from the time this building was the opulent residence of Las Palmas' early governors.

The museum's four sections include fascinating accounts of Columbus' voyages, the Canary Islands' historical role as a staging post for transatlantic shipping, pre-Columbian America and the city of Las Palmas. Don't miss the model galleon on the ground floor, which particularly impresses children. Upstairs is an art gallery with some striking canvases from the Hispanic-Flemish school, and some more recent 19th- and 20th-century works by Canarian artists.

Catedral de Santa Ana   CATHEDRAL
(Map p42; Calle Obispo Codina 13; ☺8am-10am Mon-Fri, 8am-10am & 6-8pm Sat, 8.30am-1.30pm Sun) The spiritual heart of the city, the brooding, grey cathedral was begun in the early 15th century, soon after the Spanish conquest, but took 350 years to complete. The neoclassical facade contrasts with the interior, which is a fine example of what some art historians have named Atlantic Gothic, with lofty columns which seem to mimic the palm trees outside. The retable above the high altar comes from Catalunya (mainland Spain) and the exquisite lamp hanging before the altar was made in Genoa (Italy). There are also several paintings by Juan de Miranda, the islands' most-respected 18th-century artist.

Museo Diocesano   MUSEUM
(Map p42; Calle Espíritu Santo 20; admission €3; ☺10am-4.30pm Mon-Fri, to 1.30pm Sat) This building is set on two levels around the Patio de los Naranjos, once home to the Inquisition. It contains a fairly standard collection of religious art and memorabilia, including centuries-old manuscripts, wooden sculptures and other ornaments, but the setting is lovely – and fragrant, with the scent of orange blossom in springtime.

You can also access the cathedral's tower (admission €1.50; ☺10am-4.30pm Mon-Fri, to 1.30pm Sat) for a stunning wide-angle view of the surrounding city and its coast.

Museo Canario   MUSEUM
(Map p42; www.elmuseocanario.com; Calle Dr Verneau 2; adult/child €3/1.20; ☺10am-8pm Mon-Fri, to 2pm Sat & Sun; ☝) The island's main museum chronicles Gran Canaria's preconquest history. It claims the heady boast of having the largest collection of Cro-Magnon skulls in the world. There are also several mummies, plus a collection of pottery and other Guanche implements from across the island. The gift shop stocks some excellent children's educational material.

FREE Centro Atlántico de Arte Moderno   MUSEUM
(CAAM, Atlantic Centre of Modern Art; Map p42; www.caam.net; Calle Balcones 11; ☺10am-9pm Tue-Sat, to 2pm Sun) The city's main modern art museum hosts some superb temporary exhibitions, while its permanent collection

focuses on 20th-century art from both Canarian and international artists. The galleries are flooded with natural light and housed in a tastefully rejuvenated 18th-century building. Confusingly, there is a second, smaller, CAAM a couple of streets away on San Antonio Abad 1 (open from 10am to 6pm, Tuesday to Saturday), which holds temporary exhibitions of modern-art installations, including short, edgy films.

Gabinete Literario HISTORIC BUILDING
(Library; Map p42; Plazoleta Cairasco) This ornate historical building dates from 1844 and was a national monument. It was the island's first theatre and retains an old-world display of faded elegance, with a gracious internal patio and rooms lined with bookcases. The place now functions as a private club, although the pricey French restaurant (La Galeria) is open to all.

Calle Mayor de Triana HISTORIC STREET
(Map p42) This pedestrianised street has long been the main shopping artery in Las Palmas. In between window shopping, look skyward to enjoy some real architectural gems, including several striking examples from the modernism school of architecture.

FREE **Casa-Museo de Pérez Galdós** MUSEUM
(Map p42; www.casamuseoperezgaldos.com; Calle Cano 6; ☺10am-2pm & 4-8pm Mon-Fri, 10am-2pm Sat & Sun) In 1843 the Canary Islands' most famous writer, Benito Pérez Galdós, was born in this house in the heart of old Las Palmas. He spent the first 19 years of his life here before moving on to Madrid and literary greatness. The house contains a reconstruction of the author's study, various personal effects and other objects relating to

his life. It is a delightful place with a pretty central courtyard. Guided tours take place hourly, but only in Spanish.

Parque San Telmo PARK
(Map p42) The Iglesia de San Telmo, on the southwestern side of the park, was one of the first religious buildings in town. Beside it is a tourist information kiosk and, in the northwestern corner, a beautiful Modernist kiosk, which these days functions as a classy cafe for breakfast, drinks and light snacks, like nachos with cheese, served on the open-air terrace.

CIUDAD JARDÍN

This leafy, upper-class suburb is an eclectic mix of architectural styles, ranging from British colonial to whitewashed Andalusian. Also here is lovely **Parque Doramas**, with its fine *dragos* (dragon trees). The park was designed by the British towards the end of the 19th century, when the UK dominated the economic life of Las Palmas.

FREE **Pueblo Canario** TOURIST VILLAGE
(www.pueblocanario.es; ☺10am-8pm Tue-Sat, to 2.30pm Sun; ⌖) Designed by artist Néstor Martín Fernández de la Torre, and built by his brother Miguel, this mock Canarian village borders the gardens of the Parque Doramas. With a restaurant, central plaza, handicraft shops and children's playground, it is designed as a pleasant bit of escapism in a quasi-traditional Canarian village. Traditional folk music is played here at 11.30am on Sundays. The *pueblo* is located on the south side of the Parque Doramas, around 500m south of Calle Leopoldo Matos, via the Paseo Marítimo and Calle León y Castillo.

Museo Néstor MUSEUM
(Pueblo Canario; admission €2; ☺10am-8pm Tue-Sat, 10.30am-2.30pm Sun) This art gallery is dedicated to the works of symbolist painter Néstor, who died in 1938, and also includes a modest collection of works by fellow Canarian artists. For directions, see Pueblo Canario.

SANTA CATALINA

Santa Catalina is an intriguing mix of city beach, multicultural melting pot, edgy port and business hub. At times you'll feel like you're in the developing world; at other times you're firmly in mainland Spain. Parque Santa Catalina is safe enough in daylight, though you can expect a fair number of down-and-outs, which increase after dark.

HAVE YOUR SAY

Found a fantastic restaurant that you're longing to share with the world? Disagree with our recommendations? Or just want to talk about your most recent trip?

Whatever your reason, head to lonely planet.com, where you can post a review, ask or answer a question on the Thorntree forum, comment on a blog, or share your photos and tips on Groups. Or you can simply spend time chatting with like-minded travellers. So go on, have your say.

Museo Elder de la Ciencia y la Tecnología

TOP CHOICE

(Museum of Science & Technology; Map p44; www.museoelder.org; Parque Santa Catalina; adult/child €5/2.50, incl 3D film €8.50/€4; ⊙10am-8pm Tue-Sun; ⓐ) This 21st-century science and technology museum is full of things that whirr, clank and hum. It occupies a revamped dockside warehouse to the east of Parque Santa Catalina and is a great space to spend a few hours. You can pilot a supersonic fighter plane, see how rockets send satellites into orbit or have a ride on the Robocoaster where a robotic arm whizzes you through a series of programmable manoeuvres. Children will be rapt at some of the displays – a space pod, interactive chroma-key screen and (perhaps not) at the graphic depiction of a baby's birth. There is also a small theatre showing a regularly changing programme of 3D films (with titles such as *Wild Ocean* and *Dinosaurs Alive*), which is great for families.

FURTHER AFIELD

FREE Jardín Botánico Canario
Viera y Clavijo   BOTANICAL GARDEN
(Botanical Garden; ⊙9am-6pm) About 9km southwest of the city, just before the village of Tafira Alta, this vast botanical garden – Spain's largest, encompassing 27 hectares – hosts a broad range of Macronesian flora from all the Canary Islands, including many species on the verge of extinction.

Buses 301, 302 and 303 pass by the garden's upper entrance. By car, take the C-811 road from Las Palmas.

🏖 Beaches

Playa de las Canteras   BEACH
The fine 3km stretch of yellow, sandy beach lies a few hundred metres west of the centre, creating a holiday-resort border to the city. There's an attractive *paseo marítimo* (seaside promenade) – the Paseo Canteras – which allows walkers, cyclists, joggers and rollerbladers to cover the entire length of the beach, free from traffic. The whole area hums with the activity of bars, restaurants, nightclubs and shops.

🏊 Activities

Playa de las Canteras is superb for swimming, strolling and sandcastle-making, but doesn't offer the world's greatest surf break. It's good for beginners, though, and you will

PEDAL POWER 47

You can cycle around the city free by registering in the local **Bici Ambiental** (www.biciambeintal.org/, in Spanish) scheme. There are five pick-up locations in town and you can borrow a bike for up to four hours. In order to borrow the bike, you must show your ID with photo (passport or driving licence) at any of the pick-up points. For more information and locations check the website.

find plenty of locals here at the weekend. You'll need your own board.

7 Mares Las Canteras   DIVING
(Map p44; www.7mares.es; Calle Tenerife 12; 1hr dive €24, 2hr initiation dive €60) Has English-speaking diving instructors and offers courses at all levels, plus wreck dives and equipment rental.

🎓 Courses

There are several language schools in Las Palmas where you can take Spanish studies.

Gran Canaria School of Languages   LANGUAGE
(Map p44; ⊙928 26 79 71; www.grancanariaschool.com; Calle Dr Grau Bassas 27) Has been in business for more than 40 years and has an excellent reputation. It offers intensive courses from €145 per week. Lodging may also be arranged.

🎉 Festivals & Events

Carnaval   CARNIVAL
Celebrated throughout the island during February or March, but particularly in Las Palmas. Two to three weeks of madness and fancy dress mark the first rupture with winter in February (the dates move depending on when Lent falls), with the bulk of the action taking place around Parque de Santa Catalina, where there is a giant outdoor stage. Annual events include the crowning of both the Carnival and Drag Queens, and the Burial of the Sardine, when a huge effigy of a sardine is paraded through the streets to the beach at Las Canteras, where it is ceremoniously buried. An extravagant fireworks display is a fitting end to the celebrations. Check www.laspalmascarnaval.com for more information.

ℹ FOLLOW THE SHOPPING BASKETS

For the freshest and cheapest produce, including everything you might need for a picnic, check out the covered markets: the best are located between Calles Barcelona and Néstor de la Torre (Map p44) and on the corner of Calle Mendizabal and Calle Juan de Quesada (Map p42) in Vegueta.

Festival del Sol   FILM FESTIVAL
A big-time gay and lesbian film festival that takes place in Las Palmas during mid-February.

Corpus Christi   CORPUS CHRISTI
This feast with movable dates takes place around June and is marked by the laying out of extraordinary floral 'carpets' in some of Las Palmas' historic streets.

Fiesta de San Juan   SAINT'S DAY
This Las Palmas festival takes place on 23 June to honour the city's patron saint. Cultural events are staged across the city, while fireworks and concerts take place on Playa de las Canteras.

✗ Eating

The choice of restaurants in Las Palmas reflects its stylish big-city feel. For the most atmosphere, head to the Vegueta and Triana *barrios*. If you are after Asian cuisine, there are plenty of Japanese and Chinese restaurants (and supermarkets) around Calle Valencia, southwest of Plaza España.

VEGUETA & TRIANA

[TOP CHOICE] **Restaurante El Herreño**   CANARIAN €
(Map p44; Calle Mendizábal 5; mains €7; ⚑) Don't miss a visit to this atmospheric place with its cavernous dining rooms and well-prepared Canarian dishes at excellent prices. Kick-start your menu with a *ración* of *mojo* potatoes and then choose from a menu that reads like a book. The service is zippy and everything is freshly made – and fresh: the market is right across the street.

La Dolce Vita   ITALIAN €€
(Map p42; Calle Agustín Millares 5; mains €10-13; ⊘closed Wed evening & Sun; ✎) Tucked down a narrow pedestrian street, the homemade pasta here is the real thing, with imaginative sauces like artichokes and almonds. The

decor is fun, with Italian film posters papering the walls, and there's a small shop selling Italian goodies out back.

Deliciosa Marta   SPANISH €€€
(Map p42; ☎928 37 08 82; Calle Pérez Galdós 23; mains €12-20; ⊘closed Tue evening & Sun) This chic place with its exposed stone wall and moody lighting has become one of the prime dining spots in town since it opened in 2007. The chef-cum-owner Poli trained in Barcelona at the famous El Bulli – and it shows, with dishes like *bacalau con espinacas a la catalana* (Catalan-style cod with spinach) and pasta with truffles. Reservations recommended.

Restaurante Amaiur   CANARIAN €€€
(Map p42; ☎928 37 07 17; Calle Pérez Galdós 2; mains €20-50; ⊘closed Sun) Next to a 19th-century palace, this special-occasion place is of similar vintage, with elegant dining rooms, parquet floors and high ceilings. Dishes like peppers stuffed with codfish, monkfish with prawns, and caviar should placate the most discerning gourmet. Reservations recommended.

Restaurante Casa Montesdeoca   CANARIAN €€€
(Map p42; ☎928 33 34 66; Calle Montesdeoca 10; mains €14-18; ⊘closed Sun) A romantic restaurant set in an exquisite 16th-century house. Dine in the gorgeous, leafy patio with its traditional wooden balconies and sunny, yellow walls. Any of the meat or seafood dishes can be heartily recommended. Reserve ahead.

La Olivia   CANARIAN €
(Map p42; www.laolivia.es; Calle Pérez Galdós 32; ⊘9am-4pm Mon-Fri) Reliably good lunchtime menu and outside seating.

SANTA CATALINA & THE PORT

[TOP CHOICE] **Thai Malacca**   THAI €€
(Map p44; Calle Diderot 14; mains €10-12; ⊘closed Sun; ✎) Hidden in the backstreets, but well worth hunting out, the Thai chef here creates authentic dishes that won't disappoint the fussiest Thai-food aficionado. The menu includes red and green curries, Tom Yum soup, Panang curry and wok dishes. Glossy dark wood, decorative orchids, and (restrained) ethnic artwork combine with stylish ceramic tableware to create a quietly elegant atmosphere.

La Marinera
SEAFOOD €€€

(Map p44; ☎928 46 88 02; Paseo de las Canteras; mains €12-16) You can spot this place from afar thanks to its distinctive position at the end of the boardwalk, surrounded by black rocks and thundering surf. The menu is exclusively fishy, with fresh fish sold by the kilo (keep an eye on the price here to avoid nasty shocks). Paella, *pescada al la sal* (fish coated in salt) and *sopa de mariscos* (seafood soup) are also good choices. Reservations recommended.

Casa Pablo
SPANISH €€€

(Map p44; ☎928 22 46 31; Calle Nicolás Estévenez 10; mains €12-35; **P**) A grand old restaurant with a knight in armour lording it over the front door. Plenty of Spanish celebrity pics adorn the walls to leave you in no doubt that this is *the* place to come in Las Palmas for solid traditional cuisine. You can be a lightweight with an excellent tapas menu if you prefer. Reservations recommended.

Natural Burguer
VEGETARIAN €

(Map p44; Avenida Mesa y López 3; mains €2.50-2.75; 🖉) South of Santa Catalina, this eco-burger joint is justifiably popular with budget-seekers and students. Veggie burgers with a choice of toppings are on the menu, as well as regular beef burgers. Extras include watercress salad, corn on the cob and *papas del abuelo* (thick-cut potato chips).

Mesón Condado
SPANISH €

(Map p44; Calle Ferreras 22; mains €5-8) This is a better-than-decent, middle-of-the-road (decor-wise) restaurant serving up a combination of Galician food, Canarian fare and more mainstream Spanish dishes. A very satisfying *menú del día* (set menu) will set you back a piffling €6 or so.

🍷 Drinking

There is no shortage of watering holes in Las Palmas. There are popular *terrazas* on Plaza España (Map p44) and lining Parque Santa Catalina (Map p44), but it's the Vegueta area, with its low-key ambience, that is the most fashionable place for a night-time tipple, particularly around Calle La Pelota.

🍸 Txiki
BAR

(Map p44; Calle Diderot 15; ⊗9pm-2am Mon-Sat) Aimed at a discerning, eco-aware crowd, this place doubles as an ecological restaurant during the day, with a night-time flipside that includes live music, theatre and exhibitions.

Macabeo
BAR

(Map p42; Calle La Pelota 18) This place oozes atmosphere and style, its cavernous interior decorated with local art and shelves of dusty bottles. A second, smaller bar with dim lighting and stone walls is perfect for locked-eyes-over-cocktails time.

Bodegón Lagunetas
BAR

(Map p42; Calle Constantino 16) One of several tapas bars on this street, this one also has a restaurant. Hang out in the bar with a *caña* (beer) and enjoy the fascinating sepia photo exhibition of late-19th-century Las Palmas.

Alambique
BAR

(Map p42; Avenida Primero Mayo 57; ⊗9pm-3am Tue-Sat) Located around 300m west of Parque San Telmo, this place is easy to miss, so look for the Mahou beer sign. Expect a chill-out setting and effortlessly stylish regulars, as well as exhibitions and occasional live music.

★ Entertainment

Pick up the monthly *La Bohemia* (www.labohemia.es) booklet to find out what is going on in town.

Auditorio Alfredo Kraus
LIVE MUSIC

(☎928 49 17 70; www.auditorio-alfredokraus.com; Avenida Principe de Asturias) A spectacular auditorium, designed by Catalan architect Óscar Tusquets, and striking in its geometric modernity. Constructed partly of volcanic rock, with a huge window and panoramic ocean views, it is the dominant feature of the southern end of Playa de las Canteras (around 1km from the waterfront tourist office). This is one of the venues for the annual summer **Jazz Festival** (www.canariasjazz.com).

Casino Las Palmas
CASINO

(www.casinolaspalmas.com; ⊗8pm-4am) If you feel like a flutter, don the glad rags, grab your passport and head for the casino within the city's prestigious Hotel Santa Catalina, built in 1904 in the heart of Parque Doramas.

Pacha
NIGHTCLUB

(Map p44; Calle Simón Bolivar 3; ⊗11pm-5.30am) Part of the Pacha empire and a super-cool place to see and be seen, the club attracts a slightly more mature crowd than the usual bump-and-grind discos.

Royal VIP NIGHTCLUB
(Map p44; Melia Las Palmas, Calle Gomera 6; ⏱11pm-4.30am) Part of the swanky Melia hotel, this nightclub welcomes a healthy mix of ages.

Teatro Pérez Galdós THEATRE
(Map p42; ☎928 36 15 09; www.teatroperez galdos.es; Calle Letini 1) Stages theatrical performances and music recitals.

Sport

Union Deportiva de Las Palmas (UD; www .udlaspalmas.net in Spanish) is Gran Canaria's premier football team. To see it in action, join the throngs heading for the 31,000-seat **Estadio Gran Canaria** (☎928 41 69 45; Calle Fondos del Segura). The stadium is located around 4.5km from Vegueta, heading southwest via the GC-23 and GC-1 highways (direction Teror).

🛍 Shopping

The long-time traditional shoppers' street is Calle Mayor de Triana (Map p42), which is as interesting for its architecture as its idiosyncratic shops. Other recommended shopping strips include Calle Cano, Calle Viera y Clavijo and the surrounding streets.

Las Palmas' super-chic shoppers' hangout is Avenida Mesa y López (Map p44). Here you'll find the mammoth department store **El Corte Inglés** (Map p44; www.elcorte ingles.es; Avenida Mesa y López 15 & 18), as well as numerous shops and boutiques. Nearby, around Parque Santa Catalina, there are plenty of cheap electronic-goods and discount shops with great deals on cameras, watches, computer equipment and mobile phones.

Fedac SOUVENIRS
(Foundation for Ethnography & the Development of Canarian Handicrafts; Map p42; Calle Domingo J Navarro 7) Head to these two adjacent government-sponsored, nonprofit stores for handicrafts. One specialises in modern design, including exquisite hand-painted silk scarves, woven shawls and modern jewellery, while next door the emphasis is more traditional and includes pottery and basketware.

**Librería del Cabildo Insular
de Gran Canaria** BOOKSTORE
(Map p42; Calle Travieso 15) Stocks lots of titles about the Canary Islands. Most are in Spanish but there are a few shelves of English guides, including Lonely Planet and similar.

Boxes & Cigars CIGARS
(Map p44; Calle Tomás Miller 80) If it's cigars you're after, this place has a dazzling range on offer, with the boxes just about as attractive as the smokes.

ⓘ Information

Internet Access

Due to the large number of immigrants in Las Palmas, the city is awash with internet cafes, generally located within *locutorios* (telephone call centres), which also offer cheap international calls.

Wi-fi is increasingly available at midrange and top-end hotels, and occasionally at public spaces and in town centres.

Money

For the highest concentration of banks with 24-hour ATM machines head for Calle José Franchy Roca, just south of Parque Santa Catalina.

Tourist Information

The regional tourist authority website is www .grancanaria.com.

Main tourist office (Calle León y Castillo 17; ⏱8am-3pm Mon-Fri) Located around 150m north of Parque San Telmo.

Bus station information office (Map p42; Estación San Telmo, Parque San Telmo; ⏱6.30am-8.30pm Mon-Fri, 7.30am-1pm Sat & Sun) Great for island-wide transport and general info.

TOURIST INFORMATION KIOSKS Parque San Telmo (Map p42; ⏱10am-8pm Mon-Fri, to 3pm Sat); **Playa de las Canteras** (Map p44; ⏱10am-7.30pm Mon-Fri, to 1pm Sat); **Parque Santa Catalina**; (Map p44; ⏱9am-2pm Mon-Fri); **Pueblo Canario** (Ciudad Jardin; ⏱9am-2.30pm Mon-Fri)

ⓘ Getting There & Away

Bus

Estación San Telmo (Map p42; www.globalsu .net; Parque San Telmo) is located at the northern end of the Vegueta district and can provide an island-wide schedule. Frequent main bus lines:

» Buses 5 and 50 express to Maspalomas (€6.50, 50 minutes).

» Buses 91 and 1 to Puerto de Mogán (€8.35, two hours).

» Buses 12 and 80 to Telde (€1.60, about 20 minutes)

» Bus 105 to Gáldar (€2.95, one hour).

The night-owl bus 5 links the capital and Maspalomas. It leaves on the hour from 8pm to 3am from Estación San Telmo in Las Palmas, and on the half-hour from 9.30pm to 4.30am from Maspalomas.

Car
There are car-rental firms at the airport, at the ferry terminal and throughout the Santa Catalina district.

ⓘ Getting Around
To/From the Airport
BUS Bus 60 runs between the airport and Estación San Telmo twice-hourly between 7am and 7pm and hourly thereafter (€2.20, 25 minutes), continuing onto Santa Catalina (€2.85, 35 minutes).

TAXI A taxi between the airport and central Las Palmas costs about €28.

Bus
Yellow buses serve the metropolitan area. Pick up a route map from the tourist office, kiosks or the bus station.

Yellow buses 1, 12, 13 and 15 all run from Triana northwards as far as the port and the northern end of Playa de las Canteras, calling by the bus station and Parque Santa Catalina.

A good way of getting an initial overview of the city is on the hop-on, hop-off **City Sightseeing Bus** (adult/child €15/7.50; ⊙9.30am-7.45pm). It departs from Parque Santa Catalina irregularly 12 times daily.

Car
Driving in Las Palmas is a pain, with the normal big-city rush-hour traffic jams and a baffling one-way street system. Most of the centre operates meter parking. Otherwise, there are several underground car parks, where you pay around €1.35 per hour. The most central are at Parque Santa Catalina, Plaza de España and at Parque San Telmo, opposite the main bus station.

Taxi
If you need a **taxi** (☏928 46 00 00, 928 46 56 66, 928 46 22 12), you can call, flag one down or head for one of the plentiful taxi stands across the city.

AROUND LAS PALMAS

Charming as Las Palmas is, it is still a noisy and chaotic city. Thankfully, if you are seeking some more mellow, albeit dramatic, surroundings, you won't have far to travel.

Starting from Las Palmas, an enjoyable one-day circuit heads first south and then cuts inland to take in the stunning mountainous terrain of the Tejeda region,

before swinging northeast back towards the capital.

Telde
POP 104,900

Telde is the island's second city and, although relatively devoid of publicised museums and sights, the historic centre is well worth exploring.

The town dates back prior to the Spanish conquest and is known for its production of stringed instruments, above all the *timple* (a kind of ukulele) – the islands' musical emblem.

◉ Sights
Look beyond the city's drab industrial shell and head for the kernel: the historic centre which comprises three distinct neighbourhoods: San Gregorio, San Juan and, arguably, the prettiest *barrio* of them all, San Francisco. Here, the narrow cobbled streets are lined with simple whitewashed houses, punctuated by the brilliant dazzle of crimson bougainvillea. This is one of the oldest quarters in the Canary Islands.

Iglesia de San Francisco　　　　CHURCH
(Plaza San Francisco; ⊙sporadic) To reach the church from the central Plaza de San Juan Bautista, take cobbled Calle Inés Chanida due west. This tranquil street runs alongside an old aqueduct with orange and banana groves below. In the church, note the three polychrome stone altars on the northernmost of the twin naves and the fine *artesonado* (coffered) ceiling.

Basílica de San Juan　　　　CHURCH
(Plaza San Juan Bautista; ⊙9.30am-12.30pm & 5-8pm) Among the grand old buildings of the San Juan area is this 15th-century church. You can't miss the gloriously kitsch 16th-century altarpiece, all gilt and gold, with a Crucifixion at its heart. The Christ figure is made from a corn-based plaster (nothing to do with toes!) by Tarasco Indians in Mexico.

...o León y Castillo   MUSEUM
...andoleonycastillo.com; Calle León y Cas-
...; ⊗8am-2pm Mon-Fri, 10am-1pm Sat & Sun)
...is museum is devoted to the city's most
famous resident, a late-19th-century politi-
cian. The building, his former home, is lovely with its galleried wooden balconies, but
the exhibits, ambassadorial credentials and
the like, may fail to thrill.

🏖 Beaches

Playa de Melinara   BEACH
This decent beach is around 5km from town
and frequented by townsfolk, rather than
tourists. A wide arc of dark sandy beach is
fronted by apartments and several inexpensive (and good) seafood restaurants. You
can follow a footpath beside the rocky coast
from here all the way to Playa de la Garita,
another popular local beach, located around
3km to the north.

❶ Information

The **tourist office** (www.telde.es; Calle León y
Castillo 2; ⊗8am-3pm Mon-Fri) is just off Plaza
de San Juan.

❶ Getting There & Away

Buses 12 and 80 run to/from Las Palmas (€1.60,
about 20 minutes, every 20 minutes).

Ingenio & Agüimes

A short bus ride south of Telde brings you
to the towns of Ingenio and Agüimes, separated from each other by the Barranco de
Guayadeque. Ingenio is best known for its
ceramics but is otherwise a plain Jane compared to its neighbour.

The historic centre of Agüimes is one of
the most perfectly restored and prettiest on
the island, so much so that the mega-luxury
hotel Villa del Conde in Maspalomas is a
pastiche of the old town centre.

◉ Sights

The pedestrian streets are lined with lovely
buildings that reflect vernacular Canarian
architecture, especially surrounding shady
Plaza del Rosario. The **Iglesia de San
Sebastián** (⊗9.30am-12.30pm & 5-7pm Tue,
Thu, Sat & Sun), with its dome of 12 large
windows (symbolising the 12 apostles),
is considered one of the best examples of
Canarian neoclassicism. The **Centro de
Interpretación** (Plaza San Antón 1; ⊗8am-

3pm Mon-Fri) shares the tourist-office building and has well-documented exhibits on
the evolution of the town's urban structure
through the centuries. You can also pick up
a brochure with mapped-out walks around
town.

✗ Eating

El Oroval   CANARIAN €€
(⏺928 78 50 53; Hotel Rural Casa de los Camellos,
Calle Progreso 12; mains €12) The restaurant
here doubles as a catering school, with
dishes based on local ingredients such as
marinated rabbit stew with potatoes and
paprika, and sweet crêpes with bananas
and caramel. The beamed, narrow dining
space is surprisingly atmospheric, given
it was once a camel's stable. Reservations
recommended.

El Populacho   CANARIAN €
(Plaza del Rosario 17; tapas €2.50; ⏺) On the
corner of the main square, this welcoming
tapas bar with its zinc bar and Art Deco
lights is housed in a former grocer's shop
(1933), as depicted in the lively murals that
cover the walls. Rumbling tummies should
opt for a generous tapas portion of *estofado
lentejas* (lentil stew).

❶ Information

Agüimes' helpful **tourist office** (www.aguimes
.es; Plaza de San Antón 1; ⊗Mon-Fri 8am-3pm)
has plenty of local information.

❶ Getting There & Around

BUS Buses 21 and 11 connect Las Palmas with
Agüimes (€3.25, 45 minutes, hourly). Bus 22
heads southeast to Arinaga (€1.30, 20 minutes,
hourly), a popular coastal swimming spot even
though it lacks a real beach.

CAR There is a paying car park on Calle
Acebuche, just outside the historic centre.

Barranco de Guayadeque

The Barranco de Guayadeque (Guayadeque
Ravine) rises up into central Gran Canaria
in a majestic sweep of crumpled ridges. For
most of the year, the vegetation here is lush
and green; if you can, visit in early spring
when the almond trees are in blossom and
the landscape is stunningly verdant and
beautiful. At the entrance of the *barranco*,
the **Centro de Interpretación** (admission
€2.50; ⊗9am-5pm Tue-Sat, 10am-3pm Sun) occupies a cave, and includes exhibits and

Local cuisine is renowned for making use of every part of the *cochino* (pig). That cute, curly tail *(templero)* was traditionally hung from the kitchen doorway to be periodically dipped into the cooking pot as a stock. A typical *tapa* here, generally accompanied by the traditional rum aperitif, is *caracajas* (pieces of fried pork liver doused in a spicy sauce). Goat is also popular, along with rabbit and veal, while seafood is, naturally enough, always a good bet – this is an island, after all. Try the much-prized *vieja* (parrot fish), a member of the sea-bream family, plus, if it's included on the menu, the local crustacean *santorra,* which is similar in appearance to the common lobster but has a distinctive rich (some would say, gourmet) flavour.

Goat's cheese is produced on several islands, though one of the best-known soft cheeses, Gran Canaria's *queso de flor,* is made from a combination of cows' and sheep's milk. The cheese, which is produced exclusively in the northern Guía area, is then infused with the aroma of flowers from the *cardo alcausí* thistle. Another scrumptious winner is the similar-tasting *pastor* cheese, produced in the Arucas region. Pick up the booklet *La Ruta de los Quesos* (in English) at larger tourist offices for more cheesy information.

Almonds are a nutty favourite ingredient of many traditional desserts, including the must-try *bienmesabe* (literally translated as 'it tastes good to me') made from ground almonds, lemon rind, honey and eggs.

Among the outstanding Gran Canaria wines is the fruity Del Monte, a perfect, if tiddly, accompaniment to meat dishes, with an alcohol content over 11.5%. Aside from *ron miel* (honey rum), which is more liqueur than rum, try the banana-based *cobana,* also produced in Gran Canaria.

!Salud!

explanations on the original inhabitants, including a mummy found in a local cave in the 19th century.

Around 4km from here, watch for the inhabited caves with their quirky exteriors, and stop for a drink at **Bar Guayadeque** (Cueva Bermeja 23), housed in a cave next door to a tiny underground chapel. Continuing on, there is a picnic ground for self-caterers and a couple of evocative cave restaurants, including **El Centro** (mains €8-10) with its warren of dining rooms reaching deep into the cave. Try the *cerdo frito con alioli de la casa* (fried pork with homemade garlic mayonnaise), which won first prize in a local culinary contest. This is a superb area for walking – continue until the road peters out by Restaurante Vega, from where there are a couple of trails with stunning views that stretch right to the sea.

Temisas

If you're driving, you can take a back road that weaves around the mountains from Agüimes to Santa Lucía de Tirajana. As the road approaches the tiny village of Temisas, set on a natural balcony, note the terracing up each side of the centre and incised into the valleys below. These terraces were worked until relatively recently. Then came mass tourism on the coast, along with less-gruelling, better-paid work, which resulted in a mass exodus from the village.

The impressive setting for Temisas, with its backdrop of impenetrable cliffs, has views across a ravine that falls away down to the sea. The village itself is sleepy and atmospheric, with original stone houses and cottages.

San Bartolomé de Tirajana

POP 3620 / ELEV 850M

San Bartolomé has no notable sights, aside from a late-17th-century church with striking stained-glass windows, but the views out over the Tirajana valley are stunning and the town makes a good base for hiking and exploring the surrounding mountainous countryside – along with the endearing Germans and their hiking sticks. There are several signposted trails.

There is a small free car park on Calle Los Naranjos opposite La Hacienda del Molino.

WORTH A TRIP

QUIRKY CASTLE

Located in pretty Santa Lucía de Tirajana, with its palm-filled valley setting, is the offbeat **Castillo de la Fortaleza** (admission €2; ⊘9.30am-3pm; 🅟). Don't be put off by the gaudy tourist-office leaflets; there is something altogether beguiling about this grey-turreted private museum.

It was built around 50 years ago, not for tourism purposes but as a folly, as well as being the home of local archaeologist, writer, artist and collector Vicente Sanchez Araña, who died in 1997, aged 77 (his devoted wife died just four months later). The museum has 16 rooms that reflect the eclectic interests and energy of this veritable Renaissance man. The most impressive room houses a well-labelled (in several languages) archaeological display of Guanche artefacts found in nearby caves. These include a tiny carved female idol: a Guanche symbol and one of only two in the world (the other is exhibited in a museum in France). Another room displays ancient armaments, including a 16th-century crossbow, while still another concentrates on local botany. Upstairs there is an art gallery with some particularly impressive watercolours by Canarian artists. This labour of love is well worth the modest admission price.

Bus 34 connects Santa Lucía with San Bartolomé de Tirajana (€1.30, 40 minutes, seven daily).

Eating

Aside from La Hacienda del Molino, there are several restaurants on Calle Tamarín in the centre of town. If you are planning a visit, try and make it a Sunday when there is a lively farmers' market.

La Hacienda del Molino　　　CANARIAN €€
(Calle Los Naranjos 2; mains €7.50-€10) This well-run hotel has an inviting bar and restaurant, with tables in a central patio or rustic stone-clad dining room. Enjoy tapas such as octopus, mussels or anchovies in vinaigrette sauce, or something more substantial such as lamb cutlets or paprika-flavoured sausages. You can also buy gourmet goodies here, including papaya and mango jams, plus see the restored namesake *molino* (mill) and learn how *gofio* is made.

Fataga

A 7km detour south from San Bartolomé brings you to the charming hamlet of Fataga, sitting squat on a small knoll humbled by lofty cliffs to the west. Its cobbled lanes are a joy to roam, especially as there are at least three bodegas in this vine-growing centre – all are well signposted but, less happily, all have sporadic opening hours.

About 1.5km north of the village, parts of **El Molino del Agua** (☑928 17 23 03; Carretera Fataga; mains €8-10) hacienda date back to the 16th century. Reopened under new ownership in 2011, the historic mill is hidden

among a grove of around 1000 palm trees, and also offers accommodation. The restaurant has tables under the orange trees and a reasonable Canarian menu.

Located on the main road, **Bar Restaurante La Albaricoque** (www.restaurante albaricoque.com; Calle Nestor Álamo 4; mains €6-8; ⊘closed Tue) is good for tapas and has sound local and international fare, including seafood croquettes and filled jacket potatoes. The main draw, however, is the outside terrace with its wall-to-wall mountain views. Pop over the road for a slice of cake for dessert at **Paparazzi** (Nestor Alamo 3).

Bus 18 (€1.30, 50 minutes, four times daily) from Maspalomas to San Bartolomé stops here.

Tejeda

POP 2347 / ELEV 1050M

Tejeda is 33km north of San Bartolomé, along a road that twists its way through splendidly rugged scenery of looming cliffs and deep gorges. It is a lovely hill village with a handsome church and steep, winding streets lined with balconied houses. There is a free car park opposite the helpful **tourist office** (www.tejedaturistica.com; Calle Leocadio Cabrera 2; ⊘11am-5pm Mon-Fri).

◉ Sights

This region is ideal for hiking and less arduous walks. The tourist office has detailed brochures of surrounding trails. Try and visit in early spring when the almond trees are in blossom.

Centro de Plantas Medicinales   GARDEN
(☑928 66 60 96; www.plantasmedicinalescanarias.com; Calle Párroco Rodriguez Vega 10; adult/child €3/free; ☺11am-3.30pm Tue-Fri, 11.30am-4pm Sat, 11.30am-4.30pm Sun) An unusual garden which centres on medicinal plants with explanations (in English). There is a small interpretation centre, and a cafe where you can fittingly end your visit with a cup of curative herbal tea.

✖ Eating

Dulceria Nublo Tejeda   BAKERY €
(Calle Hernández Guerra 15) The gastronomic highlight in town is this sublime pastry shop with delicious local treats freshly baked on the premises. Try the almond cakes coated in chocolate and take home a jar of delicious *bienmesabe* (almond-and-honey spread).

Cueva de la Tea   CANARIAN €
(Calle Hernández s/n) If you want to stay in the area, check out the quaintly named **Fonda de la Tea** hotel. It also owns this restaurant on the main street, west of the church, where you can enjoy a selection of tapas for just €10, accompanied by panoramic views from the outside terrace.

Around Tejeda

CRUZ DE TEJEDA

The greenish-grey stone cross from which this spot takes its name marks the centre of Gran Canaria and its historic *caminos reales* (king's highways), along which it is still possible to cross the entire island. The site is one of the most popular coach-tour destinations from the resorts, so is usually swarming with tourists; hence the souvenir stalls and donkey rides.

From the lookouts here you can contemplate the island's greatest natural wonders: to the west is the sacred mountain Roque Bentayga and, in clear weather, you can see the towering volcanic pyramid of Teide on neighbouring Tenerife; to the southeast, the island's highest peak, Pozo de las Nieves, and the extraordinary emblem of the island, Roque Nublo (1803m), which as often as not is enveloped in cloud. Dropping away to the northeast is Vega de San Mateo.

Walking here doesn't present any great challenges, but take water, dress warmly and leave the Jimmy Choos at home. Generally, you'll follow well-paved and signposted paths that snake their way around rock formations often obscured by cloud. The half-hour walk from Cruz de Tejeda to Roque Nublo is especially recommended. You can get information and tips from Hotel El Refugio or the tourist office in Tejeda. If you are feeling peckish, **Restaurante Yolanda** (www.asadoryolanda.com), located right on the crossroads, is good for grilled meats and homely cakes.

Bus 305 (€3.75, two hours, three daily) from Las Palmas passes by on its way to Tejeda.

LOCAL KNOWLEDGE

ROGER BRADLEY: HIKING GUIDE

I firmly believe that Gran Canaria is one of the last great hiking destinations in Europe still to be truly discovered, especially by the British. Although the local government is gradually clearing and signposting walking trails, there has long been a lack of detailed walking maps. In 2010 I published a guide detailing 25 great hikes around the island – and I'm already working on the 2nd edition!

Top hike My favourite area for hiking is around Artenara, which is both beautiful and fascinating, with the largest number of occupied cave houses on the island.

Favourite scenery I always prefer to hike in areas where there are small villages, rather than in the absolute outback where you can walk for hours without seeing a soul. I enjoy stopping in a bar for a beer, seeing what people are growing in their allotments and just having a chat.

Best advice Hire a car and get away from the overbuilt beach resorts! The interior is breathtakingly beautiful and dramatic, and the roads are, overall, very good and comparatively traffic-free – except on Sundays.

ROQUE BENTAYGA

A few kilometres west of Tejeda village rises the Roque Bentayga (1404m). It's signposted but you will need your own transport. Around the Roque and surroundings there are various reminders of the Guanche presence here – from rock inscriptions to granaries and a sacred ritual site.

POZO DE LAS NIEVES

Those with their own wheels can drive 15km southeast of Tejeda to this, the highest peak on the island at 1949m. Follow the signs for Los Pechos and keep an eye out for the military communications post that sits atop the rise. On a clear day the views are breathtaking. Due northwest of here stands the distinctive Roque Nublo.

Vega de San Mateo

Descending from the barren, chilly heights of Tejeda, the landscape shifts and changes and, as you approach San Mateo, the sweeping *vega* (plain) becomes a gently undulating sea of green. As with most of the northern strip of the island (especially the northeast), the area is busily cultivated and agriculturally rich, as well as an important vine-growing region.

This area is densely populated; most of the island's population lives in the north. The town is memorable mainly for its dramatic setting, along with the farmers market held every Saturday and Sunday behind the bus station (just follow the shopping baskets). If you are here in September, try to come on the 21st for the *romería* (pilgrimage) and celebrations of the patron saint, St Matthew.

Bus 303 (€2.40, 30 minutes) comes up from Las Palmas every 30 minutes.

Santa Brígida & Caldera de Bandama

En route to Las Palmas, the next town of any note is Santa Brígida, about 9km east of Vega de San Mateo. A rather drab place, it's lifted by a pretty park and narrow, tree-lined streets at its heart. There are sweeping views from the parish church over fields and palm groves to the central mountains. Stop at the **Casa del Vino** (Calle Calvo Sotelo 26; admission free; ☺10am-3pm Mon-Fri) with its modest display of wine-making implements, plus the more entertaining option of tasting (and purchasing) local wines.

Back on the road to Las Palmas, after 4km there's a turn-off for the Caldera de Bandama, one of the largest extinct volcanic craters on the island, 1km in diameter, with superb views. Close by is **La Atalaya**, the prime pottery-producing village on the island, where you can buy lovely ceramics, then stress about transporting them home.

Bus 311 (€1.30, 30 minutes) leaves virtually hourly from Las Palmas to the village of Bandama, passing through La Atalaya, which takes you close to the crater.

THE NORTHWEST

As on most of the islands, Gran Canaria's fertile north presents a gently shifting picture from its rugged, mountainous interior and the southern beach resorts and dunes. Dramatic ravines, intensively tilled fields and terraces, and forests of pine trees, covered with mossy lichen, typify the landscape as you wind along twisting roads, and pass myriad villages and hamlets. Only as you reach the west does the green give way to a more austere, although no less captivating,

MARKET TIME

The towns and villages are the scene of some interesting small markets, most of which sell local cheeses, cold meats and bakery goods, as well as local souvenirs and trinkets. They make for an easy-going morning away from the bustle of the resorts. Markets generally last from 9am to 2pm and include the following:

» **Puerto de Mogán** (Friday) One of the most touristy.

» **San Fernando** (Wednesday and Saturday)

» **Arguineguín** (Tuesday and Thursday)

» **Teror** (Saturday and Sunday)

» **Vega de San Mateo** (Saturday and Sunday)

» **San Bartolomé de Tirajana** (Sunday)

DOGS, BIRDS & BANANAS

So how did the Canary Islands get named? After the trilling native canary birds perhaps? Or after the canary-yellow colour of the bananas that grow here? Or (yet another unlikely explanation) after the Latin word for dog (canus), because members of an early expedition discovered what they considered unusually large dogs? (Still others held that the natives of the island were dog eaters. Nice...)

A more plausible theory claims that the people of Canaria, who arrived several hundred years before Christ, were in fact Berbers of the Canarii tribe living in Morocco. The tribal name was simply applied to the island and later accepted by Pliny. How Canaria came to be Gran (Big) has a couple of predictably feeble explanations: either because the islanders put up a big fight while resisting conquest, or the island was thought to be the biggest in the archipelago. Evidently, they didn't have great tape measures in those days – as we know all too well, Tenerife and Fuerteventura are larger.

landscape: the west coast is the most dramatic on the island.

Teror

POP 13,045 / ELEV 543M

In spite of its name, Teror, 22km southwest of Las Palmas, does anything but inspire fear. The central Plaza Nuestra Señora del Pino and Calle Real are lined with picturesque old houses, painted in bright colours with leaning walls and wooden balconies. The only jarring building is the modern Auditorio de Teror, just west of the basilica. Aesthetics aside, it has admirably provided the town with a welcome cultural venue. There's a farmers market in the plaza on Saturday mornings, with stalls selling local goodies like the deliciously garlic-laden *chorizo de Teror* (sausage), which should scare off those vampires for a while. The Sunday market is larger and more commercial.

◉ Sights

The main joy in this town is just wandering around the historic centre snapping photos. Aside from this, try and check out the following.

Casa de los Patronos de la Virgen MUSEUM
(Plaza Nuestra Señora del Pino 3; admission €3; ⊙11am-4pm Mon-Fri, 10am-2pm Sun) One of the loveliest buildings here houses this modest 17th-century museum. Pleasantly musty, it's devoted to preserving 18th-century life and is full of intriguing odds and ends, mostly from the Las Palmas family, who used it as a second home.

Basílica de la Virgen del Pino CHURCH
(Plaza Nuestra Señora del Pino 3; ⊙8am-noon & 2-6pm) Dominating the square is this neoclassical 18th-century church, home to Gran Canaria's patron saint. According to legend, the Virgin was spied atop a pine tree in the nearby forest in the 15th century, which turned Teror into a quasi-Fatima pilgrimage site. The church interior, a lavishly gilt-laden affair, sees the enthroned Virgen illuminated in her place of honour at the heart of a lavishly ornate altarpiece, surrounded by angels. It's a pity about the piped religious music, but the sign to turn off your mobile phone is spot on, stating that 'you don't need a mobile to talk to God'.

★ Festivals & Events

Fiesta de la Virgen del Pino RELIGIOUS FESTIVAL
The Virgen del Pino is the patron of the island and Teror is the religious capital. This festival, held during the first week in September, is not only a big event in Teror, it's the most important religious feast day on the island's calendar. Events include processions, a livestock fair and plenty of music and dancing.

✖ Eating

El Rincón de Magüi ITALIAN €€
(Calle Diputación 6; mains €6-12) Very popular pizzeria and restaurant with outside tables, plus a brick-clad dining room decorated with ceramic plates and photos of well-fed celeb diners like former Spanish PM Aznar.

JUST A SPOONFUL OF RUM

Generally associated with dancing bare-foot on a Caribbean beach (preferably under a grove of coconut palms), rum has also long been produced here, dating back to the days of the sugar plantations. The local product has a superb international reputation, being famed for both its heart-warming flavour and, yes, even the medicinal properties. Feeling a tad feverish? Then have a glug of *ron miel* (a mead rum with honey) – it sure beats an aspirin.

❶ Getting There & Away

Buses 216, 220 and 229 connect with Las Palmas (€2.20, 30 minutes, hourly); bus 215 with Arucas (€1.30, 20 minutes, hourly).

Arucas

POP 33,800

Nicknamed the 'pearl of Gran Canaria', Arucas is a great day out from Las Palmas. It is a handsome, compact town with pedestrian streets lined with elegant historic buildings and a lovely flower-filled park.

◉ Sights

The town is a delight to just stroll around. From the Iglesia de San Juan walk down Calle Gourié to Calle León y Castillo, flanked by colourful colonial-style buildings. Turn right into Plaza Constitución, situated across from the lovely town gardens and home of the late-19th-century modernist *ayuntamiento* (town hall) and a couple of pleasant terrace bars.

Iglesia de San Juan   CHURCH
(⊙9.30am-12.30pm & 4.30-7.15pm) The extraordinary, neo-Gothic church stands sullen watch over the bright white houses of Arucas in a striking display of disproportion. The church has a Sagrada Familia (Gaudí) look with its elaborate pointed spires and was, fittingly, designed by a Catalan architect. Construction started in 1906 on the site of a former *ermita* (chapel) and was completed 70 years later. Within, a fine 16th-century Italian Crucifixion hangs above the altar; the wooden Cristo Yacente (Reclining Christ) is similarly impressive, together with three magnificent rose windows.

FREE Jardines Municipales   GARDENS
(Calle Heredad) The municipal gardens are laid out in French style with fountains, pavilions, sculptures and tropical trees, including the rare evergreen soap bark tree (*Quillaja saponaria*) and several magnificent dragon palm trees. Calle Heredad flanks the gardens on the southern side of the plaza, dominated by the beautiful neoclassical **Heredad de Aguas de Arucas y Firgas** building, completed in 1908 and now housing the local water board.

FREE Municipal Museum   MUSEUM
(Jardines Municipales; ⊙10am-8pm Mon-Fri, to 1pm Sat) The gardens house the town's main museum, which has a permanent exhibition by Canarian painters and sculptors, plus temporary shows.

FREE Destilerías Arehucas   RUM DISTILLERY
(www.arehucas.com; ⊙10am-2pm Mon-Fri) More to the taste of many visitors are the free guided visits to this rum distillery. The tour culminates in a complimentary tipple and the opportunity to buy a few bottles for those summertime *mojitos* back home.

Jardín de la Marquésa   GARDENS
(www.jardindelamarquesa.com; adult/child €6/3; ⊙9am-1pm & 2-6pm Mon-Sat) Northwest of town, on the road to Bañaderos, this lovely botanical garden is owned by the Marquésa de Arucas (along with the Hacienda del Buen Suceso). Lushly planted with more than 2500 different plants, trees and cacti, there are ponds, places to sit and a greenhouse with banana trees. The admission fee includes a detailed guide identifying the plants on display.

✖ Eating & Drinking

Tasca Jamon   TAPAS €
(Calle Gourié 5) Enjoys an ace position on this narrow pedestrian street with soul-stirring views of the church from the outside tables. Enjoy good basic tapas like wedges of crumbly Manchego cheese with crusty white bread.

La Arabesca   BAR
(Calle León y Castillo 21) This dusky pink building is home to a sophisticated, intimate bar.

La Dolorosa   BAR
(Calle Párroco Cárdenes 5) The most stylish place in town with its trendy cocktail bar, complete with music videos.

ℹ️ Information

The **tourist office** (Calle León y Castillo 10; ⊙9am-5pm Mon-Fri, 10am-1pm Sat) can assist with accommodation.

ℹ️ Getting There & Away

Buses 205, 106 and 210 provide an hourly service to/from Las Palmas (€2.20, 25 minutes). Bus 215 runs hourly to Teror (€1.30, 15 minutes).

Around Arucas

If you have wheels (preferably four), take the steep, well-signposted route to **La Montaña de Arucas**, 2.5km north of town. From here there's a splendid panorama of Las Palmas, the northern coast of the island, orchards, banana groves and, less happily, hectare upon hectare of plastic greenhouses. The restaurant here, **El Meson de la Montaña** (mains from €7), has fabulous views and is touristy but good. Solid choices include onion pie with cured ham, and fillet steak with truffles. Vegetarians have slim pickings, aside from lavish salads and a fine apple cake.

Moya

POP 8300 / ELEV 490M

The spectacular 13km drive between Arucas and Moya hugs the flank of the mountain, providing gee-whiz views of the northern coast. Moya is an unpretentious working town with some traditional Canarian architecture, including the lovely **Casa-Museo Tomás Morales** (www.tomasmorales.com; admission free; ⊙9am-2pm & 4-8pm Mon-Fri, 10am-2pm Sat), opposite the 16th-century church on Plaza de la Candelaria, with its stunning views of the *barranco* (ravine). Once home to the Canarian poet, who died in 1922 aged just 37, the museum includes a music room with a 170-year-old clavichord, a small hall used for classical concerts and a pretty walled garden with grapefruit trees and cacti.

Buses 116 and 117 run to/from Las Palmas (€2.85, one hour, 15 daily).

Santa María de Guía

POP 8430

Just off the main C-810 highway, 25km west of Las Palmas, Santa María de Guía (or just Guía) is an atmospheric small town which was temporarily home to the French composer Camille Saint-Saëns (1835-1921), who used to tickle the ivories in the town's 17th-century neoclassical church.

In the 18th century, the town and surrounding area were devastated by a plague of locusts. To rid themselves of this blight, the locals implored the Virgin Mary for help. This remains a tradition and on the third Sunday of September the townsfolk celebrate La Rama de las Marías by dancing their way to the doors of the church to make offerings of fruits. The town is also known for its *queso de flor* (flower cheese), which you can find at the local supermarkets, markets and delicatessens.

Buses 103, 105, 150 and 151 (€2.70, 50 minutes) pass by roughly every half-hour on their way from Las Palmas.

Around Santa María de Guía

Around 3km east of town lies the **Cenobio de Valerón** (www.cenobiodevaleron.com; Cuesta Silva s/n, Santa Maria de Guía; adult/child €2.50/1; ⊙10am-6pm Tue-Sun; 🅿), a fascinating ancient site consisting of over 350 caves, silos and cavities of varied size which were used to store grain in pre-Hispanic times. Located on deep slopes, separated by steps and walkways, there are informative plaques throughout explaining the history and archaeology of the site, as well as the volcanic geology of the area.

Gáldar

POP 22,763 / ELEV 124M

This charming town was the capital of the *guanartemato* (kingdom) in pre-Hispanic times and is justifiably famous for its extraordinary archaeological sights. It has a bustling and attractive historic core centred around the gracious Plaza de Santiago with its neoclassical Santiago de Gáldar church. The square is also home to one of the oldest *drago* trees on the island, dating back to 1718, and located in the patio of the 19th-century Casas Consistoriales, where the **Tourist office** (www.galdarturismo.es; Casa Consistoriales, Plaza de Santiago 1; ⊙10am-2.30pm Mon-Fri) is situated.

Locals are justifiably proud of their native son Antonio Padrón who, in the 1960s, was just starting to be seriously recognised in the European art world when he tragically died of an allergic reaction to penicillin at just

48 years old. His paintings are wonderfully colourful and distinctive, many inspired by the geometric motifs of the Guanches. The **Casa Museo Antonio Padrón** (Calle Drago 2; ⊘9am-2pm Mon-Fri) is located at the artist's former studio.

Getting There & Around

BUS Bus 105 (€2.95, one hour) heads east for Las Palmas roughly every half-hour. Southbound, bus 103 (€1.30, 20 minutes, hourly) links Gáldar with Agaete and Puerto de las Nieves.

CAR There are two free car parks on Calle Real de San Sebastián as you approach town from the direction of Las Palmas.

TAXI **Radio Taxi** (⊘928 88 35 38) is a reliable company.

Agaete & Puerto de las Nieves

POP 5640

The leafy town of Agaete, 10km southwest of Gáldar, is well worth a brief stop. The pretty main street of Calle de la Concepción is flanked by typical Canarian buildings, some with the traditional wooden balconies, while in the centre of town stands the handsome main church.

Situated just 1km away is Puerto de las Nieves, the island's principal port until the 19th century but now better known as the terminal for fast ferries linking Gran Canaria with Tenerife. It is a small place with black pebbly beaches, but the mountainous setting is lovely with stunning views south along the Andén Verde. The place has a tangible fishing-village feel and the buildings, with their brilliant blue trim against dazzling white stucco, look as though they have been transplanted from some Greek island. The port is most famous, these days, for its excellent seafood restaurants and gets packed out by locals at weekends.

From the jetty you can see the stump of the **Dedo de Dios** (God's Finger), a basalt monolithic rock that was a serious tourist attraction until it took a tumble in a 2005 hurricane. Take a look at the photos outside its namesake restaurant.

◎ Sights

Iglesia de Nuestra Señora de la Concepción   CHURCH
(Plaza Constitución, Agaete; ⊘sporadic) Built in 1874, this handsome church is strikingly Mediterranean in style and home to two parts of the renowned 16th-century Flemish triptych by Joos van Cleve. Although these

---

DON'T MISS

PRE-HISPANIC PAINTED CAVES

A serious sum of money has gone into creating the **Cueva Pintada Museum & Archaeological Park** (⊘902 40 55 04, 928 89 57 46; www.cuevapintada.com; adult/child €6/free; ⊘9.30am-7pm Tue-Sat, 11am-6.30pm Sun; 1½hr guided tours 12.30pm in English, 2.30pm in German; 3pm in French; ▣), one of the island's most impressive and memorable sights. Although you can visit independently, the highlight of the visit is the painted caves, which are only open at set times (too many to list here!) and a guided 90-minute tour is highly recommended. You can reserve in advance via telephone or just turn up at the allotted time, although there is a limit of 20 people on each tour.

This guided visit starts with a half-hour 3D film about the pre-Hispanic indigenous people, their lifestyle and culture and the subsequent Castilian occupation. The tour continues via walkways above the 5000-sq-metre excavated site where you can clearly see the remains of cave houses dug out from the volcanic rock.

Before entry into the Cueva Pintada, there is a short explanatory film about how the pigments were created and applied, and possible theories as to the meaning of the geometric symbols – most likely related to the lunar and solar calendars. In order to prevent further deterioration to the paintings, you can only view the zoned-off caves for up to four minutes. Apparently, during a 10-year period from 1972 the colours of the pigments were reduced by a shocking 50% due to the constant stream of visitors. Finally, the tour visits several replicas of indigenous houses, accompanied by short explanatory films about the construction, society and economy of the native people. There is also a small gallery of excavated pieces discovered by local residents when they dug out their basements, including pottery, seals and jewellery.

Gran Canaria is a kiddie wonderland with plenty of natural, manufactured or theme-parked stuff to do. The **beaches** are the most obvious attraction and those in the southern resorts come complete with all variety of boat rides. In Puerto Rico you can go dolphin-spotting with **Spirit of the Sea**. Further west in **Taurito**, the whole place resembles a family-themed park with several pools (and pool tables) plus an abundance of amusements geared towards children and accommodating grown-ups. Theme parks are prolific in these parts, particularly around **Playa del Inglés**, where you can choose from camel rides, zoos, water parks, Wild West shows and a few more things besides. On a more highbrow note, even the most museum-jaded tot cannot fail to be impressed by the model galleons at the **Casa-Museo de Colón** in Las Palmas, with its colourful Columbus history. For a more hands-on, how-the-hell-does-it-work experience, tag after the school trips at the superb **Museo Elder de la Ciencia y la Tecnología** science museum, also in the island's capital.

are not always on view to the public, you can see a copy of the centre panel in the tiny chapel, **Ermita de las Nieves** (☺11am-1pm Mon-Sat, 9-11am Sun), just back from the water at Puerto de las Nieves.

Museo de la Rama   MUSEUM
(Calle Párroco Alonso Luján 5; admission €1.50; ☺10am-2pm Tue-Fri, to 1pm Sat & Sun) Next to the church, this small museum honours the town's most important annual festival: La Rama, with explanations, history and displays, including the quaint papier-mâché figures with their giant heads who supposedly represent popular characters in the town.

FREE **Huerto de las Flores** BOTANICAL GARDENS
(Calle Huertas; ☺Mon-Fri 9am-1pm) This 19th-century garden has more than 300 tropical plants and is a leafy retreat on a hot day.

✨ Festivals & Events

Fiesta de la Rama   FESTIVAL
An extraordinary festival that takes place around 4 August, with origins that lie in an obscure Guanche rain dance. Nowadays, locals accompanied by marching bands parade into town brandishing tree branches and then get down to the serious business of having a good time.

🍴 Eating

Aside from one indifferent pizzeria, seafood takes pride of place on the restaurant menus in Puerto de las Nieves.

Restaurante Las Nasas   SEAFOOD €€
(Calle Nuestra Señora Nieves 7; mains €8-10; ☺closed Tue) There's a great atmosphere

in this former warehouse with its old-fashioned black-and-white interior, jolly model boats, high ceilings and a small open-air terrace overlooking the ocean. It's also usually the busiest restaurant along this seafood strip, which is always a good sign.

Restaurante el Cápita   SEAFOOD €€
(Calle Nuestra Señora Nieves 37; mains €8-10; ☺closed Mon) Another sound choice, with a reasonable €7.50 *menú del día*. The fresh fish dishes can't be faulted, though the service may see you twiddling your thumbs when it's crowded.

Cofradía de Pescadores   SEAFOOD €€
(Muelle Puerto Nieves; mains €8-10) Next to the port, with an outdoor terrace, you can dine on the catch of the day along with the fishermen – and there's no better recommendation than that. Try the speciality, *fritura de pescado* (lightly fried seafood), or choose from a selection of 30 tapas *para picar* (to taste).

Restaurante Dedo de Dios   SEAFOOD €€
(Carretera Puerto Nieves s/n; mains €8-9; ☺closed Tue) A cavernous restaurant hung with ferns in a lovely old building overlooking the beach and the rocky remains of the poor old Dedo. It fills up with large, boisterous families at weekends and has a vast menu of mainly fish and seafood dishes.

ℹ Information

The municipal website is www.aytoagaete.es.
Tourist office (Calle Nuestra Señora Nieves 1, Agaete; ☺10am-2pm & 5-7pm Mon-Fri, 10am-2pm Sat)

WORTH A TRIP

HILLTOP ARTENARA

A back road climbs eastwards up the valley from Aldea de San Nicolás to **Artenara**; the highest village in Gran Canaria (1770m), with dramatic views of a huge volcanic crater that are truly breathtaking (from Mirador de Unamuno); this is one of several signposted miradors. On the other side of the village, Mirador de la Atalaya overlooks several **troglodyte caves**, some still inhabited, as well as the distant peak of El Teide in Tenerife.

One cave that is right in town now houses the **tourist office** (Calle Parroco Domingo Baez 13; ☺8am-3pm Mon-Fri). It is part of a cave museum complex that you can visit and which is furnished traditionally with illustrative panels (in English). In the centre of town, the late-18th-century **Iglesia de San Matías** (Plaza San Matías) is a delightful small church with a carved wooden ceiling, frescoed altar and Art Nouveau stained-glass windows. There are a couple of reasonable restaurants on the plaza. Alternatively, head round the corner to **Bar La Esquina** (Calle Parrocco Dominguez Baez 2) serving solidly reliable traditional dishes and with an outside terrace from where there are yet more sweeping panoramic views.

Bus 220 runs hourly from Las Palmas (€4.90, two hours). No buses connect the village with Aldea de San Nicolás.

Getting There & Away

BUS Bus 103 links the town and port with Las Palmas (€4.05, 1¼ hours) at least hourly. Bus 101 heads south for Aldea de San Nicolás (€3.75, 50 minutes, four daily).

BOAT From Puerto Nieves, **Fred Olsen** (☑902 10 01 07; www.fredolsen.es) operates six fast ferries (adult/child €49/23) a day for the hour-long trip to Santa Cruz de Tenerife. There is a free bus connection to Las Palmas (Parque Santa Catalina). Returning, the bus leaves Las Palmas 1½ hours before the ferry is due to depart.

CAR There's a free car park in Agaete, opposite the botanical gardens on Calle Huertas.

Aldea de San Nicolás

Usually known as San Nicolás de Tolentino, this rather scruffy town has little to excite the senses – it's the sort of place you only hang around in because the arse has fallen off your car. The lure here is the travelling, not the arriving. The road between Agaete and San Nicolás takes you on a magnificent cliff-side journey. If you head southwest in the late afternoon, the setting sun provides a soft-light display, marking out each successive ridge in an ever-darker shadowy mantle. There are numerous lookouts along the way to take in the rugged views.

The approach from Mogán and the south (see p69), though lacking the seascapes, is almost as awesome.

Bus 38 (€3.65, one hour, five daily) runs between Puerto de Mogán and Aldea de San Nicolás. Bus 101 (€3.75, 50 minutes, four daily) runs between Agaete and San Nicolás.

Around Aldea de San Nicolás

Heading north out of town, take a detour to **Puerto de la Aldea**, with its small harbour, a couple of seafood restaurants and, for self-caterers, the shady **Parque Ruben Día** with its stone tables and benches set under the pine trees. After your blow-out meal of bread, cheese and *cerveza* (beer), enjoy a stroll along the promenade and check out the small black stony beach.

Also just out of town, in the hamlet of Artéjévez, is the well-signposted **Cactualdea** (☺10am-6pm; adult/child €6/3), which claims to be the largest cactus park in Europe, with over 1200 species of the prickly plant, plus a replica Guanches' cave. Expect the usual insipid theme-park eating options; take a picnic if you can.

PLAYA DEL INGLÉS & MASPALOMAS

POP AROUND 40,000

This is Gran Canaria's most famous holiday resort and a sun-splashed party place for a mainly northern-European crowd. That said, during the day (and out of season) it has a more upmarket appearance than you may expect. This is not Benidorm, nor even Los Cristianos in

Tenerife. In the centre you are more likely to stumble across expensive hotels or smart apartment blocks than Dot-and-Alf-style English pubs. On the downside, there is virtually nothing that is even halfway Spanish here; everything is tourist-driven and the only languages you'll need are German or English. The town plan is also undeniably soulless, with the neatly traced boulevards and roundabouts betraying all the town-design spontaneity of a five-year plan.

At night, most of the action takes place in and around the Yumbo Centrum, with the leather handbags and wallets in the stores replaced by leather gear in steamy gay bars. The vaguely wholesome, bustling family atmosphere evaporates as the discos (both straight and gay) swing until dawn, barrels and bottles are drained by the dozen in bars, and the drag shows, saunas and sex shops all do a roaring trade.

The only natural items of genuine interest are the impressive dunes of Maspalomas, also home to some of Gran Canaria's most luxurious hotels and the island's largest golf course. The dunes fold back from the beach and cover 400 hectares, and their inland heart has been declared a nature reserve with restricted access.

There are bus stops all over the resort, including a couple beside Yumbo.

◉ Sights & Activities

Dunas de Maspalomas   DUNES
In 1994 these fabulous dunes were designated a national park. The best view of them is from the bottom of Avenida Tirjana. Stroll through the arches of the Hotel Riu Palace Maspalomas to the balcony, which is surrounded by a botanical garden displaying many shrubs and plants native to the Canaries. There is a small information office here with sporadic opening hours. Although the dunes look too pristine to blight with footprints, you *can* walk on the sand, but do

STREETSCAPES

In Maspalomas the street names are revealing – Avenida del Touroperador Saga Tours, Avenida del Touroperador Alpitours, Neckermann, Tui, Thomson and so on and so on. No plain old streets (*calles*) either – all avenues, no matter how small.

respect the signs and keep to the designated trails. Alternatively, you can go the full Sahara and opt for a camel trip with **Camello Safari** (☑928 76 07 81; adult/child €30/15; ☺9am-4.30pm).

Centro de Talasoterapia   SPA
(Thalassotherapy Centre; ☑928 77 64 04; www.gloriapalaceth.com; Hotel Gloria Palace, Calle Las Margaritas s/n, San Agustín) Massive and luxurious, this is Europe's largest thalassotherapy centre, occupying a huge 7000-sq-metre complex attached to Hotel Gloria Palace. It is nothing short of breathtaking and offers fabulous seawater treatments that leave your skin as smooth as a baby's bum and your mind as light as a feather. A day's dunking and use of the various appliances costs from €60.

Theme Parks

There's a multitude of theme parks with brochures and advertising everywhere. The following are the pick of the bunch. The tourist office can advise on appropriate bus routes and times.

Palmitos Park   ZOO
(www.palmitospark.es; adult/child €28/21; ☺10am-6pm; ⊞) Located a few kilometres north of the resort area, this is a subtropical oasis crammed with exotic flora and 1500 species of birds, along with an aquarium, orchid exhibit, reptile house, petting farm and animals such as wallabies and orang-utans. A dolphin show opened here in 2011.

Mundo Aborigen   ABORIGINE WORLD
(www.mundoaborigen.com; Carretera Playa del Inglés-Fataga; adult/child €10/5; ☺9am-6pm; ⊞) Situated 6km along the road north to Fataga, where around 100 model Guanches stand in various ancient poses designed to give you an idea of what life was like here before the conquistadors turned up to build theme parks.

Camel Safari Park La Baranda   CAMEL RIDES
(Carretera Playa del Inglés-Fataga; 1hr ride €25; ☺9am-6pm; ⊞) Has 70 camels and is located in a lush property with palms and avocado and citrus trees. There is also a restaurant, a bar and a small zoo.

Aqualand   WATER PARK
(www.aqualand.es; Carretera Palmitos Park; adult/child €25/18; ☺10am-5pm; ⊞) An enormous water park with miles of rides and slides.

IT'S A GAY OLD LIFE

Gran Canaria is the gay honey-pot of the Canaries, and Playa del Inglés is Europe's winter escape playground. There are several hotels and apartment blocks that cater towards gay and lesbian guests. A seemingly endless string of bars, discos and clubs are crammed into the Yumbo Centrum, which is predominantly a gay scene, although this doesn't stop small numbers of lesbians and straights from wading in. Little happens before midnight. From then until about 3am the bars on the 4th level of the Yumbo Centrum bear the brunt of the fun, after which the nightclubs on the 2nd level take over.

At dawn, people stagger out for some rest. Some make for the beach at Maspalomas, across the dunes, which are themselves a busy gay cruising area.

The annual **Festival del Sol** gay and lesbian film festival attracts international film-makers and takes place in Playa del Inglés in mid February.

For more information about gay clubs, events, accommodation and personal classifieds, check the following websites: www.colectivogama.com (in Spanish); www.gaymap.info; and www.grancanariagay.com.

Watersports

Although surfing is possible here (the best waves tend to break off the western end of Maspalomas by the lighthouse), this is not mind-blowing surfing territory. Windsurfers are better off heading east, beyond the resorts to Bahía Feliz, Playa Aguila and, best of all, **Pozo Izquierdo**, which is for experienced windsurfers. At the other end of the scale, for many, the only energy left after partying all night will be for getting down to the beach for a gentle swim. Beaches, from east to west, are Playa de las Burras (San Agustín), Playa del Inglés and Playa de Maspalomas. They all link up to form the one beach.

Club Mistral   WINDSURFING
(☑928 15 71 58; www.club-mistral.com; Carretera General del Sur, km 47, Playa de Tarajalillo; 6hr beginner's windsurfing course adult/child €140/120) In Bahía Feliz, rents bodyboards, surfboards, ocean kayaks, windsurfing boards and equipment. It also organises windsurf safaris.

Dive Academy Gran Canaria   DIVING
(☑928 73 61 96; www.diveacademy-grancanaria .com; Calle La Lajilla s/n, Arguineguín; initiation dives from €46, advanced open-water 5 dives €270) Has a free minibus to pick up plungers from their hotels and take them to the dive academy, due west of town. Both boat and shore dives are available.

Canaries Extreme   KAYAKING
(☑606 58 01 03; www.canariasextreme.com; Avenida EE UU 43; kayak tours per day €75) If you are looking for a watery pursuit more adrenalin-boosting than a glass-bottom boat, this outfit organises single- and double-kayak tours all around the coast.

Other Sports

To enjoy an exhilarating (and free) 5km walk, simply follow the promenade that extends eastwards from Playa del Inglés. The path follows a track that is sometimes at shore level and sometimes above it.

Happy Biking   CYCLING
(☑928 76 68 32; www.happy-biking.com in German; Hotel Continental, Avenida Italia 2; bike hire per day from €7; ⊙8.30am-7pm Mon-Sat) Now there's a nice name! Happy Biking rents out a range of cycles and also organises cycle tours, mostly quite gentle, which start at €30, including bike hire, transport and a picnic.

Free Motion   HIKING
(☑928 77 74 79; www.free-motion.net; Hotel Sandy Beach, Avenida Alféreces Provisionales s/n; bike hire per day from €9, tours per day from €45) This slickly run company offers a range of tours for small groups, and has bikes and quads for rental. The same company also offers guided walks with a choice of four hiking trips: Roque Nublo, Green North, Lake Tour and the daunting-sounding Summit Tour; all priced at around €45. The company will arrange transport to/from various resorts on the coast, including Puerto Rico and Puerto de Mogán, for a small fee.

Happy Horse   HORSE RIDING
(☑679 86 70 57; www.happy-horse.org; 3hr trek €54) Another happy (and unrelated) company organises horse treks in the hinterland

southeast of town. Pick up from your hotel is included in the price.

🏄 Beaches

Playa del Inglés
BEACH

Aside from the magnificent Maspalomas dunes, the main attraction for the thousands of annual visitors to the island's quintessential package-tour destination is the resort's beach, a magnificent and vast sandy beach stretching 2.7km from San Agustín in the east to Maspalomas in the west.

✕ Eating

The resort is predictably swarming with restaurants, with the normal mix of Chinese buffets, Argentinean grills, bland international and that increasingly rare breed – authentic Spanish.

TOP CHOICE El Salsete
MODERN CANARIAN €€

(☑928 77 82 55; www.elsalsete.com; Calle Secundino Delgado, Edificio Jovimar Bloque 1, Locales 4-5; mains €9-12; ☝) Hop in a taxi to this place, which is devilishly difficult to find in the north of the San Fernando district. Although unassuming from the outside, step within and sample the food, and you could be at a cutting-edge new restaurant in Barcelona. Dishes are creative in taste and presentation, and use only market-fresh ingredients. Reservations recommended.

Casa Vieja
CANARIAN €€

(www.grillrestaurantelacasavieja.com; Calle El Lomo 139, Carretera de Fataga; mains €7-15) Just north of the GC-1 motorway, along the road to Fataga, this restaurant is run with passion. The 'Old House' has a real *campo* (countryside) feel. Plants festoon the low roof, canaries trill and the menu is unwaveringly authentic; try the grilled meats. There is live traditional music from 8pm nightly.

Samsara
FUSION €€€

(☑928 14 27 36; Avenida Oasis 30; mains €15-18; ☺7pm-11.30pm Mon-Sat) Located across from the Palm Beach Hotel, a giant Buddha statue sets the appropriate tone. Portions are huge and aimed to share with the emphasis on Asian favourites like Thai red curry with shrimps and spring rolls with three dipping sauces. Desserts are more Western (read deliciously calorific), including chocolate brownies with coconut ice cream, and fresh strawberries. Reservations recommended.

Restaurante La Toja
MEDITERRANEAN €€

(☑928 76 11 96; Edificio Barbados II, Avenida Tirajana 17; mains €8-13; ☺closed Sun lunch) A quality establishment blending the best of cuisines from France and Galicia. Try the veal in Marsala wine or troubling-sounding elephant's ear with chips (actually a thin fillet of steak). The prices are reasonable given the fancy atmosphere and food.

Mundo
FUSION €€

(☑928 76 10 63; Apartamentos Tenesor, Avenida Tirajana s/n; mains €12; ☺closed Mon; ☝) An oasis of fashionable sophistication, Mundo opened in 2005 and has seriously raised the culinary game in these parts. Think American-diner-meets-Japanese, with a spruce-minimalist dining room, retro black-and-white tiles and cherry-red chairs. Try the black pasta with king prawns, if it's on the menu. Reservations recommended.

🍷 Drinking & Entertainment

The Yumbo Centrum transforms into a pulsating clubbers' scene at night – Babylon is the flashiest and best of the gay discos here. There are straight and gay places in the centre and you could stagger around Yumbo Centrum – as many do – for weeks and not sample all the nightlife options.

For the more mature party animal **Boney M** (Avenida Tirajana 11; ☺8pm-5am) plays charttoppers from the '70s, '80s and '90s. But don't worry, it's not a grab-a-granny scene – quite! For live Irish music, **Dunes & Tunes** (Beach Blvd s/n, Playa del Inglés; ☺8.30pm-late) is authentic – right down to the Guinness on tap.

Check the online party guide at www.maspalomas-tonight.com for a virtual club and disco tour.

🛍 Shopping

The main shopping centres are north of the centre in San Fernando and Bellavista. In them you can buy everything from children's wear to electronics. A good tip is to keep on looking, despite the enormous temptation to buy everything as soon as you see it – you may well save even more money if you shop around.

Yumbo Centrum
COMMERCIAL CENTRE

(www.cc-yumbo.com; Avenida EE UU; ☺24hr) There are more than 200 businesses in this four-level commercial centre. You can buy shoes, leather goods, perfume and anything else you fancy, tax free, although the

---

ℹ️ IT'S A LONG WALK FOR A SWIM

The Playa del Inglés beach is 2.7km long, with apartments and hotels that stretch from the shoreline to the San Fernando area, some 2km inland. Although there are buses that head to and from the beach, they may not coincide with your timetable. So if you have booked somewhere here and it is suspiciously cheap, be sure to check the exact location; there are far pleasanter parts of the island to stretch your legs.

---

quality should be checked. There are also supermarkets on the premises.

Fedac   CRAFTS
(Centro Insular del Turismo, cnr Avenida España & Avenida EE UU; ⊙10am-2pm & 4-7.30pm Mon-Fri) If you're after local handicrafts, visit the small Fedac shop located within the Cabildo tourist office. Fedac is a government-sponsored nonprofit store, with prices and quality that are a good standard by which to measure those of products sold elsewhere. You'll also get a guarantee with your purchase.

ℹ️ Information

Free Motion (www.free-motion.net; Hotel Sandy Beach, Avenida Alféreces Provisionales s/n; per 30min €2; ⊙9am-8pm Mon-Fri, to 6pm Sun) Internet access.

Main tourist office (www.grancanaria.com; cnr Avenida España & Avenida EE UU; ⊙9am-8pm) Just outside the Yumbo Centrum, with maps, helpful staff and public toilets.

Playa del Inglés tourist office (Commercial Centre Anexo 11, Local 20; ⊙9am-8pm) Smaller tourist office with a convenient location on the main beach.

ℹ️ Getting There & Away

Buses link regularly with points along the coast, westwards as far as Puerto de Mogán and eastwards to Las Palmas. For Las Palmas (€5.85, about 50 minutes), take bus 5 (night bus), 30 or 44 (nonstop). Pick up *horarios* (timetables) at the tourist office – one for the south of the island and one for the north.

ℹ️ Getting Around

To/From the Airport

Bus 66 runs to/from Gando airport (€3.85, one hour, hourly) until about 9.15pm. For a taxi,

budget for about €30 for Playa del Inglés and €35 for Maspalomas.

Bus

Global (www.globalsu.net) runs buses to many of the theme parks listed earlier. The fare for a standard run within town is €1.10.

Car

If you must take your car down to the beach, there's a large paying car park beside Playa del Inglés. Street parking costs a reasonable €0.30 for 30 minutes up to €2.40 for three hours (between 10am and 9pm).

Taxi

You can call a **taxi** (☎928 76 67 67), and taxi stands abound and are reliable. From Playa del Inglés, no destination within the urban area costs more than €8.

AROUND PLAYA DEL INGLÉS & MASPALOMAS

Puerto Rico & Arguineguín

While Maspalomas has redeeming features, in the shape of its natural dunes and superbly unnatural nightlife, its resort cousins further west are a good example of how greedy developers can destroy a coastline that shares a similar setting to Italy's Amalfi coast. Around every corner it seems there is yet another resort surrounded by steep banks of apartment blocks stretching into the hinterland. How some of these poor tourists get to the beach is a puzzle; crossing the main road is hazardous enough, and then it can be a long walk – especially if you have to return for your sunblock!

Parts of the port area of Arguineguín still remain true to its roots as a small, active fishing settlement, but it's a nondescript town with a couple of rather scrubby beaches. If you are here at lunchtime, check out the **Cofradía de Pescadores** (mains from €8; ⊙closed Wed & Sep), which, despite the plastic tablecloths and disarming six-language menu, buys its catch of the day direct from the fishing boats. Arguineguín is also home to a well-respected diving school (see p64).

Puerto Rico is a good example of appalling town planning: the original fishing village has disappeared under a sea of concrete, with the apartment blocks stacked up like stadium seats against the mountains. The beach is pleasant but certainly not large enough to cater for the number of beds here. The only escape is the multitude of boat trips that depart from the harbour, including the dolphin-spotting **Spirit of the Sea** (☎928 56 22 29; www.dolphin-whale.com; adult/child €22/12.50), offering two-hour trips in glass-bottom catamarans. A percentage of your ticket price goes towards marine research and conservation. **Lineas Blue Bird** (☎629 98 96 33; return €10) offers similar trips, with seven hourly services on a glass-bottom ferry to/from Puerto de Mogán from 10.30am to 4.30pm and eastwards to Arguineguín from 10am to 5pm.

The resorts further west, including Playa del Cura, Playa del Tauro and **Taurito**, are of a similar ilk. At least the latter has made an effort to gear itself to families, with a vast landscaped lido with lagoon-style pools, tennis courts, minigolf, gym equipment, bars and sun beds on the, albeit, grey sandy beach. The waters here are flat, smooth as glass and safe for swimming.

Buses connect Puerto Rico and Arguineguín with Maspalomas and Playa del Inglés (€1.60, 30 minutes) and with Puerto de Mogán (€1.25, 15 minutes) and Las Palmas (€6.15, 1 hour 50 minutes), roughly every half-hour.

Puerto de Mogán

After Taurito, a couple of kilometres of rugged coastline recall what this whole southern stretch of the island must have been like 45 years ago, before mass tourism descended on the Canaries.

Finally you round a bend; below you is a tempting crescent of sandy beach and next to it, a busy little yacht harbour and fishing port. Puerto de Mogán, although now largely given over to the tourist trade, is light years from its garish counterparts to the east. Thankfully, even the recent construction inland is more aesthetically pleasing, including the new luxury Hotel Cordial Mogán Playa.

Although its nickname 'Venice of the Canaries' may be a tad of an exaggeration, the architecture and bridged waterway are as pretty as a chocolate box, and the whole place exudes an air of opulence and charm. In the heart of the port, low-rise apartments have wrought-iron balconies, brightly coloured trim and are covered in dazzling bougainvillea.

On the downside, the place gets packed with envious tourists from the other resorts during the day, particularly on Friday morning when a street market takes over part of the town. Stalls sell the usual overpriced belts, bags and shell jewellery and, if you are staying here, it's a good day to leave.

Sights & Activities

Tucked among the restaurants and bars on the Calle Los Pescadores, the simple **Ermita de San Fernando** church dates back to 1955. You can take a peek inside during Mass at 6pm on Tuesday and Saturday.

Puerto de Mogán is the main centre for diving on Gran Canaria, with caves and wrecks just offshore.

Atlantik Diving DIVING
(☎689 35 20 49; www.clubdemar.com; Hotel Club de Mar, Playa de Mogán s/n; single dive with full equipment €40) Offers courses at all levels, from a Discover Scuba experience (three hours, €90) to Dive Master (minimum 20 days, €570).

Canary Diving Adventures DIVING
(☎928 56 54 28; www.canary-diving.com; Hotel Taurito Princess, Playa de Taurito) Run by a couple of Irish brothers and offers guided boat dives (from €30), four-hour (and longer) PADI certification courses from €360 and one-day beginner courses in their pool for €75.

STRESS-BUSTING TREATMENTS

The word is out that, increasingly, over-stressed executives are seeking holidays that offer more than, well, doing nothing (ie nodding off on the beach). Thalassotherapy is a long-time fashionable health treatment, based on warmed-up sea water, designed to relieve stress and other more physical aches and pains. Whether or not it works (some of its claims for cellulite control seem a little bit dubious), it is still a sensual experience in its own right and often does wonders for skin ailments. There are centres throughout the island, including at the Hotel Puerto de las Nieves, the Hotel Gloria Palace near Playa del Inglés and at the magnificent Villa del Conde in Maspalomas.

✖ Eating

There are plenty of cafes and restaurants with pleasant *terrazas* offering fresh fish.

 Jack El Negro CANARIAN €€
(Pasage Pescadores 6; mains €12) Housed in one of precious few original fishermen's cottages here, this restaurant has carafe-loads of earthy atmosphere. It is named after a legendary Caribbean pirate and run by Italian owner Claudio since 1970 (hence the Chianti bottle candleholders). A speciality is the steaks cooked to a tee on a *parilla* (open grill). But everything is good here, ranging from the *potage canario* (vegetable soup) to the pizzas.

La Cucina ITALIAN €
(Calle Corriente 8; pizzas from €6.50) Run by Italians, this tiny place is predominantly a takeaway but has a few outside tables and, at the time of writing, was hoping to expand to another floor. The pizzas come highly recommended, and there is also a good range of pasta dishes and salads, plus the obligatory creamy tiramisu.

Patio Canario SEAFOOD €€€
(www.restaurantemogan.com; Urbanización Puerto de Mogán; mains €15) This popular place enjoys an ace position with two sprawling terraces overlooking the small harbour. The menu includes such dishes as oven-baked king prawns with fresh coriander. Alternatively, tuck into a straightforward plate of grilled sardines; you'll never open a tin again.

La Bodeguilla Juananá MEDITERRANEAN €€
(Plaza Mayor s/n; mains €12) Tucked into the corner of grandly named Plaza Mayor, in front of the yacht harbour, this restaurant is run with passion. The decor has an African theme and the gastro-flair dishes include daily specials like black pudding fried with an avocado and garlic sauce. Only downside is the overpriced drinks.

La Tortuga GERMAN €€
(50 Front Line, Harbour; mains €9-12; ✍) Well-prepared German-inspired dishes; includes a vegetarian menu.

❶ Getting There & Around

BUS There is no shortage of buses heading east to Puerto Rico and Playa del Inglés (€1.50, 15 minutes). Bus 1 (€8.35, two hours) departs hourly for Las Palmas. Ferries also run between the port and Puerto Rico (see p67).

CAR There are two underground car parks; the cheapest is on Calle La Mina, signposted as you come into town (€5 maximum per day), and there are generally spaces. There is blue-zone street parking throughout the centre (€3 per four hours).

Mogán

Just as Puerto de Mogán is a relief from the south coast's relentless armies of apartments, bungalows and Guinness on tap, so the GC-200 road north from the port is another leap away from the crowds. As it ascends gradually up a wide valley towards Mogán, just 8km away, you pass craggy

---

BEACHES DETOUR

If you want more space on the sand, there are several choice beaches on the coast-hugging GC-500 road, west of Playa del Inglés. Follow the signs to the town hospital and Puerto de Mogán from the centre (top of Avenida Tirajana), passing Holiday World on your left. The road climbs past palm plantations and the golf course, Meloneras Golf. At km 7 watch for the **Pasito Bea** sign, turning left on the rough approach that leads to a small black sandy cove secluded by rocks, which is mixed nude and clothed.

After a quick dip, continue along the road, which winds around arid hills and, after 1.2km, comes to **Playa de Carpinteras**. Follow the track east of the main beach here, park on the cliffs and you will discover an idyllic, little-known (until now!) broad arc of sand with shallow water backed by sloping dunes. Known as the **Playa de Montaña Arenas**, you can clamber around the rocks due east of here to reach the beach, which, again, is mixed nude and clothed. The third beach worth recommending is at km 9.2. **Playa de Triana** is a black pebbly beach, with parking on the main road; note that you will be expected to wear your togs here!

Follow the road a further 4km to a roundabout, where it rejoins the GC-1 heading towards the vastly more commercial beaches of Puerto Rico and beyond.

PACK A PICNIC

Consider substituting sand in your sandwiches and sunbeds on the beach for a picnic with civilised tables and benches, coupled with idyllic lakeside surroundings. Head 2.5km beyond Mogán and take the recently surfaced GC-605, surrounded by truly bucolic scenery with massive rocks, lofty mountains and clusters of palm and pine trees. After 21.5km you come to the **Cruz de San Antonio** mirador, from where there are dramatic views of the lake and snaking road below. There is a lovely signposted walk to Inagua from here (10km). The road continues winding through the Pinar de Pajonales pine woods until you reach your destination: the **Presa de las Cuevas de las Niñas** lake and those strategically positioned picnic tables by the water. The journey will take you around 50 minutes max. Alternatively, you can head on to Tejeda, and the highest peaks on the island.

mountains and orchards of avocados, the main crop in these parts.

Mogán is a relaxed, unspoilt small town in a lovely mountainous setting. Although there are few places to stay here, it is becoming quite a culinary hotspot.

✕ Eating

For the best choice of restaurants and bars head for the winding main street of Calle San Jose.

Art Bodega MEDITERRANEAN **€€**
(Calle San Jose 17; tapas from €2, mains from €7.50; ⊙closed Sat) Grab a table on the terrace with its pretty views of the ravine out back, complete with bubbling brook. Tapas include bruschetta with a range of toppings, tasty pizzas and a handful of traditional Canarian dishes. The German owner prides herself on using primarily organic ingredients; there is also a permanent exhibition here of striking ceramic art.

Gladiatore ITALIAN **€€**
(Calle San Jose s/n; pasta from €11, pizzas from €7.50) Housed in a typical Canarian house with original floor tiles and intimate dining spaces. Italian owner-cum-chef Tonino ensures an authentic Italian culinary experience; he makes his fresh pasta and pizzas to order, so slip into 'Slow Food' mode (which, after all, did originate in Italy). After dinner you can hip-sway off those calories in the upstairs music bar (from 8.30pm); it's a winning combination.

Casa Enrique CANARIAN **€€**
(Calle San Jose 7; mains from €8) Serves up sound Canarian dishes, superb coffee and cakes.

Zumo Mix BAR **€**
(Calle San Jose 24; juices €3) Delicious and unusual fresh juice concoctions like aloe vera, lemon and strawberry, plus snacks.

Around Mogán

From Mogán, the GC-200 winds off to the northwest, travelling 26km through some spectacularly craggy mountains to Aldea de San Nicolás, sadly blighted by the surrounding sea of plastic greenhouses. Stop for a glass of fresh papaya juice at **Las Cañadas** (www.restaurantelascanadas.com), around 8km from Mogán on your left-hand side. This is an agreeably quirky restaurant and bar with stunning views plus the added appeal of turtles, a chameleon and a small museum with old agricultural equipment, radios and the like. You can also buy local honey and the largest avocadoes you have ever seen (when in season).

The winding road continues through **Los Azulejos**, a colourful rock formation created by different-coloured minerals of brilliant greens, yellows and ochres. To avoid a head-on collision, take your photos from the signposted **Fuente de los Azulejos Mirador** lookout.

Fuerteventura

📞 928 / POP 69,500

Includes »

Best Places to Eat

» El Cangrejo Colorao (p74)

» Casa Santa María (p77)

» Frasquita (p80)

» Restaurante Avenida (p84)

» Casa Rústica (p86)

Best Places to Stay

» Hesperia Bristol Playa (p214)

» Casa Isaítas (p214)

» Hotel Rural Mahoh (p214)

» La Gaviota (p214)

Why Go?

Fuerteventura lies just 100km from the African coast, and there are striking similarities in the landscape, as well as the houses, with their North African–style flat roofs for collecting rainfall. In other ways, Fuerteventura emulates its neighbour Lanzarote, only with more colours. Its volcanoes resemble piles of saffron, chilli and coriander; surreal triangles of exotic spices.

Most visitors, however, are more interested in mastering the waves and the wind than contemplating the abstract aesthetics of its scenery. The second-largest island in the archipelago (after Tenerife), Fuerteventura has year-round sunshine and the biggest and best beaches in the Canaries.

The main tourist resorts lie at opposite ends of the island. At the northern tip is Corralejo, beloved of the British sun-seekers, while deep down south lies Morro Jable, largely frequented by Germans, and a markedly staider place.

The island was granted the status of a Biosphere Reserve by Unesco in May 2009.

When to Go

There's no bad time to visit Fuerteventura; it really does live up to its year-round spring reputation. The winter months, December to February, can be slightly cooler with prevailing winds, but are still pleasant. April to May is ideal, temperature-wise, although Easter can equal crowded beaches.

During the autumn months, the average daytime temperature hovers around the agreeable 20°C mark, while the nights gradually become cooler. July and August are busy with Spanish holidaymakers, as well as families travelling with school-age children.

Getting Around

Tiadhe (www.tiadhe.com) provides a limited bus service, with just 17 routes covering the whole island.

Driving is a pleasure here; the terrain is flat and the roads excellent. **Cicar** (www.cicar.com) is a reliable car-rental choice.

Cycling similarly presents few hilly challenges and, provided you avoid the hottest time of the day, can be an enjoyable transport choice.

Taxis are handy for short hops, but costly for exploring further.

THREE PERFECT DAYS

Day One

Heading north from the capital, take the coast-hugging FV-1 passing the **Parque Natural de Corralejo**, with its miles of pristine golden beaches. After stopping for a swim, continue on to Corralejo's harbour and a ferry jaunt to **Isla de Lobos** for a stroll along trails and beside coves. Enjoy freshly barbecued sardines at the *chiringuito* before ferrying back and continuing on to **El Cotillo**. Here, kick back on the sand, check out the surfers and have a harbour-front sun-downer and snack.

Day Two

Start off in leafy **Pájara**, with a quick confessional at the extraordinary Aztec-inspired church. Wind your way on the scenic mountainside FV-30 road to lush **Betancuria**. Take your pick from the two intriguing museums here, but make **Casa Santa María** your lunch spot. Continue north to **Tefía**, via more camera-clicking scenery, and visit the **Ecomuseo la Alcogida**. Carry on to beachside **Los Molinos** for a seafood *tapa* and a sunset over the sea.

Day Three

After an early-morning coffee in lovely **La Oliva**, check out the current contemporary art exhibition at the **Casa de los Coroneles**, a perfect example of traditional 18th-century architecture. Just round the corner, there are more superb canvases at the **Centro de Arte Canario**. Next stop is the capital, **Puerto del Rosario**, for a stroll around the centre, graced by more than 100 sculptures, and a look at the classic early-20th-century **Casa Museo Unamuno** historic museum.

Getting Away from It All

» **Pozo Negro** (p80) Enjoy fresh seafood, a quiet beach and the surrounding craggy peaks.

» **Corralejo** (p82) Desert-like dunes that are never crowded; don't forget the drinking water (or compass).

» **Playa de Barlovento de Jandía** (p91) The antithesis of the beach resorts, with a wild, dramatic beauty.

DON'T MISS

Ordering a plate of local goat's cheese when you see it on the menu. Creamy, nutty and utterly delicious, it is often served with olives as tapas.

Best Beaches

» **Playa de la Mujer** (p81) Unspoiled sandy beach on the northwest coast, popular with surfers and swimmers.

» **Bubbles** (El Cotillo; p86) Windswept wild beach on the north coast, attracting an enthusiastic surfing crowd.

» **Playa del Matorral** (p89) A holiday brochure-style 4km of golden sand with family-geared activities.

Best Museums

» **Casa de los Coroneles** (p81) Home to some fascinating historical and art exhibitions.

» **Museo Artesania** (p76) Intriguing museum with 3D films, crafts – and cheese.

» **Museo de la Pesca Tradicional** (p86) An insightful look at traditional fishing on the island.

Resources

» Official tourism site: www .fuerteventuraturismo.com

» Rural tourism and accommodation: www .acantur.es

» Current affairs: www .sunnyfuerteventura.com

» Online news: www .fuertenews.com

History

Fuerteventura has had several names in history, ranging from the Roman's unimaginative Planaria ('Plains', due to the island's overall flatness), to the considerably more exciting Fuerteventura (Strong Adventure), which dates from the first European conquerors. Ruled by the Norman nobleman Jean de Béthencourt, the conquerors turned up in 1405 to find the island divided into two tribal kingdoms separated by a low, 6km-long wall: Jandía, on the southern peninsula, as far north as La Pared; and Maxorata, which occupied the rest of the island.

Béthencourt established a permanent base, including a chapel, in the mountainous zone of what came to be known as Betancuria, with Santa María de Betancuria evolving as the island's capital. The choice of location was determined by the natural water supply which is still in evidence: this is one of the lushest regions on the island. The mountainous location also created a measure of natural defence against those dastardly pirate raids.

New settlements spread slowly across the island and, in the 17th century, Europeans occupied El Cotillo, once the seat of the Guanche Maxorata kingdom. At this time, the Arias and Saavedra families took control of the *señorío* (the island government deputising for the Spanish crown). By the following century, however, officers of the island militia had established themselves as a rival power base in La Oliva. Los Coroneles (the Colonels) gradually took virtual control of the island's affairs, enriching themselves at the expense of the hard-pressed peasantry. You can learn more about their reign by visiting their extraordinary former home: Casa de los Coroneles in La Oliva.

The militia was disbanded in 1834 and, in 1912, the island, along with others in the archipelago, was granted a degree of self-administration with the installation of the *cabildo* (local authority).

❶ Getting There & Away

AIR

Fuerteventura airport (928 86 05 00; www .aena.es) is 6km south of Puerto del Rosario in El Matorral. There are plenty of charter and regular flights from all over Europe. Major operators from other Canary Islands and the Spanish mainland include the following:

Iberia (www.iberia.es)

Spanair (www.spanair.com)

ROAD DISTANCES (KM)

	Puerto del Rosario	Corralejo	El Cotillo	Caleta de Fuste
Corralejo	32			
El Cotillo	58	20		
Caleta de Fuste	10	36	56	
Costa Calma	64	90	87	56

Approximate distances only

Binter (www.binternet.com)

Islas Airways (www.islasairways.com)

Ryan Air (www.ryanair.com)

BOAT

The following ferries serve Fuerteventura.

Acciona Trasmediterránea (in Puerto del Rosario ☑902 45 46 45; www.trasmediterranea.es) Runs a weekly service from Puerto del Rosario to Arrecife, Lanzarote (€30, 2½ hours) at 9pm on Saturday, a weekday service to Las Palmas de Gran Canaria (€36, 4½ hours) and to Santa Cruz de Tenerife (€38, nine hours).

Fred Olsen (www.fredolsen.es) (☑902 53 50 90; www.fredolsen.es) Ferries leave six times daily from Corralejo for Playa Blanca (adult/child €21/10, 20 minutes) in Lanzarote. You can buy tickets at the port in Corralejo.

Naviera Armas (www.navieraarmas.com; Puerto del Rosario ☑902 45 65 00 Corralejo & Morro Jable ☑928 54 21 13) Runs a ferry from Puerto del Rosario to Las Palmas de Gran Canaria (€47, 6½ hours) at 11.30am on Tuesday, Wednesday and Friday. Six daily ferries leave Corralejo for Playa Blanca, Lanzarote (adult/child €18/9). From Morro Jable, daily ferries leave at 6.30pm for Las Palmas de Gran Canaria (€43, three hours) and twice-weekly ferries run to Santa Cruz de Tenerife (€43, 10½ hours).

PUERTO DEL ROSARIO

POP 35.110

Puerto del Rosario, the island's capital, is home to more than half the island's population. It's a relatively modern little port town that only really took off in the 19th century. If you fly to the island, or use the buses, you may find yourself passing through. It can appear a confusing city with sprawling suburbs and no apparent centre, which makes finding shops, restaurants and bars a head-scratching business.

N

0 — 20 km
0 — 10 miles

To Arrecife (Lanzarote)
To Playa Blanca (Lanzarote)

ATLANTIC OCEAN

Isla de Lobos

Majanicho
Bubbles
El Hierro
Corralejo
Faro de Tostón
Parque Natural de Corralejo (Grandes Playas)
Los Lagos
El Cotillo
Lajares
El Burro

FV-10
FV-101

Montaña de Tindaya (401m)
Villaverde
La Oliva
FV-1

Esquinzo
Tindaya
La Matilla

Playa de la Mujer
Los Molinos
FV-207
Tetir
FV-10
Puerto del Rosario

FV-211
Ecomuseo la Alcogida
Tefía
Casillas del Ángel
Playa Blanca
Airport

Los Llanos de la Concepción
Valle de Santa Inés
La Ampuyenta
FV-20

Parque Natural de Betancuria
Mirador Morro Velosa
Betancuria
Antigua
Calete de Fuste

Ajuy & Puerto de la Peña
Gran Montaña (708m)
FV-621
FV-30
Las Salinas

Pájara
Tiscamanita
FV-2

FV-605
Tuineje
Pozo Negro

FV-20
FV-2

Playa de la Pared
La Pared
El Brasero
Gran Tarajal
Las Playitas
Playa del Gran Tarajal

Playa de Barlovento de Jandía
La Lajita
Giniginamar
Tarajalejo

Costa Calma

Pico de la Zarza (807m)
Parque Natural de Jandía
Playa de Sotavento de Jandía

Faro de Jandía
Cofete
Península de Jandía
FV-2

Puerto de la Cruz
Playa del Matorral

Punta de Jandía
Morro Jable

To Las Palmas de Gran Canaria
To Las Palmas de Gran Canaria

ATLANTIC OCEAN

Fuerteventura Highlights

1 Try a dish of traditional goat stew and the famous Majorero cheese; they are both culinary winners on this island

2 Get in touch with your artistic side and check out the cutting-edge modern art at La Oliva's **Casa de los Coroneles** (p81)

3 Treat yourself to a touch of aromatic thalassotherapy at the beachside **Balneario Thalasso** in Caleta de Fuste (p80)

4 Dine on catch-of-the-day seafood while gazing over the waves at pretty **Corralejo** (p82)

5 Kick off your shoes and

do cartwheels in the soft, powdery sand at **Parque Natural de Corralejo** (p82)

6 Be dazzled by the verdant valley location of lovely **Betancuria** (p76)

7 Catch the waves at **Isla de Lobos** (p83), just one of Fuerteventura's super-cool surfing spots

ℹ DISCOUNT BUS CARD

If you intend to use buses fairly frequently, it is worth investing in a **Tarjeta Dinero (€12)** discount card. Tell the driver your destination and he will endorse your card; it represents about a 30% saving on each trip.

Buses do not accept €20 or €50 notes, so it's a good idea to stock up on change if buying individual tickets.

The good news is that the town hall has recently made the city more tourist-friendly by revamping the promenade and pedestrianising a wide street in the centre of town. In the absence of any significant art museum, the city has also been graced by more than 100 sculptures by local and international artists. These are located throughout the capital and are another positive sign that Puerto is trying to gild its somewhat tarnished image.

History

Puerto del Rosario, once little more than a handful of fishermen's cottages, became the island's capital in 1860, due to its strategic position as a harbour.

Until 1956 it was known as Puerto de las Cabras, named after the goats for which it had long been a watering hole (before becoming the main departure point for their export in the form of chops). In an early rebranding exercise, it was renamed the more dignified Puerto del Rosario (Port of the Rosary).

When Spain pulled out of the Sahara in 1975, it sent some 5000 Legión Extranjera (Foreign Legion) troops to Fuerteventura to keep a watch on North Africa. The huge barracks in Puerto del Rosario is still in use, although troops now number less than 1000.

◉ Sights

Pick up a *Puerto on Foot* guide from the tourist office; it has an easy-to-follow map showing 16 of the most centrally located sculptures. Newly pedestrianised Avenida 1 de Mayo leads west from the main church and is lined with shops and bars.

FREE **Casa Museo Unamuno** MUSEUM
(Calle Rosario 11; ⊗9am-2pm Mon-Fri). This small museum honours the philosopher Miguel de Unamuno, who stayed here in 1924

after being exiled from Spain. His crime was criticising the dictatorship of Primo de Rivera, both verbally and in writing. He later escaped to France before returning to his position as lecturer and Rector at Salamanca University in Spain when the Republicans came to power in 1931.

The ground-floor house has been turned into a period piece, with four rooms furnished from Unamuno's day, including the bedroom (complete with chamber pot) and his study with original desk. There are brochures available in English.

✨ Festivals & Events

Puerto del Rosario dons its party threads to celebrate the **Fiesta de la Virgen del Rosario**, held annually on the first Sunday of October, to honour the capital's patron. Processions accompany the image of the Virgin as she is carried around the town.

✗ Eating

Eating out can be rewarding, with some good choices and modest prices. The local **mercado** (market; Calle Garcia Escámez s/n) is a prime place to pick up a wheel of *queso artesanal de cabra* (organic goat's cheese) or at least to ask for a sample.

El Cangrejo Colorao SPANISH €€€
(☏928 85 84 77; Calle Juan Ramón Jiménez 2; mains €12-18) There's a pleasing old-fashioned elegance about this seafront restaurant with its bow-tied, white-tablecloth ambience. The menu mainstays includes meaty stews with mushrooms, and ham and mussels prepared in a variety of ways, including filled with lamb. There is a €17 *menú del día*. Bookings recommended.

Ali Baba's MIDDLE EASTERN €
(Avenida Ruperto González Negrin 3; kebabs €4.50; ☏) This is a superior kebab house. Crisp, fresh salad, lean spit-roasted meat, and some interesting combos like a Yufka vegetarian (traditional wheat wrap with falafel, salad and feta) are included on the menu. There is an outside terrace.

La Terraza del Muelle SEAFOOD €€€
(☏928 86 16 35; Carretera Los Pozos; mains €15-20) One of a new breed of sophisticated seafood restaurants to open up on the promenade. Push the boat out with the succulent Cantabrian lobster served with dried fruits and nuts. Reservations recommended.

FOR CHEESE LOVERS...

More than any other Canary island, Fuerteventura's traditional cuisine is simple and essentially the result of poverty. One of the keys remains the quality and freshness of the ingredients.

Given that there are more goats than people on Fuerteventura (honest!), goat stew is very popular. But it is the goat's cheese that is the real winner. In fact, so renowned is the Majorero cheese that, just like a fine wine, it bears a *denominación de origen* (proof of origin) label, certifying that it is indeed from the island and the genuine product. It's the first Canary Island cheese to receive this accolade, and the first goat's cheese in Spain to bear the label.

At the heart of the process is the Majorero goat, a high-yielding hybrid of goat originally imported from the Spanish mainland. The cheese is ideally purchased young and soft, with a powdery white rind that becomes yellow with age. One of Europe's top goat's cheeses (and not unduly goaty in flavour), Majorero is rich and buttery with a nutty flavour that goes particularly well with fruit. The wheels are often sold with a coating of oil, corn meal or paprika to preserve them. The best place to buy your wheel of *queso* is at a local produce market, where there will always be several *queserías* (cheese stalls). Ask for a taste.

 Drinking & Entertainment

Puerto del Rosario has a modest nightlife scene geared for the locals.

Camelot NIGHTCLUB
(Calle Ayose 6; ☺11pm-3am Mon-Sat) This bar has a medieval theme and a bank of music-video screens mixed in with DJs and disco. You can catch live music performances here, too, although the quality can be patchy.

Pata Negra NIGHTCLUB
(Calle León y Castilla 3; ☺9pm-late Mon-Sat) An enticing little spot with a good list of cocktails, regular live music and a boisterous weekend crowd post-midnight.

ⓘ Information

City tourist office (www.puertodelrosario.org, in Spanish; Avenida Marítimo s/n; ☺8am-3pm Mon-Fri) Small, glassed-in office on the seafront, opposite Hotel Roquemar, with information on the city.
Provincial tourist office (www.fuerteventura turismo.com; Almirante Lallermand 1; ☺8am-3pm Mon-Fri) Regional tourism information.

ⓘ Getting There & Away

Bus
Tiadhe (☎650 53 28 66; www.tiadhe.com) buses leave from the main bus stop just past the corner of Avenida León y Castillo and Avenida Constitución. The following are some of the more popular services from Puerto del Rosario:
BUS 1 Morro Jable via Costa Calma (€9, two hours, at least 12 daily)

BUS 2 Vega del Río de Palmas via Betancuria (€3, 50 minutes, three daily Monday to Saturday)
BUS 3 Caleta de Fuste via the airport (€2.10, 30 minutes, at least 18 daily)
BUS 6 Corralejo (€3.10, 40 minutes, at least 18 daily)
BUS 7 El Cotillo (€4, 45 minutes, three daily)

ⓘ Getting Around

One municipal bus does the rounds of the city every hour. Catch it at the bus station (Estación de Guaguas).

Despite the sprawling nature of the town, the grid system of streets makes navigating reasonably easy. There's a large, free car park just beyond the market heading eastwards on Avenida Marítimo. Call ☎928 85 00 59 or ☎928 85 02 16 for a taxi.

To/From the Airport
Bus 3 makes the trip to the airport. It takes 10 to 15 minutes and costs €1.10. A taxi will rack up about €7.

THE CENTRE

Central Fuerteventura offers the most geographically diverse landscape on this overwhelmingly desert-covered island. The soaring mountains of the Parque Natural de Betancuria are contrasted in the south by the wadi-style palm-tree oasis of the Vega del Río de Palmas. The west and east coasts are characterised by rocky cliffs interspersed

ℹ️ WHEN'S THE NEXT BUS?

In 2011 a new service was introduced to facilitate bus transport around the island. Essentially, you can now use your mobile phone to find out what time the next bus will be arriving at any bus stop here. Simply text the word PARADA followed by a space and the number of the bus stop to ☎928 10 01 20 and within a few seconds you will receive an SMS message giving you the approximate time remaining before the next bus will arrive. You find the number of the bus stop displayed in a small inbuilt panel at the bus stop (it will be something like 101000). The cost of the call is the same as those to other local mobile phones. Not all the bus stops have their numbers displayed, however; if you check the website www.fuerteventuratransportes.com and click on Líneas Horarios, you can download a list of all the bus stops on the island with their number. So, even if there is no number visible, that stop will still be in the system.

with small black-pebble beaches and simple fishing hamlets.

In further contrast, the central copper-coloured plains around Antigua are dotted with old windmills dating back a couple of centuries. It is the sort of landscape that makes you wish you had invested in that wide-angle camera lens. It has some of the most scenic drives on the island, particularly around Betancuria and Tefía.

Betancuria

POP 688

Wonderfully lush, this pretty hamlet is tucked into the protective folds of the basalt hills and is a patchwork of dry-stone walls, palm trees and simple, whitewashed cottages. Lording over it all is a magnificent 17th-century church and courtyard.

Jean de Béthencourt thought this the ideal spot to set up house in 1405, so he had living quarters and a chapel built. To this modest settlement he gave his own name, which, with time, was corrupted to Betancuria. During the course of the 15th century, Franciscan friars moved in and expanded the town. Amazingly, given its size, it remained the island's capital until 1834. Fuerteventura's proximity to the North African coast made it easy prey for Moroccan and European pirates who, on numerous occasions, managed to defy Betancuria's natural mountain defences and sack it.

◉ Sights

If you approach from the north, look for the ruins of the island's first **monastery** on your left, built by the Franciscans. For such a small place, there is plenty to see here.

Museo Artesania   MUSEUM
(adult/child €6/3; ⊙10am-4pm; 👪) This place is unabashedly tourist-orientated but still well worth visiting. The German owner, Reiner Loos, bought the original rambling building in the 1990s and spent several years collecting traditional handicrafts, ancient agricultural tools and similar, as well as lushly landscaping the garden. Your entrance covers several permanent exhibits, plus a craft centre where you can see the craftspeople at work; you can also taste the local cheese. The highlight, however, is an expertly produced 3D underwater film of the local coastal sea life, including the rare green turtle. There is a second, longer film which concentrates more on Fuerteventura's landscape and environment. Reiner also owns Casa Santa María, the best restaurant in town.

**Museo Arqueológico
de Betancuria**   MUSEUM
(Calle Roberto Roldán s/n; admission €2; ⊙10am-5pm Tue-Sat, 11am-2pm Sun) Archaeology buffs should check out this modest, but interesting, museum which concentrates on the indigenous Guanche tribes and includes a skeleton that was found in a local tomb and is thought to be between 600 and 1000 years old. There are also some artefacts from the Roman occupation. The admission includes an excellent brochure in English.

Iglesia de Santa María   CHURCH
(Calle Alcalde Carmelo Silvera s/n; admission €1.50; ⊙10am-4pm Mon-Sat) This church dates from 1620, and has a magnificent stone floor, wooden ceiling and elaborate baroque altar. Don't miss the sacristy with its display of vestments, its altar ware and its carved wooden ceiling in shades of gold and red. Pirates destroyed the church's Gothic predecessor in 1593.

Festivals & Events

Locals honour the patron saint on 14 July, **Día de San Buenaventura**, in a fiesta dating from 1456.

Eating

TOP CHOICE Casa Santa

María MODERN CANARIAN €€€

(928 87 82 82; www.restaurantecasasanta maria.com; Plaza Santa María de Betancuria 1; mains €12-22) Opposite the church, this restaurant looks like it has been transplanted from Andalucía. The outside dining space is set around several courtyards with bubbling fountains, plants and flowers, while the interior is sumptuous with warm stone walls, antiques and a gallery of black-and-white photos of *feria* (fair) time in Ronda (Málaga). The menu includes all manner of goaty offerings – from roasted to fried with cheese and chutney, as well as more hearty dishes like roasted lamb with wild young asparagus, and colourful salads where goat's cheese, once again, takes pride of place.

Valtarajal CANARIAN €

(Calle Juan de Béthencourt s/n; raciónes from €5) This cosy place has a good choice of *raciónes* (large tapas), as well as homemade cakes.

Getting There & Around

Bus 2 (€2.50, 50 minutes) passes through here three times daily (except Sunday) on its way between Puerto del Rosario and Vega del Río de Palmas, a short distance south.

There's a small, free car park south of the centre.

Around Betancuria

This area encompasses some great scenery and superb far-reaching vistas. For a start, a couple of kilometres north of Betancuria, on the FV-30, there's a handy lookout (on both sides of the road) that explains the various mountain peaks that loom on the horizon. Further on, the **Mirador Morro Velosa** offers mesmerising views across the island's weird, disconsolate moonscape. You can stop at the bar located here, with its large picture windows and exhibition space for subjects related to the landscape and environment.

The view is almost as spectacular at the col over which the FV-30 highway climbs before it twists its way north through Valle de Santa Inés, a hiccup of a village. Stop at the central **Bar La Pinta** (10am-6pm Tue-Sun) to pick up a chunk of *queso de cabra;* you can taste it first at the bar. This place also sells local handicrafts.

In pretty **Casillas del Ángel**, on the FV-20, the petite **Iglesia de Santa Ana** contains an 18th-century wooden carving of St Anne. For a superb meal, try La Era (928 53 81 80; Carretera General de Casillas del Ángel; mains €12-17; closed Tue) at the western end of the town. A long, low ochre building, the elegant dining room attracts business bods from all around with its menu of traditional, superbly prepared local dishes. Advance reservations essential.

Heading south of Betancuria for Pájara, you soon hit the small oasis of **Vega del Río de Palma** (Fertile Plain of the Palma River).

FUERTEVENTURA AROUND BETANCURIA

A SPORTING CHANCE

Fuerteventura is a superb year-round destination for the sports enthusiast. Although surfing the waves or sailing the breeze are the most famous sports here, there are less adrenaline-spiked activities available. Fuerteventura's peaceful but stark landscape offers some great walking opportunities, with oases, volcanic craters, abandoned haciendas and rugged coastlines awaiting the intrepid. The Isla de Lobos nature reserve is also excellent for walkers; turning right as you hop off the ferry will take you on a circular tour of the island. There's also a climb up Caldera de la Montaña here – well worth it for the dizzying views.

Leaving behind those hiking trails, mountain biking in Fuerteventura is a completely different experience. 'Cycling in the interior is a bit like cycling on the moon', one enthusiast was heard remarking. Most resorts, including Corralejo, have bicycle rental outfits.

If you fancy swinging a golf club, Caleta de Fuste is home to the island's first and only PGA championship-rated golf course, the Fuerteventura Golf Club. Or make use of the blustery climate by kite flying. If you're in Corralejo in early November you may catch the three-day festival on the beach, when hundreds of colourful kites speckle the blue sky like a flock of brilliantly coloured butterflies.

As you proceed, the reason for the name becomes clear – the road follows the course of a near-dry watercourse still sufficiently wet below the surface to keep alive a stand of palms. If you're feeling peckish for surf-and-turf or a chicken green curry with lemongrass and coconut, **Don Antonio** (☏928 87 87 57; mains €12-14; ☉Sun, Wed, Thu 11am-5pm) has an eclectic menu and is superb. Located next to the church, the restaurant is open for dinner by advance reservation only.

Antigua

POP 7000

This is a fair-sized town but a fairly dull place with not much to retain you, aside from a quick dip into the 18th-century **Nuestra Señora de Antigua** (☉10am-2pm). One of the island's oldest churches, it has a pretty pink-and-green painted altar.

Scarcely 1km north of here is the **Molino de Antigua** (adult/child €2/1; ☉10am-6pm Tue-Fri & Sun), a fully restored windmill with a cacti garden, an audiovisual display and a bar and restaurant. There is also a gift shop, with all proceeds going directly to the craftspeople.

Bus 1 (€2.10, 30 minutes) passes through here en route between Puerto del Rosario and Morro Jable.

Around Antigua

You'll require your own transport to access these small towns.

LA AMPUYENTA

If you can time your visit for Saturday afternoon, around 5pm Mass, the 17th-century **Ermita de San Pedro de Alcántara** merits a stop. The *ermita* (chapel) is surrounded by a stout protective wall built by the French from the Normandy area. Within, the walls of the nave are decorated with large, engagingly naive frescoes that date from 1760. Although the Cistine chapel comparisons on the publicity are a trifle far fetched, the murals are undeniably stunning in their pastel colours and simple execution. They contrast dramatically with the more sophisticated works embellishing the wooden altarpiece.

TISCAMANITA

POP 260

Visit this tiny hamlet, 9km south of Antigua, to see a working mill (and find out what a hard grind it all was). The **Windmill Interpretation Centre** (admission €2; ☉10am-6pm Mon-Sat) highlights a praiseworthy restoration project and has all the information about windmills you could possibly want to know; there's a free guide in English. If there is wind, you can sit under the lovely pomegranate tree and try fresh *gofio* (ground, roasted grain used in place of bread in Canarian cuisine).

Pájara

POP 3100

Pájara is a leafy oasis set amid a desert-style landscape. But what has really put the place on the map is its unique 17th-century **Iglesia de Nuestra Señora de Regla**. The exterior is Aztec-inspired with its animal motifs. The simple retables behind the altar have influences flowing back to Latin America – in this case, Mexico – and are more subdued than the baroque excesses of mainland Spain (stick a coin in the machine on the right at the entrance to light them up). Don't forget to look up; there's a magnificent carved wooden ceiling.

✖ Eating

There are several reasonable restaurants and one exceptional place to stay in town (see p214).

(see p214).

WORTH A TRIP

AJUY & PUERTO DE LA PEÑA

If you have your own wheels, a 9km side trip from Pájara takes you northwest to Ajuy and contiguous Puerto de la Peña. A blink-and-you'll-miss-it fishing settlement, its black-sand beach makes a change from its illustrious golden neighbours to the south on the Península de Jandía. The locals and fishing boats take pride of place here, and the strand is fronted by a couple of simple seafood eateries serving up the day's catch.

There's a low-key coastal walking track heading right (north) as you face the water, leading for a few minutes along the windy rocks, with some lovely views.

STUNNING DRIVES

The drive between **Betancuria** and **Pájara** on the FV-30 is one of the most spectacular on the island, although possibly not for those suffering from vertigo. The narrow road twists and turns steeply between a flowing landscape of volcano peaks and lava fields, with the sea visible (at times) in the far distance. In springtime, the peaks are surprisingly lush; a vivid green contrasting with the rich ochres and reds of the soil.

The journey via **La Pared** south towards **Península de Jandía** is almost as dramatic. Fuerteventura ranks as relatively flat when compared to Lanzarote and the other islands to the west, but you would never think so as you wend your way through this lonely and spectacularly harsh terrain.

La Olla de la Bruja   SPANISH **€€**
(☎609 61 32 40; Calle Nuestra Señora de Regla 19; ☉11am-7pm; mains €7-10) This welcoming place is run by cheery Maike from Germany who reflects her love of cooking in such dishes as *chorizo a la sidra* (chorizo in a cider sauce) and savoury crêpes. The place has a laid-back appeal, with board games and books to keep you entertained. It will open for dinner with advance reservations.

La Fonda   SPANISH **€€**
(Calle Nuestra Señora de Regla 25; mains €7-12) La Fonda has a pleasant rustic ambience, with stone walls and wooden ceilings, as well as ropes of garlic, legs of ham and strings of chilli hanging from the ceiling to add to the atmosphere. The food here is good, honest and hearty.

ⓘ Getting There & Around

Bus 18 (€3.10, 30 minutes, three times daily) runs between Pájara and Gran Tarajal. There are no services to the north.

You can leave your car in an empty parking lot south of town, opposite the Casa Isaítas rural hotel.

Caleta de Fuste

This smart, well-landscaped resort exudes an opulent southern-California feel, particularly around the sprawling Barceló mini-village, which fronts the main beach. Caleta is convenient for the airport and, if you're travelling with a young family, the wide arc of sand and shallow waters are ideal. However, if you are seeking somewhere intrinsically Canarian, look elsewhere; this is a purpose-developed tourist resort. In all fairness, though, it is a relaxing place with some good hotels and restaurants.

⛱ Beaches

The resort is fronted by a white sandy beach, complete with volleyball net and **camel rides** (30-min ride €12). It is ideal for families, although a poor relation compared to the rolling dunes and endless sands of Corralejo and Jandía.

⚐ Activities

Watersports

Deep Blue   DIVING
(☎606 27 54 68; www.deep-blue-diving.com; orientation dive €20; ⊞) Conveniently situated beside the port, for up to four dives, each dive costs €33, reducing to €24 for more than 12 dives. There are beginner courses for PADI certification; specialist courses, including ones for children (€41); and snorkelling (€12, one hour).

Surf School   SURFING
(☎620 84 64 15; www.fuerteventurasurfschool.com; 1-3-day courses €40-100) A long-established surf school located behind the tourist office.

Fuerte Fun Center   WINDSURFING
(☉10am-5pm Sun-Mon) On the far side of the beach, this reliable choice offers four-hour beginner courses for €80, including windsurfing equipment hire. Gear hire costs €35/60/195 per half-day/day/week.

Boat Trips

Oceanarium Explorer   BOAT TRIPS
(☎928 16 35 14; Puerto Castillo; ⊞) This outfit runs a range of family-friendly activities, including half-day fishing trips (€90), and boat trips (adult/child €40/20) where you might catch sight of dolphins and whales.

Golf

Fuerteventura Golf Club   GOLF
(www.fuerteventuragolfclub.com; 18 holes €52) This club has top-whack facilities, including

CATCHING THE WAVES

The sea offers most of the action in Fuerteventura. From Caleta de Fuste, Morro Jable and Corralejo, you can both dive and windsurf. The waters off Corralejo are good for deep-sea fishing and the nearby curling waves draw in surfers. Kiteboarding has fast gained popularity, too, thanks to regular wind gusts on the coast.

You can also pick up the handy *Surfers' Map* available from most tourist offices; it lists all the surfing outfits, as well as surf camps, speciality stores and at least one surf cafe (for surfing the web and meeting like-minded souls). The map also marks and rates the top surfing beaches on the island.

Water-sports tuition and equipment rental are listed throughout this chapter.

a pro shop and resident PGA professional, and covers a vast 1.5 sq km.

Cycling

Caleta Cycles   CYCLING
(☑676 60 01 90; Centro Comercial Los Geranios; 4/6hr tours, €35/45) This British-run place organises guided bike tours and also rents bikes (one day €8).

Thalassotherapy

Balneario Thalasso   SPA
(☑928 16 09 61; www.barcelo.com; Calle Savila 2) You can't miss the glass building behind the beach with its giant 'Thalasso' sign. An hour massage costs €60 (including Thai, chocolate and the intriguing-sounding anti-stress Chinese chimes massages). An aromatic face massage will set you back €39. Thalassotherapy is also available at the Barceló Club El Castillo.

✕ Eating & Drinking

[TOP CHOICE] Frasquita   SEAFOOD €€
(Playa de Caleta de Fuste; mains €8-10; ☺closed Mon) This is one of the best restaurants on the island to come to for fresh seafood, despite its very plain appearance and white plastic tables and chairs. Make sure you sit in the glassed-in dining room overlooking the beach rather than the front terrace, which mysteriously overlooks the car park out back.

Puerto Castillo Restaurante   ITALIAN €€
(Avenida Castillo s/n; mains €9-12; ☺closed Sun) Beside the *castillo* (castle), this 1st-floor restaurant has sea views from a vast terrace and an elegant ambience in the dining room. Reborn as an Italian restaurant in early 2011, the pasta is freshly made and the pizza is definitely upper crust – it's no surprise then to learn the new owner is from Rome.

Beach Cafe   BAR €
(Playa de Caleta de Fuste; cocktails €5.50) Sip a cocktail in the glassed-in terrace overlooking the main beach. There's a weekend line-up of live music here, including a hip-swaying salsa class on Saturday nights.

ℹ Information

Tourist office (Centro Comercial Castillo; ☺9am-3pm Mon-Fri) Shares a space with the police station and is surprisingly sparse on information, given the popularity of the place.

Around Caleta de Fuste

Just south of Caleta, in Las Salinas, is the **Museo de la Sal** (Salt Museum; adult/child €5/free; ☺10am-6pm Tue-Sat), with audiovisual displays that explain the history of salt and demonstrate how it is extracted from the sea.

A few kilometres south, follow the signs to **Pozo Negro**. This 5km drive is stunning and you'll probably pass a lot of walkers en route. Palm plantations, green meadows, herds of goats and craggy peaks typify the scenery. This tiny fishing community is the antithesis of Caleta de Fuste; there are just a cluster of cottages, some brightly painted fishing boats and two popular seafood restaurants, with little to choose between them in the fresh-fish stakes. **Los Pescadores** (mains €9) specialises in paella and has a terrace on the beach. Pozo Negro is popular with windsurfers, but bring your own gear.

THE NORTH

Road to La Oliva

The FV-10 highway travelling westwards away from Puerto del Rosario to the interior of the island takes you through a landscape that typifies Fuerteventura. Ochre-coloured soil and distant volcanoes create a barren landscape of shifting colours and shapes, depending on the position of the sun. Before crossing the ridge that forms the island's spine, the road passes through the sleepy hamlets of **Tetir** and **La Matilla**. The tiny 1902 chapel in the latter is a good example of the simple, bucolic buildings of the Canaries – functional, relatively unadorned and aesthetically pleasing.

About 7km south of La Matilla, along the FV-207, and 1km beyond the village of Tefía, is the **Ecomuseo la Alcogida** (adult/child €5/free; ☺10am-6pm Tue-Sat), a restored agricultural hamlet complete with furnished houses, outbuildings and domestic animals (though the chained-up dogs have a troubling un-eco feel). Overall, it's an interesting glimpse into the tough rural life of the not-too-distant past, with local artisans working in some of the settlement's buildings making lace and wicker baskets. There are explanations in English, plus a gift shop and bar.

Follow the road out of Tefía and swing right (east) on the FV-211 for Los Molinos. This is another lovely drive with the road curving around low-lying hills with isolated lofty palms and herds of goats. On the way you can't miss the old windmill used to grind cereals for the production of *gofio*, sitting squat across from a distinctive white-domed observatory.

The road continues to wind its way over the crest of the hill before descending dramatically beside a gaping gorge to tiny **Los Molinos**. Expect just a few simple houses overlooking a small, grey, stony beach with cliff trails to the east and plenty of goats, geese and stray cats. If you do stop here, make a point of having a seafood meal at beachside **Restaurante Casa Pon** (mains €8-10) while gazing over Atlantic breakers.

A couple of kilometres north of here, along a rough track, lies the **Playa de la Mujer**, an enticing stretch of sand, particularly popular with surfers.

Tindaya is a sprawling village where much of the island's Majorero goat's cheese is produced. Despite the lack of high-street delis (and the lack of a high street!) you can go right to the source here and buy your wheel of *queso* from **Queson Tindaya** (Calle Salamanca 12; ☺8.30am-2pm Mon-Sat). For more cheesy information, see the boxed text on p75.

Bus 7 from Puerto del Rosario to El Cotillo passes through Tetir, La Matilla and Tindaya three times daily. Bus 2 (€1.50, 20 minutes, twice daily), between Puerto del Rosario and Vega del Río de Palmas, passes by Tefía. There are no buses to Los Molinos, but it is a well-surfaced, scenic road if you are driving.

La Oliva

POP 2300

One-time capital of the island, in fact if not in name, La Oliva still bears a trace or two of grander days. The weighty bell tower of the 18th-century **Iglesia de Nuestra Señora de la Candelaria** is the town's focal point of sorts, with its black volcanic bulk contrasting sharply with the bleached-white walls of the church itself.

◎ Sights

Art and history enthusiasts will have plenty to keep them smiling in this town.

FREE **Casa de los Coroneles**   MUSEUM
(☺10am-6pm Tue-Sun) This 18th-century building looks more like a child's toy fort than a simple *casa* (house). In fact, its name means House of the Colonels and it has an interesting history. From the early 1700s, the officers who presided here virtually controlled the island. Amassing power and wealth, they so exploited the peasant class that, in 1834, Madrid – faced with repeated bloody mutinies on the island – disbanded the militia.

The building has been aesthetically restored, retaining its traditional central patio and wooden galleries; the ground floor now houses temporary exhibitions of world-class modern art. These include audiovisual installations, as well as paintings and photography. The 1st floor concentrates on the history of the building, including an entertaining audiovisual presentation comprising interviews with several of the elderly local population, such as a former servant of the aristocratic family who last lived here. Don't miss the simple chapel with its original tiled floor. Adjacent to the *casa*, the perfect cone of the volcano is an example of nature's own art. To get here, follow the signs from the centre of town.

TOP CHOICE **Centro de Arte Canario**   ART GALLERY
(Calle Salvador Manrique de Lara s/n; admission €4; ☺10am-5pm Mon-Sat) Another highlight

FUERTEVENTURA FOR CHILDREN

The main attraction has to be the **beaches**, many of which have fine white sand and shallow waters that are safe for paddling tots. For a man-made water adventure, the massive **Baku Water Park** (www.bakufuerteventura.com; admission adult/child €20/14; ☺10am-6pm) in Corralejo has ten-pin bowling, crazy golf and a driving range, as well as wave pools and kamikaze-style slides and rides.

There are plenty of **boat trips** throughout the resorts, which families may enjoy. At Caleta de Fuste, Oceanarium Explorer has a daily **dolphin-** and **whale-spotting trip**, while in Corralejo, El Majorero sails to the **Isla de Lobos**, where there is a lovely Robinson Crusoe–style beach and the possibility to explore the island via pedal power. Alternatively, if you don't object to zoos, **Oasis Park** in La Lajita has mammals, birds and sea life, plus shows and camel rides.

is this art museum, with its garden of sculptures and galleries containing works by such Canarian artists as César Manrique, Ruben Dario and Alberto Agullo. Two galleries are devoted to the national award-winning watercolourist Alberto Manrique (no relation to César), displaying his landscapes and more surreal, mainly interior, scenes. The gallery is located close to Casa de los Coroneles; follow the signs from the centre of town.

Casa Cilla Museo del Grano   MUSEUM
(admission adult/child €1.20/free; ☺9.30am-5.30pm Tue-Fri & Sun)
Located about 250m north of the church, on the road to El Cotillo, this small museum is devoted to grain – both its production and the harsh life of the farming cycle in general.

❶ Getting There & Away

Bus 7 (€2.20, 35 minutes) between Puerto del Rosario and El Cotillo passes through three times daily.

Corralejo

POP 12,000

Your opinion of this place will depend wholly upon where you are standing. The former fishing village near the harbour and main beach still has charm, despite the number of tourists, with narrow, uneven streets, good seafood restaurants and even a fisherman's cottage or two. Venture inland a couple of blocks and you find the predictable could-be-anywhere resort with Slow Boat buffets, fish and chips and a grid system of streets. It could be worse: the buildings are low-rise and you can still find the occasional local Spanish bar.

What makes Corralejo, however, are the miles of sand dunes to the south of town, sweeping back into gentle sugar-loaf rolls from the sea and fabulous broad sandy beaches. Protected as a nature park, no one can build on or near them...for now, that is. Unfortunately, a couple of monolithic concrete eyesores from the Riu hotel chain managed to get here before the regulation was in place.

🏖 Beaches

Parque Natural de Corralejo   BEACH
This nature park stretches along the east coast for about 10km from Corralejo. It can get breezy here, hence the popularity with windsurfers and kiteboarders. The locals have applied their ingenuity to the sand-sticking-to-the-suntan-lotion problem by erecting little fortresses of loose stones atop shrub-covered sandy knolls to protect sun-worshippers from the wind. The area is also known as **Grandes Playas** and is free to enter; sunloungers and umbrellas are available for hire in front of the two (eyesore) luxury hotels.

**Playas Corralejo Viejo &
Muelle Chico**   BEACH
The small beaches surrounding the town's harbour have fine sand and shallow water – and also serve as a year-round canvas for sand sculptors.

⊙ Sights & Activities

Most of the activities here are centred on the sea, with the main surfing beaches accessible by taxi. For landlubbers there are walking and cycling options, and a nine-hole golf course opened here in 2009.

Watersports

Dive Center Corralejo   DIVING
(☎928 53 59 06; www.divecentercorralejo.com;
Calle Nuestra Señora del Pino 22; dives from €30)
This respected outfit has been operating
since 1979. Located just back from the
waterfront, you can take the plunge with a
beginner course or, if you're already an
experienced diver, opt for a more
advanced option, including night diving
and underwater photography.

Fuerte Snorkelling   SNORKELLING
(☎680 85 61 22; www.fuerteservices.com; Paseo
Marítimo Bristol s/n; adult/child €35/30; ⊕) You
can go snorkelling on the Isla de Lobos with
this long-established operator, visiting two
sites and with a maximum of eight people
per excursion.

Pro Surf Fuerte Billabong   SURFING
(☎639 50 17 77; www.prosurfuerte.com; Galera
Beach s/n; 1-day course €45, advanced 3-day course
€120) Corralejo is a justifiably popular base
for surfers, with phrases like 'the Hawaii of
Spain' commonly bandied about. This outfit offers courses, including equipment and
insurance, plus transport to the waves.

Flag Beach Windsurf Center   SURFING
(☎928 86 63 89; www.flagbeach.com; Calle General Linares 31; ⊕) Out at Grandes Playas, Flag
Beach rents out boards (from €12 per day)
and bodyboards (from €10 per day), plus
runs a great beginner's course for €45. It

offers a range of watersports; check it out
also for accommodation arrangements and
children's courses.

Flag Beach Windsurf Center   WINDSURFING
(☎928 86 63 89; www.flagbeach.com; Calle General Linares 31; ⊕) Flag Beach has beginner
windsurfing courses for €270 for three days
and windsurf hire from €25 per hour. The
staff are also excellent kiteboarding instructors, with an introductory two-day course
costing €220.

Ventura Surf Center   WINDSURFING
(☎928 86 62 95; www.ventura-surf.com; Calle Fragata s/n; 1½hr course from €45, gear hire per hr
from €25) Conditions along much of the coast
and in the straits between Corralejo and
Lanzarote – the Estrecho de la Bocaina – are
ideal for both windsurfing and kiteboarding.
This place is on the beach at the end of Calle
Fragata, south of the centre of town.

Boat Trips

El Majorero   BOAT TRIPS
(☎616 986982; Estacíon Marítimo; adult/child
€18/9; ⊕) One-hour minicruises in glass-
bottom boats to the Isla de Lobos leave at
1pm daily, plus 4.15pm and 5.15pm according to demand. The company also operates
a regular ferry to the islet with five daily
departures from 10am to 4.30pm (adult/
child return €15/7.50). The last boat back
leaves at 5pm. Buy your tickets from the
kiosk at the port.

WORTH A TRIP

ISLA DE LOBOS

The bare, 4.4-sq-km Isla de Lobos takes its name from the *lobos marinos* (sea wolves)
that once lived there. They were, in fact, *focas monje* (monk seals), which disappeared
thanks to the hungry crew of French explorer Sieur de la Salle, who ate them (rather than
each other) to stave off starvation in the early 15th century. The good news is that they
are being gradually re-introduced to the island; check out the website www.gobiernode
canarias.org/medioambiente (in Spanish) for more information.

It is well worth joining an excursion to the islet from Corralejo. Once you've disem-
barked you can go for a short walk, order lunch at the quayside *chiringuito* (seafood
restaurant; reserve when you arrive if you intend to lunch there) and head for the
pleasant, small beach.

Take your binoculars as it's a popular birdwatching destination, plus you may spot a
shark or two, as they are common in the waters around Lobos. The island is also great for
surfing, so bring your board and don't worry, the sharks are hammerheads – a distant
(harmless) relation to Jaws. The island is also popular with divers and snorkellers.

The cheapest and fastest way to get here is on the **Isla de Lobos ferry** (adult/
child return €15/7.50) operated by El Majorero. Departing Corralejo at 10am, noon, 1pm,
3.15pm and 4.30pm, it leaves the island at 10.15am, 12.15pm, 1.45pm, 4pm and 5pm.
El Majorero also offers minicruises to the island in glass-bottomed boats).

CYCLE THE COASTAL ROUTE

Although you can drive the rough coastal road from **Corralejo** to **El Cotillo**, it is particularly well suited to cycling (or hiking), as it is virtually flat. Take the track north of the Corralejo bus station on Avenida Juan Carlos 1. This graded dirt road winds between volcanic lava fields, shifting to a more desert-like landscape after 5km. At 8km you reach the tiny fishing community of **Majanicho**, the houses clustered around a small inlet complete with scenic bobbing boats and the smallest chapel you have ever seen. From here you can detour along the FV-101 asphalt road to **Lajares** (7km) for a spot of light refreshment at one of the fabulous bakeries there (see p88), or continue on your way to El Cotillo. You will pass white, sandy beaches, interspersed with black rocky coves, and a couple of the most popular kiteboarding and windsurfing beaches in these parts. Coming direct from Corralejo you arrive at El Cotillo's lighthouse, Faro de Tostón, after 20km, where you can check out the Museo de la Pesca Tradicional. Alternatively, pedal (or plod) on to the centre of El Cotillo (4.5km), past the scrubby desert setting of Los Lagos.

Siña Maria 111   FISHING
(☑617 78 22 49; Estacíon Marítimo; angler/spectator €60/50) Deep-sea fishing trips take place between 8am and 1.30pm Monday to Saturday, and the skipper will cook your catch for lunch and keep the beer flowing.

Cycling & Hiking

Easy Riders Bikecenter   CYCLING
(☑928 53 53 62; www.extreme-animals.com; Calle Las Dunas s/n; 4hr trip €32; ☺10am-5pm) Organises year-round guided excursions with flexible times according to demand.

Natoural Adventure   HIKING
(☑664 84 94 11; www.natouraladventure.com; 4/6hr trek €40) Offers several different treks with distances ranging from 6km to 12km with varying levels of difficulty.

✖ Eating

The pedestrian area around Corralejo's small port is home to plenty of restaurants with outside terraces for ultimate people-watching potential.

TOP CHOICE Restaurante Avenida   SPANISH €
(Calle General Prim 11; mains €5.50-12; 🍴) Despite the location, just behind the Hesperia Bristol Playa hotel, this place is always heaving with a cheerful, local Canarian crowd who are here for the no-nonsense food. It's a great rustic atmosphere with beams and chunky darkwood furniture. The seafood dishes start at just €5.50 for grilled squid; roasted meats include lamb, chicken, rabbit and pork.

La Factoria   ITALIAN €
(Avenida Marítimo 9; pizzas from €6.50, pastas from €8; ☑) Situated right on the beach in the old harbour, the owner is from Bologna,

so knows a thing or two about pasta, which is made here daily. The pizzas are similarly authentic with thin, crispy bases and tasty toppings – *mama* would definitely approve. The cappuccino is the best in town.

El Andaluz   SPANISH €€
(Calle La Ballena 5; mains €10-14; ☺6.30-10pm Mon-Sat) This place continues to attract rave reviews from readers. The colourful interior has just a few tables, so get here early to secure a seat. The *menu degustación* (€18.50) is a good deal with meat and fish choices. Dishes use more herbs and vegetables than the Spanish norm and there's a tasty leek pie for vegetarians.

La Cañaña Asturiana   SPANISH €€
(Avenida Marítimo 3; mains €8-12) This restaurant has a superb position on the seafront and the menu here offers something different: traditional Asturian cuisine with dishes like Asturian stew, rabbit in cider and tuna-stuffed onions. Tastier than they sound – promise!

The Lemon Tree   BRITISH €€
(Calle Crucero Baleares; mains €7.50-10; ☺closed Tue night & Wed) Cajun chicken, gammon steak with pineapple, scampi, jacket potatoes and that '60s classic – chicken Kiev. Buzz and Maureen have a nostalgic British menu and a steady clientele of regulars. And, yes, there's banana split for dessert.

Cafe Latino   MEDITERRANEAN €
(Calle La Ballena; sandwiches €4.50, mains €6-7) This place on the waterfront has a French Riviera feel with its stripy umbrellas and classy look, but the menu is surprisingly down-to-earth, inexpensive and perfectly acceptable as long as you are not expecting cordon bleu.

Antiguo Café del Puerto
SPANISH €

(Calle La Ballena 10; tapas from €2) Warm and inviting, with rag-washed walls, good wines and 50-plus tapas (although some sound better than they taste).

 Drinking & Entertainment

Finding a drink in Corralejo doesn't pose a problem. Bars, discos and, if you must, karaoke clubs take up much of the **Centro Comercial Atlántico** (Avenida Nuestro Señora del Carmen) as well as the custard-yellow shopping centre further down the road, on the corner of Calle Anguila.

 Rock Island Bar
NIGHTCLUB

(www.rockislandbar.com; Calle Crucero Baleares s/n; ☺7.30pm-late; ☎) Over the last 21 years, Mandy and musician husband Gary have made this bar one of the most popular in town. There is acoustic music nightly, playing to an enthusiastic music-loving crowd.

Waikiki
NIGHTCLUB

(Calle Arístides Hernández Morán 11; ☺10am-late) Although this place doubles as a restaurant during the day, the best time to come is at night when a mix of surfers, party animals, families and friends gather in a hibiscus-fringed beachside setting to sip cocktails and enjoy the late-night music scene. The piña coladas are sublime.

Zazamira
CAFE

(Calle La Iglesia 7; ☺Wed-Mon 10am-11pm) Elbowed down a narrow street near the harbour, this is the healthy option with fresh juices like papaya and orange and ginseng-spiked coffee. Alcoholic options too.

Mojito Beach Club
BAR

(Avenida Marítimo s/n; ☺11am-late) Hip new place opened in 2011 on the waterfront with a menu of exotic *mojitos,* plus live music from 9.30pm.

 Shopping

Unless you are looking for souvenir place-mats or kiss-me-quick caps, your best option for local shopping, including several of the national chains, is the stretch of Avenida Nuestra Señora del Carmen from west of the tourist office until Calle Crucero Baleares.

No Work Team
OUTDOOR GEAR

(Avenida Nuestro Señora del Carmen 46) One local surf-wear label to check out is No Work Team. You'll find good-quality, comfy duds for men, women and children, with an unmistakeable surfing feel.

 **Information**

Locutorio Francis (Calle Acorazado España 1; per hr €2; ☺10am-10pm) Internet access.

Tourist office www.corralejograndesplayas .com; Avenida Marítimo 2; ☺8am-2pm Mon-Fri, 9am-2pm Sat, Sun & holidays) Located on the seafront near the harbour with shelves full of brochures.

 **Getting There & Away**

Bus

The bus station is located on Avenida Juan Carlos I. Bus 6 (€3.10, 40 minutes) runs regularly from the bus station to Puerto del Rosario.

Bus 8 (€2.90, 40 minutes, 13 daily) heads west to El Cotillo via La Oliva.

Car & Motorcycle

Cicar (☏928 82 29 00; www.cicar.com) has an office right at the Centro Comercial Atlántico's entrance and has good prices, with an economy car from around €150 for a week's rental.

For motorcycles, stop by the originally named **Rent A Bike Club** (☏928 86 62 33; Avenida Juan Carlos I 21; ☺9am-1pm & 5-8pm Mon-Sat, 9am-1pm Sun), opposite the bus station. You can rent scooters and motorcycles from €40 and €65 per day respectively, with full insurance.

 **Getting Around**

The town is easy to navigate and there is plenty of free on-street parking, especially in the side streets off the main Avenida Nuestro Señora del Carmen.

Call ☏928 86 61 08 or ☏928 53 74 41 for a taxi. A trip from the town centre to the main beaches will cost about €7. There's a convenient taxi rank near the Centro Comercial Atlántico.

El Cotillo

POP 4400

This former fishing village has real character; it's a bit scruffy in places, but that's all part of the charm. Unfortunately, the cranes have arrived – and not the winged variety. At least the development continues to be low-rise and, particularly around Los Lagos, the architecture is more imaginative than most.

Once the seat of power of the tribal chiefs of Maxorata (the northern kingdom of Guanche Fuerteventura), El Cotillo has been largely ignored since the conquest. The exceptions to the rule were the cut-throat pirates who occasionally landed here plus the slowly growing invasion of less violent sun-seekers who prize the area's unaffected peacefulness.

◎ Sights

Museo de la Pesca Tradicional   MUSEUM
(Museum of Traditional Fishing; Faro de Tostón; ⊘Tue-Sat 10am-6pm; adult/child €3/1.50) This interesting museum opened in 2008 and is located in the town's distinctive stripy lighthouse, next to the original lighthouse (not open to visitors). Climb the 64 steps for panoramic sea views and then visit the various galleries. There is English information available and several insightful mini videos about traditional fishing methods.

FREE **Castillo de Tostón**   CASTLE
(⊘9am-noon & 1-4pm Mon-Fri, 9am-1pm Sat & 9am-3pm Sun) This tubby *castillo* is not really a castle, more a Martello tower. There's a sight-and-sound exhibit, a display of arsenal and you can climb to the top for sweeping views of the surf beach.

✦ Activities

Watersports are the main activity here. The local authorities are planning to designate the western coastal regions south of El Cotillo a national park; see the boxed text Protecting the Coastline.

Experienced surfers only should make for a spot known as **Bubbles** north of the centre, which is not as innocuous as it sounds. Waves break over reef and rocks; you can pick out the casualties on the streets of El Cotillo and Corralejo. To get here, you'll need your own transport.

PROTECTING THE COASTLINE

Introduced by the local *cabildo* (government authority), plans were underway in 2011 to designate much of Fuerteventura's northwest coast a national park (similar to that of Lanzarote's Parque Nacional de Timanfaya). Stretching roughly from Los Molinos up to Playa del Majanicho, this would protect this wild, unspoiled region from being blighted from construction. It would also regulate watersports, ensuring, for example, that windsurfing, kiteboarding and surfing have designated areas – which makes good safety sense.

Dive Inn   DIVING
(☎928 86 82 63; Calle Felix de Vera Guerra s/n; single dive €35) The friendly staff here will take you to all the best spots for scuba diving (courses and equipment hire available) and can help out with tips about the surrounding area. Snorkelling gear is available for those who prefer to float on the water's surface, and there's also a nifty snorkelling course available (€35).

✗ Eating

The town has some of the north coast's finest restaurants, with the catch of the day reigning supreme.

TOP CHOICE **Casa Rústica**   MEDITERRANEAN €€
(Calle Constitución 1; mains €7.50) This place has enjoyed long-time popularity with visitors and locals alike. A comfortable rustic dining room with a few street-side tables is the setting for a diverse range of well-prepared dishes. The cuisine is Spanish with an Italian flourish, like gnocchi with mascarpone and *Jamón serrano* (cured Spanish ham). There's an inexpensive daily menu (€9).

El Mirador   SEAFOOD €€
(Calle Muelle de los Pescadores 19; ⊘closed Thu) Sitting just above the picturesque harbour, the staff here are exceptionally friendly and the food is consistently good. There is an emphasis on rice dishes with several paellas, including vegetarian, Valencian and seafood, as well as black rice choices and creamy rice with king prawns.

Restaurante La Vaca Azul   SPANISH €€
(Old Harbour; mains €10-12; ⊘closed Tue) This place enjoys prime position overlooking the pebbly beach, although the surreal rooftop cow (floodlit in lurid blue at night) has the best spot. The menu includes paella, mixed fish grill (minimum two people) and unusual sides like marrow with honey.

Aguayre   FUSION €€
(Calle La Caleta 5; mains €7.50; ✎) A trendy Tex Mex–cum-Italian-cum-vegetarian restaurant. Come here with an appetite and tuck into one of the piled-high salads, California wraps or a sizzling Diavola pizza with chilli, salami and red onions.

La Marisma   SEAFOOD €€
(Calle Santo Tomás; mains €12) A suitably nautical interior and a menu including superbly prepared seafood.

WIM GEIMAERT, ENVIRONMENTALIST

Wim Geimaert is the founder of the **Clean Ocean Project** (www.cleanoceanproject.org), established in 2002 to protect and preserve beaches. Geimaert organises regular beach cleanings in Fuerteventura, as well as elsewhere on the Canaries and the Spanish mainland. He has also established three shops in Corralejo, El Cotillo and Lajares that sell eco-friendly surf gear to raise money for ocean-pollution awareness. Geimaert is also a keen windsurfer and kiteboarder.

Top beaches My favourite beaches are mainly on the northwest coast, especially Playa de la Mujer. The Corralejo Grandes Playas are also superb. I often head for El Burro here, which is great for windsurfing and surfing.

Secret spot I love spending the day at Playa Esquinzo, located on the northwest coast 5km south of El Cotillo, as it is wild and beautiful, but little known.

Day off I enjoy going for long hikes when I have a chance. One of my favourite walks starts right outside the Clean Ocean Project shop in Lajares. It is a signposted trail to La Oliva (9.5km) and passes some stunning scenery. On Fuerteventura there are also many hidden beaches on the northwest coast.

Mare Alta TAPAS €
(Calle 3 Abril 1978 s/n; tapas from €2.50) Belgian-owned tapas bar with an imaginative choice and lovely courtyard setting.

Azzurro MEDITERRANEAN €€
(Carretera Al Faro; mains €12; ⊘closed Mon) Overlooking the beach at Los Lagos, this place offers quality pasta and seafood.

🛍 Shopping

Clean Ocean Project CLOTHES
(www.cleanoceanproject.org; 11 Calle del Muelle de Pescadores) Stop by this ecologically aware place that stocks cool surf wear in soft greens and blues. The business donates a percentage of all profits to beach-cleaning days and antipollution awareness. There are branches in Lajares and Corralejo; check the website for more information and see the boxed text about the owner Wim Geimaert.

Cycle & Surf Shop SURFBOARDS
(☑610 31 69 86; Calle 3 Abril 1978 s/n; surfboards per day €12.50, body boards per day €7.50, wetsuits per day €5; ⊘10am-2pm & 5-7pm) English-run shop across from the sports stadium which also rents out bicycles (per day €10).

❶ Getting There & Away

Bus 7 (€4, 45 minutes) for Puerto del Rosario leaves daily at 6.45am, noon and 5pm. Bus 8 (€2.90, 40 minutes, 13 daily) leaves for Corralejo. There is plenty of car parking on the streets of the town, although the one-way system is a tad confusing. There is also plenty of parking near the *castillo*.

THE SOUTHEAST

Tarajalejo & Giniginamar

These two quiet fishing hamlets go about their business largely undisturbed by tourists, despite Tarajalejo's new four-star Bahia Playa hotel. Their small, grey beaches are nothing spectacular but reasonably uncrowded. Stop for a drink at the simple **Beach Bar Tarajalejo**, with its straw umbrellas on the beach. This is a popular spot for windsurfers.

Just west of the FV-2 highway outside Tarajalejo, **El Brasero** (☑638 74 81 67; Carretera Gral Tarajalejo) comprises a large, reliably good **restaurant** (mains €12), a swimming pool (free for diners) and an adjacent modest **aquarium** (adult/child €5/2.50; ⊘10am-7pm) with around 120 species of fish. It also runs **Centro Hípica** (☑699 24 46 23; per hr €20) for horse riding and trekking.

Bus 1 (€5.50, one hour 20 minutes, hourly) between Puerto del Rosario and Morro Jable stops at Tarajalejo (not in Giniginamar).

La Lajita

This little fishing village presents yet another black-sand and pebble beach and cove with colourful fishing boats and an

WORTH A TRIP

A GOOD-TIME TOWN: LAJARES

Located 13km southwest of Corralejo via the FV-101 and the FV-109, the modest main street in Lajares has a laid-back feel. A handful of foreigners have opened up an enticing combination of restaurants, shops, surf bars and outstanding bakeries. Fancy a slice of dense chocolate torte or some creamy cheesecake topped with berries or an alternative Scandinavian-style breakfast with boiled eggs and cheese? Then check out **Pastelo**. If you prefer an exquisite French tart (no pun intended), nip over the road to tiny **El Goloso**. For something altogether more substantial, stop in at super-cool **Canela Café**, with its diverse menu that includes creamy pumpkin curry (€7.50) and the surf-and-turf choice of steak and prawns with garlic butter (€15.50). There's live acoustic music here on Friday nights.

One of the better craft markets is also held here on Saturday mornings. Failing that, check out one of the island's only second-hand clothes stores: **Pandora**, which also sells fashionable new threads. Nearby **La Vaca Loca** has hand-knitted jumpers. If you are travelling on to El Cotillo, consider taking the minor road just east of the centre, direction north to Majanicho, then following the coastal road to El Cotillo (see the boxed text p84).

unspoiled waterfront. However, a sprawl of unimaginative apartment blocks stretches all the way to the highway. At its southern exit is one of the island's largest theme parks: **Oasis Park** (www.fuerteventuraoasis park.com; Carretera General de Jandía s/n; adult/child €18/10; ☉9am-6pm; [image]). Here you can wander around the little zoo, populated by monkeys, exotic birds and other animals, and see various shows, which include sea lions, birds of prey and parrots. You can also join a 35-minute **camel trek** (adult/child €8/4). If plant life is more your thing, visit the park's botanical garden, with more than 2300 types of cacti.

Bus 1 (€5.75, 1½ hours, hourly) stops at the highway exit to town, from where it's a short walk south to the complex.

PENÍNSULA DE JANDÍA

Most of the Península de Jandía is protected by its status as the Parque Natural de Jandía. The southwest is a canvas of craggy hills and bald plains leading to cliffs west of Morro Jable. Much of the rest of the peninsula is made up of dunes, scrub and beaches.

It is said that German submarine crews used to hole up along the peninsula occasionally during WWII. Just imagine the paradise they found with not a single tourist, not one little apartment block; only them and their mates!

According to other stories, Nazi officials passed through here after the war to pick

up false papers before heading on to South America. One version of the story even has hoards of Nazi gold buried hereabouts – so bring your bucket and spade.

The only real way to explore the peninsula is via car; the roads are a combination of graded, unsealed and surfaced. A 4WD is recommended for exploring the Playa de Barlovento and surrounding beaches.

Costa Calma

Costa Calma, about 25km northeast of Morro Jable, is a confusing muddle of one-way streets interspersed with apartments, commercial centres (at least eight!) and the occasional hotel. The long and sandy beach is magnificent, but the whole place lacks soul or anything historic; its lifeline being the (mostly) German tourists.

🏃 Activities

Fuerte Fun Centre   WINDSURFING
(☎928 53 59 99; www.fuerte-surf.com; ☉9.30am-6pm) If catching the breeze with a sail and a board appeals, this place on the beach runs windsurfing courses, including a four-hour introductory course (€80), and also rents equipment (from €20 per hour). English and German are spoken.

Acuarios Jandia   DIVING
(☎928 87 60 69; www.acuarios-jandia.com; [image]) This well-established company runs a wide range of courses, from pool dives for tots (€25) to advanced open-water dives (€241).

✕ Eating & Drinking

Rapa Nui   CAFE €
(Commercial Centre Bahia Calma; sandwiches €2; ⊙closed Sun) A good choice on a sunny day (and there are plenty), this place has a lovely terrace with sea views. It runs the adjacent surf shop and school and serves sandwiches, snacks, ice cream (made on the premises), cocktails and coffees to a primarily young and tanned surfing crowd.

Bar Synergy   BAR
(Centro Comercial Costa Calma; ⊙7pm-3am Mon-Sat) Head here for a *mojito* sundowner; it's about as hip as Costa Calma gets, with a dark-pink interior and lightweight mainstream music.

La Pared

Located on the west coast, this is another hot spot for surfers. As you approach the mottled black basalt and sandy beach, look for the *queso artesano* sign on your right where you can pick up a wheel of local organic goat's cheese. For surfing courses and board rental, stop by **Adrenalin Surf School** (☑928 94 90 34; www.adrenalin-surfschool.com; 4hr beginner course €40). Overlooking the beach, **Restaurante Bahía La Pared** (☑928 54 90 30; mains from €13) specialises in fresh fish and seafood paella. The restaurant also runs an adjacent swimming-pool complex, complete with kiddie slides, which is free for diners.

Playa de Sotavento de Jandía

The name is a catch-all for the series of truly stunning beaches that stretch along the east coast of the peninsula. For swimming, sunbathing and windsurfing, this strand is a coastal paradise, with kilometre after kilometre of fine, white sand that creeps its way almost imperceptibly into the turquoise expanse of the Atlantic.

For 10 hyperactive days each July, its drowsy calm is shattered by daytime action and frantic nightlife as the beach hosts a leg of the **Windsurfing World Championship** (www.fuerteventura-worldcup.org), which celebrated its 25th anniversary in 2010 and attracts windsurfers and kiteboarders from around the globe.

Various driveable trails lead down off the FV-2 highway to vantage points off the beach – its generous expanses mean you should have little trouble finding a tranquil spot on the sand.

If you want to do a bit of cyberspace research before arriving, check out www.playasdejandia.com (in Spanish).

Morro Jable

POP 9040

More staid than its northern counterpart Corralejo, Morro Jable is almost exclusively German. The beach is the main attraction, with pale golden sand stretching for around 4km from the older part of town. It's fronted by low-rise, immaculately landscaped apartments and hotels. Back from the beach, the charm palls somewhat with a dual carriageway lined with commercial centres and hotels. The older town centre, up the hill, provides a glimpse of what the town must have looked like before the charter flights started landing.

🏖 Beaches

Playa del Matorral is the main beach here and it's magnificent, stretching eastwards for over 4km from Morro Jable. A family-friendly beach, it's great for indulging in a variety of watersports, churning a pedalo or just collapsing on the sand. The beach rarely gets crowded, but for true solitude head for the beaches 7km further east, although they are accessible only with your own transport.

🏃 Activities

Understandably, most of the activities here are based in, on or near the sea.

Centro de Buceo Felix   DIVING
(☑928 54 14 18; www.tauchen-fuerteventura.com; Avenida Sakvadir 27; 1hr dive €26) Organises daily dives at 1pm.

Mark Robinson's Wasser Sports   WINDSURFING
(☑928 16 80 00; www.robinson.de, in German; 10-12 hr beginner course €170, board rental per hr €25) Part of the luxurious Robinson's resort, situated on Playa del Matorral.

Magic   BOAT TRIPS
(☑900 50 62 60; www.magic-paradise.eu; 5hr cruise adult/child €54/28; 🚼) Operates a couple of smart catamarans out of the port. Sailing at 10am or 10.30am (also at 4pm from May to October), cruises include a barbecue lunch and allow plenty of time for swimming and snorkelling.

QUALITY CRAFTS

Throughout Europe, government-endorsed art and crafts shops equal a hike in prices and are places to avoid for euro economisers. In Fuerteventura, however, they have the equation right for their *Tiendas de Artesanía*: the artisans determine the prices and receive 100% of the profits.

The government's role is solely to verify the authenticity of the craft in question, which is, unfortunately, quite important these days, given the prolific sale of Chinese-imported lacework, and similar. Look for the distinctive stamp of guarantee, with its green border for creative handicrafts and brown border for traditional handicrafts. All the labels should be numbered and contain the details of the artisan. Look for the shops in the Molino de Antigua, Betancuria, Puerto del Rosario and, yes, even at the airport.

Orlando Rent a Car CYCLING
(928 54 00 65; Apartmentos El Matorral bajo, Avenida Jandía; bike hire per day €8) Conveniently located near the Cosmo Centro Comercial, rents out bikes for one day or longer, including insurance.

✕ Eating

You can get the usual bland international cuisine and fast food at innumerable places among the apartments, condos and shopping centres along Avenida Saladar. Head into the older part of town for seafood and more authentic choices.

Restaurante Posada San Borondón SPANISH €€
(Plazoleta Cirilo López 1; mains €8-16) Somewhere a little more interesting and offering a variety of Spanish food, including delicious grilled sole. It's easy to find, right next to the steamship exterior, complete with portholes and funnels, of Bar Barco.

La Gaviota SEAFOOD €€
(Calle Tomas Grau s/n; mains €8-12) One of the better restaurants on this seaside strip. Go for a plate of *pimientos padron* (small green peppers) as a starter, followed by a plate of simple grilled tuna.

La Laja SEAFOOD €
(Calle Tomas Grau s/n; mains €12) A good seafood choice located on the corner of the boardwalk (you can climb down the stairs by the church).

Drinking & Entertainment

The main nightlife action is along the beach-front part of the resort. A cluster of pubs is concentrated in the Cosmo Centro Comercial. You could also head for **Stella Discoteque** (Avenida Saladar s/n), 450m further on – look for the twin bronze lions and you are nearly there.

Surf Inn BAR
(Cosmo Centro Comercial; ☺7pm-3am Mon-Sat) Re-opened in 2011 after a major revamp, this place is aimed at a younger late-night crowd who like to check out surfing and snowboarding videos in between quaffing cocktails.

Olympia BAR
(Centro Comercial Playa Paradiso, Avenida Saladar s/n; ☺10am-1am) With comfortable wicker furniture, a central bar and picture windows overlooking the seafront, this place is perfect for post-dinner cocktails; the music is pretty chilled out as well.

Shopping

There's a small Thursday **market** (Avenida Saladar; ☺9am-1.30pm) in a car park due west of the tourist office. With most stalls run by Moroccans and Africans, you'll be lucky to find anything that smacks particularly of the Canaries.

Cosmo Centro Comercial COMMERCIAL CENTRE
(Avenida Saladar) This large centre has plenty of shops selling tax-free goodies.

❶ Information

Cosmo Office (Cosmo Centro Comercial, Avenida Saladar; per hr €4; ☺9am-1pm & 5-10pm Mon-Fri, 5-10pm Sun) Offers speedy internet connection.

Tourist office (www.pajara.es, in Spanish; Cosmo Centro Comercial, Avenida Saladar; ☺8am-3pm Mon-Fri) Lots of brochures and helpful staff.

Getting There & Away

The port, Puerto de Morro Jable, is 3km by road from the centre of town.

Bus 1 runs to Puerto del Rosario (€9, two hours, at least 12 daily) between 5.45am (weekdays) and 10.30pm. Bus 10 (€8.80, 1¾ hours, three daily), via the airport, is faster. Bus 5 (€2.45, 40 minutes) to Costa Calma runs frequently.

ⓘ Getting Around

There is a large, free car park next to the tourist office in the Cosmo Centro Comercial. Finding a spot in the older part of the town can be problematic. To call a taxi, ring 928 54 12 57.

To/From the Airport

Bus 10 (€7.50, 1½ hours, three daily) connects the town with the airport; taxis cost around €75.

Around Morro Jable

Much wilder than their leeward counterparts, the long stretches of beach on the windward side of the Península de Jandía are also harder to get to. You really need a 4WD to safely negotiate the various tracks leading into the area.

PUNTA DE JANDÍA

Although the road here is gradually being re-surfaced, at the time of research only the first 2km was asphalted. The rough track gets plenty of use, though, so is in pretty good nick. From Morro Jable it winds out along the southern reaches of the peninsula to a lone lighthouse at Punta de Jandía.

Puerto de la Cruz is located a couple of kilometres east of the lighthouse. A tiny fishing settlement and beach, it is a popular weekend retreat for locals. Two modest *chiringuitos* open only at lunchtime and serve up the local catch to tourists passing en route to the island's westernmost point. There's little to choose between them.

COFETE

About 10km along the same road from Morro Jable, a turn-off leads northeast over a pass and plunges to Cofete (7km from the junction), a tiny peninsula hamlet at the southern extreme of the Playa de Barlovento de Jandía. Sandy tracks, negotiable on foot or by 4WD, snake off to this wind-whipped strand. **Restaurante Cofete** (☑928 17 42 43; mains €6-12; ☺11am-7pm) does drinks and excellent snacks and has a more sophisticated menu than you'd expect from a restaurant that's literally at the end of the road. It serves fresh fish as well as *carne de cabra en salsa* (goat in sauce).

PLAYA DE BARLOVENTO DE JANDÍA

This is a wild length of coast that can get very windy, though the flying sand doesn't seem to deter the nude bathers. Take care swimming here: the waves and currents are more formidable than the generally calmer waters on the other side of the island.

CANARIES CONSERVATION

Morro Jable is home to the **Sodabe Turtle Reserve**, where loggerhead turtles are being reintroduced after an absence of some 100 years. The programme dates back to January 2007 when 145 loggerhead turtles were successfully hatched on the nearby west coast beach of Cofete in the Parque Natural de Jandía.

The beaches here are only the second site in the world selected for such a translocation of eggs; the first is in Mexico. The eggs came from a turtle colony in the southern islands of Cape Verde, which has similarities to the beaches and environment here, namely in the quality of the water, the sand and, above all, the consistently warm climate. The turtle eggs are hatched in artificial nests and, before they can crawl away to an uncertain future, the baby turtles are transferred to special tanks at the reserve's 'nursery' until they are strong enough to swim without water wings. At this stage they are microchipped and released into the sea.

The hope is that when they are all grown up they will return to their Cofete home to lay eggs themselves so the species will once again spontaneously breed on the island. The project organisers hope to repeat the hatching at least every five years in an attempt to reverse the depletion of this species of marine turtle.

Another significant conservation project on the island concerns the endangered Mediterranean monk seal, which is being gradually introduced back to the Isla de Lobos, just off Corralejo. Check out the website www.gobiernodecanarias.org/medioambiente (in Spanish) for more information.

Lanzarote

928 / POP 141,940

Best Places to Eat

» Lilium (p97)
» La Bodega de Santiago (p110)
» La Cantina (p102)
» El Risco (p107)

Best Places to Stay

» Hotel Diamar (p215)
» Finca de Arrieta (p216)
» Caserío de Mozaga (p216)

Why Go?

A Unesco biosphere reserve, Lanzarote is an intriguing island with an extraordinary geology of 300 volcanic cones, yet ticks all the right good-time boxes. There are great beaches, interesting sights and plenty of restaurants and hotels. The landscape has a stark and otherworldly appearance, with the occasional bucolic, palm-filled valley juxtaposed with surreal crinkly black lava fields. Long associated with package tourists and pie-and-chips resorts, times are finally changing and there has been a marked increase in the number of independent travellers to the island. In response, the government has undertaken an island-wide initiative to signpost walking trails, and rural accommodation options have increased.

The island's major sights have been aesthetically developed by the late César Manrique, a Lanzarote native and artist. He still has a considerable impact on the island via a cultural foundation that promotes Lanzarote's conservation, culture and architectural integrity.

When to Go

Lanzarote is, happily, a year-round destination due to its consistent spring/summer weather. Busier months tend to be July and August, when Spaniards take their holidays, while cheaper airfares from other European destinations are normally most plentiful during the autumn and spring (aside from Easter week).

The island's annual carnival in February–March pales very slightly compared to that in Tenerife or Gran Canaria, but is still celebrated with great gusto. There are processions, music and general merriment.

Getting Around

Driving on Lanzarote is a cinch. A good car-hire choice is **Cabrera Medina** (www.cabreramedina.com), with branches all over the island. Alternatively, the bus network is fine for major towns.

THREE PERFECT DAYS

Day One

Head for the extraordinary **Parque Nacional de Timanfaya**, where a bus trip gets you up close and personal to this otherworldly landscape. Next, appreciate a more benevolent side of nature at nearby **El Golfo** by enjoying a seafood lunch overlooking the surf. Take the coastal road south past surreal caves and emerald-green ponds, winding up at the man-made and modern **Marina Rubicón** with its designer shops, classy bars and relaxing restaurants overlooking the bobbing boats.

Day Two

Wise up on Manrique at the **Fundación César Manrique** and admire its extraordinary lava-field setting. Next, head for the **Jardín de Cactus**, displaying a myriad of prickly cacti. Many consider your next stop, the **Jameos del Agua**, to be Manrique's pinnacle achievement, while nearby **Cueva de los Verdes** is a natural wonder. Next, take in the awesome views from the **Mirador del Río**, before returning south to Arrecife for dinner in a castle at **MIAC Restaurant**, with its adjacent contemporary art gallery – another feather in Manrique's entrepreneurial hat.

Day Three

Designate your driver and start your tipple trail at the **Monumento al Campesino restaurant**, enjoying local food and wines. Nearby, wine cellar **Bodega Mozaga** dates from 1880 and has won awards for its deliciously fruity *malvasía*. Another excellent wine cellar, **Bodega Tinache**, has 20 hectares of vines en route to Timanfaya; go for the dry Malmsey and *moscatel*. Take a hiccup of a sidestep to **La Geria** with a visit to **Bodega Stratvs**, a new, young winery with excellent fruity reds. Wind up your trip at the adjacent **Bodega Rubicón**'s small viticulture museum, which also offers free tastings.

Getting Away from It All

» **Puerto Calero** (p112) Enjoy a gentle, sea-hugging stroll to the secluded Playa Quemada.

» **Explore the interior** (p111) Ditch the map and drive inland, discovering unspoiled hamlets and stunning views.

» **Orzola** (p104) Escape the sunbed-striped beach resorts and check out the natural, white sandy coves on the far northeastern coast.

DON'T MISS

Taking a hike, walk or even a short stroll in the island's volcanic interior, where there are sign-posted trails to encourage you to stride out.

Best Beaches

» **Playa Quemada** (p112) Picturesque, black volcanic beach with excellent seafood restaurants.

» **Playa Mujeres** (p114) Golden sandy beach, popular with surfers.

» **Playas Caletones** (p104) Series of wild, natural beaches and coves in the far northeast.

Best Markets

» **La Recova Market** (p98) Daily produce and crafts market.

» **Haría Market** (p106) Weekly produce and *artisanía* (crafts) market.

» **Marina Rubicón** (p113) Twice weekly souvenir and crafts' market, overlooking the harbour.

Resources

» Restaurant website: www.eatlanzarote.com

» Annual sports events: www.clublasanta.com

» Rural eco-friendly accommodation: www.stayecochic.com

» Online magazine: www.lanzarotemagazine.co.uk

History

Lanzarote has experienced more than its fair share of misfortune. It was the first island to fall to Jean de Béthencourt in 1402 and was subsequently made the unneighbourly base for conquering the rest of the archipelago. Many locals were sold into slavery and those remaining had to endure waves of marauding pirates from the northwest African coast. Today's popular tourist site, the Cueva de los Verdes, was a refuge for those unable to flee to Gran Canaria, but of course couldn't protect their homes from large-scale looting. British buccaneers, such as Sir Walter Raleigh, also got in on the plundering act and, by the mid-17th century, the population had dwindled to a mere 300.

Just as the human assault seemed to be abating, nature elbowed in – big time. During the 1730s, massive volcanic eruptions destroyed a dozen towns and some of the island's most fertile land. But the islanders were to discover an ironic fact: the volcanic soil proved a highly fertile bedrock for farming (particularly wine grapes), which brought relative prosperity to the island.

Today, with tourism flourishing alongside the healthy, if small, agricultural sector, the island is home to nearly 142,000 people, not counting all the holiday blow-ins who, at any given time, can more than double the population.

ⓘ Getting There & Away

AIR

Guasimeta airport (☑928 84 60 00; www .aena.es) is 6km southwest of Arrecife. Major operators from other Canary Islands and the Spanish mainland:

Iberia (www.iberia.es)

Air Europa (www.aireuropa.com)

Spanair (www.spanair.com)

Air Berlin (www.airberlin.com)

Binter Canarias (www.bintercanarias.com)

Islas Airways (www.islasairways.com)

BOAT

The following ferries serve Lanzarote.

Acciona Trasmediterránea (in Arrecife ☑902 45 46 45; www.trasmediterranea.es) Runs a weekly ferry on Wednesday at midnight (€33, 8 hours) from Arrecife to Las Palmas de Gran Canaria. Buy tickets at the ferry terminal up to one hour before embarkation or via the website. A weekly ferry also runs to Santa Cruz de la Palma (€28, eight hours) and Santa Cruz de Tenerife (€29, six hours).

ROAD DISTANCES (KM)

	Yaiza	Playa Blanca	Puerto del Carmen	Arrecife
Playa Blanca	14			
Puerto del Carmen	13	29		
Arrecife	23	39	38	
La Caleta de Famara	25	40	25	16

Approximate distances only

Fred Olsen (☑902 53 50 90; www.fredolsen .es) Ferries (adult/child €21/10, 20 minutes, six times daily) link Playa Blanca with Corralejo on Fuerteventura. It runs a free ferry bus service between Playa Blanca and Puerto del Carmen.

Naviera Armas (www.navieraarmas.com) Has five daily ferries (€43, 7 hours, 30 minutes) between Arrecife and Las Palmas de Gran Canaria and six sailings daily (adult/child €18/9, 25 minutes) between Playa Blanca and Corralejo on Fuerteventura. There are also four weekly ferries to Santa Cruz de Tenerife (€36, 11 hours, Tuesday, Wednesday, Thursday and Saturday) at 11am.

ARRECIFE

POP 53,920

Arrecife is a small, manageable city with a pleasant Mediterranean-style promenade, an inviting sandy beach and – it has to be said – a disarming backstreet hotchpotch of sun-bleached, peeling buildings, elegant boutiques, rough bars and good (and bad) restaurants. The sights are scarce, yet interesting, and include a couple of castles, a fashionable cultural centre and a pretty lagoon. If anything, Arrecife's most notable quality is that it's a no-nonsense working town that earns its living from something other than tourism.

History

The single biggest factor behind Arrecife's lack of pizzazz is that it only became the island's capital in 1852. Until then, Teguise ruled supreme. In 1574 the Castillo de San Gabriel was first constructed (it was subsequently attacked and rebuilt) to protect the port. Its shorter and squatter younger sibling further up the coast, the Castillo de San José, was built in 1776–79.

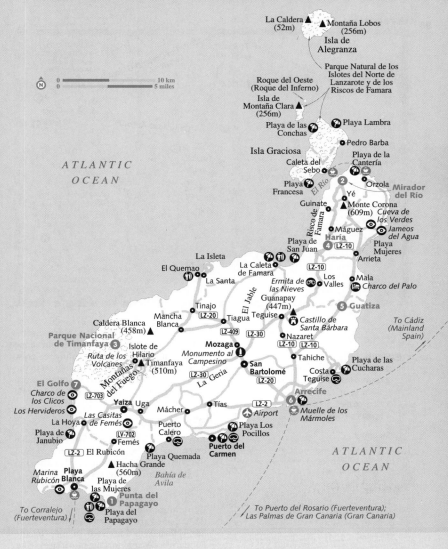

Lanzarote Highlights

❶ Kick back on the golden sandy beaches of **Punta del Papagayo**, on the wild south coast (p114)

❷ Enjoy heady sweeping views from mountain-top **Mirador del Río** (p105)

❸ Lace up your walking shoes and explore the magnificent **Parque Nacional de Timanfaya** (p109)

❹ Experience an oasis of green at lush, palm-filled **Haría** (p106)

❺ Get spiky at Manrique's fabulous **Jardín de Cactus** in Guatiza (p103)

❻ Be a high-flyer on the dance floor at Arrecife's **Star's City** disco (p98)

❼ Enjoy a simple plate of freshly barbecued sardines at an oceanfront **El Golfo** restaurant (p110)

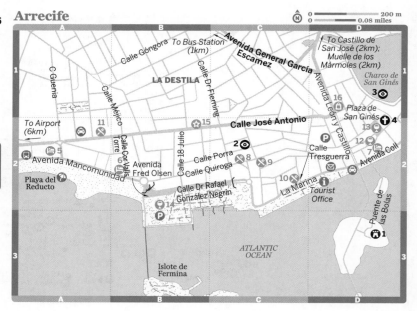

Arrecife

⊚ **Sights**

1 Castillo de San Gabriel D3
2 Centro Insular de Cultura El
   Almacén...C2
3 Charco de San Ginés..........................D1
4 Iglesia de San Ginés D2

🛏 **Sleeping**

5 Hotel Diamar A2
6 Hotel Lancelot....................................B2
7 Hotel Miramar D2

🍴 **Eating**

8 Café Nizar C2
9 Domus Pompeii...................................C2
10 La Tavernetta C2
11 Lilium...A2

🍷 **Drinking**

12 Bar Andalucía D2
13 La Tentacion.......................................D2
14 Star's City B2

🎭 **Entertainment**

15 Ococo B2

🛍 **Shopping**

16 La Recova Market................................D1

By the close of the 18th century, a semblance of a town had taken uncertain shape around the harbour. As its commerce grew and the threat of sea raids dropped off in the 19th century, the town thrived and the move of the island's administration to Arrecife became inevitable.

⊙ Sights

Arrecife is easy to navigate. With the notable exceptions of the Castillo de San José and the port, everything of interest is located in a tight area around the centre.

⌜TOP⌟ Museo de Arte
⌞CHOICE⌟ Contemporáneo   MUSEUM

(MIAC; Carretera de Puerto Naos; adult/child €2.50/free; ⊙11am-9pm) Converted in 1994 by the Fundación César Manrique into a sleek, contemporary art museum and restaurant, the **Castillo de San José** was built in the 18th century to deal with pirates and provide unemployed locals with a public-works job scheme. Today it houses the most important collection of modern art in the Canaries. Aside from a couple of early works by Manrique himself, artists such as Miró, Millares, Rivera, Sempere and Tápies are on show.

The surreal volcanic landscape on Lanzarote is best appreciated by striding out on foot. The local government has recently made this a lot easier by clearing, signposting and renovating 10 historic walking trails in a substantial project known as the Red de Diez Senderos Turísticos y Recreativos (Ten Tourist-Orientated and Recreational Walking Paths). Look for this written in Spanish on large signs throughout the island, which also include a detailed map showing the respective routes and all those essential details such as length of walk, type of terrain and level of difficulty, plus the flora and fauna, and the points of interest to be found along the way.

You can also check the website www.cabildodelanzarote.com (in Spanish); use the *buscador* (search) box to find the link. The maps will, it is hoped, eventually be published in a booklet; check at any tourist office for an update.

Charco de San Ginés LAGOON
(Avenida César Manrique) This attractive small lake with its colourful boats and resident seagulls could be a picture postcard, Portofino-style place. Instead, the buildings and restaurants here are a beguiling combo of mildly down-at-heel and freshly whitewashed, with blue trim.

FREE **Centro Insular de Cultura El Almacén** CULTURAL CENTRE
(☑928 81 01 21; Calle José Betancourt 33; ⏰8am-3pm Mon-Fri) Another vibrant gallery space is this cultural centre housed in a former warehouse that has had a stylish makeover, once again influenced by Manrique. Being extensively reformed at the time of research, when it re-opens the venue promises, once again, to have regular art exhibitions, a cinema and bar-cum-restaurant where you can enjoy live music at weekends.

Castillo de San Gabriel CASTLE
Located on a little islet just off the seafront promenade, this castle is scheduled to re-open as a history museum, but no fixed date was available at the time of research. Call or check at the tourist office for an update.

Iglesia de San Ginés CHURCH
(Plaza de San Ginés; ⏰before & after Mass) Dating from 1665 and featuring a statue of the island's patron saint who originated in Cuba.

🏖 **Beaches**
If you fancy a dip, the city's main beach, **Playa del Reducto**, is lovely: an arc of pristine pale golden sand fringed with lofty palm trees and a promenade. It is safe for children, reasonably clean and, generally, surprisingly empty. You can also stride out south from here on a coastal walk to Puerto

del Carmen (12 kilometres, about three hours).

🎊 **Festivals & Events**
Carnaval CARNIVAL
Celebrated with gusto throughout the island during February or March, but particularly in Arrecife, Carnaval festivities kick off the week before Ash Wednesday.

Día de San Ginés PATRON SAINT
The day of the island's patron saint is 25 August and it's celebrated with a major fiesta in even the smallest *pueblo* (village). In Arrecife, the streets surrounding the Iglesia de San Ginés are home to the most revelry.

🍴 **Eating**
Fish lovers should head for the Charco de San Ginés, which is surrounded by breezy seafood restaurants. Elsewhere, there's a smattering of outdoor cafes and restaurants on Calle Ruperto González Negrín and La Marina.

TOP CHOICE **Café Nizar** MIDDLE EASTERN €€
(Calle Luis Morote 19; mains €8-12; ⏰closed Sun; ☑) The Syrian owner-cum-chef serves Middle Eastern fare that is deliciously authentic. Try the meze of seven dishes (€15), which includes hummus, *moutabel* (spicy aubergine dip) and *tabouleh*. More substantial meaty dishes are also available.

TOP CHOICE **Lilium** MODERN CANARIAN €€
(www.restaurantelilium.es; Calle José Antonio 103; mains €7-9) Forget the uninspired location; this small place takes its cooking seriously. There are plenty of culinary surprises, such as a succulent lobster and papaya salad. Order the cheese and paprika bread to accompany your meal.

BONO BUS

If you are planning on making a few trips, invest in a Bono Bus card, which can save you around 30% off the fare. The cards cost €12 or €22 (depending on how many trips you are planning on taking) and are purchased at bus stations. Tell the driver your destination and the amount will be deducted from your card via a stamping machine.

MIAC Restaurant MEDITERRANEAN €€€
(☎928 81 23 21; Castillo de San José; mains €15-30) Situated in the Castillo de San José, this is Arrecife's greatest gastronomic-cum-visual experience. Glide down the spiral staircase and order some wonderful meat and fish dishes in the grooviest possible setting. The huge wraparound windows overlook the port and the decor is the usual Manrique mix of airy and inventive. The bow-tied service completes the dress-for-dinner feel.

Domus Pompeii ITALIAN €€
(Calle José Betancourt 19; pizza from €7, pasta from €8; ☑) The owner of this trattoria is from Pompeii, so expect faux-Roman surroundings and delicious thin-crust Neapolitan pizzas, plus homemade pasta with simple, fresh sauces. The complimentary *limoncello* liqueur is a nice touch.

La Tavernetta MEDITERRANEAN €€
(cnr La Marina & Calle Tresguerra; mains €6-9; ☑) La Tavernetta has all-day fussy-family appeal with a vast menu that includes bacon-and-egg breakfasts, healthy salads, juicy steaks and a decadent chocolate soufflé.

 Drinking

Star's City BAR
(Arrecife Gran Hotel, Avenida Fred Olsen) You can't miss this looming, green, glass skyscraper that, unsurprisingly, was built before Manrique returned to the island and initiated strict building guidelines. Like it or loathe it, there's no avoiding the fact that this 17th-floor bar has unbeatable panoramic views. Open daily for coffee and cocktails, there's a disco here on Friday and Saturday from 10pm.

Bar Andalucía BAR
(Calle Luis Martín 5; ☺closed Sun) Open since 1960, this bar sports Andalucian tiles, paintings for sale and straight-from-Seville

tapas, such as stuffed peppers and *patatas alioli* (fried potatoes with garlic-spiked mayonnaise).

La Tentacion BAR
(Plaza de las Palmas; ☺closed Sun) Across from the Iglesia de San Ginés, with good wines and tapas, including some Cuban-inspired choices like *yucca frita* (fried yucca).

 Entertainment

There's plenty of nightlife choices in town, ranging from gritty local bars to intimate chill-out cafes. The main moving-and-shaking clubs are located on one short strip of central Calle José Antonio. They're open from around 10pm until approximately 4am.

Ococo NIGHTCLUB
(Calle José Antonio 62) Ococo is a one-club-fits-all kind of place with pool tables, sports screens, darts, white-leather sofas and delicious alco-fruity drinks, such as a mango sorbet cocktail. It morphs into a disco Fridays and Saturdays from 11.30pm.

 Shopping

For the highest concentration of shops head for pedestrianised Avenida León y Castillo.

La Recova Market MARKET
(☺9am-2pm Mon-Sat) Located between Avenida León y Castillo and Charco de San Ginés, stalls here sell everything from artisan crafts to organic cheese; there are second-hand stores on Saturday.

 Information

Main tourist office (☎928 81 31 74; La Marina s/n; ☺8am-2pm Mon-Fri) Located in a fabulous bandstand rotunda–meets–tourist office building on the promenade.
Redes Servicios Informática (Calle Coronel Bens 17; per hr €1.80; ☺9am-1.30pm & 5-8pm Mon-Fri, 9am-1pm Sat) Internet access.
Tourist office (☎928 84 60 73; ☺9am-7pm Mon & Wed, 9.30am-9.30pm Tue & Thu, 9am-9.30pm Fri & Sat, 10.30am-9.30pm Sun) There's a second smaller tourist office in the airport arrivals hall.

 Getting There & Away

Arrecife Bus (☎928 81 15 22; www.arrecifebus.com) has a frequent service around the area, departing from the bus station and including the routes following. Otherwise services are minimal. Three buses on weekdays (two daily on weekends) head north for Orzola (€3.25,

1½ hours), from where you can get a boat out to Isla Graciosa.

BUS 1 Costa Teguise (€1.20, 20 minutes, every 20 minutes)

BUS 2 Puerto del Carmen (€1.60, 40 minutes, every 20 minutes)

BUS 6 Playa Blanca (€3.25, 1½ hours, 12 daily)

Car & Motorcycle

You will find plenty of rental companies, especially around Avenida Mancomunidad and Calle Dr Rafael González Negrín.

❶ Getting Around

A couple of *guaguas municipales* (local buses) follow circuits around town, but you're unlikely to need them. Street parking is limited. There is free parking besides El Charco de San Ginés. Alternatively, head for the waterfront Gran Hotel, fronted by an underground paying car park. There's a taxi rank beside the tourist office on La Marina and another on Calle José Antonio. Otherwise call ☑928 80 31 04.

To/From the Airport

Lanzarote's airport is 6km south of Arrecife. Buses 22 and 23 (€1.20, 20 minutes) run between the airport and Arrecife every 30 minutes or so between 7.10am and 10.40pm Monday to Friday (between 8.40am and 10.40pm on weekends). A taxi will cost about €11.

To/From the Port

Muelle de los Mármoles is about 4km northeast of central Arrecife. Bus 1 calls in at the port. A taxi costs about €4.50.

AROUND ARRECIFE

Costa Teguise

Northeast of Arrecife is Costa Teguise, which is perfectly pleasant provided you are not expecting cobbled streets and crumbling buildings. This is a purpose-built holiday resort, built on a grid system, with bustling shopping centres, family-geared beaches and watersports, plenty of mediocre (and better) bars and restaurants but, inevitably perhaps, no real soul. There's not even an original fishing village at its heart.

The most appealing beach is Playa de las Cucharas. Those further south suffer unfortunate views of the port and industry near Arrecife. The Centro Comercial Las Cucharas shopping centre is the resort's focal point.

◉ Sights & Activities

Lanzarote Aquarium　　　　　　　AQUARIUM
(www.aquariumlanzarote.com; Centro Comercial El Trébol; adult/child €12/8; 🅿) This is the largest aquarium in the Canary Islands, and children, in particular, will enjoy it. It has three touch pools and a shark tank, plus plenty of colourful fish and sea critters viewed from an underwater tunnel.

TOP CHOICE Olita Treks　　　　　　HIKING
(☑619 16 99 89; www.olita-treks.com; Centro Comercial Mareta; walks from €35) Conducts excellent local walks, which cover turf such as the Isla Graciosa, the island's volcanoes and various coastal stretches. Walks are either half- or full-day; the price includes pick-up and transport.

Calipso Diving　　　　　　　　　　DIVING
(☑928 59 08 79; www.calipso-diving.com; Centro Comercial Calipso; one dive €30) Long-established and a reliable choice for courses and dives; there is equipment hire for experienced divers.

Aquatis Diving Center　　　　　　DIVING
(☑928 59 04 07; www.diving-lanzarote.net; Playa de las Cucharas; one dive €28, aquarium dive €149) Offers similar to Calipso, as well as the more unusual opportunity to dive surrounded by sharks at Lanzarote Aquarium.

Zoo Park Famara　　　　　　KITEBOARDING
(☑634 88 40 68; www.zooparkfamara.com; Avenida Marinero 5; 3hr course €25) Take advantage of the steady local winds; prices include equipment.

Bike Station　　　　　　　　　　CYCLING
(☑628 10 21 77; www.bikelanzarote.com; CC Maretas s/n; bike rental per day/week €14/70) Rents bikes and arranges tours (from €30) of the island.

✕ Eating

There's no shortage of restaurants, although English pub fare seems to be more prevalent than traditional Canarian cuisine.

Patio Canario　　　　　　SEAFOOD €€
(Plaza del Pueblo, Avenida Islas Canarias; mains €9-14) This place specialises in fresh seafood from Isla Graciosa and Galicia on the Spanish mainland. The outside terrace is set in an attractive courtyard surrounded by an international clutch of restaurants, including Mexican, Swiss and Indian.

LANZAROTE FOR CHILDREN

There's plenty going on for children on the island. Several of the Manrique sights should keep them suitably gobsmacked, while the southern resorts have plenty of kiddie-geared activities. The island's most touted attraction is the **Guinate Tropical Park**, with its birds, aquarium, botanical garden and various shows. There are plenty of sea-themed activities, aside from the ubiquitous glass-bottom boats. **Submarine Safaris** in Puerto Calero submerges to the watery depths, while high riders can contact **Paracraft** (☎619 06 86 80; www.lanzarote.com/paracraft; Playa Chica, Puerto del Carmen; ⏲10am-6pm), which offers parascending (10 minutes, €80). If the sea starts to pall, Costa Teguise's **Aquapark** (☎928 59 21 28; Avenida Teguise s/n; adult/child €21/15; ⏲10am-6pm) has the usual assortment of rides and slides.

☆ Entertainment

Jazz Mi Madre! LIVE MUSIC
(Calipso Centre, Local 1; ⏲Tue-Sun 9.30pm-3.30am) At last! A place that doesn't play head-banging techno or cheesy pop for the masses. Expect live jazz and blues played by accomplished musicians and a more mature, albeit enthusiastic, foot-tapping crowd.

ⓘ Information

Tourist office (☎928 59 25 42; Avenida Islas Canarias s/n; ⏲10am-5pm) Ask for the brochure detailing three walks around town and beyond, ranging from 4.6km to 10km.

ⓘ Getting There & Away

Bus 1 (€1.20, 20 minutes, about every 20 minutes) connects with Arrecife (via Puerto de los Mármoles) from 7am to midnight.

Tahiche

The **Fundación César Manrique** (César Manrique Foundation; ☎928 84 31 38; adult/child €8/free; ⏲10am-6pm) is an art gallery and a centre for the island's cultural life. Only 6km north of Arrecife, it was home to Manrique, who enjoys a posthumous status on the island akin to that of a mystical hero. He built his house, Taro de Tahiche, into the lava fields just outside the town. The subterranean rooms are, in fact, huge air bubbles left behind by flowing lava. It's a real James Bond hideaway, with white-leather seats slotted into cavelike dens, and a sunken swimming pool. There's a whole gallery devoted to Manrique, plus minor works by some of his contemporaries, including Picasso, Chillida, Miró, Sempere and Tàpies. Tragically, in September 1992, only six months after the foundation opened its doors, Manrique was killed a few yards away in a car accident.

From Sala 10, have a look out the large picture window at the striking modern building semisubmerged into the lava field and topped by a series of cupolas. Formerly owned by a wealthy architect from Tenerife, it was bought by the foundation in early 2011. Watch this space.

At least seven buses a day stop here on their way from Arrecife to Teguise. Look for the huge mobile sculpture by Manrique dominating the roundabout, and walk 200m down the San Bartolomé road.

Teguise

POP 15,825

Teguise, 12km north of Arrecife, has a North Africa–meets–Spanish pueblo feel. It is an intriguing mini oasis of low-rise buildings set around a central plaza and surrounded by the bare plains of central Lanzarote. Firmly on the tourist trail, there are several shops here selling flowing garments and handmade jewellery. There are also restaurants, bars and a handful of monuments testifying to the fact that the town was the island's capital until Arrecife took the baton in 1852.

Maciot, the son of Jean de Béthencourt, moved here when it was a Guanche settlement and married Teguise, daughter of the one-time local chieftain. Various convents were founded and the town prospered. But with prosperity came other problems, including pirates who plundered the town several times, reaching a violent crescendo in 1618 when an armada of 5000 Algerian buccaneers overran the town, hence the ominously named Calle de la Sangre (Blood Street).

Teguise is completely taken over by a mammoth and very touristy Sunday-morning market, complete with burger stalls and human statues. Unless this is your thing, visit another day, although surprisingly, there is a dearth of places to stay in town.

◎ Sights

Wandering Teguise's pedestrianised lanes is a pleasure in itself. Several monasteries dot the town; look out for the Franciscan **Convento de Miraflores**, the **Convento de Santo Domingo** and the **Palacio de Herrera y Rojas**.

TOP CHOICE Museo de la Piratería MUSEUM
(Castillo de Santa Bárbara; www.teguise.es; adult/child €3/€1.50; ⊘9am-4pm Mon-Sat; 👪) Opened in the spring of 2011, this modest yet fascinating museum is located in the imposing 16th-century **Castillo de Santa Bárbara**. This is the oldest castle in the Canaries and really looks the part, perched up on Guanapay peak with sweeping views across the plains. The exhibits detail the numerous attacks Lanzarote suffered at the hands of pirates from across Europe and Africa during the 16th century, when Teguise was the island's capital.

Palacio Spínola HISTORICAL BUILDING
(Plaza de la Constitución; adult/child €3/€1.50; ⊘9am-3pm Mon-Fri) Palacio Spínola was built between 1730 and 1780 and passed to the Spínolas, a prominent Lanzarote family, in 1895. Nowadays it serves as both a museum (of sorts) and the official residence of the Canary Islands government. It has an impressive frontage and pretty internal courtyard and deserves a leisurely perusal, although many of the furnishings are clearly a few decades more modern than their surrounds.

⚔ Festivals & Events

Fiesta de Nuestra Señora del Carmen takes place annually on 16 July in celebration of the town's saint, with plenty of dancing in the street and general merriment.

LANZAROTE TEGUISE

CÉSAR MANRIQUE

César Manrique is the island's most famous native son and his influence is everywhere, ranging from the obvious, like his giant mobile sculptures adorning roundabouts, to the (thankfully) unseen: the lack of high-rise buildings and advertising billboards.

Born on 24 April, 1919, Manrique was initially best known as a contemporary artist. Influenced by Picasso and Matisse, he held his first major exhibition of abstract works in 1954 and, 10 years later, his art career reached its pinnacle with an exhibition at New York's Guggenheim Museum. But Manrique never forgot his birthplace and returned home in 1968, after his successful US tour, brimming with ideas for enhancing what he felt to be the incomparable beauty of Lanzarote.

He began with a campaign to preserve traditional building methods and a ban on roadside hoardings. A multifaceted artist, Manrique subsequently turned his flair and vision to a broad range of projects, with the whole of Lanzarote becoming his canvas. In all, he carried out seven major projects on the island and numerous others elsewhere in the archipelago and beyond. At the time of his death, he had several more on the boil. See p93 for an itinerary of Manrique's sites.

On the grand scale, it was primarily Manrique's persistent lobbying for maintaining traditional architecture and protecting the natural environment that prompted the *cabildo* (government) to pass laws restricting urban development. The growing wave of tourism since the early 1980s has, however, threatened to sweep away all before it. But Manrique's ceaseless opposition to such unchecked urban sprawl touched a nerve with many locals and led to the creation of an environmental group known as El Guincho, which has had some success in revealing – and at times even reversing – abuses by developers. Manrique was posthumously made its honorary president.

As you pass through villages across the island, you'll see how traditional stylistic features remain the norm. The standard whitewashed houses are adorned with green-painted doors, window shutters and strange onion-shaped chimney pots. In such ways, Manrique's influence and spirit endure.

LAGOMAR

En route from Tahiche to Teguise, you reach the sleepy small town of **Nazaret**. In the centre, look for a sign to **Lagomar** (adult/child €5/2; 10am-7.30pm Tue-Sun). Carved into the rock face, with fanciful chimneys, cupolas, miradors and winding staircases, this gallery, museum, restaurant and bar has a New Mexico–meets-Morocco look. Regular exhibitions are held, while a small museum recounts the interesting history of the building. It was designed for Omar Sharif by Jesus Soto, a prominent Lanzarote architect. The actor apparently lost it to a local property developer in a spectacularly unsuccessful game of bridge. Stop for a drink in the bar, set around a white puddle of a pool with tunnels and cosy seating, or consider a meal in the excellent restaurant with Middle Eastern and Mediterranean specialities.

✗ Eating

TOP CHOICE La Cantina FUSION €€
(📞928 84 55 36; Calle Leon y Castillo 8; mains €8-10; ⊘closed Mon; 🖉) Run by Benn and Zoe, an enthusiastic young English couple, this restaurant is in one of the oldest houses on the island, dating back some 500 years. It's all lofty ceilings and warm, wood fittings, and has the characteristic original central patio. The menu includes both Canarian and Asian-inspired sharing platters, like the Thai mixed starter with chicken satay and fishcakes. A typical main is a spicy lamb tagine. Zoe's chocolate brownies have a strong local following, while Benn's love of good local wines accounts for the presence of some excellent, hard-to-find vintages on the menu. Reservations recommended.

Casa Leon MEDITERRANEAN €€
(Calle Leon y Castillo s/n; mains €8-10; ⊘closed Mon; 🖉) This small restaurant shares its locale with a health-food centre and alternative-therapy centre. The cuisine is eclectic Mediterranean with choices like red lentil and tomato soup, risotto with tofu, and Atlantic cod; there is a generous buffet on Sunday. The ambience is laid-back and cosy, with warm colours, Moroccan lamps and provocative artwork.

ℹ Getting There & Away

Numerous buses, including 7 and 9 (€1.20, 30 minutes) from Arrecife, stop in Teguise en route to destinations such as Orzola and Haría. There are also buses and organised tours to the town's Sunday market from Costa Teguise, Puerto del Carmen and Playa Blanca.

San Bartolomé & Around

Starting life as the Guanche settlement of Ajei, San Bartolomé (population 17,452) ended up in the 18th century as the de facto private fiefdom of a militia leader, Francisco Guerra Clavijo y Perdomo, and his descendants. The **Museo del Tanit** (www.museo tanit.com; Calle Constitución 1; adult/child €6/3; ⊘10am-2pm Mon- Sat), set in an 18th-century Canarian house, concentrates on the last 200 years of local life, with artefacts, equipment and exhibitions. English explanations are available.

A couple of kilometres northwest of town, on the Tinajo road, rises the modernistic, white **Monumento al Campesino** (Peasants' Monument), erected in 1968 by (surprise, surprise) César Manrique to honour the thankless labour that most islanders had endured for generations. Adjacent stands the **Museo del Campesino** (admission free; ⊘10am-6pm), which is more a scattering of craft workshops, including weaving and ceramics.

Most people come here to eat – ironic for a monument dedicated to those who habitually endured hunger – at the **restaurant** (mains €7-12; ⊘12.30-4pm). The dining room is vast, circular and sunken, complete with tunnel. There is a good wine and rum list, and well-prepared local cuisine, accompanied by Canarian music. Try the traditional starter of *papas, queso y gofio* (potatoes, local cheese and *gofio* – ground, roasted grain used in place of bread in Canarian cuisine), followed by a typical main like chicken casserole with garlic and potatoes.

Three kilometres southwest, en route to Yaiza, is the **Museo del Vino El Grifo** (www.elgrifo.com, in Spanish; admission, incl glass of wine, €4; ⊙10.30am-6pm). The former bodega (traditional wine bar) and winery of the El Grifo company, winemaking equipment – some dating back to 1775 – is on display here, and you can buy all sorts of wine-drinking requisites and indulge in a little wine tasting. Right next door, **Bodegas Baretto** is another long-established and highly respected winery offering free tastings and selling local cheese and homemade *mojo* (Canarian sauce made with either red chilli peppers, coriander or basil).

The region has several excellent winery routes, including one between San Bartolomé and Tinajo, which includes the small but excellent **Bodega La Vegueta** (⊙8am-3pm), **Bodega Tinache** (⊙9am-2pm & 4-8pm), **Bodega Vega de Yuco** (⊙7.30am-3.30pm) and **Bodega Mozaga** (⊙8.30am-3pm Mon-Fri). They are well signposted.

THE NORTH

Lanzarote's northern towns and villages are typically clusters of whitewashed buildings surrounded by what looks like a felt-covered landscape of lichen and lava fields. The principal attractions are the combined works of nature and César Manrique, including a pair of breathtaking lava caves, cactus gardens and a stunning lookout created out of an old gun emplacement.

ECO RESORT

How is this for something different? Stay in an authentic Mongolian yurt in a totally eco-friendly resort powered by wind and solar. Organic fruit, veg and wine can be part of your welcome pack and the resident chickens can keep you in eggs. Owners Tila and Michelle also include a battery-cum-petrol hybrid car for guests booked into their deluxe Eco Yurt Royale. Other perks include the option of windsurfing and surfing lessons (one of their three sons is the number two surfing champ on the island) and advice on local hikes. The yurts are wonderfully furnished with just the right ethnic touches, perfect for a chilled-out stay. For more information see p216.

Guatiza & Charco del Palo

Just north of tiny Guatiza is the **Jardín de Cactus** (Cactus Garden; adult/child €5/2.50; ⊙10am-6pm), signalled by an 8m-high spiky metal cactus. According to reliable sources, the garden was Manrique's favourite attraction. Built in an old quarry, it comes over as more a giant work of art than a botanical garden. There are nearly 1500 different varieties of cactus, every single one labelled. There is a restaurant and bar on site if you want some refreshments.

If you fancy bathing (or even shopping!) in the buff, a few kilometres north of Guatiza is the naturist resort of **Charco del Palo**, with pleasant sandy beaches and rocky coves. To get here, take the narrow road to the beach just south of Mala.

Arrieta

POP 1929

The main attraction of the fishing village of Arrieta is the small beach **Playa de la Garita**, a combination of volcanic rock and sand with a congenial beach bar and restaurant where you can relax with a beer and tapas.

There are also some good seafood restaurants in town which get packed out with locals at weekends. Right on the main road with a sea view terrace, **Almanecer** (La Garita 46; mains €8-10) is a favourite. Unpretentious, the menu really does depend on what is freshly caught in the nets that day; typically sea bass, blue marlin or grouper.

Bus 9 (€3.25, 1½ hours, three daily weekdays, two on weekends) from Arrecife to Orzola calls in here.

Malpaís de la Corona

The 'Badlands of the Crown' are the living (or dead) testimony to the volcanic upsurges that shook the north of the island thousands of years ago. Plant life is quietly, patiently, winning its way back and it is here that you can visit two of the island's better-known volcanic caverns.

Lava is the hallmark of Lanzarote. So, unsurprisingly, after the lunar wonders of the Parque Nacional de Timanfaya, the flow of visitors is strongest here, at the site of an ancient lava slide into the ocean. The cavernous Cueva de los Verdes and, further 'downstream', the hollows of the Jameos del

Agua – adapted by César Manrique into a kind of New Age retreat-meets-bar – are an easy 1km walk from each another.

These two sights are well signposted, around 4km northwest of Arrieta.

TOP CHOICE **Cueva de los Verdes** CAVE
(☎928 84 84 84; adult/child €8/free; ⏰10am-6pm) Cueva de los Verdes is a yawning, 1km-long chasm, which is the most spectacular segment of an almost 8km-long lava tube left behind by an eruption that occurred 5000 years ago. As the lava ploughed down towards the sea (more than 6km of tunnel is above sea level today, and another 1.5km extends below the water's surface), the top layers cooled and formed a roof, beneath which the liquid magma continued to slither until the eruption exhausted itself.

You will be guided through two chambers, one below the other. The ceiling is largely covered with what look like mini-stalactites, but no water penetrates the cave. The odd pointy extrusions are where bubbles of air and lava were thrown up onto the ceiling by gases released while the boiling lava flowed; as they hit the ceiling and air, they 'froze' in the process of dripping back into the lava stream.

Anyone with severe back problems might think twice about entering the cave – there are a few passages that require you to bend at 90 degrees to get through. Similarly, it's no place for claustrophobes.

The visit is worthwhile in itself for a great visual gag deep inside the cave. No, we're not telling – and urge you in turn to keep it quiet from your friends. Guided tours, lasting about 45 minutes and available in English, take place when there are 50 people waiting, which usually doesn't take long to happen. Concerts of mainly jazz and blues are held here from September to April, organised by **Musical Candelaria** (☎649 99 09 56).

Jameos del Agua CAVE
(☎928 84 80 20; adult/child €8/free) The first cavern you reach at Jameos del Agua resembles the nave of a vast marine basilica. Molten lava seethed through here en route to the sea, but in this case the ocean leaked in a bit, forming the startling azure lake at the heart of the Jameos. Manrique's idea of installing bars and a **restaurant** (⏰7.30-11.30pm) around the lake, adding a pool, a concert hall seating 600 (with wonderful acoustics) and the subtly didactic Casa de los Volcanos, was a pure brainwave.

Have a closer look into the lake's waters. The tiny white flecks at the bottom are crabs. Small ones, yes, and the only known examples of *Munidopsis polymorpha* (blind crabs) away from the deepest oceans. Do heed the signs and resist the temptation to throw coins into the water – their corrosion could kill off this unique species. Like the Cueva, access for the mobility impaired is not really possible – there are a lot of steps.

Orzola

Most people just pass through this northern fishing town on their way to Isla Graciosa. It's a pity, though, because this region has some stunning strips of sand, as well as several good seafood restaurants flanking the port, where you can be sure that the fish is flapping fresh.

Bus 9 from Arrecife runs here (one hour), corresponding with the departure times of the ferry to Isla Graciosa.

Beaches

Playas Caletones is a rarely crowded series of coves and beaches, collectively known as the Caletones. They are located just east of town and have a natural, untamed beauty, with fine white sand and shallow lagoons.

Just north of Orzola, **Playa de la Cantería** is another beautiful sandy beach, flanked by cliffs, and famed for its big breakers (which can be dangerous for swimming).

Minor Canaries

The string of tiny islets flung out north of Lanzarote are known as the Minor Canaries and, together with Isla Graciosa, are part of a nature reserve. Although access to the smaller islands is generally limited to researchers, Isla Graciosa may be visited.

ISLA GRACIOSA

This island is recommended for the ultimate stress-busting break. A day should suffice; anything longer would be for the keenest surfers (and the surfing here is world-class) or for those seeking longer-term peace and quiet. See the Accommodation chapter for overnight options.

About 600 people live on the island, virtually all in the village of Caleta del Sebo, where the Orzola boat docks at the attractive, recently revamped harbour. Behind it stretches 27.5 sq km of largely barren

Although the Lanzarote cuisine does not vary dramatically from that of its neighbours, there are some culinary stars. The addictive *papas arrugadas* (wrinkly potatoes) are generally accompanied by a choice of three *mojo* sauces here (not always the Canarian case), including *mojo verde* (with parsley), *mojo de cilantro* (with fresh coriander) and the classic *mojo picón* (with a spicy chilli kick).

Latin American influences are reflected in several dishes and, for red-blooded appetites, the steaks are typically prime-cut Argentinian beef. Other popular meaty choices for Lanzarotians include goat, baby kid and rabbit; exactly the same choices favoured by their Guanche ancestors who, by all accounts, were not the greatest fishermen. If you fancy a heart-warming homey stew, look for the classic *puchero*, traditionally made with various cuts of meat, fresh root vegetables and chickpeas.

Seafood lovers should look for the indigenous *lapa*, which is a species of limpet, traditionally grilled (which releases the flesh from the shell) and accompanied by a green *mojo*. Note that, although they do not look as appealing, the black-fleshed *lapas* are tastier than the orange variety.

Do try the local wines while you are here (see the itinerary on p93), particularly the prize-worthy dry white *malvasía* (Malmsey wine). The vines flourish in the black volcanic soil and are planted in small craters to protect them from the wind. The grapes are planted and harvested manually, resulting in high labour costs. When you buy a bottle of local wine you actively contribute to the preservation of a traditional method of viniculture in danger of dying out.

scrubland, interrupted by five minor volcanic peaks ranged from north to south. About a 30-minute walk southwest of Caleta del Sebo is delightful little Playa Francesa; there's also the lovely long sandy beach of Playa de las Conchas, and Playa Lambra, another sandy stretch, on the northern end of the island.

On a windy day Caleta del Sebo can seem a cross between a bare Moroccan village and a sand-swept Wild West outpost. This place is worlds away from the tourist mainstream. There are no sealed roads and the main form of transport seems to be battered old Land Rovers.

The downstairs restaurant at **Pensión Enriqueta** (Calle Mar de Barlovento 6; mains €6) has an inexpensive daily menu and excellent seafood dishes.

If you feel like accelerating out of first gear, boogie on down to **Las Arenas** (Calle Mar de Barlovento s/n; ☺from 12.30am Fri & Sat), a disco pub at the back of the Enriqueta that only opens its steamy doors to revellers after midnight.

Biosfera Express (☎928 84 25 85; www .biosferaexpress.com; Orzola harbour) runs five boats daily from Orzola across to the island (adult/child €11/7, 20 minutes, 8am, 10.30am, 1pm, 4.30pm and 6.30pm). It can get very rocky between Orzola and Punta Fariones, so you may want to pop a seasickness pill.

Consider taking the outbound 8am or 10.30am sailing, which allows time to explore before taking the last boat (departure times from the island are 7am, 9.30am, 11.30am, 3.30pm and 5.30pm). A cheaper option and a possibility if you want to travel outside these times is available by calling **Danny Romero Toledo** (☎676 90 18 45; adult/child €7.50/4), who runs a small private ferry. To get around the island, consider using pedal power. There are a couple of well-signposted bike-hire places that can help you reach those far-off beaches.

THE NORTHWEST

The island's northwest arguably offers visitors the most rewarding look at Lanzarote's natural beauty. It's a place of attractive, unspoiled towns, some great escapes and stunning panoramic views.

Mirador del Río

About 2km north of Yé, the Spanish armed forces set up gun batteries at the end of the 19th century at a strategic site overlooking El Río, the strait separating Lanzarote from Isla Graciosa. Spain had gone to war with the US over control of Cuba, and you couldn't be too careful! In 1973 the ubiquitous César Manrique left his mark, converting the gun emplacement into a spectacular bug-eyed lookout point.

Mirador del Río (☎928 52 65 51; adult/child €4.50/2.25; ☻10am-6pm) has a good bar and souvenir shop. There are vertiginous views of the sweeping lava flows – frozen in time – that fall to the ocean, and of Isla Graciosa and the surrounding volcanic islets.

Guinate

The main reason for visiting the village of Guinate, about 5km south of Mirador del Río, is the **Guinate Tropical Park** (www.guinatepark.com; adult/child €14/6; ☻10am-5pm), home to around 1300 rare and exotic birds, a penguin pool and other animals, including monkeys and meerkats. The parrot show is best avoided, unless you enjoy birds on bicycles and the like.

Just beyond the park is another fine (and completely free) **lookout** across El Río and the islets.

Haría

POP 4894

Eminent Canarian author Alberto Vásquez-Figueroa described Haría as '*without doubt the most beautiful village on the island, if not the world*'. Although a tad exaggerated, the village really does have a pretty bucolic setting, in a palm-filled valley punctuated by splashes of brilliant colour from bougainvillea and poinsettia plants. In the 17th and 18th centuries, locals traditionally planted a palm tree to celebrate a birth (two for a boy, one for a girl!). Later, this North African–style oasis became a popular spa for wealthy Canarians.

The central pedestrian avenue, Plaza León y Castillo, is shaded by eucalyptus trees, and is the site of a superb Saturday morning craft and produce market.

For superb local cuisine and atmosphere, head for family-run **El Cortijo de Haría** (Calle El Palmeral 6; mains €7-9; ☻lunch Fri-Wed) located in a typical Canarian house with several beamed dining rooms, cheery staff and reliable food prepared for the local, rather than tourist, palate. The *mojo* and Canarian soup (lentil or chickpea) are excellent, and the menu specialises in roasted meats, including suckling pig. The family makes several products for sale, including bottles of *licor de la Abuela* (Grandma's liquor), touted as being a powerful aphrodisiac. The fig jam may be a safer bet.

Bus 7 (€2.90, 45 minutes) connects Haría to Arrecife via Teguise and Tahiche four times daily weekdays and three times daily on weekends.

La Caleta de Famara

Years before he hit the big time, César Manrique whiled away many a childhood summer on the wild **beach** of La Caleta de Famara. It's one of the best sandy spots on Lanzarote and a place where you don't have to fight for towel space on the sand. This low-key seaside hamlet, with its dramatic cliff views, has a youthful, bohemian vibe and makes few concessions to the average tourist, aside from a few choice restaurants overlooking the surf.

Famara's excellent waves offer some of Europe's finest breaks, along with **El Quemao**, around 15km due south (but only suitable for very experienced surfers). If you don't fancy taking a board, then come here to watch the surfing, which is some of the best you will see throughout the Canaries. Pedro Urrastarazu at **Famara Surf Shop** (☎928 52 86 76; www.famarasurf.com;

COMPETITIVE SPORTING EVENTS

» **Ironman Lanzarote** (www.ironmanlanzarote.com) Europe's oldest official Ironman race (triathlon); May

» **Volcano Triathlon** (www.clublasanta.com) Triathlon aimed at all levels; May

» **Wine Run Lanzarote** (www.clublasanta.com) Half marathon through the wine region with option for wine tasting; June

» **Open water swims** (www.clubvulcano.org) Covering the 2.6km between Lanzarote and Fuerteventura, this race is open to all ages; October

» **Music Marathon Festival** (www.musicmarathonfestival.com). Marathon, including roller-skating option, with live music along the course; October

LOCAL KNOWLEDGE

KIRSTY JONES: WORLD-CHAMPION KITEBOARDER

I've been going to Lanzarote on holiday with my parents since I was 15 and that's where my passion for surfing and windsurfing began. When I was 16 I decided to try windsurfing one very windy day on Puerto del Carmen beach – from then on I was addicted to the energy and power of the wind and waves. About four years ago, after travelling to many places around the world with my job as a professional kiteboarder, I decided to buy a house on Lanzarote.

Top kiteboarding beach Aside from Famara, I love to kiteboard on the Playa del Risco, which most tourists don't know about. It's at the bottom of the gigantic Mirador del Río cliffs in the north, and quite a tough hike down and back (especially carrying your gear!), but the views are incredible and once you finally walk onto the deserted white sandy beach at the bottom, it's worth every step.

Secret spot One of my favourite places is actually right in front of my house in Charco del Palo, but under water! Whenever the wind drops, there is a place off the rocks here where I can spend hours free diving and snorkelling and exploring the amazing underwater world. There are stunning caves and rock formations, all types of fish and the water is crystal clear.

And on land? I love to explore the rocky shoreline of the northeast and northwest coast and look for driftwood and other interesting things that the tide and waves have brought in, which I then use to decorate my back yard.

El Marinero 39; 1-day surf school €39; ⊘10am-8pm) rents boards and offers courses at various levels.

✗ Eating

TOP
CHOICE **El Risco**　　　　MODERN CANARIAN €€
(Calle Montaña Blanca 30; mains €6-12) El Risco has a superb location, with a terrace overlooking the sea, and a nautical blue-and-white interior. Owner Gustavo recommends his fish and goat dishes, but has also introduced a menu of pizzas and savoury crêpes. The result makes this a winner for diverse dining choices. The atmosphere is pleasantly informal.

Restaurante Sol　　　　SEAFOOD €€
(Calle Salvavidas 48; mains €6-13; ⊘closed Mon) Located in a simple blue-and-white building fronting the sea, come here for grilled fish or fried baby squid. This place gets packed out with noisy local families at weekends – always a good sign.

ⓘ Getting There & Away

Bus 20 (€1.95, 50 minutes) connects Arrecife with La Caleta de Famara. It leaves La Caleta de Famara at 7.30am, 9am and 5.30pm and sets off from the capital at 7am, 8.30am, 2pm and 5pm, Monday to Friday only.

Tiagua

About 10km south of La Caleta, and 8km northwest of San Bartolomé, the open-air **Museo Agricola El Patio** (www.museoelpatio .com; Calle Echedey 18; adult/child €6/3; ⊘10am-5.30pm Mon-Fri, to 2.30pm Sat; ⓗ) recreates a 19th-century traditional farmer's house (complete with wine cellar) and provides an insight into traditional aspects of the island's culture. Signage – including some irritatingly edifying texts – is in English. You can taste local goat's cheese and a selection of *malvasía* and muscatel wines. You'll see loads of old equipment and furniture, a windmill and the odd camel or donkey chewing the cud.

Tiagua is on the bus 16 (€1.30, 30 minutes) route from Arrecife to La Santa. Bus 20 (€1.30, 25 minutes) to La Caleta de Famara also calls in here.

INLAND & WEST COAST

The interior and west coast of Lanzarote are within easy reach of popular tourist haunts to the south, but can seem a world away in terms of crowds, infrastructure and activities. These are reasons enough to explore this area, along with its striking abstract

THE BARD'S FAVOURITE TIPPLE

Shakespeare was reputedly quite fond of a regular swig of 'sack' – which is what *malvasía* (Malmsey wine) was often called in his day. There are numerous references to the tipple in his works. Mind you, he probably had a vested interest in promoting this 'nectar of the gods' (as it was also known): in his role of poet laureate, he was granted a generous boozy allowance from the Crown of 268 free gallons of the wine every year.

landscape of towering black mountains and odd stone circles that have more to do with growing vines than with any pagan cult.

If you don't have your own wheels, there are organised tours to the wineries in this region. Buses are sporadic, at best, to this part of the island.

La Geria

Near San Bartolomé, the LZ-30 is one of the most interesting and enjoyable drives you can take on the island. A well-surfaced road, it winds southwest through the area of La Geria, passing what has to be one of the oddest-looking vine-growing regions around. Local viticulturists have found the deep, black lava soil, enriched by the island's shaky seismic history, perfect for the grape. The further south you go, the more common are these unique vineyards consisting of little eye-catching dugouts nurtured behind crescent-shaped stone walls, known as *zocos*, implanted in the dark earth.

◉ Sights

The *malvasía* produced here is a good drop and along the road you pass a half-dozen bodegas where you can buy the local produce at wholesale prices. There are a couple of new kids on the bodega block, as well, which are worth checking out.

Bodega Rubicón   WINERY
(☏928 17 37 08; www.vinosrubicon.com; Ctra La Geria, km 2; ☺9am-6pm) This bodega is housed in part of a former 17th-century *cortijo* (farm), which, these days, includes

a fine restaurant. It will cost you just €1.50 to taste three wines in the bodega, including the exceptional award-winning muscatel. You can also take a look at the modest, but interesting, museum, complete with historic wine press. The restaurant is a good place to taste the local cheese to accompany your glass of *vino*.

Bodega La Geria   WINERY
(☏928 17 31 78; www.lageria.com; Ctra La Geria, km 5; ☺10am-8pm Mon-Sat, 11am-7pm Sun) The La Geria wine cellar, established at the end of the 19th century, was the first bodega on the island to offer guided visits and sell wines to the public. You can pick up bottles of dry or semi-*dulce* (semi-sweet) *malvasía* (among others) for around €6.50. There's also a good little bar/cafe.

Bodega Stratvs   WINERY
(☏928 80 99 77; www.stratvs.com; Ctra La Geria, km 18; tour €10; ☺9am-8pm) Opened in 2008, Stratvs is a slick operation providing excellent one-hour tours for aficionados that include wine and cheese tasting. The gourmet shop and restaurant have a sophisticated appeal. The family also runs a farm and raises goats: some of the latter end up (organically) on the menu. Tours should be reserved in advance either via phone or the website.

✯✯ Festivals & Events

Fiesta de la Vendimia is a jolly festival in mid-August at Bodega La Geria. Newly harvested grapes are poured into a vast vat for everyone to have a good trample upon (fortunately, they don't find their way into a wine bottle!).

✗ Eating

El Chupadero   SPANISH €
(☏659 59 61 78; www.el-chupadero.com; tapas €4-8.50) This German-owned bar and restaurant is located 4km north of Uga on the LZ-30 road. Enjoy homemade soups, plus great tapas like garlic prawns, all washed down with dry local *malvasía* wines on a terrace overlooking the vineyards. The simple whitewashed decor, with beamed ceilings, plenty of plants and classy artwork, is one of the most stylish in these parts. There are live jazz concerts here on Sunday evenings.

Parque Nacional de Timanfaya

The eruption that began on 1 September 1730 and convulsed the southern end of the island was among the greatest volcanic cataclysms in recorded history. A staggering 48 million cubic metres of lava spurted and flowed out daily, while fusillades of molten rock were rocketed out over the countryside and into the ocean. When the eruption finally ceased to rage after six long years, over 200 sq km had been devastated, including 50 villages and hamlets.

The **Montañas del Fuego** (Mountains of Fire), at the heart of this eerie 51-sq-km **national park** (☏928 84 00 57; adult/child €8/4; ☺9am-5.45pm, last bus tour at 5pm), are appropriately named. When you reach the Manrique-designed lookout at a rise known as the Islote de Hilario, try scrabbling around in the pebbles and see just how long you can hold them in your hands. At a depth of a few centimetres, the temperature is already 100°C; by 10m it's up to 600°C. The cause of this phenomenon is a broiling magma chamber 4km below the surface.

Some robust scraps of vegetation, including 200 species of lichen, have reclaimed the earth in a few stretches of the otherwise moribund landscape of fantastic forms in shades of black, grey, maroon and red. Fine copper-hued soil slithers down volcanic cones, until it's arrested by twisted, swirling and folded mounds of solidified lava – this is one place where you really must remember to bring your camera.

The people running the show at Islote de Hilario, near the restaurant, gift shop and car park, have a series of endearing tricks. In one, they shove a clump of brushwood into a hole in the ground and within seconds it's converted by the subterranean furnace into a burning bush. A pot of water poured down another hole promptly gushes back up in explosive geyser fashion; you have exactly three seconds to take that impressive snap.

The Manrique-designed **Restaurant del Diablo** (☏928 84 00 56; menú del día €15; ☺noon-3.30pm; ℗) is a gag in itself – whatever meat you order you can watch sizzling on the all-natural, volcano-powered BBQ out back. Note, too, Manrique's wonderful light fittings in the form of giant frying pans. The food here is none too impressive, but, hey, who's here for the cuisine? Vegetarians might feel a bit left out, though, with all that smoking rabbit, T-bones and chicken. In the midst of all this carnivorous activity, there's a good list of local wines, some available by the half-bottle. Reservations are recommended.

Included in the admission price of the national park, tan-coloured buses take you along the exciting 14km **Ruta de los Volcánes**, an excursion through some of the most spectacular volcanic country you are ever likely to see. The trilingual taped commentary has a fascinating eyewitness account by local priest Don Agustín Cabrera, including the following surreal-sounding scene: '…the earth suddenly opened near Timanfaya. The first night an enormous mountain rose up from the depths of the earth and from its point issued flames which continued to burn for 19 days'.

Buses leave every hour or so and the trip takes about 30 minutes. By about 10am there can be long queues to get into the park, so you may find yourself waiting for a tour.

North of the park, on the same road, is the **Mancha Blanca Visitors Centre** (☏928 84 08 39; www.mma.es; Carretera de Yaiza a Tinajo Km11.5; ☺9am-5pm), which has excellent audiovisual and informative displays about the park, including a simulation of a volcanic eruption. There are **camel rides** (€12, 20min) nearby.

FIRE WALKS

It is possible to walk within the Parque Nacional de Timanfaya – but you'll need to plan in advance and you'll be part of a select group of just seven people. The 3.5km, two-hour **Tremesana guided walk** (in Spanish and English) leaves from the Mancha Blanca Visitors Centre at 10am on Monday, Wednesday and Friday. Reserve a spot by phone or in person – at the time of research, you needed to reserve at least six months in advance if you wanted to walk in high season. Try calling a day or two before and see if there's been a cancellation. The much more demanding **Ruta del Litoral** (9km, six hours) takes place once a month (no fixed date) and you need to reserve in person and be judged fit enough to handle the pace and the terrain. Both walks are free.

Yaiza

POP 9664

Yaiza is something of a southern crossroads, so you'll probably pass through (several times) on your travels. It's a tidy, whitewashed town and the recipient of numerous awards for cleanliness. For sights, try the local church, **Nuestra Señora de los Remedios**, which was built in the 18th century and features a lovely blue, white and gold painted altarpiece and a folkloric painted wooden ceiling.

There's no specific reason for hanging about, but if you arrive at lunchtime and are feeling peckish, you'll be able to find a few pleasant-enough restaurants, plus the excellent **La Bodega de Santiago** (☑928 83 62 04; Calle Garcia Escámez 23; mains €15-17; ⊙closed Mon). Located at the entrance to Yaiza and fronted by a magnificent ficus tree, this place is recommended by the local priest (it's a long story...) and deservedly so. The building dates back a couple of hundred years and is ideal for courting couples, with several intimate dining rooms and a background of soothing classical music. The menu is traditional Canarian, with an emphasis on meaty choices like pork and orange, suckling lamb chops, and similar. Reservations are recommended.

El Golfo & Around

The former fishing village of El Golfo has a laid-back, bohemian feel, with its cluster of traditional buildings and lack of tourist-geared tat for sale. It's a fabulous place to come at sunset, with several bars overlooking the thundering surf. There is no shortage of inviting eating options, either. On the waterfront there is a string of seafood restaurants, including **Restaurante Placido** (Avenida Marítima 39), **Lago Verde** (Avenida Marítima 46), where you can also enquire

---

SMOKED SALMON FOR TEA?

Next to Yaiza, the tiny village of **Uga** is famous for its freshly smoked salmon, available on better restaurant menus throughout the island. You can buy it at **Ahumaderia de Uga** (☑928 83 01 32; Carretera Uga-Yaiza 1; ⊙10am-1.30pm & 4-6.30pm Mon-Fri, 10am-2pm Sat; €32 a kilo) on the main street; look for the sign.

---

about renting an apartment, and **Costa Azul** (Avenida Marítima 7), which has a fabulous position next to the crashing waves and is filled with boisterous local families on Sundays.

Just south of El Golfo is one of the most dramatic and scenic stretches of road on the island: the LZ-703, flanked by the shifting colours of the volcanic peaks on one side and the sea and a string of small black-sand beaches on the other.

The beach fronting the **Charco de los Clicos** is worth taking a look at. The Charco itself is a small, emerald-green pond, just in from the beach; the colour comes from the algae in the water. This was the famous backdrop for Raquel Welch who slipped into *that* fur bikini in the iconic publicity still for the '60s *One Million Years BC* movie. Back to the present, the visual paint palette is further enhanced by the wonderfully colourful and textured volcanic rock surroundings. It is not safe to swim here though, as it can get very rough.

Along the coast road, which eventually leads to La Hoya, stop by **Los Hervideros**, a pair of caves through which the sea glugs and froths. After about 6km you reach the long Playa de Janubio, behind which are **Las Salinas de Janubio**, salt pans from where sea salt is extracted (up to around 15,000 tonnes a year).

THE SOUTH

The island's south is home to the most popular resorts and attracts family groups looking for an easy-going, sunny time, punctuated by deep-sea-fishing excursions and boozy nights out.

Puerto del Carmen

With sunshades four lanes deep, this is the island's most popular beach and its oldest purpose-built resort. If you are seeking an iota of Canarian atmosphere, head for the El Varadero harbour, at the far west of the beachfront, which still has a faint fishing-village feel, with its bobbing boats and uninterrupted ocean views. Otherwise the centre remains a primarily Brit-geared resort with restaurants and bars competing for the cheapest bacon-and-eggs breakfast and the largest (and loudest) Sky Sports screen. The main street is Avenida Playas, a

Lanzarote has several stunning drives, particularly around the wine country. Lesser known is the LZ-702, which you pick up just before Uga if you are coming from the west (Arrecife, Puerto del Carmen etc). The road climbs and winds between fields of goats and surprisingly verdant valleys against a backdrop of sea to the west and low-lying peaks to the east.

Pass through the hamlet of Las Casitas de Femés (2.3km), carry on to **Femés** (8km). Look for the sign to **Femés Quesería Rubicón** (Plaza San Marcial 3; ⊙10am-8pm Mon-Sat, 10am-3pm Sun), one of the best places to buy the local goat's cheese on the island; better still, you can taste it first. Priced at just €6 a kilo, choose between smoked, fresh, semicured, or coated with paprika or traditional *gofio* (ground, roasted grain used in place of bread in Canarian cuisine). Afterwards, you can nip across the road to the **Balcón de Femés** (Plaza de Femés) for a coffee, accompanied by a magnificent view stretching all the way to the coast. There is a signposted scenic footpath from the Plaza de Femés to Playa Quemada (11km), which takes around four hours.

Continue the drive winding down to **Playa Blanca** (8.3km), surrounded by wide valleys and with the seascape opening up ahead of you.

gaudy ribbon hugging the beach with shops, bars and restaurants.

🏖 Beaches

Yes, **Playa Grande** is crowded and neatly striped with sunbeds and parasols, but, beneath all this, it remains a spectacular 1200m-long beach excellent for families, with shallow waters and good amenities, including toilets and ice creams.

A couple of kilometres north of Playa Grande, the golden, sandy arc of **Playa Los Pocillos** is a kilometre long and known for its windy but calm waters, which create perfect conditions for windsurfers.

🏃 Activities

The main activities seem to be kicking back with a beer or flaking out on the beach but there's no lack of opportunity for something less supine, including walking the length of the 6km of beaches. There is also a designated cycle path here. Diving is deservedly popular, as well as jet skiing and banana and paracraft rides.

Watersports

The following are tried and trusted diving and surfing operators. For diving, prices start at around €32 per dive with your own equipment, and €39 including rental. Surfboard rental costs around €6 per hour.

Safari Diving   DIVING
(☑928 51 19 92; www.safaridiving.nl; Playa de la Barrilla 4) Offers a range of courses

including an introductory scuba diving session for novices for €60.

Canary Island Divers   DIVING
(☑928 51 54 67; www.canaryislanddivers.com; Calle Alemania 1; single dive €35) Also offers one-hour bubble-maker courses for children (€40).

Manta Dive Centre   DIVING
(☑928 51 68 15; www.manta-diving-lanzarote .com; Calle Juan Carlos I 6) One of the longest-established centres, offers single dives (€32) and packages.

El Niño   SURFING
(☑928 59 60 54; CC La Hoya) Good choice for surfers.

Cycling

Renner Bikes   CYCLING
(☑629 99 07 55; www.mountainbike-lanzarote .com; Centro Comercial Marítimo, Avenida Playas s/n; bike rental per day €24) A good central place for renting a bike.

Horse Riding

Lanzarote a Caballo   HORSE RIDING
(☑928 83 03 38; www.lanzaroteacaballo.com; Carretera Arrecife-Yaiza; 2hr excursion €50; ⊙10am-6pm; 🚗). Guided treks provide a great way to see the landscape. Other activities on offer include 20-minute camel rides, and ponies and wagons for the tots.

🍴 Eating

Among all the sauerkraut, fish and chips, and other delights on offer along the Avenida Playas pleasure zone, you'll occasionally stumble across a place offering some local cuisine. For a more traditional Spanish choice, take a walk to the old port.

Casa Roja SPANISH €€€
(Avenida Varadero s/n; mains €12-15) Enjoying possibly the best location in town, this low-key place overlooks the pretty harbour. The menu is appropriately seafood-based, with the obligatory tank of potential dinner mates at the entrance.

Blooming Cactus VEGETARIAN €€
(Calle Teide; mains €7-10; ☺Thu-Sun; 🖉) A rare vegetarian restaurant on Lanzarote. Typical dishes include *keftedes* (vegetable patties), moussaka, curries and *stefado* (vegetable stew). Tapas, snacks and cakes are also available, as well as vegan and wheat-free options. Cooking courses are also regularly held here.

Restaurante La Cañada CANARIAN €€€
(Calle César Manrique 3; mains €12-15; ☺closed Sun) Located just off Avenida Playas, this restaurant lovingly prepares Canarian specialities, including oysters (from €3.50 each), roasted goat, salt-coated sea bass and delicious *papas arrugadas* (wrinkly potatoes). Finish off your meal with that retro culinary classic: crêpe Suzette.

🍷 Drinking & Entertainment

The bulk of the bars, discos and nightclubs in Puerto del Carmen are lined up along the waterfront Avenida Playas and include Irish pubs, karaoke bars and the inevitable smattering of sleazier options. If you're after maximum-density partying, try the Centro Comercial Atlántico, where you'll find such bars and disco pubs as Waikiki, Paradise and Dreams.

Cervecería San Miguel BAR
(Avenida Varadero s/n; ☺10.30am-3am) A good spot near the harbour for a plate of steamed mussels washed down with cold beer on tap, including Guinness, Fosters and John Smith's Bitter.

César's NIGHTCLUB
(www.cesars.net; Avenida Playas 14; ☺10pm-6am) Popular nightclub attracting a breezy, hedonistic young crowd.

Buddy's NIGHTCLUB
(Calle Tenerife 18; ☺10pm-3.30am) A cool, laid-back club that attracts a mixed-age clientele with its nightly live jazz and blues.

❶ Information

Network Xpress (Centro Comercial Marítimo, Avenida Playas; per hr €2). Internet access.

Tourist office (www.puertodelcarmen.com; Avenida Playas s/n; ☺10am-9pm Mon-Fri, to 1pm Sat) Halfway along Playa Grande.

❶ Getting There & Around

BUS Buses run the length of Avenida Playas, making frequent stops and heading for Arrecife (€1.80) about every 20 minutes from 7am to midnight.

Fred Olsen (☎901 10 01 07; www.fredolsen .es) runs a free ferry bus service which leaves from the Varadero (the port jetty) in Puerto del Carmen at 9am and 5pm for Playa Blanca, to link with the ferry to Corralejo on Fuerteventura. In the reverse direction, free buses for Puerto del Carmen meet the 9am and 5pm ferries in Playa Blanca. The morning run continues to Lanzarote's airport.

CAR Parking is a nightmare here, particularly in mid-summer. Head for the paying car park on Calle Juan Carlos or the nearby Biosfera Shopping Centre (Calle Juan Carlos), which also has plenty of parking space.

Puerto Calero

A few kilometres west of Puerto del Carmen – and its complete antithesis – Puerto Calero is a pleasant, relatively tranquil yacht harbour lined with cafes and restaurants. It sports a jaunty maritime vibe that sees plenty of locals in deck shoes. There is a waterbus that leaves from Puerto del Carmen five times daily (€5; ☺10.30am, noon, 1.30pm, 3pm & 5pm; 15 min).

🏖 Beaches

Around a half-hour walk (1.5km) from the port, due south, and with beautiful mountain and sea views en route, is **Playa Quemada**, an unspoiled and secluded black volcanic beach with superb seafood restaurants.

◉ Sights & Activities

Museo de Cetáceos MUSEUM
(www.museodecetaceos.org; adult/child €8/5; ☺10am-6pm Tue-Sat; 🖟) Appropriately fronted by a 12m-long skeleton of a Bryde's whale found in Canarian waters near Tenerife, this natural history museum is devoted to dolphins and, in particular, whales, with information on the 24 species to be found in the surrounding waters. The exhibit

includes audiovisual displays, life-size exhibits, photographs and whale sounds. It re-opened in early 2012 after extensive reforms.

Squalo Diving Center DIVING
(☏928 84 95 78; www.squalodiving.com) English-run outfit offering PADI courses, including a night dive course (€270) and a digital underwater photography course (€190).

Karolines Cruceros BOAT TRIPS
(☏928 84 96 22; www.karolinescruceros.com; adult/child €56/28) You can snorkel, swim or just quaff champagne (included in the price) on this day-long cruise which includes lunch.

Submarine Safaris BOAT TRIPS
(☏928 51 28 98; www.submarinesafaris.com; adult/child €52/30; ⏱10am, noon & 2pm) The yellow sub makes one-hour dives, to a depth of 30m.

Mizu I FISHING
(☏928 51 43 22; www.sportfishinglanzarote.com; angler/companion €85/60) Skippered by the well-regarded Tino García, the boat will transport you to the nearby depths as you search for mako sharks and other big fish. You'll be picked up from your hotel and taken to Puerto Calero. All equipment is included in the price.

⚑ Festivals & Events

César Manrique-Puerto Calero International Regatta is a prestigious yachting regatta that takes place during mid-October off Puerto Calero. It includes the TP 52 racing class – the Formula 1 of the international regatta world.

✕ Eating

Amura MEDITERRANEAN €€€
(☏928 51 31 81; mains €14-18) Keep walking with your nose in the air, past all the English-themed bars and restaurants, until you reach this eye-catching vast terrace commanding sweeping sea views. The menu includes quietly gourmet treats like lobster and wild mushroom ravioli with sea urchins, and suckling pig with gnocchi and green-apple foam.

La Cabaña MEDITERRANEAN €€€
(☏650 68 56 62; Mácher; mains €13-16; ⏱Tue-Sat 7pm-late) A speedy 15-minute drive away is the tiny hamlet of Mácher; home to La Cabaña. This restaurant is run by an enthusiastic and experienced English

couple with a superb reputation for innovative Med-inspired dishes. Menus change weekly, but a typical dish would be wild salmon carpaccio with crab cakes and a beetroot and vanilla dressing.

Playa Blanca

If you are looking for sand between your toes, rather than a rollicking nightlife, Playa Blanca is not a bad choice. Despite the presence of an American fast-food chain at the beach, it is a quiet resort that has not yet spiralled completely out of control. The Blue Flag main beach has very pale sand (hence the name Playa Blanca) and good facilities. That said, you're better off crossing the ocean to Corralejo on Fuerteventura, where the beaches and dunes easily outclass Playa Blanca's. Check out also the island's latest swanky port, Marina Rubicón. There is a good arts and crafts market here on Wednesday and Saturday mornings.

✦ Activities

There are numerous activities on offer here. Pick up the leaflets at the tourist office.

Catlanza BOAT TRIPS
(☏928 51 30 22; adult/child €59/39) The 74ft-long Catlanza sails to Papagayo Bay where it drops anchor and lunch is prepared while you enjoy the complimentary bar, jet skiing, snorkelling – or just sunning on the deck.

Rubicat BOAT TRIPS
(☏928 51 90 12; Marina Rubicón; adult/child €55/33) Offers similar trips, plus sailing classes and trips to Isla de Lobos.

Cala Blanca DIVING
(☏928 51 90 40; www.calablancasub.com; Centro Comercial el Papagayo) Offers individual dives, courses and a charmingly named 'Sea Baptism' option (€60) for absolute beginners.

Rubicon Diving Center DIVING
(☏928 34 93 46; www.rubicondiving.com) Offers similar to Cala Blanca, including a six-dive package for €225.

✕ Eating

Restaurante Casa José SPANISH €€
(Plaza Nuestra Señora del Carmen 8; mains €7-11; ⏱closed Sun lunch) Opposite the church, this modest restaurant, with its traditional green paintwork, has a kitchen-sink informal atmosphere and excellent seafood dishes.

El Maño   SPANISH €€

(Marina Rubicón; mains €10-15) Trip along the long wooden bridge in the marina to reach this rare Spanish restaurant surrounded by international culinary neighbours. The menu includes dishes from all over the country, including gazpacho from Andalucía, *cochinillo a la segoviana* (Segovian-style suckling pig) and a Valencian-style paella.

El Almacen de la Sal   SEAFOOD €€€

(Paseo Marítimo 12; mains €12-35; ⊘closed Tue) Located in a former warehouse for salt, this waterfront restaurant sports elegant decor and a terrace on the boardwalk. Push the boat out with one of the fish dishes, including hake served in a crust of salt and *cod pil pil* (a spicy tomato and chilli sauce). Meat dishes and a couple of vegetarian pasta options are also available, and there's a cheaper lunchtime menu. It's about halfway between the port and the main beach.

Casa Pedro   SPANISH €€

(Paseo Marítimo 77; mains €7-12) Fabulous seafront location, and reliably good regional and seafood dishes.

❶ Information

Tourist office (⊘8.30am-12.30pm & 2-5pm Mon-Fri, 8.30am-12.30pm Sat) Located in a kiosk on pedestrianised Calle Limoner.

❶ Getting There & Away

Bus 6 (€3.15, one hour) runs at least six times daily between Playa Blanca and Arrecife via Puerto del Carmen. Free **Fred Olsen** (✆902 53 50 90; www.fredolsen.es) buses leave Puerto del Carmen (9am and 5pm) to connect with the 10am and 6pm ferry departures here for Corralejo on Fuerteventura. The service also meets the 9am and 5pm ferries arriving from Corralejo. The morning run continues to Lanzarote's airport.

Punta del Papagayo

This promontory is a *reserva natural protegido* (protected nature reserve). The road beyond the rickety toll barrier (€3 per vehicle) is dirt, but quite manageable even in a small car. Or take the easy way and hop aboard the **Taxi Boat Papagayo Beach** (✆928 59 61 07; return trip adult/child €15/7.50; ⊘10am-5pm), which sets out four times daily from Playa Blanca with a pick-up stop at Marina Rubicón.

The southeast coast leading up to Punta del Papagayo is peppered with a series of pretty golden-sand coves and beaches, including Playa del Papagayo and the picturesque and secluded 90m-long **Playa Mujeres**, west of the *punta*. It has fine pale golden sand and is particularly popular with snorkellers and surfers.

Tenerife

☎922 / POP 906,854

Best Places to Eat

» Tasca (p123)

» Bar El Peton (p129)

» Restaurante Mil Sabores (p134)

» Casa Rural la Asomada del Gata (p128)

Best Places to Stay

» Hotel Alhambra (p219)

» Hotel la Quinta Roja (p219)

» Senderos de Abono (p220)

» Hotel Aguere (p218)

Why Go?

Tenerife, the biggest and best-known Canary Island, receives over 10 million visitors a year, most of whom head straight to the tourist resorts of the south. But step beyond the lobster-red sunloungers, lap dancers and best bitter on tap and what you'll find is a cultured and civilised island of extraordinary diversity.

This potpourri of experiences includes tropical-forest walks and designer-shop struts; dark forays into volcanic lava; a sexy and sultry Carnaval celebration that's second only to Rio, and a stash of museums, temples to modern art and creaky old colonial towns. But above all else this is an island of drama, and nothing comes more dramatic than the snow-draped Pico del Teide, Spain's tallest mountain and home to some of the most fabulous hiking in all the country.

When to Go

Tenerife is famed for its eternal spring-like climate and therefore anytime is prime time here. However, there are some moments of the year that are better than others. Sun-worshippers will probably find May to June and September offer the best combination of hot sun and lower crowds. Surfers will find the best waves between December and March, and scuba divers the calmest waters in July and August. Teide can be hiked at any time but deep winter can see snowfall closing the mountain and high summer can be too hot.

Best Old Towns

» **La Laguna** (p126) Combines old-fashioned elegance with youthful zeal.

» **La Orotava** (p136) The finest colonial architecture in Tenerife.

» **Garachico** (p139) Quaint fishing port hemmed by beautiful scenery.

Best Hikes

» **Teide** (p142) Simply the most spectacular walk in the Canaries.

» **Barranco de Masca** (p144) A thrilling descent through a steep gorge.

» **Pico Viejo** (p142) Teide's forgotten peak.

» **Llano de los Loros** (p130) Beautiful, family-friendly forest stroll.

Resources

» Official tourism site: www.todotenerife.es

» The latest on climbing Teide: www.reservas parquesnacionales.es

» Website of the islands' biggest English-language newspaper: www.island connections.eu

Getting Around

TITSA (Transportes Interurbanos de Tenerife SA; www.titsa.com) runs a spider's web of bus services all over the island, as well as within Santa Cruz and other towns.

Car-rental agencies are almost as plentiful on the island as English pubs, so you shouldn't have a problem, even if you want same-day rental. The generally reliable international chains are present in all major resort areas and the airports.

You can take a taxi anywhere on the island – but it is an expensive way to get around. You are much better off hiring a car.

THREE PERFECT DAYS

Day One

Start your tour in **Santa Cruz**, fawning over the classical works in the **Museo de Bellas Artes**. Next head up to some natural art in the **Parque García Sanabria**. Get a load of how creative modern Spain can be in the **TEA**, a modern art gallery. Then learn about life many yesterdays ago at the **Museo de la Naturaleza y El Hombre** and finish your day with a stroll to the **Auditorio de Tenerife**.

Day Two

Explore the gracious streets of pretty **Garachico**, on the island's northwest coast, in the morning before driving west towards wild **Punto de Teno** at the very end of Tenerife. Hold onto the edge of your seat on the drive to spectacular **Masca** and then drop down to the seaside for some bucket-and-spade fun at **Los Gigantes** and **Puerto de Santiago**.

Day Three

Stick your head high above the clouds in the stunning **Parque Nacional del Teide**. The fit and fearless can make an all-day hiking assault on the summit; the fearless but not so fit can take it easy in the cable car ride to just below the summit. Everyone can enjoy the easy walk around the **Roques de García**.

Getting Away from It All

» **Anaga Mountains** (p129) Dense forest dripping in life and little-trodden hiking trails.

» **Porís de Abona** (p147) Tiny, tranquil and our favourite east coast beach

» **Las Américas** (p149) Not the most obvious place to get away from it all, but if you really want a do-nothing break from the nine-to-five, this is the place

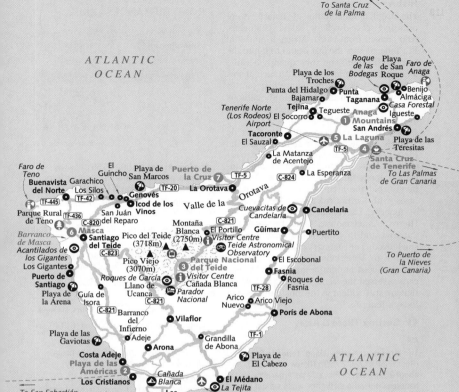

Tenerife Highlights

1 Do a Darwin and check out the magnificent **Anaga mountains** (p129), the oldest geographical region on the island

2 Put on your party frock for a night on the town at the neon-framed hot spots in **Playa de las Américas** (p149)

3 Hike around the fabulous moonscape of **El Teide** (p140)

4 Check out the great wave of the **Auditorio de Tenerife** (p119) in Santa Cruz de Tenerife

5 Visit **La Laguna** (p126), the best-preserved historical quarter on the island

6 Be overawed by tiny **Masca** (p144) and its extraordinary setting

7 Enjoy the salty sea breezes of the charming resort of **Puerto de la Cruz** (p131)

History

The original inhabitants of Tenerife were primitive cave-dwellers called Guanches, who arrived from North Africa around 200 BC. Tenerife was the last island to fall to the Spanish (in 1496) and subsequently became an important trading centre. As such, it was subject to invasions by marauding pirates and, in 1797, from the British in the famous battle of Santa Cruz, when Nelson lost his arm during the fight.

In 1821 Madrid declared Santa Cruz de Tenerife, by then the island's main port, the capital of the Canaries. The good and great of Las Palmas de Gran Canaria remained incensed about this until 1927, when Madrid finally split the archipelago into two provinces, with Santa Cruz as provincial capital of Tenerife, La Palma, La Gomera and El Hierro. As economic links between the Canaries and the Americas strengthened, a small exodus of islanders crossed the ocean, notably to Venezuela and Cuba. In later years affluent emigrants and Latin Americans reversed the trend, bringing influences that are still evident in the music and food of today's Tenerife.

❶ Getting There & Away

AIR

Two airports serve the island. **Tenerife Sur** (Reina Sofía; ☎922 75 95 10; www.aena.es), about 20km east of Playa de las Américas, handles international flights, while almost all interisland flights (plus a few international and mainland services) use the older and smaller **Tenerife Norte airport** (Los Rodeos; ☎922 63 56 35). Here you'll find an exchange booth, several car-rental agencies, a bar and a moderately helpful information booth.

BOAT

FERRIES FROM SANTA CRUZ Buy tickets for all companies from travel agents or from the main Estación Marítima Muelle Ribera building in Santa Cruz (from where the Fred Olsen boats leave). Naviera Armas has its base further to the south.

Acciona Trasmediterránea (☎902 45 46 45 in Madrid; www.trasmediterranea.com; Estación Marítima Muelle Ribera) runs a weekly ferry at 11pm every Friday from Santa Cruz de Tenerife that makes the following stops:

» Las Palmas de Gran Canaria (from €24, four hours, one to two times daily)

» Puerto de Rosario, Fuerteventura (from €28, 21 hours, 11.30pm Friday)

» Arrecife, Lanzarote (from €28, 24 hours, 11.30pm Friday)

ROAD DISTANCES (KM)

	Santa Cruz de la Tenerife	Puerto de la Cruz	Los Cristianos	Puerto de Santiago
Puerto de la Cruz	74			
Los Cristianos	158	140		
Puerto de Santiago	73	40	27	
Parador Nacional de Teide	128	90	64	40

Approximate distances only

Naviera Armas (☎902 45 65 00; www.navieraarmas.com) runs an extensive ferry service around the islands from Santa Cruz:

» Las Palmas de Gran Canaria, Gran Canaria (€41.90, 2¾ hours, 20 weekly)

» Morro Jable, Fuerteventura (€17.85, seven hours, 8pm Sunday)

» Puerto del Rosario, Fuerteventura (€12.50, 11½ hours, 3pm Monday, Tuesday and Thursday)

» Gran Tarajal, Fuerteventura (€5.65, 10 hours, two weekly)

» Arrecife, Lanzarote (€27.17, 11 hours, six weekly)

» Santa Cruz de la Palma, La Palma (€13.40, six hours, 6.30pm Tuesday and Thursday)

» Valverde, El Hierro (from €6.71, 8¼ hours, 3.30pm Monday, Wednesday and Friday)

Fred Olsen (☎902 10 01 07; www.fredolsen.es) has four to six daily high-speed ferries from Santa Cruz to Agaete in the northwest of Gran Canaria (€64, 1¼ hours), from where you can take its free bus onwards to Las Palmas (35 minutes).

FERRIES FROM LOS CRISTIANOS Ferries come in and out of the Los Cristianos port day and night. Two ferry companies operate from here, Naviera Armas and the faster, but more expensive, Fred Olsen. Buy tickets for all companies from travel agents or from the main Estación Marítima building inside the Los Cristianos port. Prices here are per person.

Routes operated by **Naviera Armas** from Los Cristianos include the following:

» San Sebastián de la Gomera, La Gomera (from €26.67, one hour, three daily Monday to Friday, one Saturday, two Sunday)

» Santa Cruz de la Palma, La Palma (€43, 3½ hours, one daily Sunday to Friday)

» Valverde, El Hierro (€23.85, six hours, Wednesday)

(Note that the boat operating on the El Hierro route is mainly used for shipping goods; luxury it most certainly is not.)

Routes operated by **Fred Olsen** from Los Cristianos include the following.

» San Sebastián de la Gomera, La Gomera (from €28.76, 40 minutes, three daily Monday to Friday, two daily Saturday and Sunday)

» Santa Cruz de la Palma, La Palma (€51.70, 2¼ hours, one daily Sunday to Friday)

SANTA CRUZ DE TENERIFE

POP 200,000

There are lots of reasons to like the bustling port city of Santa Cruz de Tenerife: evocative, brightly painted buildings, sophisticated and quirky shops, interesting art galleries, an excellent museum and a tropical oasis of birdsong, fountains and greenery in the city park. Despite all this, though, maybe the very best reason for visiting is that this is an energetic, workaday and wholly Spanish city that's a world away from the package tourism resort towns of the south of the island. The city also has an excellent bus system, making it a sensible base for exploring Tenerife's northeast.

History

Alonso Fernández de Lugo landed on Tenerife in 1494 to embark on the conquest of the final and most-resistant island in the archipelago. La Laguna, which is a few kilometres inland, initially blossomed as the island's capital. Santa Cruz de Santiago (as Santa Cruz de Tenerife was then known) remained a backwater until its port began to flourish in the 18th and 19th centuries. Only in 1803 was Santa Cruz 'liberated' from the municipal control of La Laguna by Spanish royal decree; in 1859 it was declared a city.

◉ Sights

The majority of Santa Cruz's sights are within easy walking distance of waterfront **Plaza España**, with its controversial centrepiece: a memorial to the fallen of the 1936–39 civil war. While the city is not packed with attractions, there are some lovely buildings and well-run exhibitions to enjoy.

TOP CHOICE **Museo de la Naturaleza y el Hombre** MUSEUM
(www.museosdetenerife.org, in Spanish; Calle Fuente Morales s/n; adult/under 12yr €3/1.50; ⊘9am-7pm Tue-Sun) The city's number one

attraction, and one of the best museums in all the Canary Islands, is this brainbending amalgam of natural science and archaeology set inside a former civil hospital. The highlights are undoubtedly the Guanche mummies and skulls; all of which are shrivelled masses of skin, hair and bone with faces dried into contorted and grotesque expressions. In addition there are informative displays on the geology and wildlife of the islands and all sorts of interactive displays with flashing buttons and big TV screens. Sadly, though, signage is only in Spanish and the translation cards handed out at the entrance do a poor job of bringing the exhibits to life (although more informative audioguides are available in English and German). There's also a cafe and gift shop.

Castillo de San Juan FORT
The central waterfront zone was undergoing a major facelift at the time of research and, aside from the docks themselves, was largely out of sight and out of mind. Walk 10 minutes southwest of Plaza España, though, along the waterfront, and you'll come to the 17th-century Castillo de San Juan. In the shadow of this protective fort there used to be an active trade in African slaves.

Auditorio de Tenerife NOTABLE BUILDING
(www.auditoriodetenerife.com; Avenida Constitución s/n) Nowadays the fort's squat, rectangular basalt form is overshadowed by the magnificent, soaring white wave of an auditorium, designed by the internationally renowned Spanish architect Santiago Calatrava and possessing a Sydney Opera House presence, as well as superb acoustics. **Guided tours** (12.30pm Mon-Sat Oct-Jun, 12.30pm & 5.30pm Mon-Sat Jul-Sep) will take you behind the scenes of this remarkable building. Tours are in Spanish only and you should reserve in advance. Just randomly turning up in the hope of looking around is something of a waste of time as there's unlikely to be anyone around and the city authorities seem to have almost criminally ignored the tourism potential of the building.

Parque Marítimo César Manrique PARK
(Avenida Constitución s/n; adult/senior/child €2.50/1/1.20; ⊘10am-7pm) Just beyond the contrasting fort and auditorium is this park, where you can have a dip in one of the wonderful designer pools or collapse on a sunlounger and drink in the beautiful view

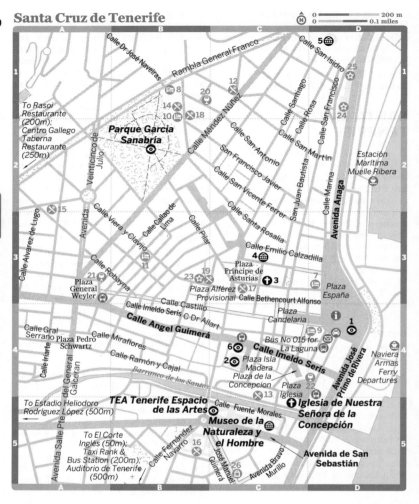

and something refreshing. It's suitable for all ages, and great for children. For more information about César Manrique, see p101.

TEA Tenerife Espacio de las Artes

ART GALLERY

(www.teatenerife.es, in Spanish; Avenida San Sebastián 10; adult/under 12yr €5/free; ⊘10am-8pm Tue-Sun) The city's slick new art exhibition space (which was opened in 2008) has an emphasis on photography, modern art and social documentary. The main exhibition halls are upstairs, while in the downstairs galleries you can watch

resident artists at work. When we last visited, the exhibitions focused on child abuse and decay of the human body. Some of the works have an overtly political or sexual message. The centre also contains a library and cafe-restaurant.

TOP Parque Garcia Sanabría

PARK

(Off Calle Méndez Núñez) On the northern fringe of the city centre, the city park is a delightful collection of Mediterranean and subtropical trees and flowers interspersed with various water features. It's the perfect place for a picnic in the shade of an Indian

Banyan tree and a lazy afternoon listening to birdsong (keep your eyes peeled for the Indian parakeets – escapees from bird cages who've made the park their home away from home).

**Iglesia de Nuestra Señora
de la Concepción** CHURCH
(Plaza Iglesia; ⏰Mass 9am & 7.30pm) Don't miss the striking bell tower of the city's oldest church, which has a tiled roof and some traditional Mudéjar (Islamic-style architecture) ceiling work. The present church was built in the 17th and 18th centuries but the original building went up in 1498, just after the island was conquered. At the heart of the shimmering silver altar is the Santa Cruz de la Conquista (Holy Cross of the Conquest), which gives the city its name. Tradition has it that Alonso Fernández de Lugo, the Spanish commander, planted it in his camp to give thanks for his 1494 victory over the Guanches.

Check out the **anteroom** to the sacristy. The altarpiece in the chapel beside it was carved from cedar on the orders of Don Matías Carta, a prominent personage who died before it was completed. He lies buried here and the pallid portrait on the wall

was done *after* his death (hence the closed eyes and crossed arms). There's also a fine painting, *La Adoración de los Pastores* (The Adoration of the Shepherds), by Juan de Miranda. The square the church sits in **Plaza Iglesia**, which was once renowned for its seedy characters, but has been tarted up and is now home to a couple of fashionable bars and brightly painted buildings.

Iglesia de San Francisco CHURCH
(Calle José Murphy) If churches are your religion then don't miss scooting by this pretty baroque church from the 17th and 18th centuries.

ROAD NAMES

Some road names are slowly being changed to new names in Santa Cruz and maps handed out by the tourist office have road names that don't always correspond to the name written on the street signs. We have used the road names written on the street signs but you can expect some confusion as names continue to change.

TENERIFE FOR CHILDREN

Tenerife is a favourite destination for families as there are plenty of sights and activities to keep the kiddies amused. Unless your tot is one of that curious breed that objects to sand between the toes (it happens!), the **beaches** in the southern resorts (as well as Puerto de la Cruz) are superb, with sandcastle-friendly sand and shallow waters. Older children can also enjoy watersports ranging from **surfing** to **diving**, or they can take to the high seas on an organised **whale-** or **dolphin-watching excursion**.

If watery pursuits begin to pall, the southern resorts of Los Cristianos and Playa de las Américas equal theme-park heaven for children. The tourist office has shelves full of brochures and flyers. Animals feature heavily, although there is nothing as straightforward as a plain old zoo; **Jungle Park** is by far the most popular animal park in the south, but even more high up the 'must do' list of children is **Siam Park**, a truly fantastic water park. Somewhat less exhilarating watery fun can be had in the numerous hotel swimming pools, or head for Santa Cruz's **Parque Marítimo César Manrique**, a wonderful complex of pools.

For something mildly more stimulating, check out the **Museo de la Ciencia y el Cosmos** in La Laguna. The island's most popular family day out is the **Loro Parque** in Puerto de Santa Cruz; even if you opt not to visit, you can't escape the publicity, with ads and stickers on seemingly every surface – moving or otherwise.

FREE Museo de Bellas Artes   ART GALLERY
(Calle José Murphy 12; ◷10am-8pm Mon-Fri, to 3pm Sat & Sun) Home to an eclectic mix of paintings by mainly Spanish, Canarian and Flemish artists, including Ribera, Sorolla and Brueghel. There's also sculpture, including a Rodin, and temporary exhibitions.

FREE Museo Militar de Almeydà   MUSEUM
(Calle San Isidro 1; ◷10am-2pm Tue-Sat) Explains the military history of the islands and is full of several centuries worth of 'technological marvels' with which to kill your fellow humans. Much of the museum is devoted to the successful defence of the city, brought alive by a superb 30m scale model of the flagship *Theseus*.

FREE Centro de Arte La Recova   ART GALLERY
(Plaza Isla Madera s/n; ◷11am-1pm & 6-9pm Mon-Fri) Located in a former market, this gallery houses temporary exhibitions of contemporary Canarian and mainland-Spanish artists.

Teatro Guimerá   NOTABLE BUILDING
(www.teatroguimera.es; Plaza Isla Madera s/n; ◷11am-1pm & 6-8pm Tue-Fri) One of the city's architectural highlights is the 19th-century Teatro Guimerá, fronted by a suitably theatrical giant mask sculpture. The sumptuous interior is reminiscent of Madrid's Teatro Real, with semicircular balconied seating and plenty of gilt.

FREE Castillo de San Cristóbal   CASTLE
(Plaza España; ◷10am-6pm Mon-Sat) Underneath Plaza España are the still-standing fragments of the former castle that once sat here. These can be accessed by an entrance on the seaward side of the plaza. There's also a small museum here recounting the history of the castle. The most famous item here is El Tigre (The Tiger), the cannon that reputedly blew off Admiral Nelson's arm when he attacked Santa Cruz in 1797. Served him right really!

🎭 Festivals & Events

As well as Carnaval (see p125), Santa Cruz plays host to a number of other festivals:

Festival de Música
de Canarias   MUSIC FESTIVAL
This is the biggest event on the serious music calendar, held annually in January and February in Santa Cruz de Tenerife and Las Palmas de Gran Canaria (on Gran Canaria). For more information, visit www.socaem.com.

Día de la Cruz   RELIGIOUS FESTIVAL
This day is observed throughout the island on 3 May, but particularly in Santa Cruz (and Puerto de la Cruz), where crosses and chapels are beautifully decorated with flowers in celebration of the founding of the city.

✕ Eating

Chairs on squares are plentiful here, due to the friendly, gregarious nature of the locals and, still more, to the sunshine. Pleasant cafe *terrazas* (terraces) include those on Plaza Candelaria and the shaded number on the fringe of Parque Garcia Sanabría, where you can sit and relax while letting your kids romp in the adjacent playground.

TOP CHOICE Tasca   TRADITIONAL CANARIAN €

(☑922 28 07 64; Calle Dr Guigou 18; menú del día €6.67; ☺closed Sun) The cultural and culinary opposite to the all-day English breakfasts of the southern resorts, this neighbourhood institution makes no allowances for confused foreigners. The waiters look like they've been doing this job forever and smiling is absolutely not a part of their job description! Despite this its laughably cheap lunch menus mean there's often a queue of locals waiting for a table and the food, which comes in huge portions, consists of hearty old-fashioned Canarian classics. Next door, and part of the same place, is a slightly smarter restaurant (mains €7 to €10) that comes alive in the evening.

Da Canio III   ITALIAN €

(Calle San Martín 76; mains €6.50-8; ☺closed Sun; ☑) Owned by Italians and serving up a better class of pizza and pasta, the dining room is tastefully decked out in terracotta and stone. The zillion-odd (well, OK, two dozen) pizza choices are ideal for fussy families, and the pasta and risottos come recommended as well.

Gom   MODERN CANARIAN €€

(☑922 27 60 58; Calle Dr Guigou 27; mains €10-15; ☺closed Sun & Mon) The modern menu at this sophisticated restaurant offers a creative take on otherwise typical Canarian and mainland fare. One of the more upmarket places in the city centre, it's the sort of place you should eat at as a treat to yourself, but it's also popular with a more informal lunchtime crowd.

Rasoi Restaurante   INDIAN €€

(Calle Perdón 5; menus €12-15; ☑) In the sometimes overwhelmingly meat and more meat Spain this Indian restaurant is a rare mix of spices and rotis. It's popular with the small local Indian population, which indicates that the food is pretty authentic.

You'll find it more formal than is normal for an Indian restaurant. Calle Perdón is a street on the right just after the bullring on Rambla General Franco.

Centro Gallego Taberna
Restaurante   SPANISH €€

(Calle Sueños 27; menú del día €8.50; ☺closed Sun & Mon) Galicia is the wet, green, Atlantic-lashed northwestern corner of the Iberian peninsula and at the restaurant inside this sky-blue Galician cultural centre you can almost taste the sea salt in the authentic Galician seafood meals it serves up. In addition the centre hosts a range of Galician cultural events and also organises flamenco and tango classes (which admittedly are not very Galician). Note that on some city maps this road is called Calle del General Sanjurjo. It's on a street on the right just after the bullring on Rambla General Franco.

La Cazuela   TRADITIONAL CANARIAN €€

(Calle Robayna 34; mains €7.50-14.50; ☺closed Sat lunch & Sun) Drenched in Canary yellow with a pretty, flower-filled terrace, this place is heartily recommended by locals for its solid traditional fare. Settle in for a long, filling lunch and try the *cazuela* (a casserole made with fresh or salted fish).

Tasca el Caminito   TRADITIONAL CANARIAN €€

(☑922 29 18 34; Callejon del Combate 10; mains €10-14) The little side street on which this restaurant is located is jammed with decent, character-infused places to eat. Our favourite, though, is this one, and our favourite thing to eat here is the *secreto Iberico* (pork served in an orange sauce with apple). If you want to look your best in a bikini then you'd best give the flan, drizzled in chocolate and cream, a miss.

El Marqués de la Noria   INTERNATIONAL €€

(Callejon Combate 10; mains €10-12) There are several fashionable places to eat on this street including El Marqués de la Noria, which serves an international mix of tastes including a fantastic seafood crêpe splashed in Roquefort cheese. The service is relaxed and friendly.

Romana   CAFE €

(Calle Villaiba Hervas 19) Join the queue for what is arguably the best ice cream in town; try the legendary ice-cream sandwich, it beats a BLT any day.

TASTY TENERIFE

Don't confuse the traditional culinary fare here with that of the Spanish mainland; there are distinctive differences, although the ubiquitous tapas of Spain are common here also. The cuisine reflects a Latin American and Arabic influence, with more spices, including cumin, paprika and dried chillies, than the Spanish norm.

As on the other islands, the staple product par excellence is *gofio,* toasted grain that takes the place of bread and can be mixed with almonds and figs to make sweets. The traditional *cabra* (goat) and *cabrito* (kid) remain the staple animal protein. The rich, gamey *conejo en salmorejo* (rabbit in a marinade based on sweet black pudding and avocado) is common, as well as stews (*potaje, rancho canario* or *puchero*) of meat and vegetables simmered to savoury perfection. Fish is also a winner, with the renowned horse mackerel *(chicharros)* of Santa Cruz de Tenerife even lending their name to the city's residents: the Chicharreros. Also recommended is the *sancocho canario,* a salted-fish dish with *mojo* (a spicy salsa based on garlic and red chilli peppers). This sauce is the most obvious contribution to the Canarian table, and is typically served with *papas arrugadas* (wrinkly potatoes; small new potatoes boiled and salted in their skins). The most typical dessert is *bienmesabe* (literally 'tastes good to me'), a mixture of honey, almond cream, eggs and rum.

If you are into self-catering, then hit the local markets. They are the best place to buy the freshest vegetables and fruit. Stalls are grouped according to the types of food they offer. One of the best markets is the **Mercado de Nuestra Señora de África** in Santa Cruz de Tenerife.

Self-Catering

Mercado de Nuestra Señora de África　　　　MARKET €
(Calle San Sebastián; ⊙11am-11.30pm Mon-Sat) This market has a Central American look with its arched entrance, clock tower and flower sellers. It's not large by Spanish standards but is still tantalising, with its mountains of fresh fruit and vegetables and variety of fish. You can also buy bread, fabulous local cheese and meats.

Drinking

Bar Zumería Doña Papaya　　　　JUICE BAR
(Calle Callao Lima 3; juices €1.80-3.40; ⊙closed Sun) Delicious fresh fruit juices, including strawberry, mango, papaya, avocado and various delectable-sounding combinations. Plenty of local workers also come here at lunchtime for a quick and simple meal.

Bar Imperfecto　　　　CAFE, BAR
(Calle San Antonio 69; ⊙9pm-2.30am Mon-Sat) Although it doesn't get busy until hot-chocolate time, the atmosphere is worth the wait. Alternative music and rock and roll is the music scene, played against a dark, wood-panelled backdrop with black-and-white pics from the silver screen.

Murphy's　　　　PUB
(Plaza Concepción s/n; ⊙5pm-2.30am Mon-Thu, 5pm-3.30am Fri & Sat, 6.30pm-2.30am Sun) This Irish pub has a predictable blarney atmosphere and Guinness on tap, but is classier than many Irish imports. Live music most weekends.

☆ Entertainment

Nightclubs

Most of the nightlife is centred around the northern end of Avenida Anaga, while there is an increasing number of live-music venues within stumbling distance of Plaza España. Venues tend to change name, management and style as frequently as their patrons change their dance-sweaty clothes. Current hot spots include **Honky Tonk Xpress** (Avenida Anaga 31; ⊙6pm-3.30am Mon-Sat) and **La Nuit** (Avenida Anaga 37; ⊙6pm-3.30am Mon-Sat).

Theatre & Classical Music

TOP CHOICE Auditorio de Tenerife　　　　LIVE MUSIC
(☏922 27 06 11; www.auditoriodetenerife.com; Avenida Constitución s/n; 🛜) Tenerife's newest and flashiest entertainment option has dramatically designed curved-white concrete shells capped by a cresting, crashing wave of a roof. It covers and significantly enhances a 2-hectare oceanfront site. The auditorium hosts fantastic opera,

dance and classical-music performances, among others.

Teatro Guimerá
THEATRE
(☑box office 902 33 33 38; www.teatroguimera.es; Plaza Isla Madera s/n; tickets €12-18; box office ☺11am-1pm & 5-8pm) The other venue for highbrow entertainment, whether music or theatre.

Sport
Santa Cruz is home to football team **CD Tenerife** (www.clubdeportivotenerife.es, in Spanish; Callejón Combate 1), which plays in Spain's second division (although at the time of writing they were on the verge of being relegated). You can buy tickets at the *taquilla* (box office) of the club stadium, **Estadio Heliodoro Rodríguez López** (Calle La Mutine s/n), or call into the club's headquarters.

Shopping
The main shopping strip is the pedestrianised Calle Castillo and surrounding streets. There's something for everyone here. Some promising deals are available on electronics and watches but there are also some great little boutiques, stocked with clothes from Spanish and international designers.

El Corte Inglés
CLOTHING
(Avenida Tres de Mayo 7) Monster-sized department store that will keep you stocked in whatever your heart desires.

It also has a restaurant and an excellent, albeit pricey, supermarket with interesting imported goodies.

Rastro
MARKET
(Calle José Manuel Guimerá; ☺Sun morning) This flea market is held along two parallel streets leading from the covered market to the coast. It's the usual mix, including pirated CDs, cut-price underwear and handmade jewellery, but is bustling and fun. Keep your money out of sight.

La Isla Bookshop
BOOKSTORE
(Calle Robayna 2) This shop has titles in English, including novels, a few Canaries guidebooks and a selection of Lonely Planet guides.

❶ Information
EMERGENCY **Police station** (☑922 84 95 00; Avenida Tres de Mayo 32)

INTERNET ACCESS **Ciber Scout** (Centro Castillo, Calle Castillo s/n; per hr €2; ☺8am-11pm Mon-Sat, 10am-11pm Sun) Also offers cheap-rate phone calls, and snacks are available.

MEDICAL SERVICES **Hospital Rambla** (☑922 29 16 00; Rambla General Franco 115)

POST **Main post office** (Plaza España 2)

TOURIST INFORMATION Scattered about the city you'll find some computer terminals in public spaces, with touch-screen information about Santa Cruz attractions. The **tourist office** (☑922 23 95 92; www.webtenerife.com; Plaza España s/n; ☺8am-6pm Mon-Fri, 9am-1pm

---

DON'T MISS

CARNAVAL CAPERS

Only Rio de Janeiro does it better and even *that* party does not overshadow Santa Cruz's efforts to make **Carnaval** (www.carnavaltenerife.com) a nonstop, 24-hour party-orgy. Festivities generally kick off in early February and last about three weeks. Many of the gala performances and fancy-dress competitions take place in the Recinto Ferial (fairgrounds) but the streets, especially around Plaza España, become frenzied with good-natured dawn-to-dusk frivolity.

Don't be fooled into thinking this is just a sequin-bedecked excuse to party hearty, though. It may sometimes be hard to see or believe, but there is an underlying political 'message' to the whole shebang. Under the Franco dictatorship, Carnaval ground to a halt and there didn't seem to be too much to celebrate. The Catholic Church's relationship with the fascists was another source of frustration so, when Carnaval was relaunched after the death of General Franco, the citizens of Santa Cruz wasted no time in lampooning the perceived sexual and moral hypocrisy of the church and the fascists. Today, you will still see a lot of people dressed for the event as naughty nuns and perverted priests, and more drag queens than bumblebees in a buttercup field. And all in the name of good, clean fun. Book your accommodation ahead – if you intend to go to bed, that is.

BONO BUS

If you'll be travelling a lot by public transport in Tenerife then it's worth investing in a BonVia or Bono Bus card. Valid on all TITSA buses throughout the island as well as the city tram network, they give a 30% discount on standard fares as well as reduced entry to some tourist attractions. Cards cost €12 or €30 (depending on how many trips you are planning on taking) and can be bought from any bus or tram station as well as some newspaper kiosks. They are valid for one year.

Sat Jan-Jun & Oct-Dec, 8am-5pm Mon-Fri & 9am-noon Sat Jul-Sep) is located in the Cabildo Insular de Tenerife building. Don't confuse it with the tourist information kiosk in front of the adjacent post office.

❶ Getting There & Away
Bus

TITSA buses radiate out from the **bus station** (www.titsa.com) beside Avenida Constitución. Major routes:

Bus 102 Puerto de la Cruz (€4.40, 55 minutes, every 30 minutes) via La Laguna and Tenerife Norte

Bus 103 Puerto de la Cruz direct (€4.40, 40 minutes, more than 15 daily)

Bus 110 Los Cristianos and Playa de las Américas direct (€7.55, one hour, every 30 minutes)

Bus 111 Los Cristianos and Playa de las Américas (€7.55, one hour 20 minutes, every 30 minutes) via Candelaria and Güimar

Bus 341 Tenerife Sur (€6.20, 50 minutes, 20 daily)

Buses 014 & 015 La Laguna (€1.30, 20 minutes, every 10 minutes)

Car & Motorcycle

Car-rental companies (some also rent out motorcycles) are plentiful. Major operators also have booths at the *estación marítima* (ferry terminal).

Tram

A flash new tram line links central Santa Cruz with La Laguna. Tickets cost €1.30 and the full journey takes 40 minutes, making it by far the most pleasant way of travelling between the two towns.

❶ Getting Around
To/From the Airport

From Tenerife Norte, TITSA buses 102, 107 and 108 (€1.35, 20 minutes) go to Santa Cruz. Bus 102 (€3.15, one hour) carries on to Puerto de la Cruz via La Laguna, only 3km from the airport.

A taxi to Tenerife Norte will cost about €15 and to Tenerife Sur, around €60.

Bus

TITSA buses provide the city service in Santa Cruz. Several buses pass regularly by the centre (Plaza General Weyler and Plaza España) from the bus station, including 910 and 914. Other local services include the circular routes 920 and 921. A local trip costs €1.05.

Car

Paid parking stations can be found underneath Plaza España and within the Mercado de Nuestra Señora de África market.

Taxi

The major taxi stands are on Plaza España and at the bus station.

THE NORTHEAST

La Laguna
POP 130,000

Often overlooked by visitors to Tenerife, La Laguna is nevertheless one of the urban highlights of the Canary Islands. An easy day trip from Santa Cruz or Puerto de la Cruz, San Cristóbal de la Laguna may have an unattractive shell of concrete blocks, but its kernel, the historic town centre, is a gem, with narrow streets lined with colourful buildings, grand old villas and idiosyncratic small shops. Its layout provided the model for many colonial towns in the Americas and, in 1999, La Laguna was added to the Unesco list of World Heritage sites. The town has a youthful energy and possibly the island's most determined *marcha* (nightlife).

◉ Sights

Canarian Mansions   HISTORIC BUILDING
La Laguna allows you to fully appreciate the beauty and eccentricity of Canarian urban architecture: bright facades graced with wooden double-doors, carved balconies and grey stone embellishments. Elegant, wood-shuttered windows conceal

cool, shady patios, which, in the best cases, are surrounded by 1st-storey verandas propped up by slender timber columns. Whenever you see an open door, peek inside – with luck the inner sanctum will also be open, but do remember that many are private residences or offices.

Calle San Agustín and the surrounding streets are lined with fine old houses. Take a look inside **Casa del Montañés** (Calle San Agustín 16). Destroyed by a fire in 2006, the tranquil patios of the **Casa Salazar** (Calle San Agustín 28) have been beautifully restored and nowadays it's home to the bishop of La Laguna. The imposing **Casa de los Capitanes** (Calle Carrera) is beside the *ayuntamiento* (town hall) and houses the tourist office. The distinctive blue facade of **Calle Carrera 66** is the former home of surrealist painter Oscar Dominguez.

Both the exterior and interior of the 19th-century **Teatro Leal** (Leal Theatre; Calle Obispo Rey Redondo 54) is a pleasingly over-the-top butterfly of a building that is sadly open to the public only during performances.

Museo de la Historia de Tenerife   MUSEUM
(Casa Lecarno; Calle San Agustín 22; adult/under 18yr €3/1.50, admission free Sun; ☺10am-8pm Tue-Sun) The documents, maps, artefacts and descriptions are interesting enough at this museum, but the 16th-century mansion itself is noteworthy, having benefited from an effective and tasteful renovation. Note the brickwork, which features Renaissance designs, on either side of the stone portico at the museum's entrance.

Iglesia de Nuestra Señora de la Concepción   CHURCH
(Plaza Concepción; ☺8.30am-1.30pm & 6-7.30pm Mon-Fri, 8.30am-1.30pm & 6-8.30pm Sat, 7.30am-2pm & 4.30-8pm Sun) The island's first church, constructed in 1502, has subsequently undergone many changes. Elements of Gothic and plateresque styles can still be distinguished and the finely wrought wooden Mudéjar ceilings are a delight. Climb the tower (€1) for stunning rooftop views.

Catedral   CATHEDRAL
(Plaza Catedral) A few minutes' walk east, this cathedral was completely rebuilt in 1913. A fine baroque retable in the chapel is dedicated to the Virgen de los Remedios. At the time of research the Cathedral was closed for major renovations; when it reopens (and there's no guessing when that will be) highlights include some fine paintings by Cristóbal Hernández de Quintana, one of the islands' premier 18th-century artists.

Iglesia de Santo Domingo   CHURCH
(Calle Santo Domingo) Originally a hermitage and expanded in the 17th century, this church also contains paintings by de Quintana. Seek out the vivid murals painted in the 20th century by Mariano Cossío and Antonio González Suárez. Temporary art exhibitions as well as a small museum showcasing the treasures of the church are also housed here.

Santuario del Cristo   CHURCH
(Santuario del Santísimo Cristo de La Laguna; Plaza San Francisco s/n; ☺8am-1pm & 4-8.45pm Mon-Thu & Sat, to 9pm Fri & Sun) At the northern end of the old quarter, this church

TENERIFE LA LAGUNA

DON'T MISS

BEHIND-THE-SCENES TOURS

Much of the interest and beauty of La Laguna is hidden away behind heavy doors and walls from prying tourist eyes; if you want to get a more in-depth feel for the town it's worth joining one of the frequent guided tours organised by the tourist office. Tours run at 10.30am, noon and 4pm Monday to Friday and 10.30am and noon Saturday and Sunday. Tours are free and are in Spanish (though with 48 hours advance notice the tourist office can cobble together a tour in English, German or French). Tours, which leave from the tourist office, take in most of the buildings and churches mentioned here as well as a number of other historic buildings that cannot be visited independently.

Tours focusing exclusively on the churches and convents cost €3 per person and last around an hour and a half. As with the general tours, they are only in Spanish unless you request otherwise 48 hours in advance. It's also possible to walk this tour without a guide but the cost is still the same. Tickets for these two tours can be bought from the Iglesia de Nuestra Señora de la Concepción.

contains a blackened wooden sculpture of Christ – the most venerated crucifix on the island. Be as respectful as possible inside, as most of the people here are praying, not sightseeing.

Iglesia y ex-convento de
San Agustín   CHURCH
(Calle San Agustín s/n; ⊙10am-8pm Tue-Fri, to 3pm Sat & Sun) This ruined church is out of bounds, but you can peer through the gap in the wall at the cactuses and other plants busy reclaiming the building's structure. The cloisters, filled with tropical plants and flowers, which are open to the public, are probably the prettiest in town. The rooms surrounding the cloisters contain an art gallery of frequently changing, and fairly ho-hum, local works.

Convento de Santa Clara   CONVENT
(cnr Calles Anchieta & Viana; ⊙4-7pm Mon-Sat & 11.30am-7pm Sun) Of the other convents, this is the most interesting, and renowned for its beautiful lattice-work wooden balcony. At the time of research it was closed for renovations, but when it reopens you should also make a bee-line for its fine 16th-century chapel.

Convento de Santa Catalina   CONVENT
(Plaza Adelantado; admission €3; ⊙10am-5pm) The Santa Clara chapel and the closed order in this convent are still active. On 15 February each year the remarkably well preserved body of Sister María de Jesús de León Delgado, who died in 1731, is put on display. The convent also contains an interesting religious museum.

Museo de la Ciencia y el Cosmos   MUSEUM
(www.museosdetenerife.org, in Spanish; Calle Vía Láctea s/n; adult/child €3/free; ⊙9am-7pm Tue-Sun; ⊞) If you enjoy pushing buttons and musing on the forces of nature, you can have fun at this museum, even if you don't speak Spanish. About 1.5km south of Plaza Adelantado, it also has a planetarium, so you can stargaze during the day. A good choice for those wanting to have their children stimulated by something other than yet another sugary ice cream.

Fundacíon Cristino de Vera   ART GALLERY
(www.fundacioncristinodevera.com; Calle San Agustín 18; adult/child €5/free; ⊙11am-1pm & 5-9pm Mon-Fri, to 8pm Sat) The town's prime arts venue houses a mixture of temporary exhibitions as well as a permanent

collection of works by acclaimed local artist Cristino de Vera.

Festivals & Events

Corpus Christi   RELIGIOUS FESTIVAL
Celebrated with gusto in La Laguna (the date changes annually, but it's always in June) and also La Orotava, where mammoth floral carpets, using tons of volcanic dirt, flower petals, leaves and branches, are painstakingly designed into intricate biblical scenes in the streets and plazas.

Romería de San
Benito Abad   RELIGIOUS FESTIVAL
Held on the first Sunday in July this, one of the most important fiestas in La Laguna, is held in honour of the patron saint of farmers and crops.

Fiesta del Santísimo
Cristo   RELIGIOUS FESTIVAL
Held in La Laguna from 7 to 15 September, this festival includes religious processions, traditional music and an impressive fireworks display.

Eating

TOP CHOICE Casa Rural la
Asomada del Gata   TRADITIONAL CANARIAN €€
(☑922 26 39 37; Calle Anchieta 45; mains €10-14; ⊙closed Mon & Tue) Hidden away inside this backstreet Casa Rural, this is easily one of the town's more popular restaurants. Home-cooked food is served in a country farmhouse–style dining room (complete with a roaring log fire in the winter). The short menu focuses on refined Canarian dishes and there's an excellent wine list.

El Tonique   TRADITIONAL CANARIAN €€
(☑922 26 15 29; Calle Heraclio Sánchez 23; mains €8-12; ⊙closed Mon lunch & Sun) Head downstairs to this cosy restaurant, its walls lined with dusty bottles of wine. These are but a sample of more than 250 different varieties quietly maturing in Tonique's cellars. The food is very good and worth the wait for a table (it's popular for lunch) and a plate of *pimientos del piquillo rellenos de merluza* (small peppers stuffed with hake).

La Folie   CAFE €
(Calle Santo Domingo 10; snacks €2.50-6) This fabulous place has a real '60s Haight-Ashbury feel with its cavernous interior, leopard-skin upholstery, murals and

» **Playa de las Teresitas** (San Andres) The beach escape of choice for residents of Santa Cruz. Offers soft Saharan sand, safe bathing, good seafood restaurants nearby and a totally Spanish vibe.

» **Porís de Abona** Our favourite east-coast beach; pretty, pocket-sized black-sand beach in a working fishing village. Largely undeveloped.

» **El Médano** Superb for windsurfing and long beach walks, but much too windy for sunbathing. Cool, international surf vibe.

» **Los Cristianos, Playa de las Américas & Costa Adeje** Several dark-sand beaches with safe bathing and lots going on. Absolutely always busy.

» **Los Gigantes** A range of attractive coves, some sandy, some rocky, but all linked by a promenade that twists and turns along the cliffs. Low key and enjoyable.

» **Puerto de la Cruz** Stunning waterfront swimming pools and a couple of calm and sandy beaches in Tenerife's classiest resort.

idiosyncratic clutter. It's a good place to seek out whether for breakfast, savoury crêpes or *mojitos*.

 Drinking

Students comprise the town's nightlife, and the bulk of the bars are concentrated in a tight rectangle northeast of the university, known as El Cuadrilátero. At its heart, pedestrianised Plaza Zurita is simply two parallel lines of bars and pubs, so there's no shortage of quaffing choice.

❶ Information

Police station (☑922 31 46 05; Calle Nava y Grimón 66)

Post office (Calle Santo Domingo)

Tourist office (☑922 63 11 94; www.visitla laguna.es; Calle Carrera 7; ⊙9am-8pm Mon-Fri, to 2pm Sat & Sun Jun-Sep, 9am-5pm Mon-Fri Oct-May) In a lovely old house with an inner courtyard; ask for the fascinating *San Cristóbal de La Laguna, World Heritage Site* brochure.

❶ Getting There & Away

There is a stream of buses going to Santa Cruz. Bus 015 (€1.30, 20 minutes) is best, as it takes you straight to Plaza España. The new tram system links the two towns. A one-way ticket costs €1.30. Buses 101, 102 and 103 also offer a regular service to Puerto de la Cruz (€3.45, one hour). If La Orotava (€2.65, 1½ hours) is your goal, take bus 108.

Finding a parking space on the streets is migraine-inducing. There's an underground pay car park beneath Plaza San Cristóbal, but if possible come on public transport.

San Andrés & Around

The village of San Andrés, all narrow, shady streets lined with fishermen's cottages painted in primary colours, is 6km northeast of Santa Cruz. It is distinguished by the now-crumbled round tower that once protected the town, plus some good seafood restaurants, which alone justify the short journey. Bustling **Bar El Peton** (Calle Aparejo; mains €7-9) is a cute little place next to the tower. There are just three or four tables that are normally buried under a mountain of superlative seafood. There are also a number of flashier, but by no means better, places on the waterfront road.

The golden sands of the **Playa de las Teresitas**, just beyond the village, were imported from the Sahara. It's a pleasant beach where the sunbathers are almost exclusively Spanish, whether local or from the mainland. Limited parking is available and it's safe for children to swim here.

There are frequent 910 buses (€1.30, 20 minutes) from Santa Cruz to San Andrés, continuing on to Playa de las Teresitas. Bus 245 goes northeast from San Andrés to the end of the road at Igueste, following another 6km of beautiful coastline.

Taganana & the Anaga Mountains

The rugged Anaga mountains (geologically the oldest part of Tenerife) sprawling across the far northeast corner of the island offer some of the most spectacular scenery in Tenerife and the whole area is littered with

WANT MORE?

Head to **Lonely Planet** (www.lonely planet.com/canary-islands/tenerife) for planning advice, author recommendations, traveller reviews and insider tips.

hiking trails. If hiking isn't your idea of fun then you can still get a feel for the mountains by driving the numerous switchbacks of the TF-12 road, which links La Laguna and San Andrés. It's also worth making the short, and steep, detour to Taganana along the TF-134. If using public transport, bus 246 travels from Santa Cruz to Taganana via San Andrés at least six times daily from Santa Cruz (€1.30, 50 minutes).

There's little to see or do in the small town of Taganana, but it's only a few more kilometres north to the coast and **Roque de las Bodegas**, which has a number of small restaurants and drink stands. Local surfers favour its beach – and, even more so, the rocky strand of **Almáciga**, 1.25km eastwards and accessible by the same bus.

For serious exploration of these mist-shrouded peaks, though, you need to leave the road behind and strike out on foot. The main visitors centre is the **Cruz del Carmen**, which sits a little under halfway between La Laguna and Taganana on the TF-12 road. Filled with tweeting birds you never actually see, the laurel forests surrounding the visitors centre are a jungle of twisted trees coated in moisture-retaining mosses. Through this forest wind several well-marked trails, including a five-minute one suitable for wheelchairs and strollers. Another easy half-hour return walk is to the **Llano de los Loros** – a stunning viewpoint. The visitors centre can supply details of much more taxing walks around here.

Punta del Hidalgo & Around

Once the pebble beaches and swimming pools around Punta del Hidalgo and Bajamar were a popular resort but today they're slightly down at heel and grotty, and the only visitors are Germans in search of winter sun and locals out for some salt air. Despite this less-than-rosy picture, the area is a pleasant break from Santa Cruz and La Laguna and the surrounding mountain

scenery is spectacular. If it's lunchtime pop by the tranquil village of El Socorro and **Restaurante Bar San Gonzalo** (Carretera General del Socorro 179; menú del día €7; ☺closed Sun pm & Mon), which is excellent for steaks and has a dining room with vineyard views. Continuing northwest from El Socorro, you reach the scrappy seaside resort of **Bajamar** (via Tejina). You can swim in large man-made rock pools awash with Atlantic rollers, which are popular with locals.

Three kilometres northeast, **Punta del Hidalgo** is a more interesting place, although don't expect any crumbling cobbles or medieval churches. Like most of the towns in this region, Punta is comparatively modern, its charm being the dramatic ocean location backed by soaring craggy mountains. Stroll along the boardwalk, stopping for a coffee, *cerveza* (beer) or fishy meal at friendly **Angelo** (Altagay Apartments; mains €8-15) across from the beach. The whole coastline here is excellent surfing country, with some of the best-quality spots on the north coast packed into a tight area – but visiting surfers shouldn't expect the locals to welcome them with open arms.

Bus 105 runs to Bajamar (€1.30, one hour five minutes) and Punta del Hidalgo (€1.30, 1¼ hours) every 30 minutes from Santa Cruz via La Laguna.

Tacoronte & El Sauzal

Tacoronte is located in the heart of one of the island's most important wine regions. Downhill from the modern town centre is the signposted **Iglesia de Santa Catalina** – a bright little whitewashed church built in the Canaries' colonial style. You'll also see a handful of traditional old houses, but otherwise there's a lack of gawp-worthy sights here. **Cristo de los Dolores**, held on the first Sunday after 15 September, is Tacoronte's big fiesta with harvest festivities and wine tasting.

Just beyond the El Sauzal exit from the motorway is the **Casa del Vino La Baranda** (☏922 57 25 35; Autopista del Norte; admission free; ☺10.30am-6.30pm Tue, 9am-9pm Wed-Sat, 11am-6pm Sun), a museum devoted to wine and its production, located in a traditional Canarian country house with an opportunity to sample the produce in the adjoining tasting room. It's a charming place, with some beautiful views of El Teide on a clear day. The museum also has a well-regarded restaurant and, during July and August, the central courtyard becomes a tasteful venue for classical-music concerts every other Tuesday from 8.30pm. The museum also organises regular wine-tasting courses.

Bus 101 links these towns to Puerto de la Cruz (€2.25, 20 minutes) and Santa Cruz (€2.15, 40 minutes) every 30 minutes or hourly (depending on the time of day).

THE NORTH

Puerto de la Cruz

POP 31,100

Puerto de la Cruz is the elder statesman of Tenerife tourism, with a history of welcoming foreign visitors that dates back to the late 19th century, when it was a spa destination popular with genteel Victorian ladies. These days the town, which attracts a classier style of tourist than the pie-and-pint crowd who happily prefer the south, is a pleasant resort with real character and interest. In fact, we'd go so far as to say that it's the most charming resort town in Tenerife. There are stylish boardwalks, beaches with safe swimming, traditional restaurants, a leafy central plaza, lots of pretty parks and gardens and plenty to see and do.

History

Until it was declared an independent town in the early 20th century, Puerto de la Cruz was merely the port of the wealthier area of La Orotava. Bananas, wine, sugar and cochineals (dye-producing insects) were exported from here and a substantial bourgeois class developed in the 1700s. In the 1800s the English arrived, first as merchants and later as sun-seeking tourists, marking the beginning of the tourist transformation that characterises the town today.

◉ Sights

Old Town HISTORICAL SITE

The Plaza Europa, a balcony of sorts built in 1992, may be a modern addition, but it blends well with the historic surroundings and is a good place to start your visit. The tourist office is here, located in the **Casa de la Aduana** (built in 1620), the old customs house, where now you can also find quality arts and crafts for sale. Opposite is the **ayuntamiento** (town hall), which was a banana-packaging factory until 1973. A short walk away is the little **Museo Arqueológico** (Archaeological Museum; Calle Lomo 9; adult/under 6yr €1/free; ◷10am-1pm & 5-9pm Tue-Sat, 10am-1pm Sun, closed Aug), which provides an insight into the Guanche way of life with its replicas of a typical cave dwelling, as well as a burial cave where pots and baked-clay adornments share the same burial area, demonstrating the Guanches' belief in an afterlife. The most interesting exhibit is a tiny clay idol – one of only a few ever found.

Southeast of the museum is the lively **Plaza Charco** (Puddle Plaza), which acquired its name because it used to flood from the sea every time there was a heavy storm (thankfully, no more). Just off the plaza is **Iglesia de San Francisco**, tacked

---

TENERIFE ACTIVE

Possibly no other island in the archipelago offers so many opportunities to burn off calories than Tenerife. Windsurfing, diving, hiking, fishing, surfing, golf and cycling are all not just possible here, but almost impossible to avoid. For watersports most facilities are concentrated in and around the southwestern resort areas, although the north coast has a wide variety of surf spots.

Tenerife is marvellous for hiking and climbing with plenty of scope, ranging from easy rambles to mountain assaults. For the most dramatic scenery, choose from the many trails within the Parque Nacional del Teide. Other attractive areas are the Anaga mountains in the northeast and around the Valle de la Orotava. There are numerous companies offering guided walks, as well as the rangers at El Teide. Check the following websites and ask at any tourist office for details:

» www.pateatusmontes.com

» www.gregorio-teneriffa.de, in German

» www.gaiatours.es

» www.caminantesdeaguere.com

Puerto de la Cruz

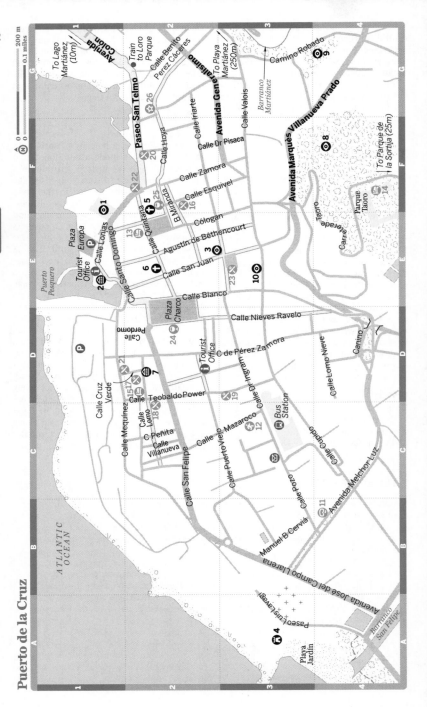

on to tiny **Ermita de San Juan**, the oldest structure in town (built in 1599). Three blocks away is **Iglesia de Nuestra Señora de la Peña de Francia**, a 17th-century church with three naves, a wooden Mudéjar ceiling and the image of Gran Poder de Dios, one of the town's most revered saints.

Several Canarian mansions, many of them in poor repair, dot the town centre. The mid-18th-century **Casa Iriarte** (Calle San Juan), once the home of intellectual Tomás de Iriarte and the site of clandestine political meetings, has seen better days. The **Torreon de Ventoso** (Calle Valois) is one of the better-kept historic buildings. The tower once formed part of the town's Augustine convent and was used to keep watch over the port.

Outside the town centre there are also some noteworthy spots, such as **Castillo de San Felipe** (⊙11am-1pm & 5-8pm Tue-Sat) beside Playa Jardín, which plays host to a variety of temporary art exhibitions and regular theatre and dance performances. Above town, the **Mirador de la Paz**, a square with great views, is where Agatha Christie was supposedly inspired to write the novel *The Mysterious Mr Quin*.

Loro Parque   ZOO
(☎922 37 38 41; www.loroparque.com; Calle Avenida Loro Parque; adult/under 12yr €32/21; ⊙8.30am-6.45pm) Travelling around Tenerife

you'll encounter so many posters, flags and stickers advertising the Loro Parque that you could be forgiven for thinking they sponsor Tenerife! But we'll give them their dues because where else can you see over 350 different species (and sub-species) of parrots (the world's largest collection) all in one place? But while parrots are the raison d'être of the park, today its animal portfolio has grown to include tigers, gorillas and chimpanzees, but for many people the real highlights are the penguin house complete with 'real' snow, the subterranean aquarium with the world's longest submarine tunnel and the dolphin and orca shows. There are also a variety of other attractions including a new HD cinema. The park is undeniably a highly impressive day out, but in our opinion it's more of a theme park than a serious conservation effort (although they do have the Loro Parque Fundacion, which supports conservation projects around the world). You could walk here from town, but it's much easier to hop on the free train that leaves every 20 minutes from outside McDonalds on Plaza Reyes Católicos.

Parks & Gardens   GARDEN
Don't miss a visit to the **Jardín Botánico** (Calle Retama 2; admission €3; ⊙9am-6pm Oct-Apr, to 7pm May-Sep), on the road out of town. Established in 1788, the botanical garden has thousands of plant varieties from all

over the world and is a delightful place in which to while away an afternoon smelling the roses. Just 1km closer to the town centre, the **Sitio Litre Garden** (Carretera del Botánico; adult/under 12yr €4.75/free; ⊙9.30am-5pm) boasts a luscious orchid collection and the town's oldest *drago* (dragon tree). Another tropical oasis is the **Risco Belle Aquatic Gardens** (adult/under 12yr €4/2; ⊙9.30am-6pm), which sits in the heart of the **Parque Taoro** south of the town centre. There's a pleasant cafe, with tables and chairs arranged out on the lawn. On the edge of the Parque Taoro is the newly redesigned **Parque de la Sortija**, another public park containing ponds, children's playgrounds, formal French gardens and lots of joggers. Currently it's a little empty of character, but give it time and once the plants and trees have matured it'll be the equal of any of the town's other parks and gardens.

Lago Martiánez   AMUSEMENT PARK
(Avenida Colón; adult/under 12yr €3.50/1.20; ⊙10am-sunset, last entry 5pm Oct-Apr, 6pm May-Sep) Designed by Canario César Manrique, the watery playground of Lago Martiánez has four saltwater pools and a large central 'lake'. It can get just as crowded as the surrounding small volcanic beaches. Swim, sunbathe or grab a bite at one of the many restaurants and bars.

🏖 Beaches

Puerto de la Cruz is home to several beaches, all of them largely sheltered from waves and perfect for young children. In the heart of the town are the rocky and attractive **coves** around the little port just below the Paseo San Telmo. Most people, though, make straight for the long sandy **Playa Martiánez** at the eastern end of the town. A large jetty filters down the anger of Atlantic swells and turns them into mere gentle rollers, perfect for learning to surf on. The beach itself consists of soft, black sand. At the opposite end of town is the **Playa Jardín**, which is more popular with locals but nowhere near as attractive as the other beaches.

Surfers wanting to get wet should head west several kilometres to **Playa del Socorro**, an average beach break that is easily maxed out (and is very wind exposed).

🏃 Activities & Tours

Der Wanderstab   NATURE HIKES
(☑922 37 60 07; www.derwanderstab.de, in German) Local guides meet hikers at the bus station, from where they set out on several hikes, including Teide and the northwest. They aim very much at a German audience, which can make things a little tricky for anyone who doesn't speak German.

El Cardumen   DIVING
(☑670 38 30 07; www.elcardumen.com, in Spanish; Avenida Melchor Luz 3) Offers a range of diving courses including an introductory 'try dive'. If you prefer to soar like a bird rather than swim like a fish, it also offers parapenting.

Mountain Bike Active   CYCLING
(Edificio Daniela 26, Calle Mazaroco; bike rental from €25 per day; ⊙9.30am-1.30pm & 5-7pm) Located across from the bus station, it organises biking trips to El Teide and around.

⭐ Festivals & Events

Not to be outdone by Santa Cruz, Puerto de la Cruz holds its own riotous **Carnaval** celebration. Other events:

San Juan   RELIGIOUS FESTIVAL
Held in Puerto de la Cruz on the eve of the saint's day (23 June). Bonfires light the sky and, in a throwback to Guanche times, goats are driven for a dip in the sea off Playa Jardín.

Fiesta de los Cacharros   FESTIVAL
Held in Puerto de la Cruz (and Taganana) on 29 November, this is a quaint festival where children rush through the streets, dragging behind them a string of old pots, kettles, pans, car spares, tin cans – just about anything that will make a racket.

🍴 Eating

Restaurante Mil Sabores   MEDITERRANEAN €€€
(☑922 36 81 72; Calle Cruz Verde 5; mains €10-16; ⊙dinner Mon-Sat, lunch & dinner Sun) Styling itself as a temple to modern Mediterranean cooking, this flash restaurant has the looks (lime-green walls decorated with blue saucepan lids!), and the tastes, down to a fine art. The service is excellent and, considering the price, the food quality truly superb. What sort of things can you expect to find on the menu? How about duck with pineapple and couscous, all manner of seafood or a perfectly combined mix of pork, apple and bacon. It's quite dressy without being formal.

TOP CHOICE **El Limón** VEGETARIAN €
(Calle Esquivel 4; snacks €4-6; 🖉) A bright vegetarian restaurant with a menu consisting of veggie burgers, seitan kebabs, salads and fresh fruit juices, among others. It also does a good-value set-lunch menu (€10), which makes for a welcome change from all the meat-heavy or fish-friendly dishes found everywhere else. The clientele is almost exclusively local.

Restaurante Magnolia SPANISH €€
(🖉922 38 56 14; Avenida Marqués de Villanueva del Prado s/n; mains €6-12; ⊘closed Tue) Close to the botanical gardens, this highly regarded restaurant, inside a glass conservatory–style building, brings the sublime flavours of Spain's Catalonia region to the Canaries. Catalonia is widely regarded as having some of the best regional cuisine in all of Spain and after you've tucked into authentic regional dishes such as seafood casserole or Catalan sausage and beans you'll be whole-heartedly agreeing.

La Rosa di Bari MODERN CANARIAN €€€
(🖉922 36 85 23; Calle Lomo 23; mains €11-17; ⊘closed Sun pm & Mon) Located in a lovely old house with several romantic dining rooms, this unassuming little place is actually one of the classiest restaurants in town. Enjoy innovative dishes like ravioli with truffles and foie gras sauce or fish with a crust of mustard.

La Papaya TRADITIONAL CANARIAN €€
(🖉922 38 28 11; Calle Lomo 10; mains €8-12; ⊘closed Wed) This long-time favourite has a series of small dining rooms with rock-face walls and a pretty patio with adjacent leafy garden. There are Canarian touches to the menu, including the succulent salmon in *malvasía* (Malmsey wine) sauce.

Meson los Gemelos TRADITIONAL CANARIAN €€
(Calle El Peñón 4; mains €7-8) Round the corner from the bus station, this is a friendly, welcoming restaurant with a great atmosphere; the house speciality is grilled meats. There's a covered interior patio and lots of locals.

Rancho Grande INTERNATIONAL €€
(🖉922 38 37 52; Paseo San Telmo 10; mains €8-10, cakes €2-3, ice creams €5-6) The service might be frumpy and uninterested, but who can resist stopping by this waterfront institution for one of its spectacularly ornate ice-cream cocktail desserts or an overtly pretty cake? The mains aren't bad either and include some more unusual dishes such as chicken curry and chilli-con-carne.

Tapas Arcón TAPAS €
(Calle Blanco 8; tapas about €4; 🖉) *Papas arrugadas* (wrinkly potatoes) with *mojo* (spicy salsa), or the Arcón special sauces of almond and sweet pepper or parsley and coriander are the must-have tapas here.

Restaurante Rustico SPANISH €€
(Punta Viento; mains €8-12) To be totally honest the food here isn't all that great, but the location, in a cave under the seaside promenade, is magnificent and diners get a fantastic view of the rocky coast. The menu spans all the Canarian and mainland standards and there's a few pasta and pizza dishes thrown in as well.

🍷 Drinking

Most nightspots are around Plaza Charco or along Avenida Generalísimo.

Ebano Café CAFE
(Calle Hoya 2; ⊘10am-midnight) This is a beautiful building with lots of original features; the sticky, sweet cakes created inside the building are also pretty beautiful. Enjoy them while sitting outside in a comfy wicker chair with a view of the church. Tapas also served.

Colours Café BAR
(Plaza Charco; ⊘8pm-2am Wed-Mon) Above a pizzeria on this energetic stretch of eateries, snag a seat by a window overlooking the square. A cocktail bar with mellow decor and Latin and African music, this is a good place to kick off your night on the tiles.

☆ Entertainment

There are several bars and nightclubs on Calle Obispo Pérez Cacéres, but names and styles change as often as the tide.

Salsa Bar NIGHTCLUB
(Calle Hoya 27; ⊘11pm-6am Mon-Sat) Get steamy, saucy and sexy at this Latin-music-themed nightclub.

❶ Information

Main post office (Calle Pozo)
Police station (🖉922 37 84 48; Plaza Europa)
Tourist office (🖉922 38 60 00; Casa de la Aduana, Calle Lonjas s/n; ⊘9am-8pm Mon-Fri, to 5pm Sat & Sun) There's a second, smaller, office in the **old quarter** (🖉922 38 08 70; Calle Puerto Viejo 13; ⊘9am-1pm & 4.30-7pm).

ℹ Getting There & Away

The bus station is on Calle Pozo in the west of town. There are frequent departures for Santa Cruz (€4.40, 55 minutes). Bus 103 is direct while Bus 102 calls by Tenerife Norte airport and La Laguna. Other popular routes include Bus 348 (€5.20, 1½ hours, 9.15am) to El Teide (returns at 4pm). Bus 343 (€12.25, two hours, six daily) runs to Playa de las Américas. Bus 363 offers an hourly service from 6am to 10pm to Icod de los Vinos (€2.65, 45 minutes) and on to Garachico (€3.15, one hour).

ℹ Getting Around

For information about bike rental, see p134.

The long-distance buses starting in or passing through Puerto de la Cruz often double up as local buses.

Taxis are widely available and are a relatively inexpensive way to jet across town (a 15-minute ride should cost under €5).

La Orotava

POP 40,000

This colonial town has the lot, it seems: cobblestone streets, flower-filled plazas and more Castilian mansions than the rest of the island put together. Along with La Laguna, La Orotava is one of the loveliest towns on Tenerife, and one of the most truly 'Canarian' places in the Canary Islands.

The lush valley surrounding the town has been one of the island's most prosperous areas since the 16th century. Most churches and manor houses here were built in the 17th century (with some dating back to the 16th century). The valley is a major cultivator of bananas, chestnuts and vineyards, and is also excellent hiking country, with a maze of footpaths leading you into Canarian pine woods, with 1200m views down over the coastal plain; see the boxed text, p138. The tourist office can also advise on routes.

La Orotava

◉ Sights

Old Town
HISTORIC SITE

La Orotava has been able to preserve the beauty of its past. Traditional mansions are flanked with ornate wooden balconies like pirate galleons, surrounded by manicured gardens. You can cover the centre on foot in just half a day.

Plaza Constitución, a large, shady plaza, is a good place to start. On the plaza's northeastern side is the **Iglesia de San Agustín**, a simple church with a pretty wooden ceiling. A few doors away stands the palatial **Liceo de Taoro** (www.liceodetaoro.es, in Spanish) building (1928): a private cultural society, but open to the public. An attractive terraced garden separates the mansion from the street and, although the building looks a tad foreboding, you can enter and have a drink at the cafe, a meal at the restaurant or check out any exhibitions that may be taking place.

Also on the plaza are the 19th-century **Jardínes del Marquesado de la Quinta Roja** (☺9am-midnight), a series of orderly, French-influenced flower gardens cascading down the hillside, crowned by a small 18th-century marble temple. They are also known as the Jardín Victoria.

Easier on the knees is the sweet-smelling **Hijuela del Botánico** (☺9am-2pm Mon-Fri), just across Calle León. This small botanical garden was created as a branch of the larger Jardín Botánico in Puerto de la Cruz. Around 3000 plant varieties are gathered here, and there are also birds and butterflies.

Back in the centre of town, the **Iglesia de la Concepción** (Plaza Patricia García; ☺11am-1pm & 5-8pm) is one of the finest examples of baroque architecture in the entire archipelago. Follow Calle Colegio (which becomes Calle San Francisco) uphill from behind the church. This street is home to several of the **Doce Casas**, 12 historic Canary mansions that are one of La Orotava's most distinguishing features. The 17th-century **Casa Lercaro** (Calle Colegio 5-7; ☺10.30am-8.30pm) is now an upmarket restaurant, cafe and *cervecería* (beer bar).

Down the street is the **Casa de los Balcones** (Casa Fonesca, Calle San Francisco 3; ☺8.30am-7.30pm Mon-Sat, to 6.30pm Sun). Built in 1692, the interior and exterior balconies feature ornate carvings and there's a small separate museum showing furniture and costumes of the period, but it's primarily a showroom for various local crafts. Across the street is **Casa del Turista** (☺8.30am-7.30pm Mon-Sat, to 6.30pm Sun), which has similar features but is less outstanding.

Museo de Cerámica
MUSEUM

(Ceramics Museum; Calle León 3; admission €2; ☺10am-6pm Mon-Fri, to 2pm Sat & Sun) This museum boasts the largest clay-pot collection in Spain. The museum is well laid out, and there are detailed explanations in several languages. The sheer size of the pots in the *Sala de Vino* is impressive, and the sepia photos are fun, but after a few dozen pots or so, there is a certain same old pottiness about the place.

Museo de Artesania Iberoamericana
MUSEUM

(Iberoamerican Handicrafts Museum; Calle Tomás Zerolo 34; admission €2; ☺9am-6pm Mon-Fri, 9.30am-2pm Sat) Head down Calle Tomás Zerolo to visit this museum, housed in the former Convento de Santo Domingo. Exploring the cultural relationship between the Canaries and the Americas, the museum exhibits musical instruments, ceramics and various artefacts.

HIKING WITH GOBLINS

Travel between La Orotava and the Teide massif and around the halfway mark you pass through the little village of Aguamansa. Just beyond this village, and a little higher up the mountain slopes, the road passes a number of parking areas away from which radiate an array of brilliantly marked walking trials. The walking here is really easy with only gentle inclines and short distances to cover (although it's simple to join routes up and create much longer walks) and is perfect for gentle family strolling. Most of the routes twist in and out of fantastic laurel forests that are like something out of a children's fantasy story; so dense is the forest that if ever fairies, elves and goblins had a home in Europe then it must surely have been here. In other areas the laurel forests are replaced with magnificent strands of ancient pine trees with girths so thick it would take two or three grown men to encircle them with their arms.

Each parking area has a signboard explaining the different routes leading away from it.

Iglesia de Santo Domingo CHURCH
Adjacent to the handicrafts museum, this church has beautifully carved doors and a rich Mudéjar ceiling.

✨ Festivals & Events

Corpus Christi RELIGIOUS FESTIVAL
Celebrated with extravagance in La Orotava (the date changes annually, but it's always in June), an intricately designed, colourful floral carpet is laid on the streets, made from petals, leaves and branches, and in the Plaza de Ayuntamiento a tapestry of biblical scenes is created using coloured sands from El Teide.

✖ Eating

Sabor Canario TRADITIONAL CANARIAN €€
(www.hotelorotava.com; Hotel Rural Orotava, Calle Carrera 17; mains €8-10; ⊘closed Sun) Exercise the taste buds with soul-satisfying traditional cuisine at this fabulous restaurant located in the leafy patio of the Hotel Rural Orotava. The building itself is a fabulous old Canarian townhouse stuffed full of memorabilia.

Zona Kiú MODERN CANARIAN €€
(Casa Lercaro, Calle Colegio 7; mains €8-12; ⊘closed Sun evening & Mon) This enticing space is *the* place to come for laidback nightlife, a morning coffee or an elegant meal. The cafe has a decadent cake choice; the *cervecería* has beer on tap and live music at weekends; and the elegant restaurant hits the right spot with innovative dishes like sole and prawn rolls in a dill sauce. And if you can squeeze in something for dessert, how about a banana tortilla?

❶ Information

Police station (☎922 33 01 14; Calle Cólogan 2)

Post office (Calle Cólogan s/n)

Tourist office (☎922 32 30 41; www.villa delaorotava.com, in Spanish; Calle Calvario 4; ⊘9am-5pm Mon-Fri) A well-marked tourist route of the town's major monuments starts here.

❶ Getting There & Away

Parking in La Orotava is an absolute nightmare. If you're not staying here then it's far better to just come by bus from Puerto de la Cruz, which is just 9km away. Buses (€1.30, 20 minutes) leave roughly every half-hour from 7am to 11pm. Bus 104 (€3.65, 50 minutes), among others, comes from Santa Cruz.

Icod de los Vinos

POP 22,200

An umbrella-shaped *drago* tree is the cause of a lot of fuss in this town. Indeed, it's worth a look, and the shady main square, Plaza San Marcos, is a lovely, leafy spot to rest and enjoy the town's white-walled church. Other than this plaza and the tiny kernel of old streets leading off it, the town is not the most inspiring of places. For restaurants and places to stay head on to neighbouring Garachico, which is many notches up on the postcard-pretty stakes.

The **tourist office** (☎922 81 21 23; Calle San Sebastian 6; ⊘9am-7pm Mon-Fri) is just off the main plaza.

◉ Sights

The pride of the town is what is touted as the world's largest and oldest **dragon tree**, which has supposedly been here for more than 1000 years. In actual fact, this statement is a little optimistic and it would be better described as the world's largest and oldest Canary Islands Dragon Tree (there are around 40 different species and sub-species of *drago* trees). Past **Plaza Constitución** (aka Plaza Pila), a square with historic Canary homes, is **Drago Park** (adult/child €4/2; ☺9.30am-6.30pm), where you can pay to get up close to the famous tree. The best view, however, is the free one from the west wall of the Plaza de la Inglesia. **Plaza San Marcos** is in the centre of town. Here you can see the **Iglesia de San Marcos**, which has an ornate silver high altar.

The second major sight here is the **Mariposario del Drago** (www.mariposario .com; Avenida Canarias; adult/child €8.50/5; ☺10am-6pm Oct-Apr, to 7pm May-Sep), a hot and sticky greenhouse full of hundreds of exotic butterflies. It's located just below the Plaza San Marcos.

ⓘ Getting There & Away

If you're driving, save yourself a headache and follow the signs towards the paid car park. Arriving by bus is easy: Bus 106 (€6.30, 1¼ hours) comes directly from Santa Cruz every two hours from 6.45am to 10.45pm. Bus 354 (€3.05, 45 minutes) comes from Puerto de la Cruz every half-hour from 7.30am to 10.30pm, and Bus 460 (€5.90, one hour 35 minutes, eight daily) makes the trip up from Playa de las Américas. The bus station is to the northeast of the town centre.

Garachico
POP 6800

A gracious, tranquil town located in a deep valley flanked by forested slopes and a rocky coastline, Garachico has managed to retain its Canarian identity and is one of the few coastal towns where you may still need Spanish to order a beer. There are no big hotels, probably because there is no real beach, though swimming in the natural, volcanic coves along the rocky coast is a rare delight.

Named for the rock outcrop off its shore (*gara* is Guanche for island, and *chico* is Spanish for small), Garachico is a peaceful place. You'd never guess the history of calamities that lies behind its whitewashed houses and narrow, cobblestone streets. Garachico was once an important commercial port, but its unlucky inhabitants suffered a series of disasters that all but finished off the hamlet: freak storms, floods, fires, epidemics and, in 1706, a major volcanic eruption that destroyed the port and buried half the town in lava, reducing it to a poor shadow of its former self.

Just outside town, you can hike trails that follow the path of the disastrous lava flow.

◉ Sights & Activities

The soul of Garachico is the main Plaza Libertad, with its towering palm trees, cafe tables and lively atmosphere. At dusk old men in flat caps play cards surrounded by sauntering couples, children kicking balls, and families. Nearby is the **Iglesia** and evocative **Convento de San Francisco** (1524). Just off the plaza is the **Iglesia de Santa Ana**, with a dominating white bell tower and original 16th-century doors.

Another rare remnant of the volcano is in the cute **Parque de la Puerta de Tierra**, just off Plaza Juan González (aka Plaza Pila), where the **Puerta de Tierra** (Land Gate) is all that's left of Garachico's once-thriving port. It was once right on the water but thanks to the eruption is now in the centre of town.

On the water you can visit **Castillo de San Miguel**, a squat stone fortress built in the 16th century, with photos and explanations of the area's flora and fauna, as well as a chronological history of the town. Sadly, the opening hours are highly erratic.

TENERIFE TIPPLES

The wine of Tenerife (and the Canaries in general) isn't well known internationally, but it's starting to earn more of a name for itself. The best-known, and first to earn the DO grade *(denominación de origen)*, which certifies high standards and regional origin, is the red Tacoronte Acentejo. Also worth a tipple are the wines produced in Icod de los Vinos and Guimar.

The Casa del Vino La Baranda in El Sauzal organises regular wine-appreciation courses. Other local tipples include La Dorada beer. Brewed in Santa Cruz de Tenerife, its lager-style taste is equal to any import from the mainland.

THE DAY EL TEIDE SWALLOWED THE SUN

These days scientists can explain exactly how a volcano erupts: magma from the earth's core explodes through the crust and spews ash, rock and molten lava over the land. But the Guanches, living in pre-Hispanic Tenerife, had a more romantic version. According to legend, the 13th-century eruption was caused when El Teide swallowed the sun. The people believed that the devil, Guyota, lived inside El Cheide, as El Teide was then known. One day he emerged from his underground lair and saw the sun. Jealous of its light, he stole it and hid it inside his lair, causing death, destruction and darkness all over the island. The Guanches begged Chaman, the sky god, for help, and the god battled Guyota inside the volcano. The Guanches knew Chaman had triumphed when one morning they awoke to see the sun back in the sky and the volcano plugged with rock, trapping the evil Guyota inside forever.

The legend coincides perfectly with what happened following the medieval eruption. An ash cloud covered the sun, and the only light the Guanches saw came from the mouth of the active volcano, leading them to believe the sun was trapped there. The volcano's toxic ash would have killed many plants and animals, and the 'battle' going on inside the volcano was probably the rumblings following the eruption. The 'plug' that safely trapped Guyota in El Cheide was new volcanic rock.

★ Festivals & Events

Romería de San Roque   RELIGIOUS FESTIVAL
Garachico's most important annual festival takes place on 16 August and the town fills with pilgrims (and partygoers) from throughout the island. San Roque (St Roch), the town's patron, was credited with saving the town from the Black Death, which arrived in 1601.

✕ Eating

 Casa Ramón   TRADITIONAL CANARIAN €
(Calle Estebam Ponte 4; mains €5-7) The wood-panelled dining room of this little restaurant, run by an elderly lady who refuses to make any concessions to the modern age, is a throwback to a bygone era. The music that accompanies your meal comes courtesy of an old cassette player, the bills are written on scraps of paper, dessert comes around in an ancient chest drawer, coffee is unheard of, the toilets are of the long-forgotten squat type and Spain's new no-smoking rule – well, what's that all about then? The food, which is 100% local seafood (and no, you won't get given a menu), is good but the portions are kind of small.

El Caletón   TRADITIONAL CANARIAN €€
(Avenida Tomé Cano 1; mains €7-18) The best position in town, with a vast terrace overlooking the volcanic rock pools. You can have a drink or ice cream or something more substantial; the menu includes a tasty *setas con gambas* (oyster mushrooms with prawns).

Information

The **tourist office** (☏922 13 34 61; Calle Esteban de Ponte 5; ☺10am-3pm Mon-Fri) stocks maps of the town and can advise on *casas rurales*.

❶ Getting There & Away

Bus 107 connects the town with Santa Cruz (€6.85, one hour 55 minutes), La Laguna, La Orotava and Icod de los Vinos, while Bus 363 comes and goes from Puerto de la Cruz (€3.15, one hour, up to 20 daily).

THE CENTRE

Parque Nacional del Teide

Standing sentry over Tenerife, formidable El Teide (Pico del Teide) is not just the highest mountain in the Canary Islands but, at a whopping 3718m, the highest in all of Spain and is, in every sense of the word, the highlight of a trip to Tenerife. The Parque Nacional del Teide, which covers 189.9 sq km and encompasses the volcano and the surrounding hinterland, is both a Unesco World Heritage site and Spain's most popular national park, attracting some four million visitors a year. Most serious hikers have heard of Teide, but few realise beforehand just how spectacular the mountain and surrounding national park is. It would be easy to pass a week in and around the park tramping the various hiking trails and not get bored.

Most casual visitors arrive by bus or car and don't wander far off the highway that snakes through the centre of the park, but that just means that the rest of us have more elbow room to explore. There are numerous walking tracks marking the way through volcanic terrain, beside unique rock formations and up to the peak of El Teide.

This area was declared a national park in 1954, with the goal of protecting the landscape, which includes 14 plants found nowhere else on earth. Geologically the park is fascinating: of the many different types of volcanic formations found in the world, examples of more than 80% can be found here. These include rough badlands (deeply eroded barren areas), smooth *pahoehoe* or *lajial* lava (rock that looks like twisted taffy) and pebble-like lapilli. There are also complex formations such as volcanic pipes and cones. The park protects nearly 1000 Guanche archaeological sites, many of which are still unexplored and all of which are unmarked, preventing curious visitors from removing 'souvenirs'.

The park is spectacular at any time of the year. Most people attempt to climb to the summit in the summer – and with the weather being at its most stable then this makes perfect sense – but to really see the park at its pinnacle of beauty, early spring, when the lower slopes start to bloom in flowers and, if you're lucky, the summit area still has a hat of snow, is best. Many visitors, having driven up from the hot coastal plains, are surprised at just how cold it can be in the national park. Deep winter in particular can see heavy snow shutting the main roads through the park and access to the summit can be closed for weeks on end.

El Teide dominates the northern end of the park. If you don't want to make the very tough five-hour (one-way) climb to the top, take the cable car. Surrounding the peak are the *cañadas*, flat depressions likely caused by a massive landslide 180,000 years ago.

Sights

Pico del Teide   LANDMARK

The **cable car** (☎922 69 40 38; adult/under 14yr €25/12.50; ☺9am-4pm) provides the easiest, most popular and most expensive way to get up to the peak of El Teide. If you don't mind paying up, the views are great – unless a big cloud is covering the peak, in which case you won't see a thing. On clear days, the volcanic valley spreads out majestically below, and you can see the islands of La Gomera, La Palma and El Hierro peeking up from the Atlantic. It takes just eight minutes to zip up 1200m.

A few words of warning: those with heart or lung problems should stay on the ground, as oxygen is short up here in the clouds. It's chilly, too, so no matter what the weather's like below, bring a jacket. The cable cars, which each hold around 35 passengers, leave every 10 minutes, but get here early (before noon) because at peak times you could be queuing for two hours! The last ride down is at 5pm. Be aware also that weather conditions often force the early closure of the cable car – strong winds can whip up suddenly and the cable car can stop running with very little notice. This is normally not a huge problem for casual visitors who've caught the cable car up the mountain as a park warden based at the top cable car station will inform everyone that it's about to stop running, but for hikers climbing all the way up the mountain and intending to take the cable car back down it can be a very serious issue indeed.

See the Hiking section (p142) if you want to tackle the mountain on foot.

Roques de García   LANDMARK

A few kilometres south of the peak, across from the parador, lies this geological freak show of twisted lava pinnacles with names like the Finger of God and the Cathedral. They are the result of erosion of old volcanic dykes, or vertical streams of magma. The

IT'S ASTRONOMICAL

One of the best places in the northern hemisphere to stargaze is the **Observatorio del Teide**, set just off the C-824 highway that runs between La Laguna and the El Portillo visitor centre. Scientists from all over the world come to study here and at its sister observatory in La Palma. You can add your name to the list of those who've seen through the mammoth telescopes scattered here if you stop by between 10am and noon any Friday from December to March. You'll need to make an appointment first. For more information, see www.iac.es.

CLIMBING TO THE SUMMIT – THE PAPERWORK

The key to climbing the summit from the top of the cable car is to plan ahead. There's a permit scheme in force that restricts the number of visitors who can climb to the summit to 150 a day. Until recently, anyone who intended to make this climb had to contact the national park office in Santa Cruz. Now, the park authorities have gone and got all hi-tech on us and it's at last possible to reserve your place online. Using www.reservasparquesnacionales.es (follow the links through to the Parque Nacional del Teide) you can make a reservation up to 2pm the day before you want to climb (as long as spaces are available!).

Should you really feel the need to make life hard for yourself it's also possible to make the application in person or by post via the **administrative offices** (☎922 92 23 71; Calle Sixto Perera González 25; ☉9am-2pm Mon-Fri) of the national park in La Orotava.

You can choose from several two-hour slots per day in which to make your final ascent to the summit. In addition to the permit, take your passport or ID with you on the walk, as you'll probably be asked to produce it, and don't miss your allotted slot or you won't be allowed beyond the barrier.

Note that bad weather conditions can mean the closure of the summit for weeks at a time. The website has details of any such closures and when they next expect it to be open to hikers.

From the cable car it's about a one-hour walk to the summit.

hard rock of the dykes has been bared while surrounding earth and rock has been gradually swept away. The weirdest of the rocks, the **Roque Cinchado**, is wearing away faster at the base than above, and one of these days is destined to topple over (so maybe you shouldn't get too close). Spreading out to the west are the otherworldly bald plains of the Llano de Ucanca.

This is the most popular spot in the park and is viewed by nearly 90% of its visitors. The car park is always crowded, but most people just leave their cars or tour buses for a 15-minute glance. If you plan to hike the relatively easy, 1½-hour trail that circles the rocks, you'll most likely be alone.

Pico Viejo   LANDMARK
Calling this mountain 'Old Peak' is something of a misnomer considering it was actually the last of Tenerife's volcanoes to have erupted on a grand scale. In 1798 its southwestern flank tore open, leaving a 700m gash. Today you can clearly see where fragments of magma shot over 1km into the air and fell pell-mell. Torrents of lava gushed from a secondary, lower wound to congeal on the slopes. To this day, not a blade of grass or a stain of lichen has returned to the arid slope. The ascent of this peak is often overlooked in the hurry to stand atop Spain, but those in the know often rate it as more impressive than the climb to the summit of Teide itself, and it's certainly much less busy

(when we last climbed it we were the only people on the mountain). It also has the advantage of not needing any special permits.

Hiking

For the family-friendly saunter around the Roques de García you won't need anything other than comfortable shoes and some warm clothes. For anything more ambitious, though, you'll need proper walking boots and poles, warm clothes, some food and water and a map and compass. If you're intending to climb Teide or Pico Viejo in the winter, when thick snow is common, you'll need full winter hiking gear including thick fleeces, a waterproof jacket, gloves and a hat, and sunglasses. Poles are an essential item and on some routes crampons wouldn't go amiss either. There are very strict rules about where you can and cannot walk in the park and you must keep to the marked trails at all times (though some of these can be very vague on the less-frequented high-altitude trails). Most importantly don't underestimate Teide: this might not be the Himalayas but it's still a serious mountain (especially in the winter) and its ocean setting means that the weather here can change unbelievably fast (see also the warning about the cable car earlier).

Guided Hikes
Park rangers host free guided walks around the mountain in both Spanish and

English. The pace is gentle and there are frequent information pauses. Even though you'll huff and puff rather more than usual because of the high altitude, the walks are suitable for anyone of reasonable fitness (including children aged over 10).

Groups leave at 9.15am and 1.30pm from the visitor centre at El Portillo, and at 9.30am and 1pm from the visitor centre at Cañada Blanca. Walks last about two hours. Groups are small, so it is essential to reserve a place in advance. Phone ☏922 92 37 71 between 9am and 2pm Monday to Friday.

Self-Guided Hikes

The general park visitor guide lists 21 walks, ranging in length from 600m to 17.6km, some of which are signposted. Each walk is graded according to its level of difficulty (ranging from 'low' – the most common – to 'extreme'). You're not allowed to stray from the marked trails, a sensible restriction in an environment where every tuft of plant life has to fight for survival.

You don't have to be a masochist to enjoy the challenge of walking from road level up to **La Rambleta** at the top of the cable car, followed by a zoom down in the lift, but neither should you take this walk lightly. People unused to serious hiking will find this a very strenuous walk. Get off the bus (request the driver to stop) or leave your car at the small road-side parking area (signposted 'Montaña Blanca' and 'Refugio de Altavista') 8km south of the El Portillo visitor centre and set off along the 4WD track that leads uphill. En route, you can make a short (half-hour, at the most), almost-level detour along a clear path to the rounded summit of **Montaña Blanca** (2750m), from where there are splendid views of Las Cañadas and the sierra beyond. For the full ascent to La Rambleta, allow about five hours (one way). If you're intending on taking the cable car back down it's vital that you allow sufficient time (and have enough food supplies) to walk back down the mountain if the cable car has to close early. Alternatively, make the Montaña Blanca your more modest goal for the day and then head back down again (about 2½ hours for the round trip).

Another long but relatively gentle route is the 16km **Las Siete Cañadas** between the two visitor centres, which, depending on your pace, will take between four and five hours (note that you'll need transport waiting for you at the end of this walk).

Maybe the most spectacular, and certainly the hardest, walk in the park is the climb to the summit of **Pico Viejo**, then along the ridge that connects this mountain to Teide and then up to the summit of Teide. Allow at least nine hours for this hike (one way) and be prepared to walk back down Teide again if the cable car is closed. In fact, for this walk it's actually better to walk to the Refugio de Altavista at 3270m on the first day, overnight there and then continue your ascent to the summit of Teide the following morning as this will allow you most of the second day to descend Teide on foot if required.

ℹ Information

The park has two excellent visitor centres: **El Portillo** (☏922 92 37 71; Carretera La Orotava-Granadilla; ⊙9am-4pm) in the northeast, with an adjacent botanical garden; and **Cañada Blanca** (Carretera La Orotava-Granadilla; ⊙9am-4pm) in the south, which has an informative 15-minute video presentation about the history, ecology, flora and fauna of the park. Both centres stock maps and hiking information as well as an excellent guidebook to the park, but at the time of research the Cañada Blanca centre was closed for renovations.

ℹ Getting There & Away

Surprisingly, only two public buses arrive at the park daily: Bus 348 (€5.20, one hour) from Puerto de la Cruz, and Bus 342 (€4.60, 1½ hours) from Los Cristianos. Both head to the park at 9.15am, arriving at the parador, and leave again at 4pm. That's good news for the countless tour companies that organise bus excursions, though not so encouraging for the independent traveller. The best way to visit is with your own car. There are four well-marked approaches to the park; the two prettiest are the C-824 coming from La Laguna and the C-821 from La Orotava (and Puerto de la Cruz). The C-821 is the only road that runs through the park, and the parador, the cable car and the visitor centres are all off this highway, as well as several miradors, where you can pull over and take *the* shot to impress the folks back home. To see anything else, you have to walk. The C-821 carries on to Vilaflor, while the C-823 highway links the park with Chío and Los Gigantes.

Vilaflor

The pretty town of Vilaflor, on the sunny southern flanks of Teide, is the highest village in Tenerife and makes a superb base for explorations of the national park. There are a number of places to stay and eat in the village, including **Restaurante La Fuente** (Plaza Vilaflor; mains €7-10), which is a simple place with tables set out on the plaza and a menu that includes big plates of sardines and goat.

THE NORTHWEST

Punta de Teno

When Plato mistook the Canary Islands for Atlantis, it must have been because of places like Punta de Teno. It's what daydreams are made of – waves crashing against a black, volcanic beach, solitary mountains rising like giants in the background, the constant whisper of lizards scurrying in the brush... This beautiful spot, the most northwestern on the island, is no secret. But it still has a wild charm that the visitors can't take away. You can fish off the point, splash along the rocky coast or just absorb the view.

Think twice about heading out here if there have been recent heavy rains, as mud and rock slides are common.

Take the highway towards Buenavista del Norte from Garachico and keep following the signs to the Punta, around 7km further on. Bus 107 (€7.85, 1½ hours) comes from Santa Cruz, but to get out to the Punta you need your own car.

MAPS & BOOKS

Maps of the island are readily available. Among the best are those by Editorial Everest. There are an equally large number of hiking guidebooks to Tenerife. Some of the best include *Walk Tenerife* and the accompanying *Tenerife Hiking Map*, both by David Brawn and published by Discovery Walking Guides; *Tenerife Landscapes*, by Noel Rochford and published by Sunflower (the same people also publish *Southern Tenerife and La Gomera Landscapes*); and Rother Walking Guides' *Tenerife*, by Klaus and Annette Wolfsperger. *Tenerife & its Six Satellites*, by Olivia M Stone, provides a fascinating glimpse of the island from a late-18th-century viewpoint.

Santiago del Teide

This small town, sitting just to the north-west of the national park boundary, as well as on the junctions for Los Gigantes and Garachico, makes a superb base for all of these places. In addition Masca and the Teno mountains are just a few minutes to the northwest and the immediate area is littered with fantastic hiking trails, which are at their best in early spring when the cherry blossoms are in bloom. There's a small **tourist office** (☎922 86 03 48; Avenida Marítima 34; ☺9am-4pm Tue-Sat) on the main square beside the church that can provide information on the many fine walking trails in the area. The town is also home to one of the better places to stay in Tenerife; see p220.

Masca

Tiny Masca must be the most spectacular village in Tenerife. It literally teeters on the very brink of a knife-edge ridge and looks as if the merest hint of a puff of wind would blow the entire village off its precipitous perch and send it tumbling hundreds of metres to the valley floor. The **Fiesta de la Consolación** takes place in the first week of December. Villagers wearing traditional dress bring out their *timples* (similar to a ukulele) and other instruments for an evening of Canarian music. The surrounding rugged and beautiful **Parque Rural de Teno** is popular for hiking – if you don't want to go it alone, **El Cardón** (☎922 12 79 38; www.elcardon.com) provides guides, setting out from Garachico, Los Silos or Buenavista del Norte on Wednesday and Saturday. **Hans Wander-Club** (☎629 24 49 70; Avenida Maritima 25; tours per person €20-38), based in Los Gigantes, organises similar tours.

A popular but demanding trek is down **Barranco de Masca** to the sea. Allow six hours to hike there and back, or do it the smart way and take a bus from Santiago del Teide to Masca at 10.35am (Bus 355), walk down the gorge and then catch the **Excursions Maritimas** (☎922 86 19 18) ferry back to Los Gigantes (€10, 1.30pm, 3.30pm and 4.30pm daily) at the end of your walk. If you need to get from Los Gigantes to Santiago del Teide in order to catch the onward bus to Masca, Bus 325 leaves Los Gigantes at 8.40am (there's another at 5.15pm). Take

TO THE END OF TENERIFE

The northwest corner of Tenerife offers some spectacular unspoiled scenery. From Garachico, head west on the TF-42 highway past Buenavista del Norte and down the TF-445 to the lonely, solitary **Punta de Teno**.

You'll have to return to Buenavista to catch the TF-436 mountain highway to Santiago del Teide. Curve after hairpin curve obligates you to slow down and enjoy the view. Terraced valleys appear behind rugged mountains, and **Masca** makes the perfect pit stop. When the highway reaches Santiago, you can head either north on the TF-28 towards Garachico, or south towards Los Gigantes, where signs point the way down to **Playa de la Arena**, a sandless beach that's nearly as pretty as Punta de Teno, though more developed.

You'll need at least a full morning to complete this route.

note of the warning sign at the start of this hike which advises that the route is not totally safe and that you undertake the hike at your own risk. Do not attempt this hike if there is even the remotest chance of rain or strong winds as the risk of rock falls and land slides is very high. If you are intending to catch the water taxi back to Los Gigantes at the end of the walk then it's advisable to take your mobile phone with you and call them if you're going to be late: they will wait for you if they know you're coming. There are sections of this hike that vertigo sufferers will have real problems traversing.

There are two 355 buses (€1.30, 30 minutes) each day to/from Santiago del Teide. The drive to Masca is so dramatic that it'll make the eyes of vertigo sufferers slam shut and tummies start twisting up in fear. However, for your own good we'd suggest you do resist the urge to shut your eyes!

Los Gigantes & Puerto de Santiago

POP 5750

These two towns have merged into one, and a worrying number of cranes can only mean more building is under way, but for the moment at least the low-rise, and low-key, town that sprawls along the rocky, cove-infested coastline is a million miles from Las Américas and is certainly one of the more attractive resort towns in Tenerife. Just to the north of the town rise the awesome **Acantilados de los Gigantes** (Cliffs of the Giants) rock walls that soar up to 600m out of the ocean. The submerged base of these cliffs is a haven for marine life, making this one of the island's supreme diving areas.

The best views of the cliffs are from out at sea (there's no shortage of companies offering short cruises) and from **Playa de los Gigantes**, a tiny volcanic beach beside Los Gigantes' port that offers a breathtaking view. If you are looking for more sunbed space, head to Playa de la Arena, a larger volcanic beach in Puerto de Santiago. Both resorts have a large British expatriate community, which means plenty of restaurants serving beans on toast.

🏃 Activities

This is the best place on the island for diving with abundant marine life. **Los Gigantes Diving Centre** (✆922 86 04 31; www.divingtenerife.co.uk; Los Gigantes Harbour; dive with equipment rental €45, introductory dive €55; ⊙9.30am-5pm Mon-Sat), an English-owned outfit, has been diving here for more than a decade. Dive excursions are run at 10am and 2pm. It also offers night dives and the opportunity to hand feed sting rays.

Equally popular are whale and dolphin trips. The waters between western Tenerife and La Gomera are among the world's best for spotting these amazing creatures. One reputable outfit is **Katrin** (✆922 86 03 32; www.dolphinwhalewatch.com; Los Gigantes Harbour; 2hr safari €25; ⊙11.30am-1.35pm), which conducts marine biology research and also takes out groups with special needs. **Nashíra Uno** (✆922 86 19 18; www.maritima acantilados.com; Los Gigantes Harbour; 2/3hr whale & dolphin cruise €25/35; ⊙11am, 2pm & 6pm) has several daily whale- and dolphin-watching trips and also offers taxi boat services from Masca back to Los Gigantes (€10).

For information on hiking tour companies based here see the Masca section.

BIOCLIMATIC HOUSING

As if to compensate for the possible environmental degradation caused by the port (see p148), Granadilla is the home of a new state-of-the-art bioclimatic housing complex. The 25 houses, which are available to rent, have been built using recycled and recyclable materials, use renewable energy for all their power, water and waste processing and are 100% carbon-dioxide free.

✗ Eating

You won't be hard-pressed to find a restaurant (most are by Los Gigantes Marina or along the Avenida Marítima), but there are slim pickings for truly good ones.

El Mesón   TRADITIONAL CANARIAN **€€**
(☏922 86 04 76; Calle La Vigilia; mains €10-14) Locals rate this large restaurant, with walls lined in wine bottles, as one of the best in town and the owner, who's quite a character, could talk the hind legs off a donkey. It serves an excellent array of seafood and traditional Canarian and mainland meat dishes (give 48 hours notice and it can prepare you a whole suckling pig).

El Baco de Nino   SEAFOOD **€€**
(Paseo Marítimo, Puerto Santiago; mains €10-15) Seaside-facing restaurant that's a little more expensive than others but its seafood gets votes of confidence from locals. The indoor seating area is fairly formal or you can get casual on the sunny terrace. The baby octopus is well worth slurping down.

**El Rincón de
Juan Carlos**   MODERN CANARIAN **€€€**
(☏922 86 80 40; Pasaje de Jacaranda 2; menús from €27; ☺dinner Mon-Sat) If you're all set to splurge, this formal restaurant is just off the main plaza in Los Gigantes. Try one of the sumptuous fit-for-a-King-Juan-Carlos menús or, if you're missing a McDonald's, try the duck burger with mustard and local cheeses. Advance reservations are a good idea.

❶ Information

The **tourist office** (☏922 86 03 48; Avenida Marítima, local 34; ☺9.30am-4.30pm Mon-Fri, to 12.30pm Sat) is on the 2nd floor of the shopping centre across from Playa de la Arena.

❶ Getting There & Around

Bus 473 (€3.75, 1¼ hours) comes and goes from Los Cristianos, and Bus 325 (€6, 1¾ hours, six daily) travels from Puerto de la Cruz. For those with wheels, it's a well-marked 40km drive from Los Cristianos.

THE EAST

The east coast of Tenerife is the forgotten coast of the island and at first glance that's hardly surprising: the landscape of the east is dry, dusty and sterile, but it is speckled with bright and colourful little villages which bring life to the otherwise stark surroundings. If you have the time then it pays to explore this region a little more. There's some pleasant low-key beach towns and a much more local vibe than can be found in the international resorts of the south coast. If you're still adamant about driving straight on past then at least do yourself a favour by taking the winding TF-28 highway, formerly the principal thoroughfare, which crawls along the mountain ridge above the coast. The alternative is a very busy motorway (the TF-1), which cruises down Tenerife's eastern coast, linking Santa Cruz to the resorts of the south in an easy 40-minute drive.

Candelaria
POP 16,000

Just 18km south of Santa Cruz is Candelaria, a busy little village where the only real claim to fame is the basilica, home to the patron saint of the entire Canary archipelago. The ornate 1950s **Basílica de Nuestra Señora de Candelaria** (☺7.30am-1pm & 3-7.30pm) sits at the edge of the town centre, overlooking a rocky beach and flanked by a plaza where nine huge statues of Guanche warriors stand guard. During the official festivities for the **Virgen de la Candelaria** celebration on 15 August, this plaza fills with pilgrims and partygoers from all over the islands. The town centre is a hop and skip north of the basilica and is a jolly seaside town overlooking a black, volcanic-sand beach. It's much more popular with locals on day trips out of Santa Cruz than it is with foreign tourists.

A couple of kilometres north of the basilica you'll find **Las Caletillas**, which is technically a separate town, although you would never know it. It's here that you'll discover a couple of hotels, places to eat and the best swimming beach. At the far northern end of the Las Caletillas strip, cheery **Meson Las Ruedas** (Avenida Generalismo s/n, Las Caletillas; mains €7) is popular with locals on account of its large portions of fresh fish, prawns, squid, octopus and other underwater delights.

The **tourist office** (☎922 50 04 15; Plaza CIT; ⊗9am-2pm & 4.30-7pm Mon-Fri) is located at the northern end of town, beside Hotel Tenerife Tour. There's another, smaller **office** (⊗9am-2pm & 3-5pm Mon-Fri) just north of the basilica.

If you're driving, take exit 9 of the TF-1 motorway. Buses 122, 123, 124 and 131 (€1.95, 30 minutes) connect the town with Santa Cruz.

Güímar & Around

POP 16,000

A rural town with views of a gauzy blue ocean in the distance, Güímar's centre is well kept and pleasant for a stroll. Most people come to see the **Pirámides de Güímar** (☎922 51 45 10; www.piramidesde guimar.net; Calle Chacona; adult/under 8yr/9-12yr €10.50/free/5.55; ⊗9.30am-6pm), featuring much-restored pyramid ruins that explore an intriguing question: could the Canarios have had contact with America before Columbus famously sailed the ocean blue? This theory was developed by renowned Norwegian scientist Thor Heyerdahl, who lived on Tenerife until his death in 2002 and based his ideas on the Mayan-like pyramids discovered in Güímar. As interesting as the pyramids and the museum are it is quite an expensive family afternoon out.

The roughly hourly buses 120 and 121 (€2.85, 50 minutes) from Santa Cruz stop at the Güímar bus station, a few blocks from the pyramids.

About 12km further south is **El Escobonal** and the **Archeological & Ethnographical Museum of Agache** (Plaza El Escobonal; ⊗5-8pm Mon-Fri), displaying all kinds of odds and ends related to Guanche and island culture. Note that the opening hours are very erratic. Continue on to **Fasnia** and the tiny **Ermita de la Virgen de los Dolores**, a chapel perched on a hill at the edge of town (off the TF-620 highway). It's usually closed, but is worth the short drive up for the panoramic views of the harsh, dry landscape.

Keep on the TF-620 past the *ermita* to reach **Roques de Fasnia**, a little town carved into the volcanic cliff. There's a tranquil black-sand beach that's rarely crowded. A bit further south is **Porís de Abona**, a charming little fishing village albeit surrounded by new housing. There's an attractive cove here, complete with fishing boats and sandy beach where you can take a dip. We rate this as one of the most attractive beaches on the east coast. German-owned **Café al Mar** (☎626 39 00 96) enjoys prime position and is good for pitta bread sandwiches and the like. The owner, Juliane, also has apartments to rent.

El Médano

Not yet squashed by steamroller development, El Médano is a world-class spot for windsurfers and kiteboarders. The laid-back atmosphere they bring with them gives the place a dab of bohemian character and it's altogether a much more pleasant place to stay than nearby

---

THE VIRGIN OF CANDELARIA

In 1392, a century before Tenerife was conquered, a statue of the Virgin Mary holding a *candela* (candlestick) washed up on the shore near modern-day Candelaria. The Guanche shepherds who found the statue took it to their king and, according to legend, the people worshipped it. When the Spanish conquered the island a century later, they deemed the statue miraculous, and in 1526 Commander Pedro Fernández de Lugo ordered a sanctuary be built. The logical explanation of the 'miracle' is that the statue was either the figurehead from a wrecked ship, or a Virgin brought by French or Portuguese sailors, who had been on the island before the Spanish conquest. In either case, the statue was swept away by a violent storm in 1826 and never found. The ornate statue that is today swathed in robes in the Basílica de Nuestra Señora de Candelaria was carved soon after by local artist Fernando Estévenez. On 15 August, the day she was supposedly found by the Guanches, the Virgin is honoured by processions, numerous Masses and a kitschy re-enactment of costumed 'Guanches' worshipping her.

Las Américas. The resort boasts the longest beach in Tenerife (2km), lined by a wooden boardwalk – ideal for evening strolls, but that same wind that makes it so good for windsurfing makes it less than ideal for sunbathing.

Activities

The sails of windsurfers and kiteboarders speckle the horizon here. There are several companies that offer classes and equipment rental, but novices note that the winds are very strong and challenge even the pros. You can rent windsurf equipment or sign up for courses at the **Surf Center Playa Sur** (☎922 17 66 88; www.surfcenter.info; lessons from €60; ⏰10.30am-7pm), just beyond Hotel Playa Sur Tenerife.

Another option for kiteboarding is the **Azul Kite School** (☎922 17 83 14; www.azulkiteboarding.com; Paseo Mercedes Roja 26; course from €145; ⏰11am-1pm & 4-7pm Tue-Sat, 11am-8pm Tue-Sat in summer).

If you prefer to live life under the waves rather than above them, **Descubare Atlantico** (☎659 19 03 68; www.descubare-atlantico .com; Calle Pescadores) offers discovery dives (€55) as well as full courses (€240 to €355).

Eating

Timón SEAFOOD €

(☎666 27 90 50; Calle Marcial García s/n; tapas €2) If you're lucky you may be able to grab one of just two outside tables on a weeny terrace above the surf. You don't have to push the boat out to sample the delicious seafood tapas here. It's also the perfect spot for a sunset *mojito* (€2.50) or three.

Café M INTERNATIONAL €

(☎699 94 73 94; Paseo Mercedes Roja 14; mains €4-8) A cheery, German-run restaurant with healthy salads, pasta and wraps, plus a terrace overlooking the surfers.

ℹ Information

Tourist office (☎922 17 60 02; Plaza Príncipes España; ⏰9am-3pm Mon-Fri, to 1pm Sat)

ℹ Getting There & Away

El Médano is just east of the Tenerife Sur airport, off exit 22 of the TF-1. Bus 470 (€3.05, one hour 35 minutes) leaves hourly to Los Cristianos, and Bus 116 (€6.20, one hour 10 minutes) leaves every two hours from Santa Cruz.

GRANADILLA PORT CONTROVERSY

Santa Cruz de Tenerife's current double-whammy position as the island's major port and capital may soon be toppled by a controversial new port project in Granadilla in the southeast of the island. Upon completion, this is predicted to be the fifth-largest port in Spain, comprising a 2.5km-long, 55m-deep breakwater, a 26-hectare area for containers, a 200-sq-metre area for general merchandise and a commercial port area of 19.5 hectares.

Despite protests from Greenpeace and local environmental agency **Ben Magec** (www.benmagec.org, in Spanish), the Commission of the EU granted approval for the controversial project in late 2006 after four years of debate. Paraphrasing European commissioner Stavros Dimas, he explained that because Tenerife is a small island, it is highly dependent on an efficient maritime transport system. He added that the main Santa Cruz port is no longer able to cope with the increasingly heavy workload of containers, thus the construction of the industrial port of Granadilla is essential to guarantee the economic security of the island in the future.

The flip side of this comes from the environmentalists who cite that the project will destroy 5km of coastline and negatively impact the island's emblematic beaches of El Médano and La Tejita. The new port is also predicted to have a severe impact on the biodiversity on the island, the natural flora and fauna, as well as local fishing and archaeological remains. According to Ben Magec, the current port is of a sufficient size to serve the island and is already integrated into the city's infrastructure. In its view, the intent of the politicians is to transform Santa Cruz into a leisure port for cruise liners.

Since the EU granted approval for the project, the arguments for and against have swayed back and forth and in and out of all manner of courts. At the time of writing the environmentalists have the upper hand and the project has been put on hold, but supporters of the project are vowing to fight on.

Los Cristianos, Playa de las Américas & Costa Adeje

POP AROUND 150,000

Don't forget to wear your shades when you first hit Tenerife's southwestern tip. You'll need them, not just against the blinding sunshine, but also the accompanying dazzle of neon signs, shimmering sand and lobster-pink northern Europeans. Large multipool resorts with all-you-can-eat buffets have turned what was a sleepy fishing coast into a mega-moneymaking resort. The sweeping, sandy beaches are some of the most lively and child-friendly on the island. The nightlife is for those with high energy and high spirits and there is a predictably dizzying array of restaurants. Where else can you eat in an 'authentic Mexican Cantina' for lunch, a 'real Parisian café' for dinner and have a drink in a blarney-themed Irish pub afterwards? Of course, all that variety leaves little room for Spanish culture to shine through.

Los Cristianos, where the old town still retains – barely – the feel of a fishing village, is the most southerly of the resorts. Just beyond is Playa de las Américas, with its high-rise hotels, glossy shopping centres and Las Vegas–style fake Roman statues and pyramids. The northern part of Las Américas is by far the most tacky and seedy part of the entire strip. The Costa Adeje flows seamlessly north of here and is home to luxury hotels and a better class of beach.

Many independent travellers bound for the western islands end up having to spend at least one night here and most aim straight for Los Cristianos, which has the best facilities for independent travellers.

The free tourist-office map is helpful, but if you're confused, do what the locals do – orientate yourself by the hotels and large buildings.

👁 Sights

Siam Park AMUSEMENT PARK
(📞902 06 00 00; www.siampark.net; Autopista del Sur exit 28; adult/3-11 yr €30/19.50; ⏰10am-6pm Apr-Oct, to 5pm Nov-Mar) Southern Tenerife's biggest theme park is the impressive Siam Park, which offers a chance to throw yourself down a 28m-high vertical waterslide,

---

Despite all the adverse publicity and warnings from local tourist offices, timeshare touts in this holiday-heaven resort continue to convince tourists that their scratch card is the one in a hundred/thousand/million winner! And the prize (usually a bottle of cheap champagne) can, of course, only be collected in person from the resort. If you go (don't!), be prepared to spend a minimum of three hours at the resort and be subjected to some of the most aggressive high-pressure sales methods employed in the world. Many people are simply unable to resist. If you do go to a presentation, don't take your chequebook, credit cards or any cash with you. Also be wary of the discount holiday-club scam. The promise is that, once you have made an initial payment, you will benefit from discounted accommodation, airline tickets, car rentals and cruises. In fact, this product is even worse than timeshare and that first payment will bring you nothing in return, except grief.

---

surf in a swimming pool, get spat out of the guts of a dragon and buy tat at a floating market in Bangkok.

🏃 Activities

The 2800 average hours of yearly sunshine mean that beaches are the star turn here, but if you just can't take another day of lying prone on a sunbed, there are other, more mildly energetic options.

Diving

The volcanic coast here makes for excellent diving, and calm waters means that even a first-timer can have a thrilling 'try dive' in the ocean. A standard dive runs upwards of €35, though the per-dive rate drops if you're planning several days of diving.

Aqua Marina DIVING
(Map p150; 📞922 79 79 44; www.aquamarina divingtenerife.com; Playa de la Vistas, Playa de las Américas; ⏰9am-6pm) Offers the standard array of boat dives, courses and speciality dives as well as plain old snorkelling for those who don't want to get their hair wet.

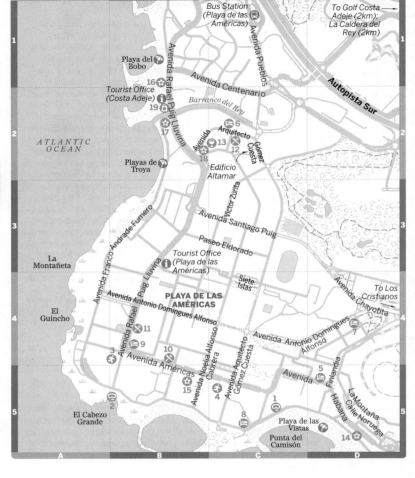

0   400 m
0   0.2 miles

To Golf Costa Adeje (2km); La Caldera del Rey (2km)

Bus Station (Playa de las Américas)

Avenida Pueblos

Autopista Sur

Playa del Bobo

Avenida Rafael Puig Lluvina

16
Tourist Office (Costa Adeje)
19
17

Avenida Centenario

Barranco del Rey

Avenida

6
Arquitecto
13
12
Gómez Cuesta
18

ATLANTIC OCEAN

Playas de Troya

Edificio Altamar

Víctor Zurita

Avenida Santiago Puig

Paseo Eldorado

La Montañeta

Tourist Office (Playa de las Américas)

Siete Islas

To Los Cristianos

Avenida Chayofita

El Guincho

Avenida Franco Andrade Fumero

Avenida Rafael Puig Lluvina

PLAYA DE LAS AMÉRICAS

Avenida Antonio Domingues Alfonso

Avenida Antonio Domingues Alfonso

11
9
10
3
15
4
Avenida Américas

Avenida Noelia Alfonso Cabrera

Avenida Arquitecto Gómez Cuesta

Avenida

Finlandia

La Montaña Calle Noruega

Habana

El Cabezo Grande

2

8
1
Playa de las Vistas
Punta del Camisón
14
5

Fun Dive Tenerife   DIVING
(Map p150; ☑645 90 87 56; www.fun-dive-tenerife .com, in German; Hotel Park Club Europe, Playa de las Américas; ☺9am-6pm) Has diving classes for children as well as PADI-regulated night diving trips. It's very much aimed at German-speaking visitors.

Sailing & Surfing

You won't have to sail far from shore before the hotel jungle of Tenerife's largest resort melts into the gentle slopes of the island. Rent a boat, take an excursion or sign up for a whale-watching trip and cruise the waters between Tenerife and La Gomera with the beautiful outline of El Teide behind you. The tourist office in Los Cristianos has a list of companies that organise all kinds of boat trips, some of which even set sail on the high seas in a pirate ship – who could resist!

The best-known surf spot in town is the creatively named Spanish Left, which is found close to the K-16 Surf shop. A long and easy left with some hollow sections, it's one of the most localised spots in Europe and is dominated by a highly aggressive local crew.

Playa de las Américas

K-16 Surf   SURFING
(Map p150; 922 79 84 80; www.k16surf.com; Calle México 1-2; surf lessons from €35, board rental per day from €12) Rents out surfboards and provides tuition for only slightly more than the price of rental.

Horse Riding
There are several riding stables in the vicinity, including **La Caldera del Rey** (648 65 04 41; www.tenerifehorses.com; San Eugenio Alto, Costa Adeje; 2hr trek €50), which also has a children's petting farm, BBQ area, climbing wall and a low rope course for children.

Golf
Constant mild weather means that Tenerife is a place where golfers can play year-round. It's not the most ecologically sound activity on the island (water is a constant problem, and golf courses need plenty of it) but that hasn't stopped sprawling courses from emerging all around Playa de las Américas.

Some of the best courses are **Golf Costa Adeje** (www.golfcostaadeje.com; Finca Los Olivos; adult/child 18 holes €87/30; 7.30am-7pm), **Golf del Sur** (www.golfdelsur.net; Urbanizacíon Golf del Sur, San Miguel de Abona; adult/child 18 holes €85/42; 7.30am-7pm) and **Los Palos Centro de Golf** (www.golflospalos.com; Carretera Guaza-Las Galletas, Km7, Arona; adult/child 9 holes €23/15; 7am-7pm). In all cases the prices quoted here are for the winter high season. In summer you can expect prices to drop by around a quarter.

Whale Watching
Companies offering two-, three- and five-hour boat cruises to check out whales and dolphins are set up at the end of Playa de Los Cristianos, near the port, and in Puerto Colón in Costa Adeje. Most trips include food, drink and a quick swim. There are several such companies but all are basically the same, with a two-hour trip costing upwards of €18. Try the Playa de Los Cristianos–based **Travelin' Lady** (Map p152; 609 42 98 87; under 10yr free; 9.30am-8pm Sun-Fri, noon-3pm Sat).

Fishing
Deep-sea-fishing jaunts start at about €49 for a three-hour trip. Get information from the kiosks set up at the western end of Playa de Los Cristianos or from a tourist office.

✳️ Festivals & Events
Canarian Food Fair   FESTIVAL
A week-long event in Los Cristianos in mid-March showcasing food and produce from all over the islands, with free tastings and an opportunity to purchase.

✖️ Eating
You won't go hungry here. The dilemma is more likely to be choosing where to go for the best quality and good value. Avoid restaurants that advertise their international cuisine with sun-bleached posters on the pavement. There's an extraordinary number of all-day English breakfast and pie-and-peas type of places. There are some hidden corners where you'll find, generally fairly mediocre, Spanish and Canarian food.

On the waterfront in the port area of Los Cristianos are a handful of kiosks, including the ever-popular **Pescaderia Dominga** (Map p152), selling fresh-off-the-boat fish. You can either buy it uncooked to take

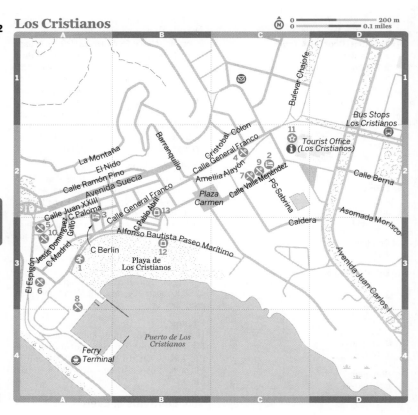

away and deal with yourself or they'll fry it up for you and then you can dangle your legs over the edge of the nearby jetty and eat the freshest and best fish picnic you'll ever have.

TOP CHOICE Le Bistrôt d'Alain

FRENCH €€

(Map p152; ☎922 75 23 36; Calle Valle Menendez 23, Los Cristianos; mains €10-15) Hidden away from the masses, this formal but unassuming restaurant serves quality classic French fare such as steak with a Roquefort sauce or more unusual dishes such as a fish stew rammed with prawns, salmon and veggies. It's one of the better-regarded places to eat in town and is understandably popular with French visitors.

Garibaldi

ITALIAN €€€

(Map p150; ☎922 75 70 60; Avenida Rafael Puig Lluvina, Playa de las Américas; mains €12-20; ☺dinner Mon-Sat) This very classy, and pricey, Italian restaurant has an air of gentility and serves its meats and pastas on a romantic patio surrounding a fountain. It's best to reserve a table in advance.

Restaurante Fortuna Nova

SPANISH €€

(Map p152; Calle Valle Menendez, Los Cristianos; mains €10-12; ☑) There's not a Yorkshire pud or all-day breakfast in sight at this great-value eatery. The food is classically Spanish and, considering the price, is of a very high standard. There's a nice shady terrace to eat on and it's popular at lunchtime with local workers, which is always a good sign.

Bar Nuestro

TRADITIONAL CANARIAN €

(Map p152; Calle San Roque 12, Los Cristianos; mains €5) A cloth-cap-authentic local bar, Bar Nuestro has a barnlike interior and an unwaveringly authentic Canarian menu that includes dishes such as chickpeas with pork sausages and grilled sardines.

Los Cristianos

Casa del Mar　　　　　　SEAFOOD €€
(Map p152; Esplanada del Muelle, Los Cristianos; mains €10-15) Enjoy views of the beach as you savour the freshly caught *lubina* (sea bass), *dorada* (sea bream) and *merluza* (hake). Of all the waterfront restaurants in which to tuck into some seafood, this one is probably the most popular with locals – high praise indeed. On the roof is a sunny terrace bar selling drinks and ice cream.

Bar Gavota　　　　　　CAFE €
(Map p152; Calle General Franco, Los Cristianos; breakfast €5) Opposite the church in Los Cristianos, this is one of the few central bars that retains its typical Spanish feel – as well as a local crowd of regulars. It's perfect for a toast-and-coffee breakfast or drinks at any time.

Rincón del Marinero　　　　　　SEAFOOD €€
(Map p152; Muelle Los Cristianos; mains €7-15) Specialising in local seafood, including a tasty *zarzuela* (fish and seafood stew), this nautical-themed restaurant has all its tables under a covered terrace (proof that there's never bad weather here).

El Faro　　　　　　MODERN CANARIAN €€€
(Map p150; ☎922 75 38 27; Avenida Américas, Parque Santiago V, Playa de las Américas; mains €20-25) For a swanky night out, El Faro fits the bill (although we must say that the fake lighthouse, which lends its name to the restaurant, is naff in the extreme). Watch the world go by from the 2nd-storey terrace as you savour the imaginatively prepared meat, fish and pasta dishes.

☆ Entertainment

Post-midnight, Los Cristianos' action takes place at the Centro Comercial San Telmo, the shopping centre behind Playa de las Vistas, when this daytime-dull little strip is transformed into a string of nightclubs pumping out music late into the night.

GETTING AWAY FROM IT ALL – TENERIFE SPAS

Holidaying can be tough, especially when there's so darn much to see and do. Thank goodness for day spas.

Around Costa Adeje, escape to **Aqua Club Termal** (☎922 71 65 55; www.aquaclub termal.com; Calle Galicia, Torviscas Alto), which, according to its promotional bumf, is the most comprehensive thermal and sports complex in Europe. It has 6000 sq metres of floor space, all dedicated to pampering. Don't miss the Turkish bath.

Vitanova Spa (☎922 71 99 10; www.vitanovatenerife.com; Calle Alcalde Walter Paetzman s/n, Playa del Duque), also in Costa Adeje, offers massages and facials as well as such scrumptious delights as a chocolate massage and an anticellulite scrub with seaweed and grapes.

The **Mare Nostrum** (Map p150; ☎922 75 75 45; www.expogrupo.com; Avenida de las Américas s/n) resort in Playa de las Américas is also sure to spoil. There are those enticing-sounding fungal wraps and electrotherapy for serious spa-goers, and massages and steam baths for those seeking to de-stress.

In Puerto de la Cruz, the Oriental Spa Garden at **Hotel Botánico** (☎922 38 14 00; www.hotelbotanico.com; Avenida Richard J Yeoward 1) has fabulous Thai decor throughout and offers a range of treatments, including body wraps, oriental massages and beauty treatments.

Jazzissimo LIVE MUSIC
(Map p150; Avenida Rafael Puig Lluvina 12, Las Américas; ☺10pm-3.30am Mon-Sat) A jazz and soul club opened by Cleo Laine and Johnny Dankworth a few years back and which has been going strong ever since.

Centro Cultural THEATRE
(Map p152; Plaza Pescador 1, Los Cristianos; tickets €3) Offers a variety of cultural events, such as Cine de Verano, a summer festival of open-air movies (in Spanish) showing nightly except Wednesday. An auditorium acts as a concert venue.

Esencia de Amor LIVE MUSIC
(Map p150; www.esenciadeamor.com; La Pirámide, Avenida Américas, Playa de las Américas) Spanish ballet and flamenco concerts are generally top billing.

Casablanca NIGHTCLUB
(Map p150; Centro Comercial San Telmo, local 17, Los Cristianos; ☺11pm-late) The most famous club in this pulsating strip heaves with gyrating bodies post-midnight.

Las Verónicas NIGHTCLUB
(Map p150; Centro Commercial Las Verónicas, Las Américas) As well as Bobby's, the Las Verónicas block has a number of other loud and boisterous nightlife options, most of which you wouldn't want to take your granny to. There have been problems with violence and drugs here and in a number of the clubs the young ladies working there seem to keep removing articles of their clothing in exchange for money.

La Pirámide LIVE MUSIC
(☎922 75 75 49; www.piramidearona.com; Avenida Américas, Las Américas; adult/child incl dinner €43/21.50) The dinner theatre at the restaurant inside a pyramid-shaped congress hall is more sophisticated than it sounds. There are opera nights on Tuesday, Friday and Saturday, and classical concerts at other times. Check first in case the schedules change. Impressive as the shows are, the food is rather less so.

🛍 Shopping

Modern shopping centres are mushrooming throughout the resorts, but for traditional Canary textiles, such as embroidered tablecloths, head to **Artenerife** (Map p150; Avenida Rafael Puig Lluvina, Playa De Las Américas). **La Alpizpa** (Map p152; Paseo Marítimo, Los Cristianos) on the seafront sells arts and crafts made by people with disabilities, with the money going to charity. **Librería Barbara** (Map p152; Calle Pablo Abril 5, Los Cristianos) is a centrally located bookshop selling English, German and French titles, plus maps and guidebooks.

ENGLAAAND, ENGLAAAND

Many people travel in order to broaden the mind, see new places and explore new cultures. Some people travel in order to relax and get away from day-to-day pressures. And then there are the people who travel to get drunk and do the same things they like to do at home. It's fair to say the northern end of Las Américas is a mecca for this type of British traveller; here are their favourite spots:

Wigan Pier (Map p150; Avenida Arquitecto Gómez Cuesta; mains €4-8) is a vast British pub serving pie and chips and all-day breakfasts. As the British touts outside will remind you every time you walk past, all the food is made with 'good British products'. There's plenty of entertainment to go with your drinking and eating, including live music, quiz nights and cabaret shows.

Down the road is **Lineker's Bar** (Map p150; Centro Comercial Starco, Las Américas) – as the name suggests, it's owned by (but not run by) former England football player Gary Lineker, and is obviously the best place in town to watch the day's football on a big-screen TV.

The two most notorious clubs are **Tramps** (Map p150; Centro Comercial Starco, Las Américas) and **Bobby's** (Map p150; Centro Comercial Las Verónicas, Las Américas). Tramps bills itself as the top club in Tenerife; with guest DJs and a real Brit's Abroad mentality, it's certainly the most memorable – though maybe not for the right reasons. Nearby Bobby's is very similar and was once the focus of a British 'fly-on-the-wall' documentary series. It was a film that probably didn't do much to improve Tenerife's international image!

LOS CRISTIANOS & PLAYA DE LAS AMÉRICAS FOR CHILDREN

There is plenty going on for children of all ages here. Along the beaches, carnival-like attractions such as bumper cars and mini bungee jumping are popular with older kids, while playgrounds on Playa de Los Cristianos and behind the Centro Comercial in Los Cristianos can keep the little ones entertained.

Away from the beaches, theme parks include **Jungle Park** (www.aguilasjunglepark .com; Los Cristianos-Arona, km3; adult/under 12yr €24/16; ☺10am-5.30pm), where the main show stars eagles that swoop dramatically over the crowd. You can also see a range of large apes and cats here, but sadly, like many wildlife parks in Spain, it's more of an animal theme park rather than a serious conservation centre.

For older children, **Karting Klub Tenerife** (☑922 73 07 03; Carretera del Cho, Arona; €14-22; ☺10am-8pm) offers go-karts and video games.

All parks have free bus services. Babysitting services can often be found through hotel receptions.

❶ Information

There are several internet cafes inside the **Centro Comercial City Center** (Avenida Rafael Puig Lluvina, Las Américas).

Police station Los Cristianos (☑922 75 71 33; Calle Valle Menendez 5); Playa de las Américas (☑922 78 80 22; Avenida Noelia Alfonso Cabrera 5); Costa Adeje (☑922 79 78 11; Sector Las Terrazas) The Costa Adeje station is beside the Palacio de Congresos.

Post office (Paseo Valero, Los Cristianos)

Tourist office Los Cristianos (☑922 75 71 37; www.arona.org; Centro Cultural, Plaza Pescador 1); Playa de las Vistas (☑922 78 70 11; Centro Comercial San Telmo); Playa de las Américas (☑922 79 76 68; Centro Comercial City Center, Avenida Rafael Puig Lluvina); Costa Adeje (☑922 71 65 39; Avenida Litoral) The Costa Adeje office is by the Barranco del Rey.

❶ Getting There & Away

Bus

Plenty of Tenerife's bright-green TITSA buses come through the area, stopping at stations in Los Cristianos and Playa de las Américas. Buses 110 (direct, €7.55, one hour, every 30 minutes) and 111 (indirect) come and go from Santa Cruz. Bus 343 (€2.25, 45 minutes) goes to Tenerife Sur airport. The same bus continues on to Tenerife Norte airport. Plenty of other buses run through the two resorts, en route to destinations such as Arona (Bus 480), Los Gigantes (473), Puerto de la Cruz (343), El Médano (470) and Las Galletas (467). The Playa de las Américas bus station is situated between central Las Américas, San Eugenio and the *autovía*. There's no Los Cristianos bus station, as such; the buses stop on Avenida Juan Carlos 1, just beyond the cross road with Avenida Amsterdam, opposite the Valdes Commercial Centre. For 24-hour bus information, call ☑922 53 13 00.

❶ Getting Around

Most of the long-distance bus routes do double duty as local routes, stopping along the major avenues of Los Cristianos and Playa de las Américas before heading out of town.

There are taxi stands outside most shopping centres. Getting a taxi at night usually isn't a problem, as most people choose to walk. A ride across town should cost between €5 and €7.

Las Galletas

Las Galletas is a small resort town a few kilometres south of the Las Américas strip. In comparison to its brash neighbour the town is as quiet as a Sunday afternoon in a library, and for many people that is its attraction. However, the town lacks any real character and the rocky volcanic beach is buffeted by unceasing winds that whip up the sands and make sunbathing something of an ordeal.

◎ Sights & Activities

Wind and water have carved the dramatic rock formations of **Montaña Amarilla** (Yellow Mountain), a volcanic mound on the coast outside town. To get here, take Avenida José Antonio Tavio (beside the Ten Bel complex) down to Calle Chasna. At the end of the street is a small car park and a path leading you down to the water. You can ramble across the rocks, enjoying a building-free view of the coast, or hike around the *montaña*.

Although the actual town is dreary, Las Galletas, together with Los Cristianos and Los Gigantes, is considered one of the best diving spots in the south. For courses, 'try dives' and excursions, head to **Buceo**

Tenerife Diving Center (☎922 73 10 15; www.buceotenerife.com; Calle María del Carmen García 22; dive with equipment rental €36; ☺9am-6pm). There are reduced costs for making multiple dives. Rent sailboats and windsurfers, or take classes, at the **Escuela de Vela las Galletas** (☎629 87 81 02; Playa Las Galletas; windsurfer/catamaran rental per hour €15/30; ☺10am-6pm Tue-Sun).

✗ Eating

The seafront road consists of a strip of English teashops serving granny's homemade cake, nice cups of tea and more than a few fried breakfasts. On a grey and windy day you can't shake the somewhat bizarre sensation of having been magically transported to a Torquay of Basil Fawlty fame.

Bar la Caleta   TAPAS €
(Calle Dionisio González s/n; tapas €3-4) A crusty, old-fashioned place that has delicious, typically Andalucian tapas, including fried peppers and *tortilla* (potato omelette).

Via Moana   SEAFOOD €€
(Playa de las Galletas; mains €10-18; ☺noon-3am summer only; ℗) Get away from the crowds at this laid-back cafe and restaurant that's right on the water. On summer nights live music or a DJ turns the place into the town's main nightspot, with an eclectic mix of jazz, folk, Celtic and rock music.

❶ Information

La Vava Pipi (☎922 73 35 92; Calle Carmen García 1; per hr €2) Internet access right across the road from the tourist office.

Tourist office (☎922 73 01 33; La Rambla; ☺8.30am-3.30pm Mon-Fri, 9am-4pm Sat & Sun) At the western end of La Rambla, the tree-lined walkway that runs parallel to the Paseo Marítimo.

❶ Getting There & Away

Las Galletas is a few kilometres off the TF-1, exit 26. Buses 467, 470 and 473 (€1.30, 30 minutes) connect the town hourly with Los Cristianos, while buses 112 and 115 (€7.25, 1¼ hours) come and go from Santa Cruz.

La Gomera

922 / POP 21,950

Best Places to Eat

» Bar-Restaurante La Hila (p162)

» Bar La Chalana (p169)

» Bar-Restaurante El Puerto (p171)

» La Casa Creativa (p166)

Best Places to Stay

» Parador Nacional Conde de la Gomera (p221)

» Apartamentos Los Telares (p221)

» Finca Argayall (p222)

» Ibo Alfaro (p222)

» Apartamentos Tapahuga (p222)

Why Go?

From a distance La Gomera appears as an impenetrable fortress ringed with soaring rock walls. Noodle-thin roads wiggle and squirm their way alongside cliff faces and up ravines, and the tiny white specks that represent houses seem impossibly placed on inaccessible crags.

Viewed from up-close, however, that rough landscape translates into lush valleys, awe-inspiring cliffs and stoic rock formations sculpted by ancient volcanic activity and erosion, and those white specks reveal themselves to be charming white-walled villages.

A paradise of natural beauty, this small, round island is not the sort of place that offers golden beaches or wild, tropical nightlife. Instead this is an island on which to lace up your hiking boots and hit the myriad walking trails that weave across this lush and spectacular island.

When to Go

La Gomera, like all the islands, is a year-round destination, but there are certain times in the year that make a visit here even more worthwhile. Most people come to La Gomera to hike, and spring (March–April) is when the trails are at their best, the weather neither too hot nor too cold and the hills carpeted in subtropical flowers. September and October are also good months and two major festivals in September add cultural colour to your visit.

History

Throughout the 15th century the Spaniards tried unsuccessfully to conquer La Gomera. When they finally managed to establish a presence on the island in the middle of the century, it was due to a slow and fairly peaceful infiltration of Christianity and European culture rather than the result of a battle. Early on, the original inhabitants were permitted to keep much of their culture and self-rule, but that changed when the brutal Hernán Peraza the younger became governor (see the boxed text, p161). The Gomeros rebelled against him, unleashing a bloodbath that killed hundreds of islanders.

After the activity of those first years, and the excitement that accompanied Christopher Columbus' stopovers on the island, there followed a long period of isolation. La Gomera was totally self-sufficient and had little contact with the outside world until the 1950s, when a small pier was built in San Sebastián, opening the way for ferry travel and trade.

Even so, it was difficult to eke out a living by farming on the island's steep slopes, and much of the population emigrated to Tenerife or South America.

❶ Getting There & Away

AIR

The **airport** (✆922 87 30 00) is just 3km outside the centre of Playa Santiago. Interisland airways **Binter Canarias** (✆902 39 13 92; www.binternet.com) connect La Gomera to the rest of the archipelago, via Tenerife, several times daily.

BOAT

Several ferries and jetfoils arrive daily at San Sebastián's busy port, which is just at the foot of the town. Most people come in on the quick jetfoils from Los Cristianos, in Tenerife.

Fred Olsen (✆902 10 01 07; www.fredolsen.es) The fastest, but most expensive, boats, running to/from Los Cristianos (Tenerife) three times daily (four on Friday; from €29 one-way, 40 minutes). Also sails to Santa Cruz de la Palma daily except Saturday (daily except Monday from La Palma; from €56 one-way, 1½ hours). At the time of research boats also ran from La Gomera to La Estaca (El Hierro) on Tuesday, Thursday, Friday and Sunday (from €60 one way, two hours) but at the time of going to print they had been cancelled.

Naviera Armas (✆922 87 13 24; www.navieraarmas.com) Heads to/from Los Cristianos (Tenerife; from €27 one-way,

ROAD DISTANCES (KM)

	San Sebastián de la Gomera	Valle Gran Rey	Hermigua	La Laguna Grande
Valle Gran Rey	27			
Hermigua	16	23		
La Laguna Grande	18	11	8	
Vallehermosa	27	16	15	13

Approximate distances only

one hour) five times daily Monday to Friday, once on Saturday and twice on Sunday. Also sails to Santa Cruz de la Palma daily except Saturday (from €37 one way, 2½ hours).

SAN SEBASTIÁN DE LA GOMERA

POP 8451

The capital of the island in every way – economically, bureaucratically and historically – San Sebastián has an appealing historic centre with shaded plazas and pedestrian-friendly streets. Its main claim to fame is that Christopher Columbus stayed here on his way to the New World, and you'll learn more about the famed explorer here than you ever did at school, as his every footstep (real or imagined) in the town has been well documented for visitors. If you've just hopped off the boat from Los Cristianos in Tenerife, you're likely to be stunned at just how different San Sebastián feels from its neighbour just over the water.

History

On 6 September 1492, after loading up with supplies from La Gomera, Christopher Columbus led his three small caravels out of the bay and set sail westwards beyond the limit of the known world. When Columbus was on the island, San Sebastián had barely been founded. Four years earlier, in 1488, there had been a terrible massacre in the wake of the failed uprising against Hernán Peraza, the island's governor. When it was all over, what had been the Villa de las Palmas, on a spot known to the Guanches as Hipalán, was renamed San Sebastián.

The boom in transatlantic trade following Columbus' journeys helped boost the fortunes of the town, which sits on a sheltered harbour and was one of the

La Gomera Highlights

1 Explore the fern-filled trails of the **Parque Nacional de Garajonay**, the *laurisilva* (laurel) forest at the island's heart (p163)

2 Be amazed by the tropical flowers, plants and fruits of the lush **Vallehermoso** (p167)

3 Soak up the beauty of **Valle Gran Rey**, with its plunging valleys and picture-perfect terraced hillsides (p170)

4 Take a cruise to visit **Los Órganos**, a rock formation that resembles a titan's set of pipe organs (p168)

5 Unwind at the **Playa de Alojera**, the island's wildest beach (p168)

6 Peer into the well that 'baptised America' and explore the colourful backstreets of the pint-sized capital **San Sebastián** (p158)

7 Munch seafood on the seashore in the laid-back beach resort of **Playa Santiago** (p168)

THREE PERFECT DAYS

Day One

La Gomera is an island seemingly tailor-made for hikers. This perfect day starts from **La Laguna Grande** and weaves in and out of magnificent, mist-drenched laurel forests before emerging, a couple of fairly easy hours later, on the summit of the island and the **Alto de Garajonay**. On a clear day Tenerife's El Teide stands snow-bound and proud in the distance and below you the tangled web of La Gomera's forests fall away. Loop back around to your car and head for a well-earned dinner at the rustic **Casa Efigenia**.

Day Two

The northern half of La Gomera is one of the most fertile places in the Canary Islands, and a day spent exploring this area will quickly turn a gardener's fingers green with envy. Start your day among the banana plants of **Hermigua** and learn the secrets of *gofio* (ground, roasted grain used in place of bread in Canarian cuisine) at the **Molino de Gofio**. Next, take the twisting coastal highway to pretty **Agulo**, for a stroll around the attractive old quarter. By now you'll be whistling up a bit of an appetite so stop for lunch at the **Restaurante Las Rosas** and listen to a live performance of **Siblo**, the whistling language of La Gomera. Continue onward to the beautiful-by-name, beautiful-by-nature **Vallehermosa**, where you can finish the day strolling down to the Playa de Vallehermosa.

Day Three

For many people the **Valle Gran Rey**, or Valley of the Great King, is quite simply the best reason for coming to La Gomera. This day will show you why. Start your morning taking breakfast overlooking an empty beach in the gardens of the **Finca Argayall**. Stroll to the town port and board a boat for a **whale- and dolphin-watching trip**. Return for a fish lunch at the **Bar-Restaurante El Puerto**, sleep it all off on one of the town's beaches and then, in the evening, head up the valley for a sundowner with a view at the **Mirador César Manrique**.

Canaries' best ports. Nevertheless, its population passed the 1000 mark only at the beginning of the 19th century. The good times also brought dangers, as, like other islands, San Sebastián was regularly subjected to pirate attack from the English, French and Portuguese. In 1739 the English fleet actually landed an invasion force but the assault was repulsed.

The fate of the town was linked intimately with that of the rest of the island. Its fortunes rose with the cochineal boom in the 19th century, then collapsed with that industry, which was unable to compete with synthetic dyes.

⊙ Sights

San Sebastián is not a town of riveting sights and must-see attractions, but just exploring the relaxed and colourful streets is interesting enough. To get a good overview of San Sebastián, head up the road to the Parador Nacional Conde de la Gomera hotel, where the Mirador de la Hila showcases the coast,

the town's square houses and the rough, dry mountains beyond.

In the town centre, most of the interesting sites are somehow related to Columbus (in either real or contrived ways), and they form a route you can follow around town. Begin at Plaza Américas, where you can get a juice in one of the terrace bars and across through Plaza Constitución, shaded by enormous Indian laurel trees.

The tourist office runs free tours of the old quarter on Wednesday and Friday at 11am.

Casa de la Aguada   MUSEUM
(Calle Real 4; ⊙8.30am-6pm Mon-Sat, 10am-1pm Sun) Just off Plaza Constitución, this place is also referred to as Casa de la Aduana and Casa Condal, since at different times it served as the customs house and the count's residence. The tourist office fills one side of this traditional Canary home, but the back is dedicated to the exhibit 'La Gomera & the Discovery of America', an interesting account (in Spanish) of Columbus' trip and Gomeran culture in those times. According

to folklore, Columbus drew water from the well that sits in the central patio and used it to 'baptise America'.

Iglesia de la Virgen de la Asunción
CHURCH
(Calle Real) This is the site where Columbus and his men supposedly came to pray before setting off for the New World. The original chapel was begun in 1450 but was destroyed by a fire. The 18th-century church here today has three naves and mixes Mudéjar (Islamic-style architecture), Gothic and baroque architectural styles. Opening hours are very erratic.

Casa de Colón
MUSEUM
(Calle Real 56; ☉10am-1pm & 5-8pm Tue-Sat) This house is built on the site where Columbus supposedly stayed while on the island, and today it houses a small museum with exhibitions on the voyages of Columbus.

Torre del Conde
FORT
(☉10am-1pm & 4-6pm Mon-Fri) Set in a park just off the coast, Torre del Conde is considered the Canary Islands' most important example of military architecture. Here, Beatriz de Bobadilla, who was the wife of the cruel and ill-fated Hernán Peraza, had to barricade herself in 1488 until help arrived (see the boxed text, below). The fort (built in 1447) was the first building of any note to be erected on the island, and is about the only one to have been more or less preserved in its original state.

Museo Arqueológico de la Gomera
MUSEUM
(Calle Torres Padilla 8; ☉10am-6pm Tue-Fri, 10am-2pm Sat & Sun Oct-May, until 7pm Tue-Fri Jun-Sep) Inside a typical Gomeran town house, this small museum showcases both the island's Guanche past and its present-day culture. Displays reveal Guanche day-to-day life and their social, political and religious structures.

Beaches

Playa San Sebastián is the town's sandy, volcanic beach and is a nice place to relax and have a swim. It's also the site of some of the town's liveliest festivals. Unlike many beaches in the Canaries, its waters are almost always calm and smooth, making it a great beach for children.

Past the port, and accessible via a small tunnel, is the smaller and prettier, though often windy, **Playa de la Cueva**. On a clear day, Tenerife seems like it's within pebble-throwing distance.

Activities

North of town, at Km8.4 on the TF-711 highway, is an interesting trail leading into the **Dehesa de Majona**, the largely uninhabited pastureland to the north of the capital. The dirt track begins near a lookout point, venturing towards the goat-herding villages of Casas de Enchereda and Casas de Juel before winding its way towards the coast and eventually joining up with sealed local roads

---

WHAT A TANGLED WEB WE WEAVE...

Governor Hernán Peraza the younger had long been hated for his cruel treatment of the islanders. When, in 1488, he broke a pact of friendship with one of the Gomero tribes and, openly cheating on his wife, began cavorting with Yballa, a local beauty and fiancée of one of the island's most powerful men, the natives rebelled. They surprised Peraza during one of his clandestine meetings with Yballa and killed him with a dart, communicating the news via Silbo (whistle) all over the island. They then proceeded to attack the Spaniards in Villa de las Palmas, the precursor to modern San Sebastián, and Peraza's deceived wife (the famed beauty Beatriz de Bobadilla) barricaded herself in the Torre del Conde, where she waited until help arrived.

Unfortunately, the story didn't end there. 'Help' showed up in the form of Pedro de Vera, governor of Gran Canaria and one of the cruellest figures in Canarian history. His ruthlessness was bloodcurdling. According to one account, de Vera ordered the execution of all Gomeran males above the age of 15, and in an orgy of wanton violence, islanders were hanged, impaled, decapitated or drowned. Some had their hands and feet lopped off beforehand, just for good measure. The women were parcelled out to the militiamen, and many of the children were sold as slaves. To complete the job, de Vera also ordered the execution of about 300 Gomeros living on Gran Canaria.

near Hermigua. The lonely route can be hiked in about eight hours (one way).

 **Festivals & Events**

For such a small place San Sebastián has a busy festival calendar. The following are just the biggest.

Fiesta de San Sebastián　　　SAINT'S DAY
San Sebastián's festival (20 January) in honour of the town's patron saint.

El Día de San Juan　　　SAINT'S DAY
St John's Day (23–24 June) sees the beach lined with bonfires to celebrate the summer solstice.

Fiestas Columbinas　　　STREET FESTIVAL
From 6 September, a week full of street parties, music and cultural events is held in San Sebastián, celebrating Columbus' first voyage.

Bajada de la Virgen de Guadelupe San Sebastián　　　SAINT'S DAY
Every five years (2013, 2018 etc) on 5 October the town celebrates its patroness saint with a flotilla of fishing boats escorting the statue of the Virgin Mary from the chapel of Punta Llana southwards to the capital.

✕ **Eating**

TOP CHOICE **Bar-Restaurante La Hila**　　　TRADITIONAL CANARIAN €€
(✆922 14 16 01; Calle Virgen Guadalupe 2; mains €7-8) If you've just got off the boat from Las Américas and the pies and peas have left you feeling down, come to this incredibly simple little locals' restaurant, which has nothing but a single fishing net for decoration, and tuck into a seafood feast that costs next to nothing but is fit for Neptune himself. Also, don't miss the *almogrote,* a local cheese-spread made of mashed goat's cheese and spicy *mojo* (Canarian sauce made with either red chilli peppers, coriander or basil).

Restaurante Breñusca　　　TRADITIONAL CANARIAN €€
(✆922 87 09 20; Calle Real 11; mains €7-12) Locals say this slightly greasy-feeling bar/diner/restaurant is one of the best spots in town to try simple, traditional Canarian fare like homemade fried calamari, meatballs and stews. The catch of the day can always be recommended.

Restaurante Cuatro Caminos　　　SPANISH €€€
(✆922 14 12 60; Calle Ruiz de Padrón 36; mains €12-15; ☻closed Sat dinner & Sun) Stews and soups, grilled meats and various mainland staples like Iberian chorizo and Galician-style octopus are served in a tiny patio dining room where plants hang from the ceiling.

Parador Nacional Conde de la Gomera　　　MODERN CANARIAN €€€
(✆922 87 11 00; Calle Lomo de la Horca; mains €15-18) The elegant restaurant at the Parador Nacional is without a doubt the most refined establishment in San Sebastián. Staff dress in local costume and the few, but consistently good, dishes are creative versions of traditional Canarian favourites.

Restaurante El Charcón　　　SEAFOOD €€
(✆922 14 18 98; Playa de la Cueva; mains €9-15) A small and fairly upmarket (for San Sebastián) restaurant dug out of the rock near the shore, El Charcón specialises in fish and Gomeran specialities like *almogrote* and *mojo*.

Bar-Restaurante La Tasca　　　INTERNATIONAL €€
(✆922 14 15 98; Calle Ruiz de Padrón 57; mains €4-10; ☻closed Sun) Dark and inviting, this intimate tavern serves mainland-style tapas alongside pizzas, lasagne and more elaborate dishes such as grilled rabbit.

> **DON'T MISS**
>
> ## MARKET MUNCHIES
>
> San Sebastián's twice-weekly fresh market, the **mercado municipal**, is a good place to get an overview of typical Gomeran goods. Pick up some local delicacies such as honey, busily made by Gomeran bees and considered some of the finest in Spain; *miel de palma* (palm honey), a sweet syrup made from palm-tree sap; *almogrote*, a spicy cheese pâté made with hard cheese, pepper and tomato, and spread on bread; and *queso gomero* (fresh Gomeran goat's cheese), a mild, smooth cheese made with local goat's milk and served with salads, as a dessert, or grilled and smothered in *mojo*, the famed Canary sauce that's another island speciality. The market is located beside the bus station.

A Genoese sailor of modest means, Cristoforo Colombo (as he is known in his native Italy – Christopher Columbus to the rest of us) was born in 1451. He went to sea early and was something of a dreamer. Fascinated by Marco Polo's travels in the Orient, he decided early on that it must be possible to reach the east by heading west into the sunset. After years of doors being slammed in his face, the Catholic monarchs of Spain, Fernando and Isabel, finally gave him their patronage in 1492.

On 3 August, at the head of three small caravels – the *Santa María*, *Pinta* and *Niña* – Columbus weighed anchor in Palos de la Frontera, Andalucía, on the Spanish mainland. But before heading across the ocean blue, he stopped off at La Gomera for last-minute provisions, unwittingly giving the island its biggest claim to fame and many future tourist attractions. One of the things it's claimed he picked up for the journey was goat's cheese, one of La Gomera's star products to this day.

Columbus set sail on 6 September, a day now celebrated in San Sebastián with the Fiestas Columbinas. His ships didn't see land until 12 October, just as their provisions and the sailors' patience were nearing their ends. The expedition 'discovered' several Caribbean islands on this trip and returned to Spain in March of the following year.

Columbus made three later voyages, but died alone and bitter in Valladolid, Spain, in 1504, still convinced he'd found a new route to the Orient rather than America.

❶ Information

Internet@Publicidad (Calle Profesor Armas Fernández; per hr €1.50)
Police station (☑922 14 10 72; Plaza Américas) On the 1st floor of the *ayuntamiento* (town hall).
Post office (Calle Real 60)
Tourist information kiosk (Plaza Américas; ⊙9am-12.30pm & 3.30-6.30pm Mon-Fri, 9am-12.30pm & 4-6.30pm Sat) This small kiosk supplies maps but little else.
Tourist office (☑922 14 15 12; www.gomera -island.com; Calle Real 4; ⊙9am-1.30pm & 3.30-6pm Mon-Sat Oct-Jun, to 5pm Mon-Sat Jul-Sep, 10am-1pm Sun yr round) A friendly, helpful place in the Casa de la Aguada.

❶ Getting There & Away

A fun and fast alternative to tackling the hairpin curves of La Gomera's highways is the water taxi operated by **Garajonay Exprés** (www.garajonay expres.com), which takes you to Playa Santiago (€5, 20 minutes, three daily) and Valle Gran Rey (€7, 50 minutes, three daily). The trip between San Sebastián and Playa Santiago takes 45 minutes by car, while the trip to Valle Gran Rey is 1¼ hours, so water taxi is definitely the faster option.

❶ Getting Around

Bus 5 (€4, 30 minutes, up to four daily) runs between the airport and San Sebastián.

Plan on using your own two feet to get around the town; San Sebastián is very walkable, and is so small that buses merely pass through, not really connecting points of interest within the town centre.

The taxi stand is on Avenida Descubridores. The only reason you might need a car is to move between the centre and the Parador Nacional Conde de la Gomera, which is a short (though steep) walk or drive away. If you're going further afield, though, a car is very useful.

There are several car-rental agencies around, and they will arrange to have a car waiting for you at the port or airport when you arrive if you book ahead. Rental agencies include the following:

Cicar (☑922 14 17 56; www.cicar.com; Estación Marítima, San Sebastián) There is also an office at the airport.
Rent-a-Car La Rueda (☑922 87 07 09; Calle Real 19, San Sebastián)

PARQUE NACIONAL DE GARAJONAY

A jungle of nearly impenetrable green that dominates the heart of La Gomera, the Parque Nacional de Garajonay encompasses one of the last vestiges of the ancestral *laurisilva* (laurel) forests that were once spread throughout the Mediterranean. This wonderland of lush vegetation contains the island's best hiking and cycling trails, and it is an essential sight for anyone visiting the island.

A universe of organisms has forged out a life in this damp, dark forest, which covers a full 10% (around 40 sq km) of the island's surface. As many as 400 species of flora, including Canary willows and holly, flourish, and nearly 1000 species of invertebrates make their home in the park; insect lovers will have a field day. Vertebrates here include mainly birds and lizards. Relatively little light penetrates the canopy, providing an ideal landscape for moss and lichen to spread over everything.

Up here, on the roof of the island, cool Atlantic trade winds clash with warmer breezes, creating a constant ebb and flow of mist through the dense forest, something called 'horizontal rain'. The tangle of trees here is absolutely vital to the health of the island. The trees act like sponges catching this moisture on their leaves and allowing it to drip down into the soil, thus feeding them and the springs of the very island itself.

The frosty fingers of the last Ice Age didn't make it as far as the Canaries, so what you see here was common across much of the Mediterranean millions of years ago. Garajonay was declared a national park in 1981 and a Unesco World Heritage site in 1986.

Lighting fires in the park is forbidden, except in a few designated areas. Free camping is also prohibited. It can get cold here, and the damp goes right to your bones, even when it is not raining. Bring walking boots, warm garments and a rainproof jacket.

✖ Eating

TOP CHOICE **Casa Efigenia** TRADITIONAL CANARIAN €€ (☑922 80 40 77; www.efigenianatural.com; Carretera General; menú €10) Make a point of taking a short detour to the town of Las Hayas, on the southern border of the park, where this local institution serves family-style meals at long communal tables. You eat whatever your charming host Doña Efigenia decides you'll eat, but don't worry it's sure to be hearty, home-style Canarian fare. Efigenia also rents rooms (double €35) and a few *casas rurales* (rural houses; €40) in the area.

❶ Information

Get maps, hiking guides and park information at the **Juego de Bolas visitor centre** (☑922 80 09 93; http://reddeparquesnacionales.mma.es; La Palmita-Agulo Hwy; ☺9.30am-4.30pm),

which is actually located well outside the park, near Las Rosas, and is difficult to access unless you arrive from the north.

Here you'll find piles of information on the park and the island in general, including a very informative guidebook to the park and a 20-minute video. In the centre's gardens and interior patio flourishes a microcosm of La Gomera's floral riches, and a small museum shows off island handicrafts and explains the park's geology and climate. The centre offers guided tours of the park on Saturday; call ahead to reserve a spot.

There's also a smaller information booth on the edge of the **Laguna Grande** (☺8am-4pm), which has hiking-route information.

❶ Getting There & Away

Unlike some other protected parks, Garajonay is extremely accessible. In fact, you won't be able to avoid it if you move much about the island, as the park exists at La Gomera's major crossroads.

The TF-713 highway cuts east to west right through the park until it meets the TF-711 at the park's western extremity. Wheeling through in your own car is certainly the quickest and most comfortable way to move about the park. Bus 1 (€5, around one hour) runs four times daily weekdays and twice on weekends between the capital and Valle Gran Rey. The route runs along a southern secondary road, branching off shortly before Alto de Garajonay and continuing westwards along a decidedly tortuous route, stopping in towns like Igualero, Chipude and El Cercado before branching north again to rejoin the main road at Las Hayas.

A minor sealed road connects the Juego de Bolas visitor centre in the north of the island to La Laguna Grande, about midway along the TF-713, between the park's eastern and western boundaries.

THE NORTH

If you have just one day to spend in La Gomera, you should probably think about spending it in the verdant north, where dense banana plantations and swaying palm trees fill the valleys, cultivated terraces transform the hillsides into geometric works of art and white-washed houses make the villages seem like something from another era. The resulting landscape is postcard-worthy at every turn, but when admiring the views, spare a moment to remember these well-manicured terraces represent back-breaking work by the local farmers –

STRIDING OUT IN GARAJONAY

Walking is the best way to revel in the natural beauty abounding here, so park the car or get off the bus and set out to explore the park on foot. Many of the trails that criss-cross Garajonay have been used by the Gomeros for hundreds of years as a means of getting around the island, and few are strenuous.

Although several guiding companies lead convenient, transport-included hikes in and around the park, it's certainly not necessary to use their services. The park's many and varied access points make it simple to plan a journey on your own and most of the routes are very well way-marked. If you don't have a dedicated walking guide to the island, the *Self-Guided Paths* booklet and the national park map available from the Juego de Bolas or La Laguna Grande visitor centres are both sufficient and the walks they describe correspond to both the park way-marking and the routes mentioned here. Experienced walkers will find the hiking in the Garajonay area fairly easy (but nonetheless rewarding). Juego de Bolas also offers guided tours here.

One popular self-guided walk begins in **La Laguna Grande**, a recreation and picnic area just off the TF-713 highway. The *laguna* refers to a barren circle of land – now used as a recreational area – that has always held an air of mystery. Islanders say it's a mystical place and that witches once practised here.

A longer walk (2½ hours one way) heads to the **Alto de Garajonay** (1487m), the island's tallest peak. The walk begins behind the restaurant at La Laguna Grande and sets off towards **El Cercado** (a town known for its pottery production), then bears left towards Los Llanos de Crispín before winding its way through native vegetation and heading southeast to the Alto. From here, cloud permitting, you can enjoy jaw-dropping, 360-degree views around the island and can even spot Tenerife, La Palma, El Hierro and Gran Canaria in the distance.

If you don't have much time to explore, you can take the easy, 20-minute loop that serves as a decent, if too brief, introduction to the park. This route is a good place to view the park's famous laurel trees.

From the Alto, you could return to La Laguna Grande (there is an alternative trail so that you don't have to completely backtrack) or continue 45 minutes downhill to **Pajarito**, where there is a bus stop. Bus 1 (€5, around one hour) comes by four times a day weekdays and twice a day weekends; it will take you towards either San Sebastián or Valle Gran Rey. For those arriving by bus, or looking for an easy parking spot, Pajarito is also a good starting point to begin a short hike up to the Alto.

Around 15 minutes walk north of Pajarito is **El Contadero**, where another track, signposted **Caserío del Cedro**, leads northeast through a beautiful valley forest. This mostly descending trail (2½ hours one way) winds its way towards the hamlet of **El Cedro**, famous for its waterfalls. It's possible to continue hiking to Hermigua, two hours away. Or, you could return to the Pajarito bus stop via Tajaqué (three hours).

the steepness of the slopes means most work here has to be done without machines.

The curvy TF-711, running 42km between San Sebastián and Vallehermoso, is the artery connecting the towns here, and it's pocked with *miradores* (lookout points) offering gorgeous views. The highway eventually meets up with the TF-713, allowing ambitious day-trippers to loop the northern half of the island and end up back in San Sebastián in time to catch the last ferry off the island.

Hermigua

POP 475

A popular home base for those on walking holidays, the go-slow town of Hermigua, 16km outside San Sebastián, is absolutely dripping with that authentic Gomeran feel. It's also often dripping with water – this is one of the greyest and dampest parts of the island. The town itself is strung out along the bottom of a lusciously green ravine stuffed full of banana plants and other subtropical flora, its houses like beads on a chain running down the middle.

MAPS & BOOKS

The 1:40,000 *La Gomera Tour and Trail* (Discovery Walking Guides) is a fairly good walking map with 70 routes described briefly in English. Other good maps include the 1:35,000 *La Gomera – Ile de Gomera,* published by Freytag & Berndt, and the 1:50,000 *La Gomera* by Distrimaps Telestar. These maps are available in bookshops. The tourist office also gives out several decent free maps of the island.

Helpful hiking guides include *Rother Walking Guide Gomera,* published by Freytag & Berndt; *Walk La Gomera,* published by Discovery Walking Guides; and *Southern Tenerife and La Gomera Car Tours and Walks,* published by Sunflower Books.

◉ Sights

Church and Convent of Santo Domingo   CHURCH

At the heart of the original village, to the right as you enter from San Sebastián, lies this 16th-century church and convent, with an intricately carved Mudéjar (Islamic-style architecture) ceiling.

Molino de Gofio   MUSEUM

(Carretera General; adult/child €2.50/free; ☺10am-5pm Mon-Sat, to 2pm Sun) This is a reconstructed windmill where *gofio* (roasted grain used in place of bread in Canarian cuisine) was once ground. The quick tour leads you around the museum and mill. Afterwards, you can taste *gofio* accompanied by sweet wine. There's also a good restaurant here.

Iglesia de la Encarnación   CHURCH

Further down the ravine you'll find the modern town, centred around this church. Its construction was begun in the 17th century and not completed until the 20th, partly due to the fact that the original construction crumbled in the early 18th century. A public park, complete with a *lucha canaria* (Canarian wrestling) ring (see p245) and plenty of ducks is to your right.

🕅 Beaches

Hermigua winds down to a captivatingly blue ocean where the crushing waves are a bit too rough for swimming (although the odd surfer pops by for a wave or two) and the beach itself feels a little forgotten about.

Better, and even quieter, is **Playa de la Caleta**, 3km southeast down the coast; follow the signs from the waterfront. It's one of the prettier black-sand and pebble beaches in the north of the island.

✕ Eating

 La Casa Creativa   TAPAS €

(☎922 88 10 23; Carretera General 56; tapas €3-6; ☑) With an outdoor terrace, cool music, superb tapas and a priceless barman, this is easily the most popular place to eat in town. The house special is the octopus salad, and after one taste you'll understand why. We wouldn't turn our nose up at the chickpea salad or the chicken curry either. There's plenty of vegetarian options and some gut-expanding cakes.

Restaurante Iratxe Taberna   SPANISH €€€

(☎922 88 07 40; Carretera General 161; mains €10-20; ☺dinner Mon-Sat) You only have to glance at the name of this restaurant, with its 'tx', to know that the food here comes from the Basque regions of Spain's far northeast. Basque food is often hailed as the best in Spain, so it should come as no surprise to hear that this restaurant, with its fabulous cod and other Basque specialities, is hailed as the gastronomic highlight of town.

❶ Getting There & Away

Bus 1 (€2.50) runs four times on weekdays and twice at weekends between San Sebastián and Vallehermoso, stopping in Hermigua along the way.

El Cedro

Southwest of Hermigua, and on the national park border, El Cedro is a rural hamlet set amid farmed terraces and laurel thickets. The ravine and waterfall known as **Boca del Chorro** (also called Boca del Cedro) runs in a roughly north–south direction through the village. The waterfalls are just to the northeast of the village. The simple chapel, **Ermita de Nuestra Señora de Lourdes**, is a 1km wander out from the hamlet.

You can grab a bite to eat at **Bar La Vista** (☺9am-7pm), which offers simple Canarian snacks and meals (€5 to €10).

To walk to El Cedro from Hermigua, ask in town for the way to the *sendero* (trail) to El Cedro and be prepared for a two- to three-hour hike. If you're not up for walking, follow the signs to El Cedro off the main highway south of Hermigua.

You can also reach El Cedro from El Contadero on the Caserío del Cedro trail in Parque Nacional de Garajonay.

Agulo

A spectacular 5km drive north of Hermigua, Agulo is a pretty scrabble of picturesque lanes and tenderly restored buildings. Founded early in the 17th century, it squats on a low platform beneath the steep, rugged hinterland that stretches back towards the Garajonay park.

The town hall has erected a number of information boards throughout Agulo, which trace out a walking tour taking in all the most important buildings. The elegant **Iglesia de San Marcos** dominates the centre; built in 1912, it's a simple temple with a high ceiling and a few interesting pieces of art.

Get a quick and shockingly cheap meal at **Bar Mantillo Los Chocos** (✆922 14 61 66; Calle El Mantillo s/n; mains €6), which specialises in roasted chicken, lentil stew and local seafood.

Las Rosas

Continuing past Agulo on the main highway, next you'll come to Las Rosas, which sits at the foot of the national park. Just before the town centre is the turn-off for the park's Juego de Bolas visitor centre.

The town's claim to fame is being the home of the Fred Olsen–owned **Restaurante Las Rosas** (✆922 80 09 16; Carretera General; mains €7-10), which is a tourist magnet on the main highway. Although the food is not very good (expect overcooked tuna fillet, various meats in overpowering sauces, watery soups), you won't regret a meal here because this is one of the few spots on the island where you can hear a live demonstration of Silbo Gomero. Don't miss the opportunity to witness the intriguing whistling. Reservations are recommended because the restaurant packs out with the tour-bus crowd.

Vallehermoso

POP 1540

This truly is a 'beautiful valley', as its name translates. Small mountain peaks rise on either side of the deep gorge that runs through town, and the green, terraced hillsides dotted with palm trees complete the picture. Like Hermigua, this makes a good base for exploring the island on foot.

Beaches

Playa de Vallehermoso is a beautiful strip of sand pounded by waves and hemmed in by tall cliffs on either side.

SILBO: FOR THE BIRDS

The first time you hear Silbo Gomero you might think that you're listening to two birds having a conversation. Alternately chirpy and melodic, shrill and deeply resonating, this ancient whistling language really is as lovely as birdsong. Silbo, once a dying art, but now being brought back to life, is steeped in history and boasts a complex vocabulary of more than 4000 whistled words that can be heard from miles away.

In pre-Hispanic Gomera, Silbo developed as the perfect tool for sending messages back and forth across the island's rugged terrain. In ideal conditions, it could be heard up to 4km away, saving islanders from struggling up hill and down dale just to deliver a message to a neighbour. At first, Silbo was probably used as an emergency signal, but over time a full language developed. While other forms of whistled communications have existed in pockets of Greece, Turkey, China and Mexico, none is as developed as Silbo Gomero.

Modern conveniences have all but killed the language, but in the past few years Silbo has gone from being La Gomera's near-forgotten heritage to being its prime cultural selling point. Silbo has been a mandatory school subject on the island since 2000, and in 2009 another lifeline was thrown to the language after it was inscribed on the Unesco List of Intangible Cultural Heritage of Humanity. This inclusion will allow more money to be pumped into the promotion of the language and is a big morale boost for *silbadores*.

BEST BEACHES

» **Playa de Alojera** Dramatic, largely deserted and a world away from anywhere.

» **Playa Santiago** A long, calm, cobblestone beach, plus a charming little village built around a small harbour. It's often sunny here when the north of the island is overcast.

» **Valle Gran Rey** This resort has several different beaches with something to suit everyone – from the wild and woolly (and nudist) to wind-sheltered suntraps. Lots of facilities.

» **Playa San Sebastián** San Sebastián's town beach is often overlooked but its sweep of black sand and calm water is ideal for families. Lots of facilities.

Sights & Activities

The heart of town is **Plaza Constitución**; bars, services and much of the budget accommodation is around here. Take time to search out the stone **Iglesia de San Juan Bautista** behind the town centre.

Just outside town towers the volcanic monolith of **Roque Cano** (650m), a town icon visible from just about everywhere.

Past the *roque,* down at the waterfront there's a **public pool** (admission €2; ◷noon-6pm Tue-Sun).

A short, signposted walk or drive northwest from the waterfront is **Castillo del Mar** (www.castillo-del-mar.com; Parque Marítimo), an old banana-packaging factory that has been converted into a beautifully rustic and windblown cultural centre hosting concerts, exhibits and a tapas bar. Sadly, at the time of research, it was closed for legal and financial reasons, but as the owners and many island folk are fighting to have it reopened, it's worth checking on the situation.

Eating

Haute cuisine it ain't, but there are a couple of bars serving tapas and simple meals on the main plaza. Self-caterers can find some fresh produce at the tiny **mercadillo** (◷9am-1pm Mon-Sat), beside the town hall.

Restaurante Parque Marítimo SEAFOOD €
(☎922 80 15 61; mains €6-8) An informal bar and restaurant by the beach, you can order paella, local fish and shellfish here while squinting at the shimmering ocean. It also has a good range of tapas.

Around Vallehermoso

LOS ÓRGANOS

To contemplate this extraordinary cliffscape (something like a great sculpted church organ in basalt rising from the ocean depths)

4km north of Vallehermoso, you'll need to head out to sea. Boats making the trip set out from Valle Gran Rey in the south of the island. The columned cliff face has been battered into its present shape by the ocean.

ALOJERA

This sleepy settlement sits in a fertile valley that stands out as an oasis of green amid dry hills. Past the town itself, at the end of a nausea-inducing and seemingly endless series of hairpin curves, you reach the reward: the breathtaking **Playa de Alojera**.

Arguably the prettiest beach on the island, this place is no secret, but it's rarely crowded. The sweeping, silty black beach is ideal for swimming – at least when there's no swell; if a big swell is running keep well away from the water. Cliffs, rock formations and natural pools offshore lend a sense of drama here that is unmatched on the island. You can eat (in your bathing suit if you like) at the beach-side **Brisas del Mar** (Playa de Alojera; mains €7-8), where the menu is a rundown of every species of Canarian fish, all served in fillets.

THE SOUTH

The sunniest part of the island, the south is endlessly changing, from dry sunburnt peaks to lush banana-filled valleys, and from stern rocky coasts to silty black-sand beaches. This is where you'll find the island's two resort areas – the modest Playa Santiago and sprawling Valle Gran Rey.

Playa Santiago
POP 560

Playa Santiago is a small, ocean-side hamlet with a sleepy village centre and a long cobblestone beach with calm waters. The place is so quiet that often the only noise is that of the wind brushing through the banana leaves, waves slapping the shore and the cock-a-dooing of cockerels.

Until the 1960s this area was the busiest centre on the island, with factories, a shipyard and a port for exporting local bananas and tomatoes. But the farming crisis hit hard, and by the 1970s the town had all but shut down, its inhabitants having fled to Tenerife or South America. In recent years, tourism has brought new life to the town. A huge luxury-hotel complex owned by Fred Olsen is doing more than its fair share to bring visitors this way, and the port has traded bananas for passengers and is now a stop for the Garajonay Exprés water taxi.

🏖 Beaches

At **Playa Santiago**, splashing in the waves, rambling along the rocky shore and marvelling over the peaceful ocean view will likely take up most of your time. You can also head to three smaller beaches, **Playas de Tapahuga, del Medio** and **de Chinguarime**, which have some sand mixed in with the rocks and are known as hippy hang-outs. Head east, past Hotel Jardín Tecina; the three lie at the end of a bumpy gravel track.

🏃 Activities

To get out on the water, you can hop on a cruise boat to go whale-watching. Tour companies include **Tina** (☑922 80 58 85; www .excursiones-tina.com; 4hr cruise adult/child €40/20), which runs tours departing Playa Santiago on Mondays. Most trips include lunch and a swim.

Tecina Golf Course   GOLF
(☑922 14 59 50; www.tecinagolf.com; Lomada del Tecina, s/n; 9/18 holes €60/100) Yet another Fred Olsen initiative, the new 18-hole golf course is the island's only one; it can be found just outside town.

🍴 Eating

Self caterers will find all the basics at **Supermercado El Paso II** (Calle Anton Gil).

TOP CHOICE **Bar La Chalana**   SEAFOOD **€€**
(Blvd Colón Laguna; mains €7-9) This delightful wooden beach shack, tucked away at the northern end of the beach, is part beach-bar with chilled out Latin beats, part restaurant with a menu heavy in the fruits of

the sea, part craft shop and part art gallery. Whichever bit appeals the most, you'll end up kicking back here for hours longer than anticipated.

La Cuevita   SEAFOOD **€€**
(☑922 89 55 68; Avenida Marítima; mains €7-15) Tucked into a natural cave beside the port, plants dangle from the ceiling and low lighting creates a cosy atmosphere. La Cuevita serves fresh local seafood, such as tuna, *vieja* (parrot fish), *lapas* (limpets) and *chocos* (cuttlefish), along with grilled meats, all served with *papas arrugadas* (wrinkly potatoes) and a tangy red *mojo*.

Restaurante Junonia   TRADITIONAL CANARIAN **€€**
(☑922 89 54 50; Avenida Marítima; mains €8-10) A local favourite with a porch out front and a welcoming, farmhouse style, Junonia serves fresh local fish and other local specialities on blue-and-white-checked tablecloths.

ℹ Information

All the town's services, including the post office, petrol station, laundrette, pharmacy, post office, police station and medical centre, are clustered around Plaza Playa Santiago in the heart of town.

Tourist office (☑922 89 56 50; www.gomera -island.com; Edificio Las Vistas, Avenida Marítima; ⊙9am-1pm Mon-Sat year round, plus 4-6pm Mon-Fri winter) On your right as you enter the town centre.

ℹ Getting There & Away

Bus 3 (€4, 30 minutes, up to five daily) links Playa Santiago with San Sebastián. Much easier are the water taxis of **Garajonay Exprés** (www .garajonayexpres.com), which take you to San Sebastián (€5, 20 minutes, three daily) and Valle Gran Rey (€5, 25 minutes, three daily) more quickly.

Call a taxi on ☑922 89 50 22.

Alajeró & Around

POP 325

The palm trees outnumber the residents in this peaceful oasis situated on a ridge high above the ocean. Alajeró is the only sizable village outside Playa Santiago in the southeast of the island. It boasts the modest 16th-century **Iglesia del Salvador**.

A good time to be in town is during the **Fiesta del Paso** in September when Gomeros from far and wide converge on

Alajeró to celebrate this chirpy procession that dances its way down from the mountains.

Alajeró is a good starting point for several **hikes**. The long-distance GR132 trail passes through town, as do the shorter PR LG 15 and 16. The latter heads downhill to Playa Santiago or, more challengingly, up to **Benchijigua**, a tiny settlement amid steep green slopes. Information plaques outlining the walks are near the church. If you want to stay in Benchijigua there are a couple of memorable *casas rurales*. Another option is to take an 8km loop trail to Magaña, along the Lomo de la Montaña and past the island's oldest *drago* (dragon tree) before returning to Alajeró. Allow 2½ hours for the journey.

If you're driving, you can see the *drago* tree by taking an unsigned left turn, 1.25km north of Alajeró, as far as an old farmhouse, from where a trail drops steeply. If you're on the bus, get off at the Imada stop and turn left down a cobbled track to join this side road. Either way, allow a good 1½ hours for the round trip.

Bus 3 (€4, 40 minutes, up to five daily) runs between Alajeró and San Sebastián, stopping at Playa Santiago on the way. The bus stop is on the main highway.

Valle Gran Rey

POP 3440

Bet you can't make it all the way down to the shore without stopping at one of the lookout points to sigh at the natural beauty of the 'Valley of the Great King'. A deep, green gorge running down to meet the island's longest beach, this is La Gomera's tourist epicentre. If you speak German you'll feel right at home, as most services here are geared towards the many Germans in search of sunshine and nature. Talking of sunshine, it's worth noting that when the rest of the island is soaking in a light drizzle the Valle Gran Rey can be happily lazing about working on its suntan.

Before you descend into the valley, you could stop at the **Ermita del Santo** in Arure, where a tiny chapel is built into the rock face and is surrounded by a recently built *mirador* showing off the southern landscape.

Also worth a stop, the **Mirador César Manrique** enjoys incredible views of Valle Gran Rey's gorge and the mountains that loom around it. The **restaurant** (mains €8-14; ⊘closed Sun dinner) serves Canarian dishes.

A few kilometres further on is another of the area's many road-side chapels: the best feature of the **Ermita de San Antonio** is the view from the plaza outside.

🏖 Beaches

Though the lush valley itself is perhaps the best the Valle Gran Rey has to offer, most people head straight to the shore. The beaches here are among La Gomera's prettiest, with calm waters and lapping waves. It's worth remembering, though, that the Valle Gran Rey is often very windy. The beach at **La Playa** is long and sandy, with bars and a waterside boardwalk nearby. Heading towards Vueltas, the **Charco del Conde** is a quieter place to splash and swim. The **Playa de las Vueltas**, beside the port, is the most wind-sheltered – and consequently often the most busy – of the town beaches. A gentle, soft black-sand beach, it's ideal for children, and the water is as calm and current-free as a pond. It also has the advantage of having a couple of bars just behind it; very handy in case mummy and daddy start to get a bit thirsty...

🏃 Activities

Boat Trips

There are a few boat operators offering whale- and dolphin-watching tours.

Oceano   BOAT TRIPS
(⛵922 80 57 17; www.oceano-gomera.com; Calle Quema 7; adult/child €37/25) Regarded as one of the best outfits, Oceano offers twice daily three- to four-hour tours throughout the year.

Tina   BOAT TRIPS
(⛵922 80 58 85; www.excursiones-tina.com; adult €33-40, child €20) Cruises around the south and west of the island, towards Los Órganos. The day-long trip could include some spontaneous whale- or dolphin-watching, as well as a little tuna fishing. Tours run every day except Saturday and Monday.

Cycling & Hiking

Landlubbers will be pleased to know that Valle Gran Rey is the starting point for an endless array of hikes and cycling trips.

Bike Station Gomera   CYCLING
(⛵922 80 50 82; www.bike-station-gomera.com; La Puntilla 7, Valle Gran Rey; bike rental per day €21; ⊘9am-1pm & 5-8pm) Island-wide bike tours.

La Gomera doesn't have any of the theme parks, zoos or water parks that make the bigger islands such kid magnets. The fun here is of a less flashy variety and depends on nature to provide the thrills.

Kids' first stop is, usually, the **beach**. The long, calm beaches of Valle Gran Rey and Alojera, where there is a saltwater wading pool for little ones, are ideal, as is San Sebastián's beach. For kids who aren't strong swimmers, pools like the one in Vallehermoso might be a better bet.

Short **boat trips** are guaranteed to brighten kids' days. The Garajonay Exprés water taxi is a thrill in itself, but even more fun are the real cruises. Trips to Los Órganos sail from Valle Gran Rey, along with half-day **whale-watching cruises**, which also sail from Playa Santiago.

You could also plan a stop in a recreational area like **La Laguna Grande**, a picnic spot and playground rolled into one where kids can happily spend an entire afternoon running and playing.

Ökotours HIKING

(☏922 80 52 34; www.oekotours.com, in German; Calle Vueltas, Vueltas, Valle Gran Rey; day hike per person €26-32; ☺10.30am-1pm & 5.30-7.30pm Mon-Fri, 10.30am-1pm Sat) Island-wide hiking tours for a mainly German clientele.

Timah HIKING

(☏922 80 70 84; www.timah.net; La Puntilla, Valle Gran Rey; day hike per person €25-31; ☺10am-1pm & 5-8pm Mon-Sat, 6-8pm Sun) Can organise longer multi-day hiking holidays. A percentage of profits goes to animal-welfare charities.

 Eating

TOP CHOICE **Bar-Restaurante**
El Puerto SEAFOOD €€

(☏922 80 52 24; Puerto de Vueltas; mains €6-15) Specialising in – what else? – fresh fish, this too-bright (the fluorescent lights lend it a bit of a fast-food air) place by the port is one of the best spots in town to try local delicacies such as grilled *peto* and *medregal* (both local fish). The clientele are mainly Spanish and the menu del día is outstanding value at just €7.

Restaurante
El Palmar TRADITIONAL CANARIAN €€

(☏922 80 53 32; Borbalán s/n; mains €8-11) Hidden among banana trees, a stone's throw from the main highway into La Puntilla, it would be easy to drive right by the Palmar, so keep an eye out for the road sign. Both the food and the atmosphere are comfy and welcoming. Try the *cazuela* (thick fish stew) and be sure to have a chat with the friendly owner.

Restaurante La Islita ITALIAN €€

(☏922 80 61 61; Calle La Playa s/n; mains €6-13; ✐) This convincingly Italian eatery serves just what you'd expect – a variety of pasta and pizza dishes with plenty of tomato, basil and oregano. The daily special is sure to please and it has plenty of options for vegetarians.

Absinia TRADITIONAL CANARIAN €€

(☏922 80 58 93; Calle Absinia, Vueltas; mains €6-10; ☺closed Sun & Jun) A cheery sidewalk terrace is the perfect spot to enjoy the house specialities – *viejas*, tuna fillet with *mojo*, and *papas* with everything.

Drinking

Club de Mar BAR

(☏606 53 91 46; Paseo Las Palmeras, La Playa; ☺11pm-5am) Occasional live music, theme nights and dance classes make this one of the liveliest nightlife options on the island.

Tambara Café BAR

(☏646 51 13 96; Calle Vueltas, Vueltas; ☺5pm-1am Thu-Tue; ✐) By day nibble on the vegetarian-friendly tapas menu (€5 to €10) and by night sip cocktails at this friendly bar, where the sound of breaking waves wafts over the breezy terrace.

Bar Cacatua BAR

(Calle Vueltas, Vueltas; ☺10am-2am) Open all day, this relaxing place serves drinks, salads and sandwiches (€2 to €7) to a mixed crowd. There's a small bar area indoors, and outside is a large, shady patio with a few scattered tables.

ℹ Information

Cyber Dragon (Calle Vueltas, Vueltas; per hr
€3.50; ⊙10am-1pm & 5-8.30pm Mon-Sat)
This groovy music store also offers high-speed
internet.

Post office (☑922 80 57 30; Urbanización La
Palomera)

Tourist kiosk(☑922 80 50 58; Carretera
General; ⊙8.30am-3.30pm Mon-Fri) This small
wooden hut is off the main highway on your
right as you head towards Vueltas.

Tourist office (☑922 80 54 58; www.gomera
-island.com; Calle Lepanto, La Playa; ⊙9am-
1.30pm & 4-6.30pm Mon-Sat, 10am-1pm Sun
Oct-Jun, 9am-2pm Mon-Sat Jul-Sep) Pick up a
map and local information here.

ℹ Getting There & Away

Bus 1 (€5, 1¾ hours) connects with San
Sebastián several times a day and leaves from
the bus station located beside the large traffic
circle at the entry to the resort. To get to
Vallehermoso, you can get off at the Las Hayas
stop and wait for bus 4 (€4.50, one hour, twice
daily Monday to Friday).

The easiest way to move around the
southern half of the island is to hop on the
Garajonay Exprés (☑902 34 34 50) water
taxi heading to Playa Santiago (€5, 25 minutes,
three times daily) and San Sebastián (€6.50,
50 minutes, three times daily). It leaves from
the port.

La Palma

📞922 / POP 86,000

Best Places to Eat

» Taburiente (p179)

» Casa Goyo (p183)

» Restaurante Chipi-Chipi (p183)

» La Vitamina (p190)

Best Places to Stay

» Hotel La Palma Romántica (p224)

» Hotel San Telmo (p223)

» Apartamentos Playa Delphin (p224)

» Pensión la Cubana (p223)

Why Go?

Perhaps more than any other island in the archipelago, La Palma, the greenest of the Canarian islands, offers the chance to experience real, unspoiled nature – from the verdant forests of the north, where lush vegetation drips from the rainforest canopy; to the desertscapes of the south, where volcanic craters and twisted rock formations define the views; to the serene pine forests of the Parque Nacional de la Caldera de Taburiente. No wonder the entire island was declared a Unesco biosphere reserve.

The absence of golden beaches has diverted many travellers' attention elsewhere and mass tourism has yet to make a major mark on 'The Pretty Island', as La Palma is nicknamed, but walkers are one group who have cottoned on to what the trails of La Palma have to offer, and what they've discovered has made them very happy indeed. We're not surprised: La Palma can make anyone happy.

When to Go

La Palma follows in the climatic footsteps of all the islands in the archipelago and is a year-round destination. As on other islands, spring and autumn offer the most pleasant conditions for hiking, with generally clear skies and warm temperatures. As the most northwesterly island La Palma catches more Atlantic cloud, and rain, than any other island and winters in the north can be quite wet. Carnaval (March/April) in Santa Cruz is an unmissable spectacle of costumes, floats and, ahem, talcum powder...

History

Long before Castilla conquered the island in the 15th century, this rugged land was known as Benahoare. The first inhabitants could have arrived as early as the 5th century BC (although there's no hard and fast evidence to set the date), and they set up an orderly society that eventually divided into 12 cantons, each with its own chief.

The island officially became part of the Spanish empire in 1493, after Alonso Fernández de Lugo (a conquistador and, later, island governor) used a tribesman-turned-Christian to trick the Benahoaritas into coming down from their mountain stronghold for 'peace talks'. They were ambushed on the way at the spot now known as El Riachuelo. Their leader, Tanausú, was shipped to Spain as a slave, but went on a hunger strike on board the boat and never saw the Spanish mainland.

The next century was an important one for the island. Sugar, honey and sweet *malvasía* (Malmsey wine) became the major exports and abundant Canary pine provided timber for burgeoning shipyards. By the late 16th century, as transatlantic trade flourished, Santa Cruz de la Palma was considered the third most important port in the Spanish empire, after Seville and Antwerp.

The sugar, shipbuilding and cochineal (a bug used to make red dye) industries kept the island economy afloat for the next several centuries, but the island's fortunes eventually took a downward turn, and the 20th century was one of poverty and mass emigration. These days around 40% of the island's workforce depends on the banana crop, but the tourism industry is quickly gaining ground.

❶ Getting There & Away

AIR

La Palma's **airport** (☎922 41 15 40, 902 40 47 04), located just 7km from Santa Cruz, is in the midst of a major expansion project. Services here include rental car agencies, a currency-exchange bureau and a small **tourist office** (☎922 42 62 12; www.tourlapalma.com; ⊙9am-1pm & 3-6pm).

Interisland airways **Binter Canarias** (www.binternet.com) and **Islas Airways** (www.islasairways.com) keep La Palma well connected to the rest of the archipelago, with several flights daily to Tenerife and Gran Canaria, and more

ROAD DISTANCES (KM)

	Santa Cruz de la Palma	Los Canarios de Fuencaliente	Puerto Naos	Barlovento
Los Canarios de Fuencaliente	25			
Puerto Naos	47	22		
Barlovento	19	42	44	
El Paso	17	22	10	34

Approximate distances only

occasional direct flights to some of the other islands.

BOAT

The **Fred Olsen** (☎902 10 01 07; www.fredolsen.es) *Benchijigua Express* ferry (€49, two hours) is a good option for those coming from Tenerife. The ferry leaves Los Cristianos, Tenerife at 7pm, and the return trip leaves Santa Cruz at 5.45am. From Tenerife, you can then continue to La Gomera or El Hierro.

Naviera Armas (☎922 79 61 78; www.navieraarmas.com) connects La Palma with the following:

» San Sebastián de la Gomera, La Gomera (€37, 2¼ hours, 4am Tuesday to Saturday, 4pm Sunday)

» Los Cristianos, Tenerife (€44, four hours, 4am Tuesday to Saturday, 4pm Sunday) All travel via La Gomera.

» Santa Cruz de la Tenerife, Tenerife (€24, four hours, 4pm Friday, 7am Tuesday, Wednesday and Friday) Travels via La Gomera.

» Puerto de la Estaca, El Hierro (€25, 3½ hours, 2.30pm Sunday)

Trasmediterránea (☎902 45 46 45; www.trasmediterranea.es) sails the ocean blue for Santa Cruz de la Tenerife, Tenerife (€23, 5½ hours, 4pm Friday). The same boat continues onto Las Palmas de Gran Canaria (Gran Canaria) and Cádiz (Andalucía) in one and three days respectively.

SANTA CRUZ DE LA PALMA

POP 18,260

The historic (and bureaucratic) capital of the island, Santa Cruz de la Palma is a compact city strung out along the shore and flanked by fertile green hills. Although it makes poor use of its gorgeous location – a huge car park acts as a barrier between

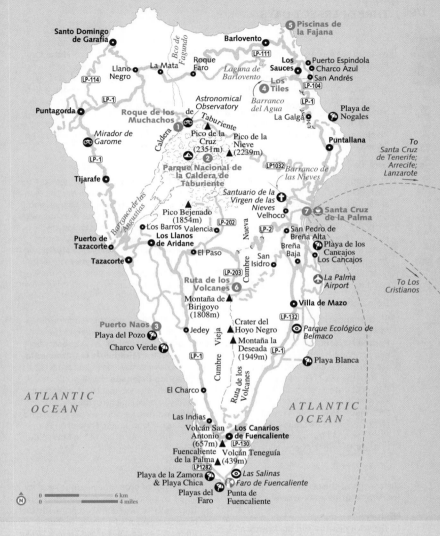

La Palma Highlights

① Peer up at the night sky from the **Roque de los Muchachos** (p188), a world-class spot for stargazing

② Explore the natural wonderland of the **Parque Nacional de la Caldera de Taburiente** (p187)

③ Bask in the sun and the breeze under the swaying palms of the black-sand beach at **Puerto Naos** (p190)

④ Grab a rain jacket and hiking boots for a trek through the enchanted junglelike forest of **Los Tiles** (p192)

⑤ Take a dip in the saltwater pools around **Piscinas de la Fajana** (p193)

⑥ Huff and puff like a moody volcano as you walk along the fabulous **Ruta de los Volcanes** (p187) hiking trail

⑦ Get tarted up like a bird of paradise and throw talcum powder at passing strangers during Santa Cruz de la Palma's hectic **Carnaval** celebrations (p180)

THREE PERFECT DAYS

Day One

Wake up in a room with a view in the romantic by name, romantic by nature, **Hotel La Palma Romántica**, a short distance from the northern town of **Barlovento**. From here drive south to the **Los Tiles biosphere reserve**, a fantastic jungle-like forest, and head out on a morning's hiking under the shadows of giant trees dripping in moss and water. Tarzan adventures over, drive the short distance to **San Andrés** for a simple fish lunch and a poke about the pretty cobbled streets. Next, drive back toward Barlovento but veer off down the steep hillside cloaked in banana plants, to the soaring cliffs around the **Piscinas de la Fajana**. The pools themselves are perfect for a bracing swim and the **La Fajana** restaurant that overlooks them is equally perfect for a sunset meal.

Day Two

Start your day exploring the pretty streets of **Santa Cruz**, not forgetting to check out the town's famous old waterfront balconies. Drive south for a seafood lunch under the roar of aeroplanes at **Casa Goyo**, which is arguably the best seafood restaurant on an island full of seafood restaurants. Continue onto quaint **Villa de Mazo** for a spot of handicraft shopping. Wallet lightened, carry on south through an increasingly barren, volcanic terrain to **Fuencaliente**, where you can check for volcanic eruptions in the excellent visitors centre at the **Volcán San Antonio** and then get up close and personal with said volcano on the short and spectacular walk along its crater rim. If time allows, make a diversion to the tip of the island and the **Playas del Faro**. Otherwise push on up the west coast to the attractive resort of **Puerto Naos** and your night stop.

Day Three

It's the central mountains that really bring visitors to La Palma, and this stunning area really lives up to the hype. From Puerto Naos, take the winding road upward to the **Parque Nacional de la Caldera de Taburiente**, where you can lace up your boots and head out on a half-day hike. The walks fanning out from the **Mirador de la Cumbrecita** are the most popular and generally the easiest. If you've got more time, and are feeling fit, then the five-hour clamber to the summit of the **Pico Bejenado** is well worthwhile. Before you start your walk, though, don't forget to call by the excellent visitor centre to learn all about the park's history and wildlife (and if you're doing one of the Mirador de la Cumbrecita walks you have to register here). Afterwards treat your sore and blistered feet to lunch in **Los Llanos de Aridane**. Then, double back on yourself and drive the short way to **El Paso**, where you can learn all about the secrets of silk at the **Museo de la Seda**. Return to Puerto Naos for a fish supper under the starlight.

---

the town and the ocean – the old town is a treasure waiting to be discovered.

History

In the 16th century the dockyards of Santa Cruz earned a reputation as the best in all the Canary Islands. Ships were made with Canary pine, a sap-filled wood that was nearly impervious to termites, making the ships constructed here some of the most reliable and longest-lasting in the world. The town became so important that King Felipe II had the first Juzgado de Indias (Court of the Indias) installed here in 1558, and every single vessel trading with the Americas from mainland Spain was obliged to register.

The boom brought economic security, but it led to problems as well. Santa Cruz was frequently besieged and occasionally sacked by a succession of pirates, including those under the command of Sir Francis Drake.

◉ Sights & Activities

Old Town   HISTORIC SITE
Chances are you'll be starting your visit either from the Plaza Constitución or from the huge ocean-front parking lot. Either way, you're a short walk from Calle O'Daly, the city's main street. Named after an Irish trader who made La Palma his home, the street is full of shops, bars and some of the town's most impressive architecture.

The 17th-century, late-Renaissance **Palacio de Salazar** (Calle O'Daly 22) is on your left soon after you enter the street from Plaza Constitución. It's now home to a government-run cultural and art centre.

Wander north along Calle O'Daly and you'll come to the palm-shaded **Plaza España**, considered the most important example of Renaissance architecture in the Canary Islands. To one side sits the imposing **ayuntamiento** (town hall; ☏922 42 65 00), built in 1559 after the original was destroyed by French pirates. Across the plaza is the ornate **Iglesia del Salvador** (◉9.30am-1pm & 5.30-7.30pm). Though the church's exterior seems more fortress than house of worship, the interior boasts a glittering baroque pulpit dating back to 1750, an ornate 16th-century wooden ceiling considered one of the best Mudéjar (Islamic-style architecture) works in all the Canaries, and several fine sculptures.

Follow the steps heading up out of Plaza de España to reach the upper town, where the shady **Plaza Santo Domingo**, with its terrace cafe, makes an excellent resting point. The **Iglesia de Santo Domingo** here boasts an important collection of Flemish paintings. Opening hours are erratic.

Head southwest on Calle Virgen de la Luz for a quick visit to the modest chapel **Ermita de Nuestra Señora de la Luz**, one of several small 16th- and 17th-century chapels in town. Another chapel, the **Ermita de San Sebastián** (Calle San Sebastián), is behind the Iglesia de San Salvador. Yet another is **Ermita de San José** (Calle San José), which has given its name to the street on which it stands. From this chapel make your way northeast towards the **Iglesia de San Francisco** (Plaza San Francisco; ◉6-7.30pm), another Renaissance church rich in works of art, the majority being unmistakably baroque.

Wander down to the waterfront to stroll alongside a series of wonderful **old houses** with traditional Canarian balconies. Many of the houses date from the 16th century and have been converted into upscale restaurants. The islanders' penchant for balconies came with Andalucian migrants and was modified by Portuguese influences. At the northern end of the seafront, the **Castillo de Santa Catalina** was one of several forts built in the 17th century to fend off pirate raids. Across the ravine and higher is a smaller one, the **Castillo de la Virgen**. Tucked away on the same hill is the 16th-century **Iglesia de la Encarnación**, the first church to be built in Santa Cruz after the Spanish conquest.

Santuario de la Virgen de las Nieves   CHURCH
(◉8.30am-8pm) For great views over Santa Cruz and the shore, take the relatively easy 2km hike north of town to La Palma's main object of pilgrimage, the 17th-century Santuario de la Virgen de las Nieves. The church sits in a peaceful spot surrounded by trees and greenery, all in typical Canarian colonial style with balconies and simple facades. Walking into the church, however, you'll leave simplicity behind to encounter a fabulously ornate interior. The plush carpet, sculptures galore and crystal chandeliers are the precursor to the Virgin Mary herself, surrounded by a glittering altar. The 14th-century sculpture is the oldest religious statue in the Canary Islands, and probably brought by merchants before the arrival of the Spaniards. Every five years the Virgin is brought down to Santa Cruz in a grand procession.

To walk from Plaza Alameda, follow the road, which becomes a signposted dirt track, westwards up the gorge of the Barranco de las Nieves. It will take nearly 45 minutes to walk up, but coming back is

---

THE SWEET TASTE OF LA PALMA

La Palma's main dishes, like those on other islands, are simple. What the island is really known for is indulgent desserts. Honey is an important food here, and historically La Palma was an important sugar producer. Most of the sugar cane is gone, but the islanders' sweet tooth remains. The honey-and-almond desserts *rapaduras* are a favourite tooth-rotter. Also tasty are *almendrados* (almond, sugar and egg cakes baked with cinnamon), *bienmesabe* (a paste of almonds and sugar) and *Príncipe Alberto* (mousse of chocolate and almonds).

Local cheeses, most made with unpasteurised goat's milk and many smoked, are worth trying. Get more information online at www.quesopalmero.es (in Spanish).

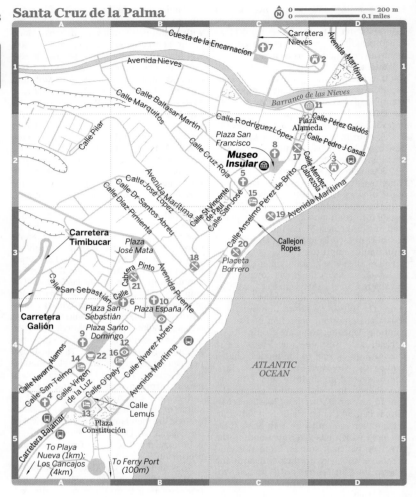

faster. By car, follow signs from the Avenida Marítima where it crosses the *barranco* (ravine), then turn right on the Carretera de las Nieves (LP-101) and continue winding up the hillside until you see signs for the sanctuary. The curve-filled 5km trip takes nearly 15 minutes. Bus 10 (€1.30, approximately 20 minutes) comes up hourly from the town centre from 7.45am until 4.45pm, and less frequently in the evenings and at weekends.

There's a bar-restaurant in the church grounds.

Museo Insular   MUSEUM

(admission €4; ☉10am-8pm Mon-Sat, to 2pm Sun Oct-Jun, to 7.30 Mon-Sat Jul-Sep) Of the couple of museums in town this, the island's main museum, is the most interesting. Here you'll find everything from Guanche skulls to cupboards of sad stuffed birds and pickled reptiles.

Museo Naval   MUSEUM

(adult/under 16yr €3/1.50; ☉10am-2pm Mon-Fri) Gaze north across leafy Plaza Alameda (a good place to sip a *café cortado* – an espresso with a splash of milk) and you'll think Christopher Columbus' ship, the *Santa María,* became stranded here. But no, it's actually the city's naval museum, known as El Barco de la Virgen (The Virgin's Boat) to the locals. At weekends it's only open when there's a cruise ship in port.

✳ Festivals & Events

As well as the annual snowy-white Carnaval celebrations, with the crazy night of talcum powder throwing, (see p180), Santa Cruz throws a few other memorable parties. These are the biggest and best known of the others.

Semana Santa
RELIGIOUS FESTIVAL
Members of lay brotherhoods parade down Calle O'Daly (Santa Cruz) in their blood-red robes and tall, pointy hoods in late March to early April.

Fiesta de Nuestra Señora de las Nieves
SAINT'S DAY
The city dons its party clothes for the celebration of the island's patron saint on 5 August.

✕ Eating

Many of Santa Cruz's nicest restaurants are located along the Avenida Marítima, especially at the far northeastern end.

TOP CHOICE **Taburiente** TRADITIONAL CANARIAN €€
(Calle Pedro Poggio 7; mains €6-10) This is a pure and simple locals' place with no unnecessary fuss. Portions are huge, but don't bother asking for a menu; it's whatever struck the owner's fancy that day, but you can be sure that whatever it was it will be traditional Canarian cuisine through and through.

La Lonja SPANISH €€€
(☑922 41 52 66; Avenida Marítima 55; mains €10-18, menú del día from €11; ☺closed Sun) Inside an old Canary house with balconies bursting with pretty flowers and overlooking the seafront, La Lonja is perhaps the city's most upscale restaurant, with a mix of Canarian, Castillian and Mediterranean fare like paella, suckling pig and roasted cheese with *mojo* (spicy salsa sauce). It can also do the more creative and unusual though, such as eel and prawns in a cream sauce.

MAKE WAY FOR THE VIRGIN

Fiesta de Nuestra Señora de las Nieves (Feast Day of Our Lady of the Snows) is the island's principal fiesta. Don't miss the parade of giants and 'fat heads' (fanciful, rather squat characters with exceptionally large heads), though the high point is the dance of the dwarves, which has been performed here since the early 19th century. Every five years (2015, 2020 etc), the Bajada de la Virgen de las Nieves is celebrated. It's a religious procession where the islanders take the Virgin around the island throughout July and August, celebrating her arrival in each important town with a big party.

DON'T MISS

THE SWEETEST-SMELLING BATTLE

Tenerife and Gran Canaria are known for their, ahem, lively celebrations of Carnaval, but unassuming Santa Cruz de la Palma also has a wild side. There's music, dancing, drinking and, of course, talcum powder. On Carnaval Monday, the good citizens of La Palma bring buckets of white, fragrant powder down to the centre of Santa Cruz and prepare to do battle with their neighbours. After loosening up with a few drinks and a little music, the snowy spectacle begins. Anyone is a target in this all-out war and the town ends the night coughing and blinking furiously, covered head to toe with talcum powder. The tradition began to mock *los indios,* Canarian emigrants who became wealthy in the Americas and returned to the island decked in white suits and Panama hats. Now it's just another excuse for a fiesta.

La Placeta   INTERNATIONAL €€
(Calle Borrero 1; mains €8-13; ⊘closed Sun; 🖉) A charming little bistro on a tiny square, La Placeta has a small menu featuring everything from lasagne to Canary *mojo,* including lots of vegetarian dishes. Downstairs, get sandwiches, desserts and tapas (€1 to €3). Head upstairs for the dining room.

Bar-Arepera El Encuentro   INTERNATIONAL €
(Calle Anselmo Pérez de Brito; arepas €2.50) Cheap and tasty, Venezuelan *arepas* (hot pockets made of corn or flour and filled with meat or cheese) are an island staple. Iron tables are set up on the shady plaza.

Heladomanía   FAST FOOD €
(Calle Vandale 8; ⊘10.30am-2.30pm & 4.30-8.30pm Mon-Fri, 10.30am-2.30pm & 5.30-8.30pm Sat, 11.30am-2.30pm & 5.30-8.30pm Sun) For some of the richest ice cream you've had in a while, pop into Heladomanía, where the artisanal ice cream is made on the spot.

Drinking & Entertainment

Santa Cruz is no mecca for night owls; on the island, Los Llanos de Aridane takes that title. But there are plenty of quiet terrace bars where you can nurse a drink or two. Along Avenida Marítima, which is lined with cafes and *zumerías* (juice bars), you'll find a family-friendly atmosphere. In town head to Calle Álvarez Abreu, the closest thing you'll find to a nightlife scene. Plaza José Mata, off Avenida Puente, also has a few bars.

Cuenta Cuento   CAFE
(Calle San Telmo 1) An old and atmospheric cafe painted in sunny colours and decorated in driftwood, this is a throwback to a bygone age and is a great place to sit with a coffee, watching the world cruise on by.

ℹ Information

Ciberplay (Calle San Francisco 1; internet access per hr €2; ⊘9am-2pm & 4.30-10pm Mon-Fri, 9am-2pm & 5-10pm Sat, 10.30am-1.30pm & 5-8.30pm Sun) Just off Plaza Alameda.

Policía Local (🖉922 41 11 50; Avenida Indios 18)

Post office (Plaza Constitución 2)

Tourist office (🖉922 41 21 06; www.tourlapalma.com; Plaza Constitución s/n; ⊘9am-2pm & 4-7.30pm Mon-Fri, 9am-2pm Sat & Sun) This small kiosk office stocks lots of information about the town and the island, whether you're interested in hiking, festivals, history or gastronomy.

ℹ Getting There & Away

Bus

Transportes Insular La Palma buses keep Santa Cruz well connected with the rest of the island. The bus stops are near Plaza Constitución and along the Avenida Marítima. Routes include Bus 1 (€5, 45 minutes) to Los Llanos de Aridane every half-hour or so. If you plan to use the bus often, you're best to buy a Bono Bus card. Cards start at €12 and represent a discount of about 20% off normal individual fares. They are on sale at bus stations, news-stands and tobacco shops and are valid on buses across the island.

Car

Having your own two wheels is the best way to tour the island at your leisure, and it's the only way to set about exploring every nook and cranny. La Palma is loaded with car-rental agencies, but most are located outside Santa Cruz.

Cicar (🖉922 42 80 48; www.cicar.com; La Palma airport) It also has an office at the port in Santa Cruz.

Oasis (🖉922 43 44 09; www.oasis-la-palma.com; Centro Cancajos local 301, Los Cancajos)

❶ Getting Around

Bus 8 (€1, 35 minutes) makes the journey between Santa Cruz and the airport every 30 minutes from 6.45am to 12.15am, stopping in Los Cancajos on the way. At weekends, the service is provided only hourly. A taxi to the airport costs about €15.

The best way to get around Santa Cruz is on foot. If you come in by car, try to find a parking spot in the large car park by the waterfront, as the narrow streets are much better enjoyed while walking. If you're in a hurry you can catch one of the buses that run up and down the Avenida Marítima (€1) or hop in a **taxi** (✆922 18 13 96).

AROUND SANTA CRUZ

Los Cancajos

A prettily manicured waterfront and a small volcanic beach are the main attractions of this cluster of hotels, apartments and restaurants 4km south of Santa Cruz; calling it a 'town' would be stretching it. Los Cancajos has none of the charm of Santa Cruz or other authentic, lived-in towns, but it nevertheless makes a good home base thanks to its abundance of quality lodging options and agreeable beach, which is one of the best on the island. There's a small **tourist office kiosk** (Playa los Cancajos; ◐9am-1pm & 4.30-7pm Mon-Fri, 10am-2pm Sat) on the waterfront.

🏃 Activities

Several activity outfits are set up in Los Cancajos. Dive with **Buceo Sub** (✆686 75 69 79; www.scuba-diving-la-palma.de; dive incl equipment from €29; ◐9.30am-6pm Tue-Sat), based beside the H10 Costa Salinas aparthotel, or **La Palma Diving Center** (✆922 18 13 93; www .la-palma-diving.com, in German; dive incl equipment €30; ◐10am-6pm Mon-Sat), in the Centro Cancajos shopping centre (on your left as you enter Los Cancajos from Santa Cruz). This last operation is aimed almost exclusively towards German visitors.

Plenty of tour operators are also set up here. **Natour** (✆922 43 30 01; www.natour -trekking.com; Apartamentos Valentina 4; guided hikes €33-45) is probably the best-regarded local hiking company and organises a variety of island-wide hiking trips under the guidance of multilingual guides.

For something a bit less energetic, don't miss taking a gentle pre-dinner stroll along

the seafront promenade. The 20-minute walk takes you past tiny coves and contorted lava flows that have been colonised by hardy plants that seem almost luminous in comparison to the black rocks on which they live.

🍴 Eating

The area around Centro Cancajos has several casual restaurants and bars, many with terraces. Self-caterers can head to the **Spar** (Urbanización Costa Salinas) supermarket near the H10 hotels.

El Pulpo SEAFOOD €€
(Playa Los Cancajos; mains €6-10; ◐closed Wed) This waterside beach shack is the place to come for fried fish, a friendly beach-bum attitude and a long and lazy lunch. What's great about it is that when the kids get bored they can run off and play on the beach while you carry on eating and drinking.

Restaurante La Fontana ITALIAN €€
(Playa de los Cancajos; mains €8-10; ◐closed Mon) Come here for tasty wood-oven pizzas, various pasta dishes and some scrummy desserts (try the delicious almond cake). It'll also package everything up so you can take it away with you.

🍷 Drinking & Entertainment

A handful of bars and terraces scattered behind the Centro Cancajos serves as Los Cancajos' nightlife centre. Although offerings vary wildly by season and night, you may find anything from DJs and dancing, to live music, to a quiet sip-your-drink-and-chat atmosphere.

❶ Getting There & Away

Bus 8 (€1, 10 minutes) passes through every 30 minutes on its way from Santa Cruz to the airport; a second bus does the route in reverse. The main bus stop is at the Centro Cancajos shopping centre.

Breña Alta

POP 6670

Just outside Santa Cruz, this rural, tranquil area isn't a major destination but it is home to a few notable sights, renowned artisans and the Parador Nacional hotel.

Kids will love **Maroparque** (www.maro parque.com; Calle Cuesta 28; adult/child €11/5; ◐10am-6pm), a small zoo where marmosets, toucans and pythons clamber, flap and slide around their cages. It's set in pleasantly landscaped gardens and is a perfect child-friendly afternoon.

THE SOUTH

With a mix of pine forests, banana plantations, agricultural land and barren volcanic wastelands, nobody could say that the landscapes aren't diverse in southern La Palma. The Fuencaliente area, at the southern tip of the island, is home to the most recent volcanic activity in the islands with several volcanic eruptions recorded in the 20th century.

Villa de Mazo

POP 4760

A quiet village 13km south of Santa Cruz, Mazo is surrounded by green, dormant volcanoes. The town is known for the cigars and handicrafts made here and for being a highlight of La Palma's winery route (www .enoturismolapalma.es), an island-wide series of driving routes that take in the best of the island by way of the pleasure of the grape.

GETTING ACTIVE IN LA PALMA

La Palma is a paradise for outdoorsy types, with excellent hiking, diving, paragliding and cycling all available. Many outfitting companies operate island-wide, so regardless of where you're based you can enjoy the activities La Palma has to offer.

Hiking

Don't come to La Palma without allowing a generous chunk of time to explore its wondrous landscapes on foot. With 850km of trails, this is the ideal place for a walking holiday. Several companies offer guided hikes; the best is **Natour** (☑922 43 30 01; www .natour-trekking.com; Apartamento Valentina 4, Los Cancajos; day-long walks with guide €33-45; ⊙9am-1pm & 5-7pm Mon-Fri), a company operating island-wide. Popular routes include the walk around the Parque Nacional de la Caldera de Taburiente, the Ruta de los Volcanes and the 'Enchanted Forest' walk through forest land in the north. The company will pick you up at your hotel or a central meeting point.

Another reputable guide service is **Ekalis** (☑922 44 45 17; www.ekalis.com; Las Indias 51, Fuencaliente; guided hikes, bike trips, caving expeditions & rock climbing per day €38), which also offers hotel pick ups.

It's not necessary to hike with a guide; La Palma offers safe walking conditions to anyone who's prepared and carries a good map. But the beauty of having a guide, other than the history and anecdotes they can share, is enjoying a long one-way trek with transport arranged at either end. Throughout this chapter there's information on notable walks, with details on how to arrange your own transport by bus or taxi.

Adventure Sports

If just plain walking seems too tame, try rock climbing or caving. Ekalis offers a variety of climbing and rappelling experiences as well as a two-hour spelunking expedition. It also offers bike rental and guided mountain biking trips, another popular activity on the island. If you're in shape, La Palma's endless climbs and dips will be thrilling, but if trudging uphill isn't your thing, guide services like those offered by **Bike'n'Fun** (☑922 40 19 27; www.bikenfun.de, in German; Calle Calvo Sotelo 20, Los Llanos; guide service per person €40, bike rental per day €15) offer transport to the top of a peak followed by a mostly downhill ride. All operators can pick you up at your hotel or a central meeting point.

In recent years, paragliding has really taken off (pardon the pun!); the island is considered one of the world's best places to glide. Try it in Puerto Naos with **Palmaclub** (☑610 69 57 50; www.palmaclub.com; Paseo Marítima; tandem glide €90-140; ⊙noon-6pm).

Diving & Kayaking

For those wanting to get out on the water, diving outfitters in Puerto Naos and Los Cancajos will hook you up with tanks, wetsuits and fins. Sea-kayaking expeditions are also available in Puerto Naos and Los Cancajos; contact Ekalis for more information.

DON'T MISS

GREAT OFF-THE-BEATEN-TRACK EATING

Some of the island's best restaurants are a short drive from Santa Cruz. For unbeatable local flavour, it doesn't get any better than this.

Restaurante Chipi-Chipi (✉922 41 10 24; Calle Juan Mayor 42, Velhoco; mains €8-13; ⊘closed Wed & Sun) This is a meat-eater's haven, with a variety of grilled meats all served with loads of *papas arrugadas* (wrinkly potatoes) and *mojo* (spicy salsa sauce made from red chilli peppers). It's located between the Santuario de la Virgen de las Nieves and the village of San Pedro, on the edge of the small hamlet of Velhoco.

Casa Goyo (Carretera General Lodero 120; mains €8-10; ⊘closed Mon) Hands-down the best seafood on the island can be had at this beach-shack-like eatery just south of the airport. Hear the roar of the planes as you savour *vieja à la plancha* (pan-grilled parrot fish) and *papas*.

Leaflets detailing the routes can be picked up in many tourist offices or downloaded from the website.

◉ Sights

Museo Casa Roja   MUSEUM
(Calle Maximiliano Pérez Díaz; admission €2; ⊘10am-2pm Mon-Fri, 11am-6pm Sat, 10am-2pm Sun) As soon as you enter town, make a left to head down to this lovely pinkish-red mansion (built in 1911) with exhibits on embroidery and Corpus Christi – a festival the town celebrates with particular gusto: streets are decorated with elegant 'carpets' made of flower petals, seeds and soil. The house itself has an impressive imperial staircase and ornate tiled floors.

Escuela Insular de Artesanía   HANDICRAFTS
(⊘8am-3pm Mon-Fri Oct-Jun, to 2pm Jul-Sep) Beyond the museum is the island handicrafts school, which runs a shop where you can buy tobacco, embroidery, ceramics, baskets and other goods. It is of course one of the best places on the island to purchase handicrafts. To get to the shop, head into the school's main patio and up the stairs on your right.

Market   MARKET
(Via de Enlace Doctor Amilcar Morera Bravo; ⊘3-7pm Sat, 9am-1pm Sun) You can also buy artisan goods at this weekend market, where produce, handicrafts and a variety of food products are sold.

Templo de San Blas   CHURCH
Down the hill from the school is this imposing 16th-century church, which sits on a small plaza overlooking the ocean. Inside, the church boasts a baroque altarpiece and several interesting pieces of baroque art. It was closed for renovations at the time of research.

Cerámica el Molino   MUSEUM
(Carretera Hoyo de Mazo; ⊘9am-1pm & 3-7pm Mon-Sat) Continue 800m down the hill (take the car unless you want to trudge back uphill) to reach this meticulously restored mill that houses a ceramics museum and workshop where artisans make reproductions of Benahoare pottery. There's a popular souvenir shop as well. You can also get here from the LP-132 highway.

✖ Eating

La Cabaña   TRADITIONAL CANARIAN   €€
(Carretera a Fuencaliente Km6; mains €7-13; ⊘closed Mon) Enjoy grilled meats, fresh fish, salads, soup, *papas arrugadas* with *mojo,* and fabulous bread cooked with anise (an island speciality) at this rustic spot just off the highway south of town. The balcony terrace affords an ocean view – although you'll have to put up with traffic noise.

San Blas   TRADITIONAL CANARIAN   €
(Calle Maria del Carmen Martínez Jerez 4; mains €5-8; ⊘closed Sun afternoon & Mon) In the centre of town, get simple dishes like pastas, salads, *chocos* (cuttlefish) with *mojo verde* (green sauce) or goat with potatoes, served on a shady outdoor terrace.

❶ Getting There & Away

Mazo is sandwiched between the LP-1 and LP-132 highways. Get here by Bus 3 (10 daily), which links Mazo with Los Llanos (€4.50, one hour), Fuencaliente (€1.90, 30 minutes) and Santa Cruz (€1.50, 20 minutes).

Parque Ecológico de Belmaco

The first ancient petroglyphs (rock carvings) found on the archipelago were discovered at this site in 1752. A 300m trail that winds around various cave dwellings once inhabited by Benahoare tribespeople is the heart of this 'ecological park', but the real attractions are the whorling, sworling, squiggling rock etchings, which date back to AD 150. There's also a museum and small shop.

Belmaco (Carretera a Fuencaliente Km7; admission €2; ⊙10am-6pm Mon-Sat, to 3pm Sun) boasts four sets of engravings, and experts remain perplexed about their meaning, though they speculate that the etchings could have been religious symbols.

Note that the ground here can be a bit rough for people with baby strollers or wheelchairs.

Bus 3 from Santa Cruz heads down this way four times daily (except weekends). The nearest bus stop is about 400m south of the cave.

Playa Blanca

Just 1.3km north along the LP-132 highway from the Parque Ecológico de Belmaco is an unmarked road that leads down to Playa Blanca ('White Beach', though 'Salt and Pepper Beach' would be a better name). A perfect picnic spot, here you'll find a tiny

---

WORTH A TRIP

TO THE END OF THE ISLAND

If you're in the mood for some scenic driving, and possibly some scenic swimming, take the LP-1282 highway far past the Princess resort complex to the very southern tip of the island and **Playas del Faro** (Lighthouse Beach) and **Las Salinas** (a salt deposit known as a bird-watcher's paradise). The black-lava rock here and crystal-blue ocean are perfect contrasts to one another, but if you do choose to swim off one of the beaches here be wary of heavy under-tows and dangerous dumping waves. Return to civilisation by following the highway, now called LP-130, north to complete the loop. Be careful at night; the road is curvy and unlit.

---

hippy hamlet with a few summer homes, a tranquil beach and a rocky coast perfect for fishing or crabbing.

Fuencaliente
POP 1856

Fuencaliente (Hot Fountain) is the best tourist base in the south of the island and offers a mix of marine and volcanic attractions. The area gets its name from hot springs that were once believed to treat leprosy, but were buried by a fiery volcano in the 17th century. Don't think that the volcanoes have gone all sleepy and tame since then; the last eruption was in 1971, when Volcán Teneguía's lava flow added a few hectares to the island's size.

You'll drive through a lovely pine forest before reaching Los Canarios de Fuencaliente, the urban centre of Fuencaliente. Note that signs often refer to Los Canarios, which is just a short version of Los Canarios de Fuencaliante.

◉ Sights & Activities

Volcanoes   MOUNTAIN
Creating a stark, at times lunar-like, landscape, the volcanoes in this area are the newest in the archipelago and are the main draw of Fuencaliente. The beauty of their low, ruddy cones belies the violence with which they erupted.

Don't miss the short but breathtaking walk along the rim of **Volcán San Antonio**. It takes just 20 minutes to walk the gravel path halfway around the yawning chasm of this great black cone, which last blew in 1949 and is now being repopulated by hardy Canary pines. Afterwards, take a look at the small **visitor centre** (adult/under 13yr €3.50/free; ⊙9am-9pm), where a seismograph constantly measuring volcanic movement in the area shows a boring but comforting straight line.

From the visitor centre, a signposted trail leads you to **Volcán Teneguía**; its 1971 eruption was the archipelago's most recent. The easy to moderate walk there and back takes about 2½ hours. If that's not far enough then you can continue onwards for a further hour (one way) down to the coast at the Faro de Fuencaliente and the end of La Palma.

Bodegas Teneguía   WINERY
(www.vinosteneguia.com; Los Canarios s/n; ⊙9am-2pm & 3-6pm Mon-Sat, 11am-2pm Sun)

WORTH A TRIP

THE SOUTHWESTERN COAST

The road up the west coast from the bottom tip of the island is full of open curves that swoop past green hills dotted with cacti and low shrubs. The highway runs along a ridge, leaving the glittering ocean a blue haze to the left. Other than the view, there's not much here, unless you count the small bar at the **mirador** 6km out of Fuencaliente in the tiny town of **El Charco**, but even so it all makes for a great detour from either Fuencaliente or even Puerto Naos.

Keep heading north and you'll travel through a series of tiny, almost uninhabited villages. Stop in **San Nicolás** for a while (it's 1km past the village of Jedey), to eat at **Bodegon Tamanca** (Carretera General; mains €8-13; ⊘closed Sun dinner & Mon), an atmospheric restaurant located in a spacious, natural cave with stone-topped tables and booths that seem to be dug into the rock. This is a meat-lover's kind of establishment, whether you like it grilled, cured or stewed. Afterwards you can purchase a bottle or two from the attached wine bodega.

After getting your fill of the craters, check out the town's other claim to fame: the wines made in this volcanic soil. The largest winery in town is Bodegas Teneguía, with white, red and sweet wines that are sold all over the island and beyond. There's also a good restaurant in the winery.

🏖 Beaches

The coast around Fuencaliente is largely inaccessible, with banana plantations, rocky outcrops and steep cliffs lining much of it. Two pleasant exceptions are **Playa de la Zamora** and **Playa Chica**, black beaches tucked side by side in coves. They're no secret but are rarely crowded. To get here, take the Carretera de Las Indias (LP-1282) past the San Antonio volcano towards the hamlet of Las Indias. Follow the curves downhill until a small sign indicates a turn-off for the *playas* (beaches) to the right.

🍴 Eating

Tasca La Era   TRADITIONAL CANARIAN €€
(Carretera Antonio Paz y Paz 6; mains €8-12; ⊘closed Wed) A farmhouse-style restaurant with a terrace and garden area, this is a charming spot for simple meat and fish dishes. Children can work up a pre-dinner appetite by racing around the restaurant gardens.

El Patio del Vino   TRADITIONAL CANARIAN €€€
(☏922 44 46 23; Los Canarios s/n; mains €9-14; ⊘closed Mon) Behind the Bodegas Teneguía is this upscale restaurant, where house soups and local game dishes are served in a tranquil and spacious dining room. It is

surprisingly formal for such a small, rural place as Fuencaliente.

El Quinto Pino   INTERNATIONAL €€
(LP-1282, Las Indias; mains €6-10; ⊘Thu-Sun; ☑) Pizzas, grilled meats and vegetables are the speciality at this tiny, family-run spot in the hamlet of Las Indias, northwest of Los Canarios.

ⓘ Getting There & Away

Bus 3 (€3.50, one hour, up to five daily) heads between Fuencaliente and Santa Cruz via Mazo. It then continues onwards to Los Llanos.

THE CENTRE

For most visitors the majority of their time on La Palma is spent in this central region, and for good reason. The bowl-shaped Caldera de Taburiente, and the national park named after it, dominate the centre of La Palma, with rocky peaks, deep ravines and lush pine forests blanketing the slopes. It offers some of the most spectacular hiking in all of the Canary Islands and a visit here is an absolute must.

The LP-2 highway, which links Santa Cruz with Los Llanos, skirts the southern rim of the park, and from the road you can sometimes see the characteristic cloud blanket that fills the interior of the caldera and spills over its sides like a pot boiling over.

Two of the island's important commercial centres, El Paso and Los Llanos (the island's largest town), are in this area, making this region the economic engine of La Palma. It's also a key banana-growing

FESTIVALS & EVENTS

Like any Spaniards worth their heritage, the Palmeros love a good party, and the year is packed with festivals and celebrations.

Each town has feast days celebrating its patron saint with several days of parades, parties and other activities. The following are some of the bigger and better events:

» **Breña Alta** (late June)

» **Breña Baja** (25 July)

» **Barlovento** (12–13 August)

» **San Andrés y Los Sauces** (early September)

» **Tazacorte** (late September)

Other festivals worthy of note:

» **Fiesta of the Almond Blossom** (January–February) A celebration of the beauty of the almond blossom in Puntagorda and of the town's patron saint, San Mauro Abad.

» **Las Cruces** (3 May) The island's crosses are bedecked in jewellery, flowers and rich clothes. Truly a sight to see.

» **San Juan** (23 June) Marks the summer solstice, and is celebrated in Puntallana with bonfires and firecrackers galore.

» **El Diablo** (8 September) Fireworks, parades of devils and grim music in Tijarife provide a graphic show of the triumph of good over evil. About 30kg of gunpowder is used in the 20-minute show honouring Nuestra Señora de Candelaria.

» **Castanets** (24 December) After Midnight Mass in Breña Alta and throughout the island, Palmero men perform skits accompanied by the noisy music of castanets.

area and, as you near the west coast, banana plantations fill the valleys. To add to the area's prestige the coast here is home to some of the island's longest, prettiest beaches and best 'resorts' (don't worry, it's all fairly low-key).

El Paso

POP 7440

The gateway to the Parque Nacional de la Caldera de Taburiente – the park's visitor centre is just outside town – El Paso is the island's largest municipality, with sprawling forests and around 8 sq km of cultivated land. The modest town centre, however, won't detain you for long. If you're driving into town, turn right at the 'Casco Histórico' sign to reach the main attractions. The **tourist office** (☎922 48 57 33; www.lapalma-cit.com; Calle Antonio Pino Pérez s/n; ☉10am-6pm Mon-Fri, to 2pm Sat & Sun) is inside the town park.

○ Sights & Activities

Museo de la Seda   MUSEUM

(Silk Museum; www.lashilanderaselpaso.com; Calle Manuel Taño 6; ☉10am-1pm Mon, Wed & Fri, 10am-1pm & 5-7pm Tue & Thu) Here you can learn the secrets of worms that are in fact caterpillars that spin dresses fit for a marriage. The silk produced here is made according to traditions that have barely changed since the industry arrived on the island in the 16th century.

**Ermita de la Virgen de la
Concepción de la Bonanza**   CHURCH

A restored 18th-century, curiously painted little chapel. Renovations mercifully left intact the splendid Mudéjar ceiling above the altar.

Finca Corazón   HORSE RIDING

(☎699 62 95 17; www.la-palma-reiten.com, in German; Custa de la Juliana, El Paso; guided excursions €50-85; ☉11am-6pm) El Paso's real appeal is its natural beauty, and a great way to enjoy it is on horseback. The German owners of this farm take equestrians of all levels on 2½- to five-hour rides in and around the national park. As with so many businesses on La Palma it's aimed more at Germans.

Hiking

HIKING

If you prefer to do the hard work yourself then El Paso is a good take-off point for the demanding, but breathtaking (in every sense of the word) **Ruta de los Volcanes**, a 19km hiking trail that meanders through ever-changing volcanic scenery and gives privileged views of both coasts as it heads south along the mountain ridge, through the heart of volcanic territory and towards Fuencaliente. This trail is part of the long-distance GR-130. Allow six to seven hours for the trek – it's demanding and is best undertaken on cool, cloudy days, as there is not much shade or fresh water along the way. The trailhead is the **Refugio del Pilar**, an expansive park with a picnic area, on the LP-203 highway, outside El Paso and off the LP-2. The walk finishes in Fuencaliente, from where you will probably have to arrange homeward-bound transport.

 Courses

The tourist office organises a range of free tours, courses and tastings. If ciggies are getting too expensive, learn how to make your own cigars on a **cigar making course** (☉11.30am Mon). On Wednesdays wine-tasting courses take place and on Fridays you can taste a variety of *mojo* sauces (we imagine that this is much more undersubscribed than the previous two!).

 Eating

Bodegón La Abuela   TRADITIONAL CANARIAN **€€**
(Calle General Tajuya 49; mains €5-12; ☉closed Thu) On your left as you leave El Paso toward Los Llanos, this home-style eatery with a terrace serves delicious rabbit and game dishes.

Parque Nacional de la Caldera de Taburiente

Declared a national park in 1954, this beautiful park is the heart of La Palma, both geographically and symbolically. Extending across 46.9 sq km, it encompasses thick Canary pine forests, a wealth of freshwater springs and streams, waterfalls, impressive rock formations and many kilometres of hiking trails. Although you can reach a few miradors by car, you'll need to explore on foot to really experience the park at its best. The morning, before clouds obscure the views, is the best time to visit (although if you want to see the classic view of clouds spilling over the caldera lips then the afternoon is the best time).

The heart of the park is the **Caldera de Taburiente** itself (literally, the Taburiente 'Stewpot' or 'Caldron'). A massive depression 8km wide and surrounded by soaring rock walls (it doesn't take much imagination to see where the name came from), it was first given the moniker in 1825 by German geologist Leopold von Buch, who took it to be a massive volcanic crater. The word 'caldera' stuck, and was used as a standard term for such volcanic craters the world over. This caldera, however, is no crater, although volcanic activity was key in its creation. Scientists now agree that this was a majestically tall volcanic mountain, and that it collapsed on itself. Through the millennia, erosion excavated this tall-walled amphitheatre.

As you explore the quiet park, all may seem impressively stoic and still, but the forces of erosion are hard at work. Landslides and collapsing *roques* (pillars of volcanic rock) are frequent, and some geologists estimate it will finally disappear in just 5000 years. See this fast erosion near the **Mirador de la Cumbrecita**, where a group of pines stands atop a web of exposed roots, clinging miraculously to the hilltop. These trees were once planted firmly in the ground, but metres of soil have been lost during their lifetime.

🏃 **Hiking**

Many trails traverse the park, but unless you plan to spend several days exploring, you'll probably stick to the better-known paths outlined here. Most are in good shape, though the trail from La Cumbrecita to the camp site is notoriously slippery and should be avoided by novice hikers, and the trail running down the Barranco de las Angustias can be dangerous in rainy weather.

Signposting is improving but may still be confusing. Although you're unlikely to get really lost (and there are usually groups of hikers out on the trail to help you if necessary), you're best off buying a detailed map, like the 1:25,000 *Caldera de Taburiente Parque Nacional*, for sale at the visitor centre. See also the excellent website www .senderosdelapalma.com for further route descriptions.

ℹ MAPS & BOOKS

Maps are available for sale at petrol stations, newspaper kiosks and bookshops. Tourist offices give out a very basic island map, but if you plan to explore, invest in a more detailed map, like the Freytag & Berndt 1:30,000 map, in English and German.

The hiking maps covering southern, central and northern La Palma given out for free at the tourist office in Santa Cruz give a good overview, and its *Hiking Guide* (in English and Spanish) is helpful too. But if you're a serious walker, you should buy a hiking guide, such as *Landscapes of La Palma and El Hierro*, published by Sunflower Books, *Walk! La Palma* by Discovery Walking Guides, or *La Palma* by Rother Walking Guides.

THE SOUTHERN END

Most people access the park from either El Paso or Los Llanos. You'll need a car, taxi or guide to cart you up to one of the miradors that serve as trailheads.

To get an overview of the park, there's no better walk than the PR LP 13 trail, which begins at **Los Brecitos** (1081m). Get there from Los Llanos by following the signs first to Los Barros and then on to Los Brecitos. The path leads through a quiet Canary pine forest, past the park camp site, across a babbling brook, and down the Barranco de las Angustias, crossing countless small streams along the way. Watch out for interesting sights like the brightly coloured mineral water that flows orange and green, the interesting shapes made by pillow lava, and rock formations like the phallic **Roque Idafe**, an important spiritual site for the Benahoaritas. This six-hour hike is popular and is suitable for anyone in average-to-good physical shape. Be careful, however, if it has rained recently or if a storm seems imminent; the 'Gorge of Fear' can quickly become a raging torrent, and people caught in its fast-rising waters have died. At the time of research half of this route was closed due to landslides blocking the trail.

When the trail is fully open the best way to tackle it is to park at Las Hoyas, at the base of the Barranco de las Angustias. From here, 4WD **taxi shuttle services** (☏922 40 35 40; per person €10; ☉8am-noon) whisk you up to Los Brecitos and allow you to enjoy the descent back to your car without backtracking.

Another option is to drive up the LP-202 from the visitor centre to the **Mirador de la Cumbrecita** (1287m), where there is a small **information office** (☉9am-7pm). The 7km drive passes turn-offs for the Pista de Valencia and the Ermita del Pino, leading you through a peaceful pine forest to sweeping views of the valley. From the car park, you can make a round-trip hike up to the panoramic views from **Pico Bejenado**; allow 2½ hours for the trek. Those with less time can take a 3km circuit trail to both the **Mirador de los Roques** and the **Mirador Lomo de las Chozas**; the final part of the loop is a flat, wheelchair- and stroller-friendly 1km trail between Lomo de las Chozas and the car park. The very best views can be had at sunrise or sunset. Take note, though, that the trails leading off from the Mirador de la Cumbrecita are by far the most popular in the park and, due to overcrowding, park authorities have enforced a strict traffic quota. If you want to drive up to the mirador you have to put your name down on a list at the visitors centre just past El Paso and wait until your turn to drive up. Sometimes the wait might only be a few minutes but at other times (weekends and in high season) it can be over an hour. If you miss your turn you must queue again.

Another excellent, moderately hard, walk is the PR LP 13.3 from the **Pista de Valencia** parking area to the 1845m-high **Pico Bejenado**. This five-hour return hike climbs up through some wonderful old pine forest before popping out on the caldera ridge for some gob-smacking views. The trail is easy to follow and it's a good choice for any reasonably fit walker who wants something less trodden and more challenging than the routes around the Mirador de la Cumbrecita, but not as demanding as the Los Brecitos trails.

THE NORTHERN END

A string of rocky peaks soaring nearly 2500m high surrounds the caldera, and the trail running along these rock walls affords a thrilling vantage point from which to observe the park and the rest of the island. A narrow dirt trail, part of the long-distance GR-131, skims the entire northern border of the park, and shorter trails branch off it and venture down deeper into the park.

One of the most spectacular sections runs between the **Roque de los Muchachos** and the **Pico de la Nieve**, which is off the LP-1032, a winding highway that branches off the LP-1 highway 3km north of Santa Cruz and snakes its way across the island, skirting the rim of the park and its northern peaks. Avoid backtracking by taking two cars and leaving one at the *pico* (the parking area is a 20-minute walk from the trail itself). Then drive (or get a ride) up to the Roque de los Muchachos, the highest point on the island at 2426m. The walk back down to the Pico de la Nieve should take four to five hours.

Numerous miradors dot the LP-1032 highway around the Roque de los Muchachos; even if you don't hike the rim, the views from up here are worth seeking out. At night, this area offers unbeatable stargazing.

ℹ️ Information

The interesting **visitor centre** (📞922 49 72 77; caldera@mma.es; Carretera General de Padrón; ⏰9am-6.30pm) is 5km outside El Paso on the LP-2 highway and offers free general information (be sure to pick up the English *Caldera de Taburiente Paths* map), detailed maps and guides and an excellent museum. The centre's 20-minute film (shown occasionally in English) in worth seeing. Bus 1 (€1 from El Paso, 10 minutes) between Santa Cruz de la Palma and Los Llanos stops by hourly.

ℹ️ Getting There & Away

No roads run through the park, and there are only three ways to access it: via the LP-202 near the visitor centre, via the track that goes from

Los Llanos to Los Brecitos, or via the LP-1032 highway in the north. There are no buses.

Los Llanos de Aridane

POP 21,045

The economic centre of the island and a true-blue working town, Los Llanos lacks the obvious charm of the capital or some of the smaller villages, but the shady plazas and pedestrian streets of the historic centre are worth exploring. Set in a fertile valley, this has historically been one of the island's richest areas, with a long tradition of cultivating sugar cane, bananas and, more recently, avocados. These days it's home to many of the island's business and services, and many young Palmeros are moving here to find jobs.

◉ Sights & Activities

Start your visit in busy **Plaza España**, the heart of the historic town. Majestic Indian laurel trees provide much-welcome leafy canopy on even the sunniest days, making this the perfect spot to picnic, people-watch or relax in a cafe. Don't miss the gleaming white **Iglesia de Nuestra Señora de los Remedios**, built in the Canarian colonial style. Explore the surrounding streets and plazas, particularly the Plaza Elías Santos Abreu (aka Plaza Chica), Calle General Franco and Calle Francis Fernández Taño, which still preserve much of their traditional character.

THE WORLD'S LARGEST TELESCOPE

No, those round, space-age-looking things squatting on the peak of Roque de los Muchachos aren't something from a theme park, and no, they're not alien spaceships come to explore earth. They are the telescopes of the island's astronomical observatory, one of the world's best places to study the night sky. Tossed out in the Atlantic, far from urban centres and city lights, La Palma is an ideal place to stargaze. More than 75% of the nights here on El Roque are clear, a statistic that's hard to beat.

Since the 2007 unveiling of the mammoth Grantecan (Gran Telescopio Canario, or GTC), the Observatorio del Roque de los Muchachos boasts one of the world's largest telescopes. The €1 million investment allows scientists to 'study the formation and evolution of the galaxies throughout the history of the universe, investigate why more stars were formed in the past than now, or observe the rings of spatial material that give birth to new planets near young stars,' the scientific director of the GTC, José Miguel Rodríguez, told the Spanish press.

Although it's the new telescope that's grabbing everyone's attention, the observatory has long been home to Europe's largest telescope and the site of important research. La Palma's observatory is linked with the Observatorio del Teide on Tenerife, and together they form the Instituto de Astrofisica de Canarias (IAC). The observatory is normally closed to the public, but until 9pm you're free to drive around.

LA PALMA TIPPLES

Since the early 16th century, when Spanish conquerors planted the first vines on the island, La Palma has been known for its sweet *malvasía* (Malmsey wine). Thanks to the merchants and colonists who came in and out of La Palma's ports, the wine acquired fame throughout Europe, and some referred to the tasty stuff as 'the nectar of the gods'. Even Shakespeare wrote about sweet Canary wine, making it Falstaff's favourite in *Henry IV* and calling it a 'marvellous searching wine' that 'perfumes the blood'. You can also find dry *malvasía* as well as a variety of reds, whites and rosé wines, especially in the areas of Fuencaliente and Hoyo de Mazo. For an alcohol-filled journey embark on the **Wine Route** (www.infoisla.org/rutadelvino), which includes 16 visitable wineries.

Although the sugar plantations have all but gone, what remains is put to good use in the production of *ron* (rum) by the last producer on the island, Ron Aldea.

Colourful **murals** and **modern sculptures** are dotted throughout the centre, making the city an open-air museum. A large map in Plaza España gives the artists' names and locations of their works.

Cyclists should check out **Bike'n'Fun** (☑922 40 19 27; www.bikenfun.de, in German; Calle Calvo Sotelo 20, Los Llanos; guide service per person €40, bike rental per day €15) for bike rentals or guided two-wheel excursions.

Festivals

On 2 June the city comes alive for the year's biggest party, **La Patrona**, held in honour of Our Lady of Los Remedios.

Eating

The cafes dotting the Plaza España are ideal for breakfast, a midday coffee break or an informal lunch.

TOP CHOICE / La Vitamina   VEGETARIAN €€
(Calle Real 29; mains €7-10; ⊙closed Sun; ☑) This is something refreshingly different to the run-of-the-mill meat and fish restaurants that are the standard when dining out in the Canaries. It's laid-back, slightly bohemian and has a range of largely vegetarian meals that put together flavours of Africa, Asia and Spain into some highly unexpected combinations.

Brasero Mar y Tierra   MODERN CANARIAN €€
(☑922 46 43 14; Calle Francis Fernández Taño 29; mains €8-11; ⊙closed Sun) Although the grilled meats and fish are delicious, the Mar y Tierra's real claim to fame is its fabulous setting inside a Canarian patio, where you can see the flames of the grill dancing and even peek above the patio walls to catch a glimpse of mountains in the distance. It has an ever-changing selection of daily specials, many of which feature that old-skool Canarian favourite, *gofio* (roasted cereal).

ⓘ Information

Post office (☑922 46 09 56; Calle General Franco 3; ⊙8.30am-8.30pm Mon-Fri, 9.30am-1pm Sat)

Tourist office (☑922 40 25 83; Avenida Dr Fleming; ⊙8.30am-7pm Mon-Fri, 9am-2pm Sat)

ⓘ Getting There & Away

Buses from the **bus station** (Calle Luis Felipe Gómez Wanguemert) include Bus 1 (€5, 45 minutes, up to 17 daily) to Santa Cruz, Bus 3 (€3.50, 40 minutes, up to seven daily) to Fuencaliente and Bus 4 (€1.70, 20 minutes, up to 21 daily) to Puerto Naos.

Puerto Naos

One of La Palma's two tourism centres (Los Cancajos, on the east coast, is the other), Puerto Naos is a town that exists almost solely for the tourists who come to relax on its beautiful black beach, rest under its palm trees, soak up the views of its glittering ocean and stroll along its beachfront promenade. Huddled around a rounded bay and protected on either side by tall cliffs, the town makes a good base for sunlovers who want easy access to the north and interior.

Activities

Lolling on the soft black-sand beach may well take up all your time here. But if you're in the mood for more excitement, try some of the following activities.

Tauchpartner SCUBA DIVING
(☎922 40 81 39; www.tauchpartner-lapalma.de; Edificio Playa Delfín 1; dive €30; ◷9.30-11am & 5-7pm Mon-Sat) Offers a range of scuba-diving classes as well as single dives.

Bike Station CYCLING
(☎922 40 83 55; Avenida Cruz Roja, local 3; bike rental per day €6-24, guided trip €38-44; ◷9am-1pm & 6-8pm Mon-Sat) Offers rentals and a range of challenging guided mountain-bike rides.

Palmaclub PARAGLIDING
(☎610 69 57 50; www.palmaclub.com; Paseo Marítima; tandem glide €90-140; ◷noon-6pm) Paragliding is quickly gaining momentum here; aficionados come from throughout Europe to take advantage of the island's ideal conditions and easy take-off and landing sites. Arrange for a tandem glide with Palmaclub, who are based inside the Kiosco Playa Morena. Prices are based on how big a cliff (250m or 950m) you choose to throw yourself off. You should book as far ahead as possible and be prepared for weather-induced cancellations.

Viajes Yadir TOURS
(☎922 40 81 06; Avenida Marítima; ◷9am-1pm & 4-8pm Mon-Fri, 9am-1pm Sat) Offers a bit of everything, from car hire to bus trips.

✖ Eating

Orinoco SEAFOOD €
(www.islalapalma.com/orinoco; Calle Manuel Rodriguez Quintero 1; mains €5-10; ◷closed Wed) It's not the kind of place that charms by looks alone, but this homey spot is the locals' favourite for fresh fish and traditional Palmero desserts.

La Roca SEAFOOD €€
(Paseo Marítima 4; mains €8.50-12) Seafood is the big deal at the laid-back beachside terrace of La Roca, where the sound of crashing waves may interfere with conversation – all the better to concentrate on dishes of fried baby cuttlefish, grouper fillet and a highly delectable serving of garlic prawns.

❶ Getting There & Away

Bus 4 (€1.70, 20 minutes, up to 21 daily) makes the trip to and from Los Llanos.

THE NORTH

The dense tropical forests, fertile hills and towering pines that create a blanket of green over the northern half of the island couldn't be further away from the volcanic, sun-baked south. This is the least-accessible, and many say most beautiful, part of the island, with rocky cliffs plunging into sapphire waters and deserted black beaches surrounded by palm trees.

San Andrés & Los Sauces
POP 5380

San Andrés, 3km off the main LP-1 highway, is like something from a storybook, with hilly, cobblestone streets that lead past low, whitewashed houses. The Iglesia de San Andrés has its origins in 1515 and is one of the first churches the Spanish conquerors built on the island, though most of what you see today was built in the 17th century. Inside, take a look at the lavish baroque altarpieces and the coffered ceiling.

Los Sauces, just north of San Andrés, is a modern town with two pretty central squares (or one big one bisected by the highway, depending on how you look at it). The grand church, Nuestra Señora de Montserrat, is on the square and has some valuable Flemish artwork inside. Named after the patron of Catalunya, this church is evidence of the many Catalans who participated in the island's conquest.

BEST BEACHES

» **Puerto Naos** The island's biggest resort has been designed with good looks in mind and the black-sand beach, bendy palm trees and cheerful promenade will certainly please your eye. Lots of facilities and great for children.

» **Piscinas de la Fajana** Clamber down the cliffs to this series of natural swimming pools that you'll most likely only be sharing with locals.

» **Los Cancajos** The island's second resort has safe swimming, volcanic black sand, good accommodation and lots of activities with which to tire out the children and children at heart.

More important (and more interesting) than anything in Los Sauces itself is the **Los Tiles biosphere reserve** just out of town.

One of several bars on the main plaza in San Andrés, the informal **Bar Miami** (Calle San Sebastián; mains €4-7) is where all the old locals hangout and feast on cheap seafood dishes.

All of the tourist facilities are in San Andrés.

Bus 2 (€3.50, 35 minutes, up to nine daily) connects Santa Cruz with the centre of Los Sauces; those heading to San Andrés will have to walk or try asking the driver to make a diversion.

Charco Azul

Beyond San Andrés on the LP-104 highway is a sign pointing the way to Charco Azul, a beautiful swimming hole 3km further on. A bit of tastefully applied concrete has been added to the volcanic rocks along the shore to make a series of natural-looking saltwater pools with sunbathing platforms between them. At the time of research the pools were closed due to a rock fall trying to smash them into oblivion, but work was underway to get them back up and running again.

Los Tiles

A biosphere reserve since 1983, the nearly 140 sq km of Los Tiles are covered with a lushly beautiful rainforest that's literally oozing with life. This moist, cool, natural wonderland is one of the most magical spots on the island, a must-explore place where you can wander among the diverse flora and fauna and the largest *laurisilva* (laurel) forest on the island.

At the helpful **visitor centre** (☎922 45 12 46; www.lapalmabiosfera.com; ☉9am-2pm & 2.30-5pm Nov-Jun, to 6.30pm Jul-Oct) you'll find maps, a video about the biosphere and a small museum. Nearby is the rustic **Casa de Metrío** (mains €7-10; ☉closed Wed), a restaurant serving grilled meats on outdoor picnic tables.

Fabulous hiking trails cut through Los Tiles' dense vegetation. The shortest walk is the steep climb up to the **Mirador Topo de las Barandas** (allow one hour for the round-trip), which leads to a spectacular view of the gorge running out of the reserve.

Even better, though, is the long, ravine-side hike to the **Marcos and Cordero Springs**, which passes through a dozen damp tunnels (bring a flashlight and rain jacket) and winds past waterfalls, through forest and alongside volcanic dikes. The hike isn't incredibly steep (except in short stretches), but it can be slick; be careful. A popular way to tackle this hike is to get a taxi from Los Tiles car park up to the Casa del Monte. From here, the hike to the springs and back should take about four hours. The park office can suggest a number of other walks including a very simple one-hour return walk that begins from the car park a few hundred metres down the road from the visitor office. Take the trail on the left-hand side of the road, next to the sign post, and basically follow it through the tunnel and gently uphill for as far as you feel like going.

❶ Getting There & Away

Coming from Santa Cruz, follow the signs to Los Tiles off the LP-1 highway. The visitor centre is 3km up LP-107, which runs alongside the lush Barranco del Agua. No buses venture up here, so you'll need either your own wheels or strong legs.

LA PALMA FOR CHILDREN

Building sand castles on the black-sand beaches of **Puerto Naos** and **Los Cancajos**, or splashing in the saltwater pools in places like **Piscinas de la Fajana** are givens, but what to do after the beach? Older kids (12 and above) will enjoy horseback riding with **Finca Corazón**, while the younger crowd will get a kick out of the animals at **Maroparque**.

Suitable hikes for kids include **Mirador de los Roques** and the **Mirador Lomo de las Chozas**, both in the Parque Nacional de la Caldera de Taburiente; at the latter, you can even take a stroller. Throw in some history by taking the 1.5km walk around the **Parque Cultural La Zarza**.

FROM LA ZARZA TO TAZACORTE

Ethereal, pristine, stoic, eerie, peaceful...choose your adjective for the lonely landscapes here on the island's northwestern coast. Pine forests, fallow fields, occasional rural settlements and sweeping views of the banana plantations by the Atlantic are the main attractions between La Zarza and Tazacorte. This is a solitary, tranquil area that was largely isolated from the rest of the island until recent times. Countless hiking trails, many of them quite challenging, provide most of the entertainment here.

The small towns of **Puntagorda** and **Tijarafe** are worth a brief stop, if only to wander the streets of their historic centres. Tijarafe is home to a small **museum** (Casa del Maestro, Calle 18 de Julio 11; ⊙4.30pm-7.30pm Mon-Fri) dedicated to traditional culture. Another branch of the museum sits almost opposite at number 4. Hours are the same. To get to the museums, follow the signs to the Casa del Maestro from the main highway.

Several lookouts offer privileged vantage points of the northwest coast's inspiring scenery. Just south of Puntagorda is **Mirador de Garome**, overlooking a majestic gorge. Further south, **Mirador del Time** looks out over Tazacorte.

For food, **La Muralla Restaurant** (☑650 02 16 64; Carretera General Aguatavar; mains €8-12; ⊙closed Sun pm & Mon), between Puntagorda and Tijarafe, offers fine dining (fresh fish, kebabs, pork chops, steak, paella), with even finer views from the breezy terrace or minimalist dining room. For something less formal **Restaurant Las Piñas** (Carretera General Puntagorda; mains €8-12; ⊙closed Thu), on the northern edge of Puntagorda, is a family-run farmhouse-like place with simple, filling local dishes such as rabbit, steaks and seafood. It does a great lunchtime *menú del día* for €8.50.

Barlovento

POP 2360

Skip the town itself in favour of the natural attractions that lie beyond, like the **Piscinas de la Fajana** – calm saltwater pools where frothy waves pound just beyond the subtle concrete barriers. About 5km east of Barlovento, on the LP-1 highway, you'll turn-off toward this starkly beautiful coastal spot, where red-tinged rocks and a savage ocean create a memorable panorama.

Dine at **La Fajana** (☑922 18 61 62; mains €7-12), which has an orchestra of crashing waves playing musical accompaniment to your fresh seafood meal.

Parque Cultural La Zarza

Two Benahoare petroglyphs are the main attraction at the **Parque Cultural La Zarza** (adult/child €2/1; ⊙10am-6pm Mon-Sat, to 3pm Sun). Heading west out along the LP-1 towards La Mata, the park is 1km past the turn-off for La Mata (it's on a curve and easy to miss – keep an eye out for the signpost). To actually see the geometric-shaped etchings, take the 1.5km circuit into the park itself. Back at the visitor centre, you can watch an informative 20-minute video about the life of the original inhabitants and take a tour around the interactive museum.

El Hierro

☎922 / POP 10,690

Best Places to Eat

» Restaurante Don Din 2 (p205)

» Casa Guayana (p200)

» Meson del Norte (p199)

» La Maceta (p204)

» Casa Juan (p203)

Best Places to Stay

» Hotel Villa El Mocanal (p224)

» El Sitio (p225)

» Hotel Puntagrande (p225)

» Parador Nacional (p224)

Why Go?

El Hierro is an island where the impenetrable cliff-lined shores and location in the middle of the Atlantic make it both literally and figuratively remote. It was once even considered the end of the world until Columbus famously sailed the ocean blue in 1492.

Although the 21st century has connected this small island to the rest of the planet, El Hierro will always feel remote. Of course, that's exactly what is so addictive about this place. It's impossible not to be entranced by the island's slow pace and simple style; by its craggy coast, where waves hurl themselves against lava-sculpted rock faces; by the pretty farmland and flower meadows of the interior; by the eerily beautiful juniper groves; and by the desolate volcanic badlands that stretch out like moonscapes in the south. The least-known of the Canary Islands, El Hierro is unique – so much so that it was declared a Unesco biosphere reserve – and utterly captivating. Don't miss this journey to the end of the world.

When to Go

El Hierro is a year-round destination, but the meadows of the highlands are ablaze with poppies and other wild flowers in spring (March) and hiking is a delight. For life at lower altitudes June to early July and September are perfect for lazing around the numerous natural swimming pools or diving into La Restinga's undersea paradise. And for cultural interest, if you're on El Hierro in late April, be sure not to miss the Fiesta de los Pastores, a colourful religious procession in honour of the Virgen de los Reyes (Virgin of the Kings).

History

Geographically speaking, El Hierro is the youngest island in the archipelago. Through the millennia, volcanic activity built up a steep island with a towering 2000m-high peak at its centre. But, about 50,000 years ago, the area was hit by an earthquake so massive that one-third of the island was ripped off the northern side. The peak and the surrounding land slipped away beneath the waves, creating the amphitheatre-like coast of El Golfo. The event would have been impressive and the ensuing tsunami may have been more than 100m high. Although El Hierro's last eruption was 200 years ago, volcanoes are still the island's defining feature. It is littered with around 500 cones, with many more underneath the lava flows and volcanic rocks that blanket much of the island.

The island's original inhabitants, the Bimbaches, arrived from northern Africa and created a peaceful, cave-dwelling society that depended on agriculture, fishing, hunting and gathering. They may have called the island Hero or Esero, possibly the origin of its modern name. Bimbaches have left interesting petroglyphs (geometrical etchings) on rocks and cave walls throughout the island; the most interesting is at El Julán.

After the Spanish conquest in the 15th century, a form of feudalism was introduced and Spanish farmers gradually assimilated with those locals who had not been sold into slavery or died of disease. In the subsequent quest for farmland, much of El Hierro's forests were destroyed.

In the 20th century many Herreños were forced to emigrate to find work. The island's economy has since recovered and is now based on cheese, fishing, fruit-growing, livestock and, increasingly, tourism. Many emigrants have returned. The struggle now is balancing the need to conserve the island's unique, Unesco-protected natural beauty with the need for economic growth. More than 60% of the island is classified as protected land, limiting growth options. That's great for conservationists, but as young islanders are forced to move away to study and find jobs, many see it as a problem.

❶ Getting There & Away

AIR

The island's small **airport** (☎922 55 37 00) is 12km outside Valverde. Interisland airways **Binter Canarias** (☎902 39 13 92;

ROAD DISTANCES (KM)

	Valverde	La Restinga	Tigaday	Las Playas
La Restinga	24			
Tigaday	15	41		
Las Playas	11	43	26	
El Pinar	16	11	27	16

Approximate distances only

www.binternet.com) connects El Hierro to Tenerife and Gran Canaria and then onward to the rest of the archipelago. At the airport you'll find car-rental offices, a bar and a shop selling maps and local products.

BOAT

El Hierro's spiffy new Puerto de la Estaca, built courtesy of the European Union, gets little traffic.

The **Fred Olsen** (☎922 62 82 00; www.fred olsen.es) ferry (€47, two hours) runs between Los Cristianos in Tenerife and El Hierro. It arrives at 12:30pm and departs at 4pm every day, except Saturday.

Specialising in cargo, though also accepting passengers, the **Naviera Armas** (☎922 55 09 05; www.naviera-armas.com; Muelle de la Estaca s/n) ship used on this route is decidedly less flashy and much, much slower than other Naviera Armas ships. It sails to Los Cristianos in Tenerife (€24, four hours, 6am Tuesday and Thursday, 7.30pm Sunday). The boat continues onto Santa Cruz de la Tenerife but only truck drivers stay on-board as it takes about five times as long as driving.

VALVERDE

POP 1630

The only landlocked Canary capital, Valverde is a rather unremarkable town set atop a windy mountain ridge overlooking the Atlantic. Its low white houses aren't as scenic as those balconied mansions of the other capitals, but when clouds don't interfere, the town offers some pretty valley views. On rare clear days you can see Tenerife's El Teide and La Gomera perfectly from the town centre. Even if you don't stay here, you'll probably have to pass through, as it's the island's centre of commerce and services.

History

Though Jean de Béthencourt conquered the island in 1405, Valverde only really came

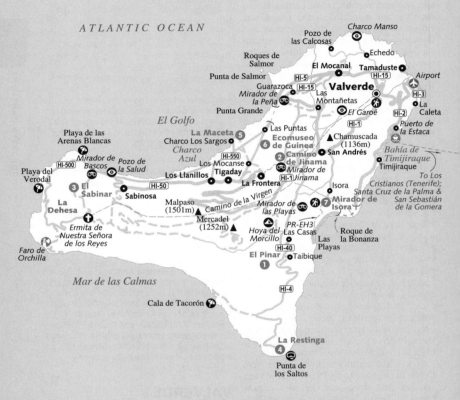

El Hierro Highlights

① Stroll among the towering pines in the pristine **El Pinar** (p202) forest

② Tackle the **Camino de Jinama** (p201), one of the island's best downhill walks, for vast views of El Golfo and the Atlantic

③ Walk among juniper trees sculpted by the wind into

eerie, gnome-like shapes at **El Sabinar** (p207)

④ Grab your mask and dive into the warm, calm waters near **La Restinga** (p203), the island's best diving spot

⑤ Splash around in **La Maceta** (p204), an overgrown rock pool battered by Atlantic swells

⑥ Measure up to the giant lizards of El Hierro and explore village houses of old at the **Ecomuseo de Guinea** (p204)

⑦ Picnic among the wildflowers at the **Mirador de Isora** (p201), with its breathtaking views to the ocean far, far below

Day One

Whether arriving by plane or boat it's the eastern half of the island that everyone sees first, but after that initial arrival most people ignore the east until their day of departure. At first glance this does indeed seem to be the least-enticing corner of El Hierro, but first impressions can often be false impressions. Leaving the port or airport, take the road south to **Las Playas**, a long stretch of cobblestone beach. It's battered by the wind, but perfect for an appetite-inducing stroll. Quell that hunger at the nearby **Casa Guayana**, which dishes up some of the finest seafood on the island. Turn the car around and retrace your steps north to either **Tamaduste**, with its calm cove and crab-filled rock pools, or **La Caleta**, with its stylish seawater swimming pools ideal for all the family. After a swim, drive up to **Valverde** and check out this pint-sized capital before heading to **El Mocanal** and your overnight stop at the **Hotel Villa El Mocanal**.

Day Two

Wake up in the **Hotel Villa El Mocanal** and drive south, and up, through a landscape that often starts off shrouded in fog before emerging into blazing sunshine and a thousand flowers around the farming town of **San Andrés**; make the short detour to the incredible **Mirador de Isora** before continuing to the majestic **El Pinar pine forests** for a walk and a picnic lunch. Next zigzag downhill through an increasingly barren, volcanic landscape to scruffy **La Restinga** and what is arguably the best scuba diving and snorkelling in the Canaries.

Day Three

El Golfo, the spectacular amphitheatre-shaped depression that so dominates the island, is for many people the most interesting part of El Hierro. Start the day by descending quickly out of the clouds of Valverde on the fast HI-5, stopping on the way at **Mirador de la Peña** for an unforgettable overview of El Golfo. Drop down to the coast and check out the quirky, and former record-breaking, **Hotel Puntagrande** and admire the coastal scenery by walking a little way (or the whole way) along the recently spruced up walk between Las Puntas and La Maceta. Return to your car and drive to the nearby **Ecomuseo de Guinea** for a dose of culture and reptiles. Feeling peckish? It's lunchtime so head to **Restaurante Don Din 2** in workaday Tigady for some excellent Canarian food. After lunch choose between the natural pools at **La Maceta** or quieter **Charco Azul** to sleep it all off and have a splash in the water. If you don't sleep for too long, finish your day by driving to the wild end of Spain and the **La Dehesa** area.

into being following a devastating hurricane in 1610. Many of the islanders fled to this small inland hamlet seeking shelter, beginning a relative boom that would eventually see the town become the seat of the *municipio* (town council) that covered the whole island. In 1926 the island's first *cabildo insular* (local government) was established here.

◉ Sights

The lure of the island lies in its natural spaces, not here in town. Still, a short stroll around can be rewarding. Start on pedestrian-friendly Calle Dr Quintero, home to shops and bars, before ducking down to the sprawling Plaza Quintero

Nuñez (known locally as the Plaza Cabildo), which acts as a splendid welcome mat for the Iglesia de Nuestra Señora de la Concepción. The church itself is a simple three-nave structure built in 1767 and crowned by a bell tower with a railed-off upper level that serves as a lookout. Inside, the polychrome *Purísima Concepción* is the town's most prized piece of artwork.

Finish your exploration of the town at the Casa de las Quinteras Centro Etnográfico (Calle Armas Martel; admission €3; ☺9am-2pm Mon-Fri, 10.30am-1.30pm Sat), where exhibits about rural island life are displayed in a small stone house. There's also a small craft shop on site.

THE ECOLOGICAL ISLAND

As your boat pulls into port, dry and rocky El Hierro might not strike you as the most beautiful of the Canary Islands, but clamber up onto the central plateau or head down to the El Golfo area and it quickly becomes apparent that first impressions can be misleading. Not only is the island enveloped in a gentle beauty, it's also home to some of the most unusual plant and animal life in the eastern Atlantic; a distinction that has earned the entire island the label of Unesco biosphere reserve. Environmentalists' attention is mainly focused on protecting the marine reserve in the Mar de las Calmas, the unique juniper trees in El Sabinar and the quiet El Pinar pine forest, but the whole island benefits from its Unesco listing, with funds going to helping the island use its unique natural resources in a sustainable way.

In early 2007 the island took its conservationist leanings to a whole new level, launching an ambitious, and still ongoing, plan to become the world's first island to depend entirely on renewable sources (like wind, water and solar) for its energy needs. This ecological mindset is seen in other ways as well, such as the island-wide plan to promote and support organic farming.

✿ Festivals & Events

A couple of times a year Valverde rouses itself from its stupor and lets its hair down for fiesta time.

Fiesta de San Isidro
Valverde   SAINT'S FESTIVAL
If you're in Valverde on 15 May, be sure to get a look at the *lucha canaria* (Canarian wrestling) showcase in the afternoon.

Fiesta de la Virgen de
la Concepción   SAINT'S FESTIVAL
The night before Valverde's biggest festival is marked with fireworks and a lively town party, while the day itself (8 December) is devoted to religious celebrations, concerts and various cultural acts.

✕ Eating

La Taberna de la Villa   INTERNATIONAL €€
(Calle General Rodriguez y Sánchez Espinoza 10; mains €5-12) Good, simple food (pizzas, pastas and tapas), a friendly atmosphere and extras like free wi-fi have made this the most popular spot in town. It morphs into a pub from midnight until 2am at weekends.

La Mirada Profunda   INTERNATIONAL €€
(Calle Santiago 25; menú €12) At this stylish bistro you don't have much of a say in what you eat, you just get to enjoy whatever the chef has prepared – soups, fresh fish and local fare with an international twist.

♟ Drinking

It doesn't get much more humdrum than Valverde, and during the week everyone heads home early. Weekends, the action (if there is any) is centred around La Taberna de la Villa, the **Tasca El Chavelazo** (Calle General Rodriguez y Sánchez Espinoza 8) next door and, if you really want a big night out, the **Fierro Lounge Club** (Calle General Rodriguez y Sánchez Espinoza 8).

❶ Information

Police station (☎922 55 00 25; ⏰8.30am-2pm & 3.30-9.30pm, closed weekend afternoons in summer) Situated inside the *ayuntamiento* (town hall).
Post office (☎922 55 02 91; Calle Correos 3)
Tourist office (☎922 55 03 02; www.elhierro. travel; Calle Dr Quintero 11; ⏰8am-3pm Mon-Fri, 9am-1pm Sat) Get maps and information about a few island attractions.

❶ Getting There & Away

Bus
The **bus station** (Calle Molino) is at the southern end of town, and routes do a good job of covering the island. From Valverde you can reach destinations including Frontera (€1, 30 minutes, up to four daily), Tamaduste (€1, 15 minutes, three daily), El Mocanal and La Restinga (€1, one hour 10 minutes, up to four daily).

Car
There are many car-rental firms in Valverde and if you reserve ahead they'll have a car waiting for you at the airport or port when you arrive.

Be sure to fill up the petrol tank before leaving Valverde, as there are only three petrol stations on the island! One is in the capital, a second in La Frontera and a third on the highway towards La Restinga.

❶ Getting Around

The easiest way to get to and from the airport is your own four wheels; car-rental agencies are happy to have a car waiting for you at the airport if you call ahead. **Taxis** (📞922 55 11 75) are a simple but pricey way to move about; it will cost about €14 to reach Valverde from the airport.

In town, you'll find a **taxi stand** (Calle San Francisco) just in front of the island transport co-op (Sociedad Cooperativa de Transportes del Hierro).

THE NORTH

The island's north coast is lined with ruggedly beautiful, but for the most part inaccessible, cliffs. The few exceptions are the delightful coves and natural volcanic-rock pools in places like Pozo de las Calcosas, Charco Manso, Tamaduste and La Caleta.

Inland, grassy fields and farms extend over much of the landscape. Due to the high altitude, a near-permanent shroud of mist and fog blankets the hilltops, making this quiet, rural area seem almost spooky in its solitude.

El Mocanal

A few minutes' drive northwest of Valverde sits El Mocanal, one of several farming villages that line the highway. Just outside the town, a well-marked turn leads down to the **Pozo de las Calcosas**, where a summer village of generations-old thatched-roof beach huts (called *pajeros*) are huddled around a few natural swimming pools. Walk down the steep, stepped path for 10 minutes to access them. Above the waterfront there's a mirador, a tiny stone chapel and a few restaurants. **Mesón La Barca** (Calle El Arenal; mains €6-15; ⊘closed

Tue) is a cheerful place, painted yellow and with a few rustic dining rooms. Fresh fish is the house speciality. Beside it is **Casa Carlos** (mains €5-16), also serving the day's catch – *atún* (tuna), *viejas* (parrot fish), *cabrillas* (comber fish) and *lapas* (limpets). Back up on the main highway the **Meson del Norte** (📞699 36 41 61; Calle Barlovento 21; mains €7-12) is a surprisingly swish and modern place that's justifiably popular with locals. The house specials are excellent and include a chickpea and chorizo stew and pork glazed in honey.

Bus 5 (€1, 20 minutes) links El Mocanal with Valverde several times daily.

Echedo

Only 3km from Valverde, Echedo is at the heart of El Hierro's wine-growing region. Its vineyards are planted behind quaint volcanic rock walls that help to block the wind that often swirls through. Far more captivating than anything in town are the **Charco Manso**, natural saltwater pools lying at the end of a lonely highway that winds down among shrubs and volcanic rock. On a fine day the clear turquoise waters are heavenly, but at high tide or when the ocean is stirred there can be strong currents here. Be especially cautious of the caves dug into the shore; peek into them on a calm day, but never swim here. The cave bottoms are pocked with tunnel-like holes called *tragadores* (literally, 'swallowers') that can suck you in as the tide ebbs.

There's a small kiosk by the *charco* that keeps sporadic hours, and for those who come prepared, there's a fine picnic area with wooden tables. For more formal eating, head into town where **La Higuera de la Abuela** (📞922 55 10 26; Calle Tajanis Caba s/n;

BEST BEACHES

Beaches are not really El Hierro's thing, but if you know where to look there are a few opportunities to get the bucket and spades out.

» **Playa de las Arenas Blancas** Pristine, uncluttered stretch of white sand interspersed with dark volcanic rocks. No facilities whatsoever and frequently dangerous swimming.

» **Cala de Tacorón** Stark volcanic coves abutting a sapphire sea with world-class diving and snorkelling opportunities.

» **La Maceta** Popular natural swimming pools set into a wave-lashed cove. Excellent for all the family. Some facilities.

EXPLORING THE ISLAND

At only 697 sq km the island seems easy to 'do' in a few days or a weekend, but keep in mind that highways here are narrow, curving things, and that very little of El Hierro's real beauty can be appreciated from a car window. Take your time to leisurely explore its coasts, its nature reserves, its towns and its forests to encounter the 'real' El Hierro.

mains €8-11; ⊘closed Tue) serves fried rabbit or goat, grilled shellfish and fresh island fish on a leafy patio once filled with an enormous *higuera* (fig tree).

Tamaduste & La Caleta

These two modest resort villages are Valverde's summer playground. Small, natural coves and beautiful waterfronts make them fantastic spots for swimming, sunbathing, relaxing and fishing, but don't expect much else from these otherwise snoring towns.

Tamaduste (10km northeast of Valverde) is the perfect place to escape from the outside world. At high tide the cove fills with water and kids dive head-first into the Atlantic. At low tide, the rough waves disappear, leaving nothing more than still pools. This is the perfect time to fish or collect crabs and ocean snails.

A few minutes further on is La Caleta, where the delightfully landscaped waterfront boasts an elegant stone-laid promenade, plenty of spots for sunbathing and aqua-blue saltwater pools, which are beautifully maintained and ideal for children (although it can get a little windy here). It used to be possible to see much-weathered Bimbache rock carvings on a rock face by the shore but, sadly, they were accidentally destroyed when the waterfront was reconstructed.

Grab a bite to eat – fresh local fish, tapas and meats in various sauces – at the family-run **Bar-Restaurante Bimbache** (☑922 96 90 14; Calle Los Cardones, Tamaduste; mains €7-12; ⊘closed Tue).

A bus connecting Valverde with the port stops three times daily in Tamaduste (€1, 15 minutes) and La Caleta (€1, 20 minutes).

Puerto de la Estaca & Las Playas

The island's only ferry port, Puerto de la Estaca becomes the centre of attention when it greets the odd ferry coming in from Tenerife. Otherwise, this place is so sleepy it borders on comatose. Five buses (€1, 50 minutes) daily link the port with Valverde. For information on ferries see p195.

Past the port, the highway curves around the coast towards Las Playas, 10km further on, slicing through a no-man's-land of rocky shores and rockier hillsides. You'll pass the little town of **Timijiraque**, where there is a small beach (watch the undertow here) and the homey **Casa Guayana** (☑922 55 04 17; Carretera General; mains €7-9), where tasty local fish is served in a cosy dining room with a handful of tables and red ruffled curtains at the window overlooking the ocean. The paella literally tastes of rock pools and the seaside! The food is so good that locals make a special effort to drive out here for lunch and reservations are sometimes required. Further along, just past a highway tunnel, look offshore to see the famed **Roque de la Bonanza**, a rock formation that soars 200m out of the water and has become a symbol of the island. Las Playas itself is a long stretch of cobblestone beach with mirror-smooth seas. It is often quite windy though.

Mirador de la Peña

Just outside the agricultural hamlet of **Guarazoca** is one of El Hierro's top sites – the Mirador de la Peña, designed by famed Lanzarote-born artist César Manrique (see the boxed text, p101). Get your camera ready: mist permitting, this mirador affords sweeping views of the valley, the gulf coast and the Roques de Salmor. Wander around short paths leading to several vantage points, then dine at the elegant **restaurant** (☑922 55 03 00; mains €10-12, menu del día €12; ⊘closed Sun dinner & Mon), with its elegant dining room dominated by a huge window looking out over El Golfo. The menu is focused on creative ways to use local ingredients, with results like Herreño pineapple stuffed with shellfish, or fish with Herreño cheese sauce. There's an informal cafe as well. Sunset is really the time to see this place at its best.

San Andrés & Around

The agricultural centre of this part of the island, San Andrés is made up of a few buildings scattered on either side of the highway; one of them is **Casa Goyo** (🖉922 55 12 63; mains €6-12), a simple, no-frills diner serving up filling local fare such as goat and rabbit on green-checked tablecloths. Talking of agriculture, the **Fiesta de la Apañada** in June sees farmers gather in San Andrés for a noisy livestock sale.

Four buses (€1, 20 minutes) daily link San Andrés with Valverde.

Gain insight into the culture of the Bimbaches by visiting the site of their ancient holy tree, **El Garoé** (🕙10am-6pm Tue-Sat). According to legend, the tree miraculously spouted water, providing for the islanders and their animals. Today we know that it's really no miracle – mist in the air condenses on the tree's leaves and gives fresh water. The tree itself is rather unremarkable, especially taking into account that the original, a variety of laurel, was felled by a hurricane in 1610; the one here today was planted in 1949. There's a small visitor centre near the tree and pretty walking trails leading to various freshwater pools. Get here along one of the two 2.7km dirt tracks that branch off the highways heading towards San Andrés. Both routes involve rocky, steep drives.

Several walking trails set off from here. Take the PR EH 7 3km to El Mocanal or 6km down to the Pozo de las Calcosas, or take the same trail 3.5km in the other direction to San Andrés.

About 3km southwest of San Andrés, turn onto the H-120 towards the **Mirador de Jinama** for soul-satisfying views over the mammoth amphitheatre that is El Golfo. Of course, depending on the day, you could be looking over a big pot of cloud soup. There's also an excellent (although windy) picnic spot and a small chapel. The H-120 highway continues on its narrow, curvy path towards the Mirador de la Peña, making it one of the island's most scenic byways.

From Jinama, you can strike out on the rocky but well-marked **Camino de Jinama**, an old donkey track that should take about 2½ hours to hike down to La Frontera and 3½ hours to return. The reverse route begins near the Plaza de la Candelaria in La Frontera.

Heading south on the HI-4 highway, you'll come to a turn-off (the HI-402) for the **Mirador de las Playas**, where there is a spectacular view of the coast below.

Isora

The cheese-producing village of Isora is a short drive (or hike, if you're up for it) from San Andrés. On the far southern side of town, perched high on El Risco de los Herreños ridge, is the **Mirador de Isora**, where the mountain falls away at your feet to reveal the smooth coast of Las Playas. The 3.5km downhill trek from the mirador to Las Playas is a popular hike with awesome views over the coast; the descent should take two hours and the round trip about five. The downward part of the hike is extremely jarring on the legs, while coming back up again will really give your heart and lungs a good workout.

If you're driving, follow the signs (just northeast of San Andrés) to Isora off the HI-4 highway. If you're walking, the PR EH 4.1km trail to Isora starts in Las Rosas neighbourhood of San Andrés.

Five buses (€1, 30 minutes) daily connect Isora and Valverde.

EATING LIKE A LOCAL

Food on El Hierro might be simple, but in our opinion it has the best food of any of the western islands. The island is very much self-sufficient and much of what you eat was grown, reared or captured on the island or off its coasts. The lack of tourists also helps to ensure that restaurants are catering mainly to a local audience, which helps to ensure a higher standard of food quality (restaurant owners know that they are relying on locals to keep coming back, whereas on touristy islands they know they're serving a here today, gone tomorrow clientele). Fresh local fish, local meat and local vegetables are often available at restaurants, especially to those who know to ask for it! Specialities on El Hierro include *queso herreño* (local soft cheese); dried figs are another favourite. The fruity white wine from Tigaday is quite good and is sold and served widely on the island.

EL HIERRO FOR CHILDREN

Although it lacks the theme parks, zoos and myriad organised activities of some of the larger islands, there's still plenty of good, clean, healthy outdoors fun for children. The various natural pools that are dotted liberally around the island offer safe swimming for all the family. The best of these are **La Maceta** and **La Caleta**. Much less frequented, but undeniably beautiful, is the **Charco Azul**. Older children will love the snorkelling and diving around **La Restinga** and everyone likes looking for dragons among the giant lizards housed in the **Ecomuseo de Guinea**. Up on the inland plateau there are plenty of chances for youngsters to burn off excess energy on the numerous fairly gentle hiking trails.

THE SOUTH

For many people this is the most beautiful part of the island. It's lush and green with an idyllic year-round climate. It's also about the only part of the Canary Islands where you'll see proper livestock farming and fields surrounded by dry stone walls. The landscape undulates gently and in February and March the whole area is nothing less than a carnival of colourful flowers. It really pays to ditch the car and follow some of the easy walking trails that criss-cross this highland region.

El Pinar

The serene El Pinar pine forest covers a long swath of the southern half of the island, casting cool shade over the volcanic terrain and providing an excellent destination for a day's hiking or a scenic drive. The lonely highway that cuts through El Pinar connects the eastern rim of the forest with the Ermita de Nuestra Señora de los Reyes on the western side of the island; countless trails branch off the main road.

On the HI-4 highway, south of the Mirador de las Playas, you'll pass **Las Casas** and **Taibique**, two small towns built along the steeply descending highway. Although they're technically independent, it's impossible to tell where one town ends and the other begins. While not a destination in its own right, this is a good place for self-caterers to buy supplies. The main attraction is the **Mirador de Tanajara**, with lovely views, and a small **ceramics shop** nearby, open whenever the owner is home. Find it just west of Taibique's town centre.

Hoya del Morcillo & Around

From the HI-4, take the HI-40 highway towards **Hoya del Morcillo** (⊗9am-9pm), a shady recreational area in the heart of El Pinar. With a football field, a playground and a picnic area, this is the perfect spot to rest among the pines. Don't miss the large-scale map of El Hierro, made with logs. A severe fire in September 2006 altered this area, and now it's a great place to marvel at the resilience of the hearty Canary pine. Their blackened trunks are proof of the fire's wrath, but the fact that they stand here today, as green as ever, shows how remarkable these trees are.

Continuing into the El Pinar forest, you come across **El Julán**, where a trail heads down to one of the island's most important cultural sites, **Los Letreros**. Here, a scattering of indecipherable petroglyphs was scratched into a lava flow by the Bimbaches. The hike is a long one that leaves behind the pine forest and heads into dry, volcanic territory. At the end (or sometimes along the trail) a guide may ask you to show your passport. Ask the guide to point out the carvings; if you don't know where to look you may pass right by the faded etchings and not know it. At the time of writing, a roadside information centre was under construction.

Continuing west, 6km past El Julán is a dirt road on your right that leads you up to the foot of **Malpaso** (1501m), the island's highest peak. The 9km of rough dirt track makes for slow going, but the ride is an adventure. The track is suitable for almost any vehicle (carry a spare tyre just in case).

La Restinga

Quickly becoming El Hierro's tourist hot spot, the once-sleepy fishing village of La Restinga is now turning into something of a resort thanks to the dozens of scuba-diving outfitters that have set up shop here. All take advantage of the underwater marvels provided by the **Mar de las Calmas** (Sea of Calm), the warm, still waters that surround the island's southwestern shore. For nondivers, there are two volcanic beaches right on the port, where the ocean is as still as bath water, if none too clean. The town itself still feels like it's being built and is certainly not what you'd describe as attractive.

The road down to La Restinga rambles through volcanic badlands. Take time to look at the funny lava shapes, ranging from *pahoehoe* or *lajial,* smooth rock that looks like twisted taffy, to hard, crumbling rock that looks like wet oatmeal. The gleaming sea stretches out before you as you descend into the town, and you can clearly make out the line between the glassy Mar de las Calmas and the windblown open ocean to the west, which is rough and choppy. Part of the sea is a marine reserve, and both fishing and diving are restricted in an effort to provide fish with a safe place to breed.

The **Fiesta de la Virgen del Carmen**, honouring La Restinga's patron saint, is celebrated on the weekend closest to 16 July with a town dance and dinner on Saturday, and a religious procession on Sunday.

🏃 Activities

There's no shortage of diving companies offering their services to divers, and everyone is offering pretty much the same thing – a €25 to €30 dive around the Mar de las Calmas, where you can expect to encounter colourful coral, majestic rock formations and a wide variety of marine life. Courses and speciality dives are also available. The companies' opening hours change daily, according to the weather and the number of dives planned. Companies include **Arrecifal** (📞922 55 71 71; www.arrecifal.com; Calle La Orcilla 30) and **El Hierro Taxi Diver** (📞922 10 40 69; www.elhierrotaxidiver.com; Avenida Marítima 4).

🍴 Eating

Delicious, fresh seafood is the main attraction at most restaurants here. Self-caterers can shop at the Spar supermarket in town.

Casa Juan   SEAFOOD **€€**
(📞922 55 71 02; Calle Juan Gutierrez Monteverde 23; mains €6-12; ⊗closed Wed & Jan) Hearty portions of fresh fish, soup, salad, *papas* (potatoes) and grilled meats are served up at this friendly place popular with locals.

ℹ️ Information

The **tourist office** (📞922 55 71 88; Avenida Marítima; ⊗8.30am-2.30pm Mon-Fri) has maps and information about the area.

ℹ️ Getting There & Away

The HI-4 highway dead-ends in La Restinga; there's no missing it. There are frequent bus services (€1, one hour 10 minutes, up to four daily) between Valverde and La Restinga.

EL GOLFO

An amphitheatre-shaped depression dominating El Hierro's northwestern flank, the green Golfo is, like the rest of the island, largely rural, with banana plantations filling

---

GETTING PHYSICAL ON EL HIERRO

El Hierro is perhaps best known as a scuba-diving destination; La Restinga is the sport's epicentre. Other popular activities include splashing around in the natural volcanic-rock pools, fishing off the shore and hiking.

The island is scored with hiking trails, including the long-distance GR trails (marked with red-and-white signs), the 10km-plus PR trails (marked in yellow and white) and the short and local SL trails (marked in green and white). The island's best-known path is the **Camino de la Virgen**, stretching from the Ermita de Nuestra Señora de los Reyes to Valverde; this 26km historic trail is walked by thousands during the fiesta Bajada de la Virgen de los Reyes (see the boxed text, p207). There are a few very demanding walks on El Hierro, such as the thigh-burning hike from Isora to Las Playas. But most of the walking, whether it be coastal strolling or countryside rambling, is fairly gentle and family-friendly – but none the less impressive for it.

WORTH A TRIP

CALA DE TACORÓN

Just before La Restinga, you'll pass the turn-off to Cala de Tacorón, an absolutely idyllic series of volcanic rocky coves that bake in a near-ceaseless sun. This is a great area for swimming and diving (many of the La Restinga–based companies come here) and it's popular with kayakers. After enjoying the water, have lunch at the rustic, covered picnic area, made with logs and branches, á la Swiss Family Robinson. If DIY lunches just aren't you then there's also a laid-back beach bar (noon-8pm, Tue-Sun) that serves an eclectic mix of dishes from wood-fired pizzas to octopus dragged straight out of the nearby water.

the low-lying coastal areas. A string of quiet hamlets, some with tempting swimming holes, are laid out along the coast, while inland, growing commercial centres like La Frontera and Tigaday serve as the economic engines of the western half of the island. To the south, a rugged mountain ridge looms like a wall hiding the rest of the island, while to the north, a desolate volcanic wasteland tempts with its peculiar beauty. More than 90% of the terrain on this part of the island is protected as some sort of reserve.

Thanks to the highway tunnel built a few years back, El Golfo is just a 10-minute drive from Valverde on the HI-5 highway. But for those who love a good scenic drive (and don't get car sick), coming in the old way, on the HI-1, snaking down over the towering mountain ridge flanking El Golfo, is rewarding – just make sure the brakes on your car are in good working order!

Las Puntas

After the tunnel, the first town you come across is Las Puntas; take the HI-55 turn-off to head down to this coastal town. Sitting right on the water, though offering no access to it, this small hamlet exists purely for the tourists who come to relax here. Its main attractions are the view and the sound of the roaring waves. A newly gravelled (and in parts even boardwalked) pathway runs between Las Puntas and La Maceta. The walk takes about an hour (one way) and is very easy (you could probably just about

manage to do it with a baby stroller) and offers sublime ocean views all the way.

From here there is a clear view of Los Roques de Salmor, an important nesting spot for various bird species and one of the last stands of the primeval Lagarto del Salmor (Lizard of Salmor).

The only spot to eat or drink close to the water, cheery La Mareta (922 55 92 72; Calle Puntagrande 3; mains €8-12; closed Mon & Tue lunch) gets lively on weekend nights. At meal time, come to enjoy tapas and seafood meals so fresh the fish on your plate will probably still be flapping their fins in protest.

Around Las Puntas
LA MACETA & CHARCO LOS SARGOS

For a swim, head down to La Maceta. This series of natural saltwater pools built along the coast is probably the pick of such places on El Hierro, and certainly the most popular with both locals and tourists. At high tide the ocean swallows the pools, making swimming dangerous. At other times, though, taking a cool dip here is a dream. There are several different pools of varying depth and wave shelter including one that is ideal for children.

La Maceta (922 55 60 20; mains €8-13; closed Wed) is a classy, and very popular, Italian restaurant just up from the pools. The enormous windows afford unbeatable ocean views or there's a breezy terrace. As you would expect, most of the dishes have a seafood bias. At weekend lunchtimes it can get busy so it's well worth reserving a table in advance. Between the restaurant and the pools are several communal barbeque areas.

From the main highway, follow the signs to La Maceta, turning down the HI-550 and taking the first sealed road to your right.

Just up the coast is Charco Los Sargos, another swimming spot with calm pools that buffer the crashing waves. It's similar to La Maceta but with less fanfare. There's a small beach shack that keeps erratic hours. From the HI-550, the turn-off is just 300m north of the turn-off for La Maceta.

ECOMUSEO DE GUINEA

The island's premier cultural site, this interesting outdoor museum (www.el-meridiano.com; admission €7.50; 10am-6pm Tue-Sat, tours 10.30am, noon, 1.30pm, 3pm & 4.45pm) is really two centres in one. The Casas de Guinea encompasses a fascinating route through volcanic caves and 20 ancient houses (four of which are visitable). The houses represent islander lifestyles through the centuries. Next door, the Lagartario is a recuperation centre for the giant lizard of El Hierro, where you can see around a dozen lizards lolling about in the sun in giant vivariums You can only visit with a guide at the times listed above. The tours are in Spanish only, except at 10.30am on Wednesdays when they run an English- and German-language tour.

Tigaday

POP 1231

The nerve centre of the La Frontera municipality, Tigaday is a commercial hub (in El Hierro terms at least) strung out along the highway. There's not much to see in the centre, but as El Hierro's second town, Tigaday is the only place on the island with shops and services to rival the capital. It even has one of the island's three petrol stations! Most shops, bars and services are along Calle Tigaday.

On Sundays a small artisan and fresh-food **market** (⊙8am-1pm; Plaza Vieja) sets up shop on Tigaday's main plaza.

✖ Eating

TOP CHOICE Restaurante
Don Din 2   MODERN CANARIAN **€€**
(✆922 55 61 48; www.restaurantedondin2.com, in Spanish; Calle La Corredera 5; mains €8-12; ⊙closed Sun) From the outside this looks like any other small-town Spanish bar, but step inside and you enter a fantastical world of culinary magic. The food is all the normal Canarian staples, but with all manner of unusual potions poured over them, and unexpected combinations. Some good examples of this are the seaweed salad

---

THE GIANT LIZARD

Imagine the Spaniards' surprise when they began to explore El Hierro and, among the native birds, juniper trees and unusual volcanic rock, they discovered enormous lizards as large as cats. Greyish-brown and growing up to 45cm in length, the lizards aren't venomous or harmful, though according to one early chronicler they're 'disgusting and repugnant to behold'.

By the 1940s these giant lizards were almost extinct, all but snuffed out by human encroachment on their habitat, introduced predators (such as cats) and climatological factors. A few survived on the Roques de Salmor rock outcrop off the gulf coast (giving the species its name, 'Lizard of Salmor'), but before long, those too had disappeared.

Then, in the 1970s, herdsmen began reporting sightings of large, unidentified animal droppings and carcasses of extra-long lizards that had been killed by dogs. To the delight of conservationists, a small colony of the giant lizards had survived on a practically inaccessible mountain crag, the Fuga de Gorreta. One herdsman was able to capture a pair of the reptiles, beginning the species' journey back to life.

In 1985 the Giant Lizard of El Hierro Recovery Plan was put into place. These days you can see it in action at the Lagartario at the Ecomuseo de Guinea, where the lizards are bred in captivity and released into supervised wild areas. At the Lagartario you can spy on a few specimens in their glassed-in cages as they soak up the sun or snack on vegetation. A guide explains the recovery efforts and the history of the giant lizard.

Giant lizards were once found on all the islands in the Canaries (each island had its own individual species), but all went to the dustbin of extinction once man, cat and dog got their hands (or paws) on them. Or had they? Just as the El Hierro Giant Lizard was rediscovered in the 1970s, scientists discovered a population of six La Gomera Giant Lizards in 1999 and then, in 2007, along came the La Palma Giant Lizard. Both these populations are only just on the brink of survival and both are classed as critically endangered (as are the El Hierro lizards).

Interestingly, in all cases it's thought that the giant lizards of today are actually quite a lot smaller than in the past. The Museo de la Naturaleza y El Hombre has some skeletons and bodies of Komodo-like giant lizards from Tenerife and Gran Canaria.

The El Hierro Giant Lizard is the only one that it's possible for the average person to see.

or the baby squid wrapped in bacon. It's very informal and very popular and you can choose between eating in the small dining room or the bar filled with fruit machines.

La Frontera

Although La Frontera is the name of the large municipality that extends over the entire gulf coast, it's also the name of a small and very peaceful settlement perched on the hillside behind Tigaday. The most important thing here is the **Iglesia de Nuestra Señora de la Candelaria**, a 17th-century construction that was redone in 1929. Inside, the three-nave church has two rows of pretty stone columns and an ornate golden altar. It sits on the **Plaza de la Candelaria**, a charming square with benches and a fountain. Behind the church, you can walk to the empty **stone chapel** perched on the hill. It's a short but steep climb and, from the top, the gulf valley spreads out before you like a patchwork quilt of fields and banana plantations.

On 15 August La Frontera celebrates the **Fiesta de la Virgen de la Candelaria** with a religious procession and a showcase of *lucha canaria* followed by a lively dance in nearby Tigaday's Plaza Vieja.

The **Camino de Jinama** begins (or ends, depending on your route) near the plaza.

Just in front of the church, **Joapira** (☑922 55 98 03; Plaza Candelaria 8; mains €6-8) is a bar with a covered terrace that also serves simple food like tapas, roast chicken and the house speciality, *carne fiesta*.

Los Llanillos & Sabinosa

There are two routes leading to the western end of the island: the flat, ocean-side HI-550, and the gorgeous but tortuously curved HI-50. Those who set out on the latter are rewarded with a beautiful drive along a mountain ridge. The hairpin curves can be challenging, though, especially if you're tempted to admire the scenery of the ocean laid out below and the surrounding rugged volcanic mountains.

The small town of Los Llanillos hugs the HI-50 highway a few kilometres out of Tigaday. Although the town itself won't detain you for long, there is a good restaurant here: **Asador Artero** (☑922 55 50 37; Calle Artero 2; mains €6-12). A cosy yet busy place, it's popular with locals who crowd in for the tasty grilled meats and chicken.

In Los Llanillos, take the turn-off for **Charco Azul**, a pristine natural cove with calm pools for swimming and hardly another soul in sight.

The highway grows steeper and curvier as it leads to Sabinosa, Spain's westernmost town. This remote little village feels as though it's at the end of the world, which in fact, until Columbus found some place called America, people thought it was. There is not much here to see, but the scenery nearby is breathtaking.

If you take the coastal highway, you'll quickly reach the famed **Pozo de la Salud** (Well of Health). You can walk down to the small *pozo*, with its waters said to cure a variety of ills, but it's all closed up and there's not much to see.

Just west of the *pozo*, down the HI-500, is **Playa de las Arenas Blancas** (White Sands Beach). Take a short road down to the coast, where indeed there are a few whitish grains of sand. They quickly melt into volcanic rock at the water's edge, though. Despite this slight abuse of the term white, it is still a fantastic spot – wild and beautiful and almost certain to be deserted. Be careful of dangerous currents if you take to the waters. There's a very simple and well-marked hour-long coastal walk starting from this beach and leading into La Dehesa area.

MAPS & BOOKS

In late 2003 a highway tunnel connecting Valverde with La Frontera was built, and the island changed the names of all its major highways. Many older maps still show the old roads. Up-to-date maps include the 1:50,000 *Tourist Map El Hierro* by Turquesa, and the satellite-generated maps given out free by the tourist office, which are sufficient for making simple tours around the island.

Hiking guidebooks remain few and far between for El Hierro in comparison with its neighbours. *La Palma and El Hierro Car Tours and Walks* published by Sunflower Books is a reliable and up-to-date guide with walks suitable for all levels of hiker.

FIT FOR A KING

The fiesta par excellence on El Hierro is the **Bajada de la Virgen de los Reyes** (Descent of the Virgin), held in early July every four years (next in 2013). Most of the island's population gathers to witness or join in a procession bearing a statue of the Virgin, seated in a sedan chair, from the Ermita de Nuestra Señora de los Reyes in the west of the island all the way across to Valverde. Her descent is accompanied by musicians and dancers dressed in traditional red-and-white tunics and gaudy caps, and celebrations continue for most of the month in villages and hamlets across the island.

You don't have to wait for the fiesta to make this iconic walk across the island. The ancient 26km Camino de la Virgen trail stretches from Valverde to the *ermita* (chapel), cutting through farms and forest on its journey across the spine of the island. Expect the well-marked walk to take eight hours. It takes in much of the island's most beautiful highland scenery – an area absolutely awash in flowers in the spring.

LA DEHESA

West of Sabinosa the island is practically uninhabited and wild volcanic landscapes dominated by fierce-looking rock formations, hardy shrubs and wind-sculpted juniper trees are the main attractions. This part of the island is called **La Dehesa** (The Pasture), and is only accessible via the arching highway that cuts through volcanic badlands where only a few low shrubs dare to survive.

Stop for a swim at **Playa del Verodal**, a curious red-sand beach that backs up to a majestic rock cliff. The beach itself is 1km off the main highway (follow the signs) and is often deserted, leaving you with your own private paradise.

As the highway nears the southern coast, you'll reach the HI-503, the turn-off for the **Faro de Orchilla** (Lighthouse of Orchilla), the most southwesterly point in Spain. Long ago robbed of its status as Meridiano Cero by Greenwich in the UK, the lighthouse is still an island icon. West of the lighthouse is a commemorative monument.

Ermita de Nuestra Señora de los Reyes

Back on the main highway, tackle a few more curves to reach this pretty white chapel, made all the more interesting because of the history and tradition behind it.

The chapel contains the image of the island's patron saint, Nuestra Señora de los Reyes (Our Lady of the Kings), because local shepherds bought her from foreign sailors on Three Kings Day, 6 January (1545). The people attribute several miracles to the Virgin, including ending droughts and epidemics.

Every four years (2013, 2017 etc) the Virgin is taken out of the chapel in a lively procession around the island. If you can't be here for this extravaganza then on the feast day of the **Fiesta de los Pastores** (25 April), the Virgen de los Reyes is taken out of out of her home in the Ermita de Nuestra Señora de los Reyes and carried to the cave where she was first kept.

El Sabinar & Beyond

From the *ermita,* continue north up windswept El Sabinar, named after the *sabinas* (junipers) that grow up here in very weird ways. Along one part of the road the way is lined with *sabinas* – though beautiful, these are not as spectacular as the wind-twisted trees further down the road at El Sabinar, which have become the island's symbol. You'll pass a turn-off to the left at a signpost indicating El Sabinar. Park here and wander among some of the most unusual trees you'll ever see. They have been sculpted by nature into wild shapes that look frozen in time.

Wear long trousers if you want to weave your way through the brush and get close to the trees, which are scattered on the hillside. These wonderfully weird *sabinas* are part of the reason that Unesco declared the entire island a biosphere reserve.

Once back at the fork, you could curl north for a further 2km to reach the **Mirador de Bascos**, a spectacular lookout that's unfortunately often cloaked in cloud. If it's a clear day, prepare for a breathtaking view.

Accommodation

Best Places to Sleep

» Fonda de la Tea (p211)

» Finca de Arrieta (p216)

» Hotel San Roque (p219)

» Parador Nacional Conde de la Gomera (p221)

Best Budget Options

» Hotel Madrid (p209)

» Pensión Magec (p217)

» Senderos de Abono (p220)

» Pensión la Cubana (p223)

Best Boutique Hotels

» Casa El Siroco (p213)

» Casa Isaítas (p214)

» Hotel Alhambra (p219)

Where to Stay

Part of the charm of this region is that every island has a distinctive character. The most popular island is Tenerife, where the high-profile tourist resorts are in the south. Puerto de la Cruz, in the north, has excellent tourist facilities, while historic La Laguna is a charming inland choice.

Fuerteventura has two main resorts: Morro Jable in the south, and Corralejo in the north, which has a pretty harbour at its heart. Lanzarote's Puerto del Carmen, Costa Teguise and Playa Blanca are the main tourist areas, while the capital, Arrecife is a good base.

Las Palmas de Gran Canaria combines a great beach with city sophistication, while the southern resorts are unabashedly family-orientated. La Palma's Los Cancajos and Puerto Naos beaches are among the best on the island, while the centre hinterland is home to atmospheric *casas rurales*.

On the smallest islands, La Gomera and El Hierro, accommodation is predominantly midrange and includes atmospheric rural accommodation.

Pricing

The price indicators in this book refer to the cost of a double room, including private bathroom and excluding breakfast unless otherwise noted. Where half-board (breakfast and dinner) or full board (breakfast, lunch and dinner) is included, this is mentioned in the price. In the budget category you may have to share a bathroom and facilities will be limited. Midrange choices often include satellite TV, private balconies and, increasingly, wi-fi, while top end offers all this, plus more, and are often located in sumptuous historic buildings.

CATEGORY	COST
€ budget	< €60
€€ midrange	€60–120
€€€ top end	> €120

Apartments

Apartments for rent are much more common than hotels. Quality can vary greatly, but they can be more comfortable than a simple *pensión* and considerably more economical, especially if there are several of you and you plan to self-cater. The two principal categories are *estudios* (studios), with one bedroom or a living room and bedroom combined, and the more frequent *apartamento,* where you get a double bedroom and separate lounge. Both have separate bathroom and a kitchenette. Also common are *aparthotels* (apartment-hotel), which function exactly like hotels in terms of service, but with large rooms that include a kitchenette – more like a small apartment.

However, many apartment complexes are contracted to tour operators and don't rent to independent travellers; even those that do may insist upon a minimum three-night stay.

In the case of privately owned apartments, most of the time the owner doesn't live in the building so there's little point in just turning up – you generally need to call ahead.

Casas Rurales

These rural hotels are generally converted farmsteads or village houses and are often a highly agreeable option for those seeking to escape the bustle of the resorts but, again, it's essential to call ahead as they usually offer limited places and there may be no-one in attendance. Many *casas rurales* are distant from public transport, so check whether a hire car is necessary or desirable. They usually represent excellent value for the charm of their setting and facilities.

Hotels, Hostels & Pensiones

Compared with mainland Spain, there are precious few *hoteles* (one- to five-star hotels) or *pensiones* (one- or two-star guesthouses) in the Canaries. Since the bulk of the islands' visitors arrive with accommodation booked in advance – usually in villas or self-catering apartments – the demand for more standard hotels is low.

In practice, there is little difference between *pensiones* and *hostales* (small hotels, not youth hostels). At the low-price, one-star end of either you may well find cramped, dank rooms and shared bathrooms (with perhaps a simple washbasin in the room), while at a slightly higher price you could find charming gems with private bathrooms

and stylish decor. *Hoteles* range from simple places to luxurious, five-star establishments with complimentary bathrobes, spa treatments and superior restaurants.

Paradores

The paradores, a Spanish state-run chain of high-class hotels with six establishments in the Canary Islands, are in a special category. They can be wonderful places to luxuriate. They also offer a range of discounts for senior citizens, under-30s and those staying more than one night. You can find current offers at www.parador.es.

Camping

For a place with so much natural beauty, there are precious few places to camp in the Canary Islands. Most islands have just one token official campsite and free camping is largely prohibited.

GRAN CANARIA

Gran Canaria arguably has the best range of accommodation in the Canaries, depending on whether you want to wake up to sounds of birdsong, the surf or surrounded by the vigour and excitement of a Spanish mainland–style city.

Las Palmas de Gran Canaria

VEGUETA & TRIANA

TOP CHOICE Hotel Madrid HOTEL €
(Map p42; ☑928 36 06 64; www.elhotelmadrid .com; Plazoleta Cairasco 4; s/d €35/45, without bathroom €30/40) This place has almost as much charm as history: General Franco spent the night of 17 July 1936 in room No 3 here (and reputedly left without paying!). The next day he flew to Spain and the rest is history. The interior is a beguiling mix of agreeable tat, priceless antiques and hanging plants; most rooms have antique

BOOK YOUR STAY ONLINE

For more accommodation reviews by Lonely Planet authors, check out hotels .lonelyplanet.com. You'll find independent reviews, as well as recommendations on the best places to stay. Best of all, you can book online.

bedheads. The downstairs bar and restaurant are atmospheric, though the menu is geared for tourists and a tad overpriced.

Hotel Parque   HOTEL **€€**
(Map p42; ☎928 36 80 00; www.hparque.com; Muelle Las Palmas 2; s/d incl breakfast €68/79; P❋@☎❋) This six-storey hotel is excellently positioned overlooking the Parque San Telmo. The best views are from the rooftop solarium and breakfast room. Rooms are large but dated, with floral curtains and a predominance of brown furnishings. More colour and style could make this a real winner, but for the moment we'll push the comfort rather than class.

Pensión Perojo   PENSIÓN **€**
(Map p42; ☎928 37 13 87; Calle Perojo 1; s/d without bathroom €17/26) A late-19th-century building with grand old doors and high ceilings plus scrupulously clean rooms washed in pale peach. The only downside is its position on an intersection that cops the full brunt of the peak-hour-traffic noise. Owner Rafael speaks Spanish only.

CIUDAD JARDÍN

Hotel Santa Catalina   HOTEL **€€€**
(☎928 24 30 40; www.hotelsantacatalina.com; Calle León y Castillo 227; s/d €139/180; P❋@☎) This historic hotel is truly magnificent, with traditional Canarian balconies, showy turrets and a red-carpet-style arcaded entrance. The rooms won't disappoint; there are king-size beds, antique bedheads, oriental carpets and plush furnishings. It exudes the class of another era, with its own casino and *hammam* (Turkish bath) and delightful views of either the sea or subtropical gardens.

SANTA CATALINA & THE PORT

Aparthotel Las Lanzas   APARTMENT-HOTEL **€**
(Map p44; ☎928 26 55 04; www.aparthotel -laslanzas.com; Calle Bernardo de la Torre 79,

2-person apt €50; ❋) These homey apartments are well kitted-out with a breakfast bar, small fridge and plenty of pots and pans. If you don't feel like whipping up eggs and bacon, you can opt for breakfast at just €3. Private balconies cost €6 more.

Apartamentos Playa Dorada   APARTMENTS **€**
(Map p44; ☎928 26 51 00; Calle Luis Morote 69; apt for 1-2 people €60, 3-4 people €75; ❋☎) These spacious apartments have enough kitchen cupboards for a family of four. The rooms have a retro '60s feel with their white plastic bar stools, tubular lights and swivel chairs. There is wi-fi access in the lobby. Go for a room with a sea view from the terrace; there's no extra cost.

Hotel Imperial Playa   HOTEL **€€**
(Map p44; ☎928 46 88 54; www.nh-hoteles.com; Calle Ferreras 1; s/d €100/120; P❋@☎❋) The lobby here sets the tone with its black tubular lamps, chocolate-brown paintwork, sage-green sofas and a magnificently quirky version of Velázquez' *Las Meninas* executed in colourful tiles. The rooms are perfectly coordinated with their striped navy-blue-and-white curtains and fabrics coupled with cool, pale parquet floors. The terraces overlook the harbour.

Around Las Palmas

AGÜIMES

Hotel Rural Casa de los Camellos   RURAL HOTEL **€€**
(☎928 78 50 53; www.hecansa.com; Calle Progreso 12; s/d €51/70; ❋) A lovely place tucked down a narrow pedestrian street in the historic centre. The restaurant (in a former camel stable) is highly rated, while the rooms are elegant yet rustic, with antiques and wooden beams and balconies. On the downside, the service can be aloof.

ONLINE RESOURCES

Casas Rurales (www.ecoturismocanarias.com) Has an extensive selection of rural accommodation throughout the islands.

Eco-Friendly (www.stayecochic.com) Specialises in eco-friendly accommodation, primarily in Lanzarote, with plans to extend to all islands.

Rural Accommodation (www.alorustico.com) A Spanish mainland website that includes some 70 choices for rural accommodation on the Canary Islands.

Country Houses (Tenerife) (www. ruraltenerife.net) Rural cottages and traditional Canarian country houses for holiday let.

SAN BARTOLOMÉ DE TIRAJANA

La Hacienda del Molino   RURAL HOTEL   €€
(☎928 12 73 44; www.lahaciendadelmolino.com; Calle Los Naranjos 2; d from €80) This delightful *casa rural* has a warm, vernacular look with lots of wood and stone. The charming rooms overlook a central courtyard where you enjoy tapas or something more substantial from the restaurant. There is a comfortable communal sitting room, complete with plasma TV and plush white sofas and chairs, plus the original mill where you can see how *gofio* is made.

Paradise Hotel Las Tirajanas   HOTEL   €€
(☎928 12 30 00; www.paradiseresorts.es; Calle Oficial Mayor Jose Rubio s/n; s/d €90/150; P@⊛☎) This place has an African-hunting-lodge look with its zebra-striped upholstery and mounted animal heads. The rooms are more mainstream luxurious, however, with wood furnishings, terracotta tiles and four-poster beds. There is also a spa, a fitness centre and a chapel if you fancy tying the knot. Located on a bluff above the town, it has spectacular views of soaring mountains.

TEJEDA

Fonda de la Tea   BOUTIQUE HOTEL   €€
(☎928 66 64 22; www.hotelfondadelatea.com; Calle Ezequiel Sánchez 22; r €95; ⊛@) This traditional stone-clad building has been tastefully transformed into a charming small hotel. Rooms are set around a Canarian-style courtyard and are tastefully decorated with plenty of terracotta tiling, pumpkin-coloured paintwork and wood. The solarium has stunning views across the valley and guests have access to the municipal pool in the summer.

AROUND TEJEDA

Parador de Cruz de Tejeda   PARADOR   €€€
(☎928 01 25 00; www.parador.es; Cruz de Tejeda s/n; r €125; P⊛☎) Re-opened in 2010 after an extensive refurbishment, the interior couples low-key sophistication with a muted earth-colour palette, accentuated by tasteful art work and framed by truly outstanding views of the surrounding gorges and cliffs. There is a luxurious spa for enjoying after your daily hikes; the staff can provide detailed maps.

Hotel Rural El Refugio   RURAL HOTEL   €€
(☎928 66 65 13; www.hotelruralelrefugio.com; Cruz de Tejeda s/n; s/d €60/74; P⊛☎) Just across from the parador, this hotel has long been a popular choice with walkers. It

ⓘ TAXES

Virtually all accommodation prices are subject to IGIC, the Canary Islands' indirect tax, charged at a rate of 5%. This tax is often included in the quoted price at the cheaper places, but less often at the more expensive ones. In some cases you will only be charged the tax if you ask for a receipt.

has an unpretentious rustic charm with a popular and reasonably priced restaurant and bar and rooms that boast appropriately great views of the surrounding striking landscape.

The Northwest

TEROR

Casa Rural Doña Margarita   RURAL HOTEL   €€
(☎928 35 00 00; www.margaritacasarural.com; Calle Padre Cueto 4; 2-/4-person apt €75/115; ☎) A beautifully restored, colonial-style 18th-century house run by lovely Queta and her husband in her late grandmother's home. There are three large and homey apartments with fully equipped kitchens, pleasant bedrooms and large sitting-cum-dining rooms with wooden beams and stone walls. There is a minimum two days' stay.

ARUCAS

TOP CHOICE Hacienda del Buen Suceso   RURAL HOTEL   €€
(☎928 62 29 45; www.haciendabuensuceso.com; Carretera de Arucas a Bañaderos; s/d €105/150; P⊛@☎) Set among lush banana plantations about 1.5km west of town, this aesthetically renovated country estate dates back to 1572. The rooms are rustic yet elegant, with lashings of white linen, beamed ceilings and parquet floors. The spa is luxurious and the whole place has an ambience of utter tranquillity. The restaurant receives mixed reviews from readers, however: consider dining in town.

AGAETE & PUERTO DE LAS NIEVES

Hotel Puerto de las Nieves   HOTEL   €€
(☎928 88 62 56; Avenida Alcalde José de Armas s/n; r €70; P⊛@☎) This hotel has an old-fashioned lobby but superb modern rooms washed in pale peach with parquet and tile floors. Choose between large rooms with sofas and chairs or smaller ones with large

ℹ PACKAGE DEALS

There are more than 500 hotels, apartment blocks and bungalows in Playa del Inglés and Maspalomas; in peak periods many are full to bursting. Consider booking a package outside Spain; you may save considerably more than what a tour operator offers. Travel agents in Britain, Ireland, Germany and the Netherlands brim with deals and last-minute offers.

terraces with sunbed space. There is a classy thalassotherapy centre with all the treatments, including an intriguing-sounding Chocolaterapia (€90).

Hotel El Cabo HOTEL €
(☑928 88 75 20; www.hotelelcabo.com; Calle Antón Cerezo 20; s/d with breakfast €50/60; ✴@) Located on the main street in town with, generally, easy parking available nearby, this small hotel has a smart corporate feel. The rooms are slickly furnished but tight on space; most overlook the street. Breakfast is the normal continental affair.

Playa del Inglés & Maspalomas

Palm Beach HOTEL €€€
(☑928 72 10 32; www.seaside-hotels.com; Avenida Oasis s/n; d from €185; P✴@🛜🏊) This hotel has been refurbished by international interior designer Alberto Pinto in a retro-chic style. Despite a mildly unprepossessing exterior, step within and it is a riot of colour and exciting modern design. In the main hall, the striped sofas are topped off with bright, colour-coordinated cushions, with massive abstracts on the walls, white tubular lambs and glass bowls of green apples. Get the picture? The rooms are all different and similarly snazzy.

Sahara Beach Club HOTEL €€
(☑928 76 07 76; www.sahara-beach-club.com; Avenida Alemania 53; bungalows from €85; P🏊) This low-rise complex overlooks the dunes and has a tranquil, homey atmosphere with recently renovated well-equipped bungalows and lovely gardens. There are private terraces with small lawns and rose bushes. The minimum stay is four days; most guests stay for several weeks.

Parque Tropical Hotel HOTEL €€
(☑928 77 40 12; www.hotelparquetropical.com; Avenida Italia 1; r €84; P@🛜🏊) A real gem in this sea of generic high-rise hotels. Dating back to the '60s, this hotel has a traditional Canarian look with wooden balconies, white stucco exterior and lush, mature gardens set amid small pools and fountains. The rooms have an Andalucian feel, with terracotta tiles, dark-wood fittings and beams combined with soothing pastel-coloured paintwork.

TOP CHOICE **Villa del Conde** HOTEL €€
(☑928 56 32 00; www.lopesanhr.com; Mar Mediterránneo 7; r €84; P✴@🛜🏊) Luxurious Villa del Conde is modelled on the historic centre of the town of Agüimes, including its neoclassical church. The rooms are set in the 'village houses', which are centred around a main plaza, complete with bandstand and terrace restaurant. It could be like Disneyland, but the architecture is executed so tastefully that it somehow works. Facilities include six pools, several restaurants and bars, a mini club and a thalassotherapy spa. There's a minimum one-week stay in July and August.

Respect Los Almendros BUNGALOWS €€
(☑+00 44 (0)20 7428 3737; www.losalmendros.es; Avenida Francia 3; bungalow €72; 🏊) One of the classiest gay accommodations located close to the dunes is this place. The bungalows are set in lush, landscaped gardens and facilities include a gym, a spa, a bar and a restaurant. Reservations are made via the UK-based company. There is a minimum stay of three nights.

Around Playa del Inglés & Maspalomas

PUERTO DE MOGÁN

Pensión Eva HOSTEL €
(☑928 56 52 35; Calle Lomo Quiebre 35; r without bathroom €20) About 750m inland, heading north from town, this excellent-value place has straightforward, light-filled rooms, a spacious rooftop terrace and – best news of all – a communal kitchen with a couple of fridges that makes self-catering (and socialising) a breeze.

La Venecia de Canarias APARTMENTS €€
(☑928565600; www.laveneciadecanarias.net; Local 328, Urbanización Puerto de Mogán; 1-/2-bedroom apt €75/110) Right in the thick of the resort's

pretty 'Venetian' quarter, with a truly lovely frontage surrounded by terrace bars, this well-managed complex has attractive, if smallish, apartments that sleep between three and five people.

Hotel Club de Mar
HOTEL €€
(☎928 56 50 66; www.clubdemar.com; Playa de Mogán s/n; d incl half-board €132, apt from €70; ❄@☒) Beside the yacht-filled harbour, the accommodation here is large, airy doubles, and apartments (between two and four people) with all the trimmings. Bag a room with a terrace overlooking the infinity pool with the beach beyond. Note that half-board is obligatory for the hotel rooms and children under 12 years receive a 50% reduction. Facilities include a spa.

Hotel Cordial Mogán Playa
HOTEL €€€
(☎928 72 41 00; www.cordialcanarias.com; d with half-board from €175; P❄@☎) The most recent addition to the town but, happily, the architecture is stunning and low-rise, with the accommodation set around a central lobby, complete with stained-glass dome. Echoing the harbour with waterways and bridges, the public areas are a delight, while the rooms are all earth colours, expensive marble and gold-and-cream striped wallpaper.

MOGÁN

TOP CHOICE Casa El Siroco
BOUTIQUE HOTEL €€
(☎928 56 93 01; www.elsiroco.com; Calle San Antonio 6, Mogán; d from €80) This charming B&B in an 18th-century former schoolhouse in the centre of Mogán has been creatively transformed by the German artist owner according to feng shui principles. The rooms are large and boldly colourful with Andrea's evocative landscape photos on the walls. There are four plant-filled

patios and a hearty cooked breakfast is included in the price.

FUERTEVENTURA

Corralejo and Morro Jable have the most beds here, although *casas rurales* are increasingly sprouting up in the rural interior.

Puerto del Rosario

Hotel JM Puerto Rosario
HOTEL €€
(☎928 85 94 64; www.jmhoteles.com; Avenida Ruperto González Negrín 9; s/d incl breakfast €55/83; ❄@☎) A solid choice, this corporate-style hotel comprises 88 rooms that are far more attractive than its looming modern exterior would suggest. Beds are big, bathrooms are plush and facilities are good. The public areas have wi-fi access and the hotel's latest addition of a restaurant has an excellent-value €8.50 *menu del día*.

Hotel Roquemar
HOTEL €
(☎928 53 15 47; Avenida Marítima s/n; s/d €25/30; ☎) Located on a busy corner across from the promenade, this 10-room hotel has pleasant enough rooms with fridges and fans. Avoid those in the interior, which can be dark; if possible, opt for the corner room No 103 with its two balconies. There is free wi-fi in the lobby.

Hostal Tamasite
HOTEL €
(☎928 85 02 80; www.hoteltamasite.com; Calle León y Castillo 9; s/d from €25/35; ❄) The Tamasite is a well-situated, two-star *pensión* (guesthouse) that has pleasant, if mildly scuffed, rooms with floral bedspreads, pine furniture and small balconies. The public areas are spacious and comfortable. Note that the elderly owner, Juana, speaks no English.

La Rosa del Taro
RURAL HOUSE €
(☎928 17 51 08; www.fuerterural.com; Atalaya Rosa del Tauro 92; 2-person house €50; P) Situated 13km southwest of the capital, these two *casas rurales* are ideal for walkers and birdwatchers. The traditional houses are simply furnished with private terraces. Solar power, recycled water (for the garden) and a refreshing lack of TV or internet signal equal a tranquil eco-friendly stay. Minimum three days.

The Centre

PÁJARA

TOP Casa Isaítas RURAL HOTEL €€
(☎928 16 14 02; www.casaisaitas.com; Calle Guize 7; s/d incl breakfast €66/84; ❄) One of the loveliest *casas rurales* on the island, the lovingly restored 18th-century stone house has two plant-filled central courtyards, traditional wooden galleries and balconies and an outside barbecue complete with giant paella pan; evening meals are an optional extra. There are just four rustic rooms, a couple of which were part of the original house.

CALETA DE FUSTE

Barceló Club El Castillo HOTEL €€
(☎928 16 31 00; www.barcelo.com; Avenida Castillo s/n; bungalows from €80; P❄@🛜🏊) This franchise is so large it deserves its own postcode. The whole place has a sumptuous feel, with bougainvillea-draped bungalows and lush landscaped gardens fronting onto the wide arc of a beach. The luxuriously marbled thalassotherapy centre offers all the latest treatments.

The North

CORRALEJO

Hesperia Bristol Playa APARTMENTS €
(☎928 86 70 20; www.hesperia-bristolplaya.com; Urbanización Lago de Bristol 1; 2-person apt €38; P❄@🛜🏊) Surrounded by bougainvillea and palms, this apartment hotel is an oasis of green. Although the apartments are starting to look a little scuffed, the accommodation is still excellent value with facilities that include three swimming pools and a handy supermarket for self-catering ease. There's a pleasant 1.2km walk from here, along the promenade, to Playa Las Clavellinas, beyond the harbour.

Apartamentos Corralejo Beach APARTMENTS €€
(☎928 88 63 15; www.corralejobeach.com; Avenida Nuestro Señora del Carmen 3; studios €75, 2-person apt €100; 🏊) Hard to miss thanks to a somewhat disarming pea-green-and-white exterior, step within and the look is fresh and modern. There is a choice of suites and apartments, both with discreet kitchenettes concealed behind smart wooden doors. The two-storey apartments are a good choice with classy marble floors,

sea views, large living space and extras, like washing machines.

Hotel Atlantis Duna Park HOTEL €
(☎928 53 61 51; www.atlantishotels.com; Calle Red 1; 2-person apt €45; P🏊) The quality is up there with the best of them at this centrally located apartment-hotel, again at winning prices. The rooms are large and comfortable with terracotta tiles, shiny marble bathrooms and large balconies overlooking the two palm-fringed pools. The bar-restaurant has live Cuban music on Fridays.

EL COTILLO

TOP Hotel Rural Mahoh RURAL HOTEL €€
(☎928 86 80 50; www.mahoh.com; Sitio de Juan Bello; s/d €40/70; P🛜🏊) This *casa rural* is hard to miss. Set in an early-19th-century stone-and-wood building, it's surrounded by a stunning cactus garden. There are nine romantic bedrooms decorated with antiques and warm colours, plus the modern conveniences of ADSL and a wi-fi zone. That said, the cockerel, which is part of a small farmyard with goats, will serve as your morning alarm. It's located around 4km north of town, just off the FV-101.

TOP La Gaviota HOTEL €€
(☎928 53 85 67; www.la-gaviota.net; studios €38, d €60; 🛜) This laid-back, neohippy place, which flies the Jolly Roger, has been lovingly created by a German couple; Ralf made most of the furniture and has scavenged ruins for old doors and the like. Every apartment is different, including one with a bedroom built into a cave. The views out to sea are sublime.

Maria Viva Surf & Dive Hotel HOTEL €€
(☎928 53 85 98; www.marea-viva.eu; Calle San Pedro 2; s/d incl breakfast €40/60; P🏊) This long-established hotel has new German owners, a new look and a new clientele of primarily surfers. Rooms are bright and well equipped, there's an outdoor pool, plus sundeck and fitness room. The breakfast is designed to ensure maximum energy for catching the waves, with everything from eggs and bacon to goat's cheese, yoghurt and muesli.

Apartamentos Juan Benítez APARTMENTS €
(☎629 17 63 48; www.apartamentosjbenitez.com; Calle La Caleta 4-6; 2-person apt €50; 🏊) This jauntily colourful apartment block is in a great position, near to the beach, as well as

to several of the best bars and restaurants in town. The accommodation comprises well-equipped and spacious modular apartments built around a central pool. All apartments have sea views and satellite TV.

The Southeast

GINIGINAMAR & TARAJALEJO

Camping El Brasero CAMPGROUND €
(☑928 16 10 01; Tarajalejo; camp site per person/tent €8/4; ⓟ🕉🛜🏊) A rare campsite on the island, and this shady site has a rare number of trees for these parts. The facilities are excellent, including a large swimming pool, a children's playground, a TV room, an adjacent restaurant (known for its barbecues) and even a small on-site aquarium.

Península de Jandía

COSTA CALMA

H10 Playa Esmeralda HOTEL €€
(☑928 87 53 53; www.h10.es; Punta del Roquito 2; s/d incl breakfast €90/120; ⓟ🕉@🛜🏊) Sporting a distinctive warm ochre exterior, this luxurious hotel enjoys prime position above the beach and has extensive facilities, including a state-of-the-art health and fitness club, tennis courts, a billiard room, a children's mini club and a discotheque with regular live acts. The rooms are restrained chic and spacious, decorated in bright yellows and greens.

Risco del Gato HOTEL €€€
(☑928 87 71 75; www.vikhotels.com; Calle Sicasimbre 2; s/d €84/141; ⓟ🕉🛜🏊) Accommodation is in spacious and luxurious suites, complete with whirlpool bathrooms, inner patio and small private garden. Located 200m from the white sandy beach of Sotovento, additional facilities include a spa centre, tennis courts, a fitness centre and three restaurants; in other words – the works.

MORRO JABLE

Apartamentos Altavista APARTMENTS €
(☑928 54 01 64; Caleta Abubilla 8; 1-/2-person apt €45/55; 🕉) Easy to find (but not so easy to park) opposite the modern church in the old town; you can't miss the multicoloured exterior. The apartments are large, have terraces and are painted a sunny yellow; several have sea views. There is also a rooftop solarium complete with pergola.

Sol Jandia Mar APARTMENTS €€
(☑928 54 13 25; www.solmelia.com; Avenida Jandia s/n; 2-/4-person apt €70/80; ⓟ🕉@🛜🏊) Part of the solidly reliable Melia hotel chain, this centrally located hotel provides excellent value, with large modern apartments brightly furnished with dark-blue fabrics and wood fittings. Landscaped gardens surround a pool and facilities include children's entertainment and squash courts.

Apartamentos Palm Garden APARTMENTS €€
(☑928 54 10 00; www.palmgardenfuerteventura.com; Avenida Saladar s/n; 2-/4-person apt €70/90; ⓟ🕉@🛜) Cascading like a ziggurat down the hillside, this huge apartment complex has airy, attractive apartments with small kitchenettes, satellite TV and terraces. If you are tired of sand in your swimsuit, there's an inviting freshwater pool. All rooms have sea views.

LANZAROTE

Although the bulk of Lanzarote's accommodation is in the main tourist resorts, alternative *casas rurales* options are increasing, particularly inland. The capital Arrecife is also home to several sound hotel choices and makes a good central base for exploring the island.

Arrecife

Hotel Diamar HOTEL €€
(Map p96; ☑928 81 56 56; www.hoteldiamar.com; Avenida Fred Olsen 8; s/d incl breakfast €54/65; 🕉@🛜) Privately owned Diamar has a boutique feel and is a welcome addition to Arrecife's hotel scene. Overlooking the beach, the large rooms are painted in cool colours with terraces overlooking the palm-fringed beach across the way. They are set around a central atrium with traditional Canarian balconies. There is wi-fi, a cafeteria and an elegant restaurant (mains from €7).

Hotel Lancelot HOTEL €€
(Map p96; ☑928 80 50 99; www.hotellancelot.com; Avenida Mancomunidad 9; s/d incl breakfast €50/62; 🕉🛜🏊) The large bright rooms have a luxurious feel with their king size beds, sexy abstract prints, plush decor and ample balconies with ocean views. There's a rooftop pool with adjacent small gymnasium, plus regular live, smoochy jazz in the bar.

Hotel Miramar

HOTEL €€

(Map p96; ☎928 80 15 22; www.hmiramar.com; Avenida Coll 2; s/d incl breakfast €45/62; ❀ ❂ ❆) Waterfront Miramar has been subjected to an adventurous paint palette in the public spaces, while the rooms are more subdued with blue-and-gold decor, fitted carpets and small balconies. Breakfast is a high, with its ocean views from the roof terrace.

Around Arrecife
SAN BARTOLOMÉ & AROUND

TOP CHOICE Caserío de Mozaga   RURAL HOTEL €€

(☎928 52 00 60; www.caseriodemozaga.com; Calle Mozaga 8; r incl breakfast €115; ❀) Northwest of San Bartolemé, in the village of Mozaga, this 18th-century family home retains its rustic authenticity with a central courtyard complete with original *aljibe* (water system). The rooms have high ceilings and are graced with family heirlooms. The restaurant (mains from €10) has an excellent reputation.

The North
ARRIETA

Finca de Arrieta   RURAL HOTEL €€

(☎928 82 67 20; www.lanzaroteretreats.com; Arrieta; yurts per week from €420) Discerning travellers can stay in a genuine Mongolian yurt with energy power from wind turbines and solar panels. Don't worry, this is more like glamping than camping: they are vast within and snugly 'furnished' with just the right amount of ethnic touches. Private terraces with BBQ, sunloungers and dining furniture equal a veritable five-star yurt experience. Owners Michelle and Tila and team can also provide daily eggs from their chickens, organic fruit and veg and invaluable advice about Lanzarote.

Apartamentos Arrieta   APARTMENTS €

(☎928 84 82 30; Calle Garita 25; 2-person apt €35) You'll find this blue-balconied apartment block on the main street, within walking distance of the beach. A modern low-rise building, it's a well-maintained place with good-sized, pine-furnished apartments and a vast rooftop terrace. Rafael, the elderly owner, only speaks Spanish.

MINOR CANARIES

Pensión Girasol   HOSTAL €

(☎928 84 21 18; Avenida Virgen del Mar s/n, Isla Graciosa; d €20-25) Located about 100m on the left from the ferry terminal, this modest place has had a recent lick of paint and offers standard, clean rooms. Those with seaview balconies are well worth the few extra euros. You'll find a breezy, casual restaurant; try the delicious grilled parrot fish. Accommodation in nearby apartments (€36) can also be arranged.

Pensión Enriqueta   HOSTAL €

(☎928 84 20 51, 685 58 25 88; www.pension enriqueta.com; Calle Mar de Barlovento 6, Isla Graciosa; d €25) This small *pensión* is situated a block back from the waterfront. The rooms are good value, being simply furnished but clean as a whistle, while the downstairs restaurant and bar are one of the liveliest places in town and dish up a similar inexpensive daily menu as the Girasol.

The Northwest
LA CALETA DE FAMARA

Apartments Famara Surf   APARTMENTS €

(☎928 52 86 76; www.famarasurf.com; El Marinero 39; 2-person apt €50, 3-bedroom bungalows €88) Owned by the surf shop, these are clean, well-equipped apartments close to the beach. They are furnished in light pine with dazzling white fitted kitchens, small serviceable bedrooms and good-size living rooms. Equally suitable for those wanting to surf or sunbathe.

Playa Famara Bungalows   BUNGALOWS €€

(☎928 84 51 32; www.bungalowsplayafamara .com; Urbanización Famara; bungalows from €60; ❆) This distinctive complex is located 2km north of the main town in between the looming Famara cliffs and the beach. The architecture comprises a modern step-terraced arrangement of semicircular holiday homes constructed from rock and lots of white stucco. Bungalows sleep between two and six, and longer stays equal good discounts.

Inland & West Coast
YAIZA

Finca de las Salinas   RURAL HOTEL €€€

(☎928 83 03 25; www.fincasalinas.com; Calle La Cuesta s/n; s/d/ste €110/140/210; ❂ ❀ ❂ ❆) This beautifully converted 18th-century hacienda is a definite treat. The vibrant colours and cactus gardens give it a Mexican feel. The rooms are spacious and tasteful; several are located in converted stables. If you have a choice, go for one in the main house. There is a gym, a spa, a sauna, tennis courts and bicycle hire on offer.

Casa de Hilario
RURAL HOTEL €€

(☑928 83 62 62; www.casadehilario.com; Calle General Garcia Escamez 19; r incl breakfast €85; ❋ ≋) There are just seven individually decorated rooms at this exceptional *casa rural*. There is an Asian-art influence throughout the hotel and all the furniture is handmade. The outside area includes a pool, a few lofty palms and some superb views. Breakfast can be enjoyed on the shady terrace. The owners also organise activities, including guided bike treks and boat rides.

EL GOLFO & AROUND

Hotelito del Golf
HOTEL €

(☑928 17 32 72; Avenida Marítima 10; d €55; ≋) There is just one hotel in El Golfo and it's this charming, friendly, family-run hotel that hasn't raised its prices in years. The rooms are bright and simply furnished with fridges and private terraces. It's worth paying the extra for a sea view. There's a small seawater pool, plus sun terrace across from the surf.

The South

PUERTO DEL CARMEN

Pensión Magec
PENSIÓN €

(☑928 51 51 20; www.pensionmagec.com; Calle Hierro 11; d €25, s/d without bathroom €18/20) There's just one standard *pensión* in Puerto del Carmen and it's a good one. Housed in a blue-and-white traditional house there are sea views from several rooms; go for No 21, with its private balcony, if you can, and are happy with a shared bathroom.

Apartamentos Isla de la Graciosa Lanzarote
APARTMENTS €€

(☑928 51 33 86; Calle Reina Sofía 20; 2-person apt €65; ❋) These two-star modern apartments are located in the older part of town. They are attractively furnished, spotlessly clean and the kitchens have pale wood fittings. There are reductions for stays of more than a night. Parking can be hard to find in these narrow streets.

Hotel Los Fariones
HOTEL €€

(☑928 51 01 75; www.grupofariones.com; Calle Roque del Este 1; s/d €82/108; P ❋ @ ☎ ≋) This

is the *grande dame* on the hotel scene; the first hotel to be built here, around 40 years ago. The rooms are comfortable, if old-fashioned; however, there are plans afoot for a major reformation. Facilities include tennis courts and minigolf.

PLAYA BLANCA

Apartamentos Gutiérrez
APARTMENTS €

(☑928 51 70 89, 636 37 28 93; Plaza Nuestra Señora del Carmen 8; s/d apt €35/40) Just by the town church, and one of the cheapest places to stay in this area. Tidy, spacious apartments (seven in all) are available, most with small balconies; a few with sea views. Owner Antonia is a delight, but speaks virtually no English, so brush up on your Spanish or your sign language.

Apartamentos Bahía Blanca Rock
APARTMENTS €€

(☑928 51 70 37; www.h10.es; Calle Janubio s/n; apt per person €58; P ❋ @ ≋) For something more stylish, this place has natty, well-run, Canarian-style apartments (sleeping up to four) in a complex just off Avenida Papagayo and a 100m stroll from the main beach. The Daisy Mini Club keeps the kiddies amused, while you can enjoy a snooze in the solarium.

Villas Kamezí
BUNGALOWS €€

(☑928 51 86 24; www.heredadkamezi.com; Calle Mónaco s/n; bungalow for up to 8 people from €225; P ❋ @ ≋) A discreet, environmentally friendly complex of 31 stunning villas with two to four bedrooms and tastefully decorated with real *Ideal Home*–style decor. It's within easy strolling distance of the Papagayo beaches, if you can be bothered tearing yourself away from the private saltwater pool. Fabulous.

TENERIFE

While finding a room is generally not a problem in Santa Cruz and in the north of the island, the same cannot be said for the southern resorts, particularly around Los Cristianos and Playa de las Américas.

Santa Cruz de Tenerife

Hotel Santa Cruz Plaza
BOUTIQUE HOTEL €

(Map p120; ☑922 28 46 01; www.stacruzplaza.com, in Spanish; Calle Cruz Verde 24; s/d €47/57; ☎) This smartly presented, central hotel, which has starched white walls offset with jet-black wooden furnishings, feels like a minimalist boutique hotel. The bathrooms come in a much more arresting palette of colours but the rooms themselves are fairly small. It's one of the better deals in town.

Hotel Contemporáneo HOTEL €€
(Map p120; ☎902 12 03 29; www.hotelcontemporaneo.com; Rambla General Franco 116; s/d €78/117; P❄@☎≋) As contemporary as the name suggests, this peach-and-white confection on one of the city's swankiest streets is probably the most popular hotel in town. Rooms have mahogany- or grey-stained hardwood floors and a plush yet understated colour scheme. The staff are exceptionally friendly and helpful.

Hotel Taburiente HOTEL €€
(Map p120; ☎922 27 60 00; www.hoteltaburiente.com; Calle Dr José Naveiras 24a; s/d from €70/77; P❄☎≋) The public areas have a fashionable minimalist look – think black glossy pots with a couple of lilies, chunky glass vases filled with green apples and plenty of mirrors and soft natural colours. The rooms are pleasant but lack the same wow factor; ask for one with a balcony overlooking the park.

Pensión Casablanca HOTEL €
(Map p120; ☎922 27 85 99; Calle Viera y Clavijo 15; s/d €15/21) In a great location on a leafy pedestrian street, the building dates from 1902. The rooms are brightly painted (you may need shades for the turquoise) with decorative finishes and floral trim. They are small but good value; the only downside is that there are only three communal bathrooms for 17 rooms, which could mean crossed legs in the corridor.

The Northeast

LA LAGUNA

Hotel Aguere BOUTIQUE HOTEL €€
(☎922 31 40 36; www.hotelaguere.es; Calle Carrera 55; s/d €51/67; @☎) The highlight of this friendly hotel is the central glassed-in patio (that now houses a popular cafe), which reeks of 1920's high-class society. Upstairs are a handful of simple old-fashioned rooms with wooden floors so highly polished you could ice-skate on them. The only real downside is that the bathrooms are very cramped and unimpressive.

Casa Rural la Asomada del Gato RURAL HOTEL €€
(☎922 26 39 37; www.laasomadadelgato.es, in Spanish; Calle Anchieta 45; d €67; ☎) Sitting behind the excellent restaurant of the same name and surrounded by lush sub-tropical plants, the four colourful rooms at this *casa rural* are quiet and comfortable and offer excellent value for money. There is a minimum-stay requirement of two nights.

Hotel-Apartamentos Nivaria APARTMENT-HOTEL €€€
(☎922 26 42 98; www.hotelnivaria.com; Plaza Adelantado 11; s/d from €96/120; P❄@) The former home of a marquis, the facade is washed in burnt sienna with traditional wooden balconies. Rooms are exquisitely done up with elegant furniture, leafy plants and earthy colours. The bathrooms are fashionably mosaic-tiled.

The North

PUERTO DE LA CRUZ

Hotel Monopol BOUTIQUE HOTEL €€
(Map p132; ☎922 38 46 11; www.monopoltf.com; Calle Quintana 15; s/d €52/96; ❄@☎≋) This old dame of a hotel, built in 1742, has a covered courtyard so filled with lush green foliage it's like being lost in the Amazon (well, after a few drinks it is). The service is low-key but efficient, and extras include a heated pool, a games room, a sauna and three sun-bronzing terraces. Original wooden balconies provide plenty of charm, while the rooms are small but well equipped.

Hotel Botánico HOTEL €€€
(☎922 38 14 00; www.hotelbotanico.com; Avenida Richard J Yeoward 1; s/d from €169/243; P❄@☎≋) The most exclusive hotel in these parts, the Botánico has beautiful gardens, a great pool area and a spa centre (see the boxed text, p153). Rooms are comfortable though not luxurious, with big balconies and all the standard amenities. If your name happens to be Bill Clinton then the 'Bill Clinton Suite' has your name all over it.

Hotel Tigaiga HOTEL €€€
(Map p132; ☎922 38 35 00; www.tigaiga.com; Parque Taoro 28; s/d from €127/191; P❄@☎≋) Judged on room quality alone, this family-run hotel, mounted like a castle on a hill, is overpriced. However, as well as a very ordinary room you get superb service,

beautiful gardens, an inviting pool and plenty of sporting and relaxation facilities.

Pensión Los Geranios
HOTEL €

(Map p132; ☑922 38 28 10; Calle Lomo 14; s/d €24/30, breakfast €2; ☎) The best-value budget hotel on one of the town's prettiest pedestrian streets. Although the building won't win any design awards, the rooms are bright, with light wood furnishings and pale-peach paintwork; several have private balconies at no extra cost.

LA OROTAVA

TOP CHOICE **Hotel Alhambra**
BOUTIQUE HOTEL €€

(Map p136; ☑922 32 04 34; www.alhambra-teneriffa.com; Calle Nicandro González Borges 19; s/d €83/109) A simply gorgeous 18th-century manor house filled with period furnishings and wonderful artwork, including a breathtaking 200m-long ceiling fresco. There are only five rooms and all are huge and well furnished in a mix of the modern and the old. The Andalucian tiled bathrooms come with bath tubs and separate showers. There's a small pool and attractive gardens. All up, this is the place for a romantic getaway in northern Tenerife.

Hotel Victoria
BOUTIQUE HOTEL €€

(Map p136; ☑922 33 16 83; www.hotelruralvictoria.com; Calle Hermano Apolinar 8; s/d from €73/90; ✹@☎) This is a seductive little number: a 17th-century mansion restored as an exquisite boutique hotel. The rooms are set around a central patio and have plenty of designer detail with textured cream wallpaper, modular light fittings and dark wooden furnishings. There's an excellent restaurant and rooftop sun terrace.

GARACHICO

TOP CHOICE **Hotel La Quinta Roja**
BOUTIQUE HOTEL €€

(☑922 13 33 77; www.quintaroja.com; Glorieta de San Francisco; s/d from €88/122; ✹@☎) This restored 16th-century manor house with its earthy-toned walls is a lovely spot in which to while away a few peaceful days. Managed by an enthusiastic young team, the rooms are centred around a gracious patio complete with fountain and wooden galleries. Rooms have cherry-coloured wooden floors, muted decor and Med-blue mosaic-tiled bathrooms.

Hotel San Roque
BOUTIQUE HOTEL €€€

(☑922 13 34 35; www.hotelsanroque.com; Calle Esteban de Ponte 32; s/d/ste from €145/210/320; ✹@☎✉) A simply stunning boutique hotel, set in a 17th-century mansion that has been converted with style and originality but without compromising on the old-Havana feel of the place. The rooms are set around two utterly gorgeous courtyards and have eye-catching designer detail, as well as spa baths and DVD and CD players. The heated outdoor pool is little short of divine.

Hotel Rural El Patio
RURAL HOTEL €€

(☑922 13 32 80; www.hotelpatio.com; Finca Malpaís 11; s/d from €67/78; ℗✹@☎✉) Just east of town, in El Guincho, is this tranquil, white-walled place tucked among plantains on a farm. The comfortable and colourful rooms are spread throughout three low-rise buildings set around a stone patio. Sitting out on the patio with a sunset drink listening to classical music is simply perfect. It's a little tricky to find so either call ahead for directions or download a map off its website. There's a minimum stay of three nights and it's closed from mid-May through to July.

The Centre

PARQUE NACIONAL DEL TEIDE

Parador Nacional
PARADOR €€€

(☑922 37 48 41; www.parador.es; d €125; ℗✉) Located in the heart of the national park, this parador was designed with little empathy for the surrounding landscape, but once inside, the rooms are attractively rustic in style, with earth colours, tasteful original landscapes and king-size beds. You pay slightly more for a Teide view. Avoid the adjacent cafeteria for anything more than a drink on the terrace; the food is overpriced and pedestrian.

VILAFLOR

Pension German
HOTEL €

(☑922 70 90 28; Calle Santo Domingo 1; s/d €20/40) Despite the name, this simple *pensión* is a lot less Germanic than you might expect. In actual fact it would be hard to imagine anything more typically like old-fashioned Spain. The rooms have little terraces and downstairs there's a bar that is a real throwback to an older Spain.

The Northwest

SANTIAGO DEL TEIDE

TOP CHOICE Hotel Señorio del Valle
RURAL HOTEL €€

(☎922 83 92 00; www.senoriodelvalle.com; Avenida Iglesia 72; s/d €57/75; P@⊙) Inside a heavily renovated manor house, with large and supremely comfortable rooms dotted with colourful works of art. There's a decent attached restaurant (mains €8 to €12) serving Canarian staples and a range of organised activities including horse riding (€8 per 30 minutes).

LOS GIGANTES & PUERTO DE SANTIAGO

Hotel Rural El Navio
RURAL HOTEL €€

(☎922 86 56 80; www.elnavio.es; d €67; P⊠) Halfway between Los Gigantes and the little town of Alcalá and ferreted away on a banana farm, this peaceful rural hotel, with old-fashioned rooms and a courtyard virtually enveloped in bougainvillea, offers nothing but peace, quiet and total tranquillity. The owners also prepare delicious home-cooked meals.

The East

GÜÍMAR & AROUND

Hotel Rural Casona Santo Domingo
RURAL HOTEL €€

(☎922 51 02 29; www.casonasantodomingo.es; Calle Santo Domingo 32, Güímar; s/d €53/69) On the edge of the attractive old quarter and inside a restored 16th-century house, this family-run hotel and restaurant is full of period charm and creaky old furniture. There's even a 'secret' white-washed central courtyard. The attached restaurant (mains €10 to €14) is one of the town's better places to eat.

EL MÉDANO

TOP CHOICE Senderos de Abono
RURAL HOTEL €€

(☎922 77 02 00; www.senderosdeabona.com; Calle Peatonal de la Iglesia 5; s/d incl breakfast €50/65; ✳⊙⊠) This rural hotel and restaurant is just across from the lovely stone church in Granadilla de Abona, a genuine working town. A converted post office, its rooms are in a series of old stone buildings with tiny courtyards, foliage-filled gardens and bucketfuls of charm. The in-house restaurant offers really superb home-cooked, local cuisine (mains €10). The only drawback is that the hot water tends to run out long before everyone has finished showering.

Hostel Carel
HOTEL €

(☎922 17 68 98; Avenida Príncipe de España 22; s/d from €35/45; ⊙) On the northern fringe of town there's great value to be found at this clean, friendly and well-run budget hotel. The rooms are large and shiny and come with balconies, some of which have vague sea views. It's something of a backpackers hangout. Breakfast is €5 extra.

The South

LOS CRISTIANOS, PLAYA DE LAS AMÉRICAS & COSTA ADEJE

Villa Cortés
HOTEL €€€

(Map p150; ☎922 75 77 00; www.europe-hotels.org; Avenida Rafael Puig Lluvina s/n, Playa de las Américas; s/d/ste from €151/190/455; P✳@⊙⊠) Designed in the style of an ultra-luxurious Mexican hacienda, this is truly sumptuous, with an exciting and dynamic colour scheme and decor. There are lots of hot yellows, oranges and blues, plus murals, exquisite original artwork and the occasional quirky touch – like the family of giant ceramic frogs just off the lobby and the mini Aztec temple outside. The gardens have streams with goldfish and a pool with cascading waterfall; the rooms are predictably stunning.

Hacienda del Sol
APARTMENT-HOTEL €€

(Map p150; ☎922 79 19 07; http://haciendadelsol.eu; Avenida Arquitecto Gómez Cuesta 5, Playa de las Américas; r €45-90, apt €60-120; @⊠) It's something of a surprise to find this stylish apartment-hotel hidden among the trash of northern Las Américas. Rooms have fully equipped kitchens and balconies or terraces with lattice-work borders, but the highlight of the complex is undoubtedly the pretty Andalucian-style gardens.

Hotel Andrea's
HOTEL €

(Map p152; ☎922 79 00 12/24; www.hotelesreveron.com; Calle General Franco 23, Los Cristianos; s/d from €31/52; @⊙) A small but neat hotel with large, if rather bleakly furnished, rooms and small glassed-in terraces (the cheapest singles don't have terraces). There's a comfy communal sitting room with TV and soft drinks. It's probably the most popular hotel in the area with independent travellers.

Playa de las Américas is one of those rare hotel jungles where you may have to swallow hard and check out one of the high-profile tour operators, which often have amazing deals. Some of the most reputable agencies are Thomas Cook-JMC, Thompson, My Travel, First Choice and Cosmos. If you decide to stake out your own accommodation anyway and are planning on spending a few nights here, try apartment agencies first. A pleasant flat for two, with a kitchen, a TV and a living area, starts at around €300 a week (generally the minimum booking period). Contact the tourist office for a full listing of agencies, or start with **Anyka Sur** (Map p150; ☑922 79 13 77; www.anykasur.com; Edificio Azahara, Avenida Habana, Los Cristianos), **Marcus Management** (Map p150; ☑922 75 10 64; www.tenerife-apts.com; Apartamentos Portosin, Avenida Penetracíon, Los Cristianos), which is aimed more at British visitors, or **Tenerife Holiday Rent** (Map p150; ☑607 14 66 77; Edificio Tenerife Garden, local 4, Playa de las Américas).

Pensión La Playa   HOTEL €
(Map p152; ☑922 79 01 98; Calle Paloma 7, Los Cristianos; s/d/tr €18/24/30) Rooms here don't exactly sparkle but they have more charm than others in this price bracket. It's common bathrooms only though and street noise can be an issue. The same family runs the popular restaurant downstairs. There are similar places nearby if this is full.

LA GOMERA

The island has, so far, kept grand-scale tourism at bay, and most lodging is in small rural hotels, family-run *pensiones*, refurbished farmhouses and apartments. By far the most appealing and authentically Gomeran places to stay are the *casas rurales* (rural houses), many of which were abandoned by emigrants and have since been refurbished for tourists. For information and to book, contact **Ecotural** (☑922 14 41 01; www.eco turismocanarias.com/gomera; Avenida Pedro García Cabrera 7, Vallehermoso).

San Sebastián de la Gomera

TOP
CHOICE **Parador Nacional Conde de la Gomera**   PARADOR €€
(☑922 87 11 00; www.parador.es; Calle Lomo de la Horca; r €110; 🅿@🛜🌊) Built to look like an old Canarian mansion, the Parador is arguably the island's top hotel. The rooms are simply but elegantly furnished, with four-poster beds, rich wooden floors and marbled bathrooms. Most rooms look out onto the gorgeous gardens, which have many examples of Canarian plants and a small pool area overlooking the ocean. The reception staff are also worthy of praise and are a credit to the parador chain.

Hotel Torre del Conde   HOTEL €€
(☑922 87 00 00; www.hoteltorredelconde.com; Calle Ruiz de Padrón 19; s €46-53, d €61-68; 🛜) The rooms' canary-yellow walls (think they did that on purpose?) add some sunshine and brightness to this well-run and very fine three-star hotel. The rooms are quiet and modern (if a little sterile) and some have views of the Torre del Conde and the pretty gardens that surround it; ask for a room with a view.

Pensión Victor   HOTEL €
(☑607 51 75 65; Calle del Medio 23; s/d €18/25) With its exterior walls covered in colourful murals depicting island life you can't possibly miss this quirky place. Once inside, the rooms are dimly lit, but it's a genuine old town house with absolutely bundles of character. Shared bathrooms only.

The North

HERMIGUA

TOP
CHOICE **Apartamentos Los Telares**   APARTMENTS €
(☑922 88 07 81; www.apartamentosgomera.com; El Convento, Carretera General; apt €36-44; 🛜🌊) Sitting on either side of the main highway coming into town are these superbly equipped and furnished apartments with stone floors and massive windows giving bird's-eye views over the valley. There's a choice of studios or larger apartments and just over the street is a small pool for guest use. Telares also rents small houses near the coast, featuring a

similar unfussy decor, generous terraces and fabulous ocean views.

Ibo Alfaro
RURAL HOTEL €€

(☎922 88 01 68; www.hotel-gomera.com; s/d €56/80; 🛜) The 17 romantic rooms here have gorgeous mountain views and an aroma of wood polish coming from the floors, ceilings and elegant furniture. The breakfast spread might be the best on the island. To get here, follow the signs up the unnamed rural road from beside Hermigua Rent-a-Car.

VALLEHERMOSO

Hotel Rural Tamahuche
RURAL HOTEL €€

(☎922 80 11 76; www.hoteltamahuche.com; Calle Hoya 20; s/d incl breakfast €55/76; P@🛜) Just outside town (it's a little hard to find; follow the signs towards Valle Gran Rey and it will be perched atop a hill to your right), there's smashing value to be found at this little B&B-style hotel. Built right into the hillside, Tamahuche climbs in a series of staircases and terraces, so don't plan to bring much luggage. Rooms, with dark wooden floorboards and wood-beam ceiling, are done in a Canary colonial style.

Hotel Triana
BOUTIQUE HOTEL €

(☎922 80 05 28; Calle Triana 13; s/d from €35/42) Old and new come together in perfect harmony at this boutique hotel near the town centre. The original stone walls of this old Canary house lend rooms a rustic air, while the minimalist decor sets it firmly in the 21st century. The more expensive rooms have little kitchenettes.

AROUND VALLEHERMOSO

Apartamentos Azul
APARTMENTS €

(☎922 80 02 17; Alojera; 2-person apt €36) Stupendously sited right on the waterfront: you only have to tumble out of your bright-blue-shuttered apartment to fall straight into the sea. The apartments themselves are fairly no-frills with a spacious kitchen and sitting area, small bedroom and constant sea breezes. The owner is rarely around so call in advance.

The South

PLAYA SANTIAGO

TOP CHOICE Apartamentos Tapahuga
APARTMENTS €

(☎922 89 51 59; Avenida Marítima; 2-person apt €50-60; 🖼) At the far end of the *avenida,* these spacious, light-flooded apartments

boast beautiful wooden balconies and marble floors, well-equipped kitchens and a rooftop pool. Make sure you get an exterior apartment, as a few open onto a cheerless and dark interior patio. All up it offers exceptional value for money.

Hotel Jardín Tecina
HOTEL €€€

(☎902 22 21 40; www.jardin-tecina.com; Playa Santiago; s/d €110/160 P🌂@🛜🖼) Sprawled along a cliff above town (a lift goes down to the beach), this is about the closest thing La Gomera has to a proper resort complex. The bungalow-like accommodation is scattered throughout a green, well-kept landscape that's so vast they even manage to conduct nature walks in the gardens! All rooms have balconies and many have ocean views.

Pensión La Gaviota
HOTEL €

(☎922 89 51 35; Avenida Marítima 35; r €27) A handful of modern, well-maintained, marine-blue rooms sitting above a busy local bar. The walls of the rooms are adorned with impressive photos and some rooms have wonderful views over a sparkling ocean.

VALLE GRAN REY

TOP CHOICE Finca Argayall
RURAL HOTEL €€€

(☎922 69 70 08; www.argayall.com; Valle Gran Rey waterfront; s/d from €80/126, without bathroom €64/100; P🖼) This is no ordinary hotel. A rural estate a 15-minute stroll outside the tourist bustle of Valle Gran Rey, the *finca* (rural estate) is a tranquil ocean-side centre focused on communal, alternative and ecofriendly living. For lodging, guests can choose options from comfortable beach shacks up to luxurious apartments with a private swimming pool. It's a blissfully chilled out place in which to loll about in hammocks, slip in and out of the swimming pool or laze about on the pebble beach out front. Most staff live on the premises, offering near-daily meditation, yoga, massage and other therapies and activities. The reception is manned only between 11am and 2pm Wednesday to Monday.

Apartamentos Baja del Secreto
APARTMENT-HOTEL €€

(☎922 80 57 09; www.bajadelsecreto.com; Avenida Marítima s/n, Charco del Conde; apt €56-87; 🖼) Location, location, location: this place, in-front of the Charco del Conde (a natural seawater pool), has the location thing sorted. The rooms, which are clean and comfortable, are much less exciting than the views (and location) but the densely vegetated grounds add a lot of charm.

Playa Calera   APARTMENT-HOTEL €€
(✆922 80 57 79; www.hotelplayacalera.com; La Playa; 2-person apt €118; @🛜🕸) This large four-star hotel fronting the sea has apartments that are more the sort of thing you'd expect to find in a swanky New York suburb rather than a hippy beach town in the Spanish sun. The open-plan rooms have beds as big as a small village, lounge areas and kitchenettes. There's a stunning pool complex overlooking the sea.

LA PALMA

Live like a local in the *casas rurales* for rent across the island. For information and reservations, contact the **Casa Turismo Rural Isla Bonita** (Map p178; ✆922 43 06 25; www.islabonita.es; Calle O'Daly 39, Santa Cruz de la Palma), which rents nearly 50 rural houses across the island.

Santa Cruz de la Palma

Unless your budget doesn't stretch beyond the *pensiones* here, it doesn't make much sense to stay in Santa Cruz itself; the best places are elsewhere.

Hotel San Telmo   BOUTIQUE HOTEL €€
(Map p178; ✆922 41 53 85; www.hotel-santelmo.com; Calle San Telmo 5; s/d from €50/60) This cute and comfortable B&B-style hotel has just eight rooms: the German owner's colourful personality is all over them and the rest of the building, from the huge lit fountain in the patio, to the eclectic art scattered about, to the orange walls that are made even brighter with glitter. At the time of research it was closed for renovations but it will be back as good as ever by the time this book hits the shelves.

Pensión la Cubana   HOTEL €
(Map p178; ✆922 41 13 54; www.la-fuente.com; Calle O'Daly 24; s/d €21/27; 🛜) One of the oldest hotels on the island, the Pensión la Cubana has recently been taken over by the owners of La Fuente and in the process it's received a bit of much-needed love and care. The quaint white-washed rooms are all wobbly floorboards and creaky doors, but none of them have private bathrooms. There's a kitchen for guest use, free tea and

coffee, a communal lounge and lots of travel advice.

La Fuente   APARTMENTS €
(Map p178; ✆922 41 56 36; www.la-fuente.com; Calle Anselmo Pérez de Brito 49; apt €37-58; 🛜) The 11 apartments are all different, but each is decorated in a casual, beachy style with modern bathrooms and equipped kitchens. There is no elevator but those willing to climb to the 4th floor are rewarded with amazing sea and town views. La Fuente also rents other apartments around town; see the website for details. The reception is closed over lunch and all day Sundays.

Around Santa Cruz

LOS CANCAJOS
Hacienda San Jorge   APARTMENT HOTEL €€
(✆922 18 10 66; www.hsanjorge.com; apt from €80; @🛜🕸) The Canary-styled Hacienda offers large and well-thought-out apartments with separate bedrooms, open-plan kitchens, uninspiring decoration and great views, but what really makes this place special are the verdant gardens filled with parrots and ducks and a fantastic pool.

BREÑA ALTA
Parador Nacional   PARADOR €€
(✆922 43 58 28; www.parador.es; Carretera de Zumacal, Breña Baja; r from €70; 🅿❄🛜🕸) This parador looks like a huge Canary farmhouse overlooking the ocean. There is a pretty pool surrounded by grass and a lovely botanical garden. Rooms are spacious and sun-filled, with a sitting area and panoramic views.

The South

FUENCALIENTE
Apartamentos & Pensión Los Volcanes   HOTEL €
(✆922 44 41 64; Carretera General 86; d/apt €26/31) A nice surprise, with newish, tasteful decor, private bathrooms and some rooms with a small balcony. Apartments are studio-style, with a kitchenette, sitting area and bed all in the same room. It's an ideal base for hikers as the owner is a keen walker with lots of route information.

Hotel La Palma Teneguía Princess & Spa   HOTEL €€€
(✆922 42 55 00; www.hotellapalmaprincess.com; Carretera La Costa Cerca Vieja 10; r from €95; 🅿❄@🛜🕸) Technically two hotels

(La Palma Princess and Teneguía Princess), this sprawling, self-contained resort complex near the waterfront (8km south of Los Canarios) is the most ambitious hotel on the island. With 625 rooms, several pools and marvellous ocean views, the overall effect is pleasing, but it's situated miles from anywhere.

The Centre
PUERTO NAOS

TOP CHOICE **Apartamentos Playa Delphin**   APARTMENTS €
(☎922 40 81 94; www.playadelphin.com; apt €48-59; 🛜) Yes, the apartments here are quite small, but we won't hold this against them because otherwise they are fantastically sited above the beach and close enough to ensure that you're lulled to sleep by the crack and whip of Atlantic waves. They have balconies equipped with sunloungers, and inside are equally well equipped with the sort of little extras such as toasters, fruit bowls and a free bottle of wine, that turns an average place to stay into a great place to stay. It's family-run and very friendly.

Sol La Palma   HOTEL €€
(☎922 40 80 00; www.solmelia.com; Punta del Pozo s/n, Playa de Puerto Naos; d from €79, apt from €83; 🅿✳🛜💺) If you don't want to self-cater, this package-tourism-style hotel is your only bet. With a sprawling, kid-filled pool overlooking the Atlantic, beige I-could-be-anywhere-in-the-world rooms and an all-you-can-eat buffet, it's your standard resort hotel but is comfortable.

Apartamentos Martín   APARTMENTS €
(☎922 40 80 46; www.aptos-martin-lapalma.com; Calle Juana Tabares 1; 2-person apt €35) Simple apartments with small kitchenettes in a sea-blue block. It's Spanish-run and very friendly, but the partition walls are thin indeed.

The North
BARLOVENTO

TOP CHOICE **Hotel La Palma Romántica**   RURAL HOTEL €€
(☎922 18 62 21; www.hotellapalmaromantica.com; Las Llanadas s/n, Barlovento; s/d from €50/62; 🅿🛜💺) The only three-star hotel this side of Santa Cruz, this excellent-value rural hotel has 44 spacious and elegant rooms, with high ceilings, terraces, lounge chairs and a

sitting area. If it's sunny (rare up here) take a dip in the outdoor pool and if it's grey slip into the heated indoor pool. There's a classy restaurant (mains €8 to €11), sweeping views of the valley and great service.

Apartamentos La Fajana   APARTMENTS €
(☎922 18 61 62; 2-person apt €30-36) There's not a massive amount of self-catering accommodation up on this northern coast, but these apartments, with views over the wild and woolly waves and the Piscinas de la Fajana, have a real away-from-the-world feel.

EL HIERRO

The most appealing lodging option is the *casas rurales*; contact **Meridiano Cero** (☎922 55 18 24; www.ecoturismocanarias.com; Calle Barlovento 89, El Mocanal) for reservations.

The North

TOP CHOICE **Hotel Villa El Mocanal**   BOUTIQUE HOTEL €€
(☎922 55 03 73; www.villaelmocanal.com, in Spanish; Calle Barlovento 18, El Mocanal; s/d from €64/80; 🅿@🛜💺) On the main highway through El Mocanal, this is the island's first boutique hotel and it defines rustic chic. Earthy-toned decor, hardwood furniture, stone construction and fabulous views make this an excellent choice. It's also one of the few places on the island that has a permanently manned reception, which we think gives it extra points.

TOP CHOICE **Parador Nacional**   PARADOR €€€
(☎922 55 80 36; www.parador.es; Las Playas; d €145; 🅿✳🛜💺) Sitting on the edge of a rocky beach, this is the island's top hotel and rooms are lovely, with hardwood floors, cool blue decor and balconies (ask for one with a view over the electric-blue ocean), though the best thing they offer is the lullaby of the crashing waves. Frequent special offers can mean you often only pay €80 for a room, but you really would need your own car if staying here.

The South
LA RESTINGA

To be honest, this isn't the island's most charming place to stay, but divers are practically obliged to, since there's an 800m to

1000m altitude difference between sea-level La Restinga and the towns up the highway – it's necessary to remain near sea level for at least 12 hours after a dive.

Casa Kai Marino   HOTEL €
(☑922 55 70 34; Calle Varadero 6; d/apt €25/36; ☎) Stunningly situated just a splish-splash-splosh from the tiny town beach, this friend-ly *pensión* has basic but perfectly adequate rooms as well as a handful of plain, spacious and well-equipped apartments.

Apartamentos Bahía   APARTMENTS €
(☑617 61 46 19; www.apartamentosbahia.info; Ave-nida Marítima 12; 1-4-person apt €30-36) These spic-and-span two-bedroom apartments are ideal for families. The open-plan kitchen and living area looks out over the blue wa-ters of the port. The furnishings are simple, but with a view like this, who needs more decoration?

El Golfo

LAS PUNTAS

Hotel Puntagrande BOUTIQUE HOTEL €€
(☑922 55 90 81; s/d incl breakfast €74/84) Las Puntas' most famous lodging is something of a tourist attraction in its own right and was once listed in the Guinness World Re-cords book as being the smallest hotel in the world. An old stone port building, it's perched on a spectacular rock outcrop that makes staying here feel like you're sleeping on a tiny rock in the middle of a vast ocean (which technically, of course, you are).

Despite the comfortable rooms it would be hard to imagine that you'd get much sleep here if a big storm were raging all around you. Add to this location a lively common room filled with the flotsam and jetsam of shipwrecks, and you get a truly memorable place to stay. The reception is normally unmanned.

**Bungalows Los Roques
de Salmor**   APARTMENTS €
(☑922 55 90 16; r up to 4 people €55-67;☀) This series of small, white-walled bungalows on your left as you enter town is an excellent option. New and well kept, they have tiled roofs, stone detailing and tasteful decor. There's also a small summer-only swimming pool. The reception is normally unmanned.

LA FRONTERA

El Sitio BOUTIQUE HOTEL €
(☑922 55 98 43; www.elsitio-elhierro.com; Calle La Carrera 26, La Frontera; r €44-56) Close your eyes and say *ommm*. Tucked away above the Frontera village centre, this 'centre for well-being' is a unique B&B and activity centre in one. The white-washed rooms, which come with little kitchens, are in a cluster of renovated stone farm buildings and have a lovely rustic look to them. They do, though, get very cold on winter nights. Various activities such as yoga, massages, hikes or bike excursions are available to guests and nonguests alike. The reception is manned from 11am-1pm only and not at all on Sundays.

Understand the
❯ Canary Islands

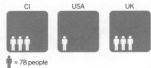

population per sq mile

CI USA UK

≈ 78 people

Canary Islands Today

The Heat is On...

And not just on the beaches. Most tourists spend their holidays in a sun-kissed Canarian cocoon, blissfully unaware of '*la crisis*' that saw a dramatic downturn in the islands' regional economy caused by the recent global recession. In 2009, the decrease in foreign visitors here equalled a drop of some €1405 million over the previous year (contributing to the massive 40% fall in the overall Spanish loss of revenue from foreign tourism: -€3500 million). On the ground, hotels slashed their room prices, restaurants and shops pulled down the shutters and new construction ground to a shuddering halt.

But it is not all doom and gloom, statistics released in 2011 revealed that the previous year saw a gradual increase in tourism of 4.9%, despite forecasts that had predicted the contrary.

» Population: 2.1 million

» GDP: €25 billion

» Annual inflation: -0.6% (2010)

» Unemployment: 29.48%

» Official Canary Islands holiday: 30 May

Diversity is the Name of the Game

One result of the economic downturn was a marked commitment by savvy officials to re-define the economic course of the islands and promote projects that were not necessarily tourist-driven. In recent years the Canaries have impressively upped their research and development capabilities in several fields. There are now two universities, an oceanographic institute, several agricultural and marine research centres and the most important astrophysics institute in the world, thanks to the clarity of the islands' skies.

As for tourism, diversity has also been the keyword here as officials demonstrate that, yes, there is life beyond the beach. *Casas rurales* (rural hotels) are sprouting up all over the islands, while activity holidays are also gaining speed. Historic trails are being signposted and mapped and the popularity of watersports, particularly windsurfing and kiteboarding,

In the Know

» When you greet Spanish people for the first time, shake hands; a second time a kiss on each cheek is common, starting on the left.

» Don't fondle fruit, veg, flowers or clothing in shops.

» No matter how hot it is, don't walk around town in your bathing suit.

Top Conversations

The economy Is it finally improving?

Smoking ban Has led to thousands of job cuts as bars have closed due to lack of business from customers who smoke.

The next fiesta Is it time to start celebrating yet?

Top Local Reads

The Canary News Weekly newspaper of local news.

Island Connections Daily news and what's on–style information.

Tenerife Magazine Online news and lifestyle pieces.

Lancelot Bilingual monthly magazine about Lanzarote.

belief systems
(% of population)

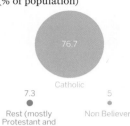

76.7
Catholic

7.3
Rest (mostly
Protestant and
Muslim)

5
Non Believers

if Canary Islands were 100 people

73 would be Canarian
13 would be European
12 would be Mainland Spanish
2 would be African

---

has soared. And, for all those stressed-out city slickers who want to chill out and avoid the Financial Times for a week, there are detox workshops, yoga retreats, meditation courses and chocolate massages (as in spas!).

People & Plans

Since the Canary Islands are so close to the coast of Africa, thousands of people searching for a better life make dangerous journeys across the Atlantic each year. In 2010 the permanent African population on the islands was around 28,136. Hundreds continue to arrive here almost daily in the hope of making a new life in Europe. Although asylum is granted to some, others are sent to one of the archipelago's several detention centres, and eventually deported. Overall the Canarios are a tolerant people; however, prejudice still exists and it is sadly worth noting that some European tourists of African origin have reported racial discrimination here, particularly in the southern resorts of Tenerife.

Plans within the archipelago include three train lines (two in Tenerife and one in Gran Canaria), with construction earmarked to begin in 2012 with a completion date set for 2017. A new marina and fishing harbour in Tenerife's Garachico is expected to be completed by late 2012 or early 2013 and should provide another boost to the economy.

After being denounced by the European Commission in 2009 for having failed to adopt sufficient conservation measures, the islands' first bioclimatic housing development, also in Tenerife, has perked up its environmental credentials. And this pales in comparison with El Hierro's plans to become the first island in the world to be electrically self-sufficient by 2012, producing all its power from a combination of wind and solar power, plus a single battery with a maximum capacity of 500,000 cubic metres. Check out www.elhierro.es for an update.

» Highest mountain in Spain: El Teide, Tenerife (3718m)

» Annual hours of sunshine: 2800 (approx)

» Number of hotel beds: 203,229

» Coastline length: 1583km

Top Books

Typical Canarian Cooking (José Luis Concepción) The classic cookbook of traditional recipes.
Crafts and Traditions of the Canary Islands (Mike Eddy) A look at the islands' traditional handicrafts.

Walking in the Canary Islands (Paddy Dillon) Includes mapped-out walks throughout the islands.
The Canary Islands through History (Salvador López Herrera) Entertaining account of the islands' history.

Natural Parks on the Canary Islands (Francisco J Macías Martín) An in-depth look at the national parks, including the fauna and flora, with colourful images.

History

There is a delightful whiff of mystery concerning the origins of the Canary Islands, including those that believe that the archipelago is, in fact, part of the remains of the legendary sunken continent of Atlantis. More plausible, though similarly intriguing, is that the islands represent the tiniest part of huge volcanoes beneath the sea. Further mystery concerns the first inhabitants, the indigenous Guanches, who were gradually driven out by waves of marauding invaders.

The first major conquest was led by French adventurer, Jean de Béthencourt at the beginning of the 15th century. Eager for fame and glory, but short on troops and provisions, he received the backing of the Castilian crown and what had started as a private French enterprise became a Spanish imperialist adventure. The last island to fall was Tenerife in 1496, marking the end of the 94-year struggle to take the islands from the proud, but ill-equipped Guanches.

The conquistadors showed no respect for the indigenous population and many were sold into slavery or succumbed to European diseases. Today, little remains of the Guanche culture, aside from the *silbo* (whistling language) of La Gomera and a slew of place names.

Cabildos insular (island governments) were founded, overseeing such joys as tax collection, developing essentials like water supplies and providing incentives for new immigrants who obediently started arriving, particularly from Europe.

Christoper Columbus also stopped by a few times en route to the Americas, which boosted transatlantic trade, but, less happily, led to the previously successful sugar production being diverted to the Americas. Wine production took up the slack, particularly in Tenerife; but eventually also suffered from increased competition from the Americas and a mass emigration to the New World ensued. As if their economic woes were not sufficient, in the early 18th century those left behind were subjected to violent volcanic eruptions.

TIMELINE

2000 BC	40 BC	AD 150
Carbon dating of archaeological discoveries reveal that Cro-Magnon were the first settlers on the Canary Islands, possibly arriving from North Africa.	An expedition lands on the islands, led by King Juba 11, the Roman Augustus' protégé who used Mogador, in present-day Western Morocco, as a base.	The famous Egyptian geographer Ptolemy fairly accurately locates the islands' position, tracing an imaginary meridian line marking the end of the known world through El Hierro.

The situation bucked up by the end of the century with the emergence of museums, schools and hospitals. The Canaries were declared a province of Spain in 1821; Santa Cruz de Tenerife was made the capital; and, in 1927, Madrid finally decided to spit the Canaries into two provinces. The economic fallout from the Spanish Civil War and World War II plunged the islands into further economic misery and, again, many Canarios opted to emigrate. Not until the 1960s did the economy start to pick up with the onset of mass tourism.

The rest is history, as they say.

... And in the Beginning

Carbon dating of the sparse archaeological finds has pushed back the known date of the earliest settlement to around 2000 BC, although earlier occupation is conceivable – and a goat's bone found in Fuerteventura has been dated back to 3000 years BC.

It is entirely possible that early reconnaissance of the North African Atlantic coast by the Phoenicians and their successors, the Carthaginians, took at least a peek at the easternmost islands of the archipelago. Some historians believe a Phoenician expedition landed on the islands in the 12th century BC, and that the Carthaginian Hanno turned up in 470 BC.

The expanding Roman Empire defeated Carthage in the Third Punic War in 146 BC, but the Romans appear not to have been overly keen to investigate the fabled islands, which they knew as the *Insulae Fortunatae* (Fortunate Isles). A century-and-a-half later, shortly after the birth of Christ, the Romans received vaguely reliable reports on them, penned by Pliny the Elder and based upon accounts of an expedition carried out around 40 BC by Juba II, a client king in Roman North Africa. In AD 150, Egyptian geographer Ptolemy fairly accurately located the islands' position with a little dead reckoning, tracing an imaginary meridian line marking the end of the known world through El Hierro.

Early (Known) Inhabitants

Tall, blond and good looking, how the Guanches actually arrived on the islands has similarly baffled historians for centuries. Could they be a result of Nordic adventurers who left the compass at home? Or Celtic immigrants from mainland Iberia, possibly related to the Basques?

Far more likely is that these first major players on the scene were actually descendents of Libyan-Berber tribes from the Maghrib; the area spanning from present-day Tunisia to Morocco. Similarities in their place names, burial practices and rock carvings suggest a link. Also, the occasional case of blue eyes and blondish hair occurs among the Berbers.

Top Historic Churches

» Iglesia de Nuestra Señora de Regla, Pájara, Fuerteventura

» Nuestra Señora de Antigua, Antigua, Fuerteventura

» Catedral de Santa Ana, Las Palmas de Gran Canaria

» Iglesia de Nuestra Señora de la Concepción, Valverde, El Hierro

» Iglesia del Salvador, Santa Cruz de La Palma

» Iglesia de Nuestra Señora de la Concepción, La Laguna, Tenerife

HISTORY ... AND IN THE BEGINNING

1312	1402	1464	1479
The Genoese explorer and seafarer, Lanzarotto Malocello, lands on the farthest north east island of the archipelago, which is how it subsequently became named Lanzarote.	On 1 May, Jean de Béthencourt, from Normandy (France) and something of an adventurer, sets out from La Rochelle with a small and ill-equipped party bound for the Canary Islands.	On learning about the Portuguese interest in the islands, the Catholic monarchs grant Diego de Herrera, the appointed lord of La Gomera, the right to attack the remaining islands.	Portugal recognises Spanish control of the Canaries under the treaty of Alcáçovas.

As far as numbers are concerned, before the 15th-century conquest it is believed that the Guanche population numbered approximately 30,000 in Gran Canaria and Tenerife, over 4000 in La Palma, over 1000 in El Hierro and a few hundred in Lanzarote and Fuerteventura.

According to a 2003 genetics research project, despite the continuous changes suffered by the population, including Spanish colonisation and the slave trade, aboriginal (Guanche) DNA lineages constitute a considerable proportion of the Canarian gene pool (42% to 73%).

The Conquest Begins

After the fall of the Roman Empire, the Canary Islands were off the radar for an incredible 1000-plus years, with virtually no written record of visits here until the early 14th century, when the Genoese captain Lanzarotto (or Lancelotto) Malocello bumped into the island that would later bear his name: Lanzarote.

On 1 May 1402, French adventurer Jean de Béthencourt, set out from La Rochelle with a small and ill-equipped party bound for the Canary Islands. So commenced a lengthy and inglorious chapter of invasion, treachery and bungling. Many Guanches would lose their lives or be sold into slavery in the coming century, with the remainder destined to be swallowed up by the invading society.

De Béthencourt's motley crew landed first in Lanzarote, at that stage governed by *mencey* (king) Guardafía. There was no resistance and de Béthencourt went on to establish a fort on Fuerteventura.

That was as far as he got. Having run out of supplies, and with too few men for the enterprise, he headed for Spain, to gain the backing of the Castilian crown. Fuerteventura, El Hierro and La Gomera then quickly fell under Spanish control. Appointed lord of the four islands by the Spanish king, Enrique III, de Béthencourt encouraged the settlement of farmers from his Norman homeland and began to pull in the profits. In 1406 he returned for good to Normandy, leaving his nephew Maciot in charge of his Atlantic possessions.

Guanches were considered elderly at age 35. They ate lots of sun-dried dates and figs that were concentrated with sugar, and this, combined with the use of mill stones to grind (gritty) grain, meant that people were toothless by their mid-20s, leading to infection – and early death.

Squabbles & Stagnation

What followed was scarcely one of the world's grandest colonial undertakings. Characterised by squabbling and occasional revolt among the colonists, the European presence did nothing for the increasingly oppressed islanders in the years following de Béthencourt's departure.

The islanders were heavily taxed and Maciot also recruited them for abortive raids on the remaining three independent islands. He then capped it all off by selling to Portugal his rights – inherited from his uncle – to the four islands. Portugal only recognised Spanish control of the Canaries in 1479 under the Treaty of Alcáçovas. (In return, Spain agreed that Portugal could have the Azores, Cape Verde and Madeira.)

Maciot died in self-imposed exile in Madeira in 1452. A string of minor Spanish nobles proceeded to run the show in the Canaries with extraordinarily little success.

1493	1501–1585	1599	1657
Tenerife provides the toughest resistance. In May, Galician Alonso Fernández de Lugo lands on the island, together with 1000 infantry soldiers and a cavalry of 150.	The Canaries' wealth leads to attacks by pirates and privateers: Ottoman Turkish admiral, Kemal Reis ventures into the Canaries, while Murat Reis the Elder captures Lanzarote in 1585.	A major offensive takes place against Las Palma de Gran Canaria during the Dutch War of Independence, with 12,000 men attacking the Castillo de la Luz, which guards the harbour.	Admiral Blake, a general under Oliver Cromwell, captures a Spanish treasure fleet, at the cost of only one ship, at Santa Cruz de Tenerife.

Christian Campaign Continues...

In 1478 a new commander arrived with fresh forces and orders from the Catholic Monarchs of Spain, Fernando and Isabel, to finish the Canaries campaign once and for all. Despite being immediately attacked by a force of 2000 men, at the site of modern-day Las Palmas de Gran Canaria, they carried the day. They went on to attack the *guanarteme* (island chief), Tenesor Semidan in an attack on Gáldar, by sea.

Tenesor Semidan was sent to Spain, converted to Christianity and returned in 1483 to convince his countrymen to give up the fight. This they did and the then commander, de Vera, subsequently suggested that some might like to sign up for an assault on Tenerife. Duly embarked, de Vera committed the umpteenth act of treachery that had marked the long years of conquest: he packed them off to be sold as slaves in Spain. But the Canarios learnt of this and forced the ships transporting them to dock at Lanzarote.

After the frightful suppression of a revolt on La Gomera in 1488, de Vera was relieved of his post as captain-general of the conquest.

The Final Campaigns

De Vera's successor was Galician Alonso Fernández de Lugo who, in 1491, received a royal commission to conquer La Palma and Tenerife. He began in La Palma in November and by May of the following year had the island under control.

Tenerife provided the toughest resistance to the Spaniards. In May 1493 de Lugo landed on Tenerife, together with 1000 infantry soldiers and a cavalry of 150, among them Guanches from Gran Canaria and La Gomera. In what was known as the First Battle of Acentejo, Lugo suffered defeat by Guanche forces who had the advantage of being familiar with the mountainous terrain.

On 25 December 1494, 5000 Guanches, under the *mencey* Bencomo, were routed in the second battle of the Acentejo. The spot, only a few kilometres south of La Matanza, is still called La Victoria (Victory) today. By the following July, when de Lugo marched into the Valle de la Orotava to confront Bencomo's successor, Bentor, the diseased and demoralised Guanches were in no state to resist. Bentor surrendered and the conquest was complete. Pockets of resistance took two years to mop up, and Bentor eventually committed suicide.

Four years after the fall of Granada and the reunification of Christian Spain, the Catholic monarchs could now celebrate one of the country's first imperial exploits – the subjugation in only 94 years of a small Atlantic archipelago defended by Neolithic tribes.

Best History Museums

» Casa-Museo de Colón, Gran Canaria

» Museo de la Piratería (pirates), Lanzarote

» Museo Arqueológico de Betancuria, Fuerteventura

» Museo Arqueológico, Tenerife

HISTORY CHRISTIAN CAMPAIGN CONTINUES...

1666

Tenerife's Garachico winemakers revolt against the emergence of a British monopoly of the wine trade, created by recent settlers, by destroying their cellars and wine.

1730–37

Massive volcanic eruptions of Timanfaya in Lanzarote. The lava flow was devastating in many ways, but created fertile ground for many crops, in particular grapes.

» Lava field, Timanfaya

1797

A British fleet led by Admiral Horatio Nelson attacks Santa Cruz de Tenerife. Sent to intercept a shipment of treasure, he famously loses his right arm in the ensuing battle.

Economic & Foreign Challenges

From the early 16th century, Gran Canaria and Tenerife in particular attracted a steady stream of settlers from Spain, Portugal, France, Italy and even Britain. Each island had its own local authority, and sugar cane became the Canaries' main export.

The 'discovery' of the New World in 1492 by Christopher Columbus, who called in to the archipelago several times en route to the Americas, proved a mixed blessing. It brought much passing transatlantic trade but also led to sugar production being diverted to the cheaper Americas. The

GUANCHE SOCIETY

The Guanche society was essentially tribal, with a chieftain or king at its head who enjoyed almost absolute rule. They lived in natural caves or simple low stone houses, while smaller grottoes and caverns were used for storing grain and as places of worship.

Economy
The economies relied on farming, herding, hunting and gathering, and their diets were based on meat (goat and fish) and *gofio,* made of toasted and ground barley; staples that are still eaten today.

Clothes & Weapons
Goat-skin leather was the basis of most garments, while jewellery and ornaments were largely restricted to earthenware bead-and-shell necklaces. Implements and weapons were fashioned roughly of wood, stone and bone.

Religion
The Guanches worshipped a god, known as Alcorac in Gran Canaria, Achaman in Tenerife and Abora in La Palma. It appears the god was identified strongly with Magec (the sun). Tenerife islanders commonly held that Hades (hell) was in the Teide volcano and was directed by the god of evil, Guayota.

Role of Women
Although living in an essentially patriarchal society, women did have some power. On Gran Canaria, in particular, succession rights were passed through the mother rather than the father. But when times got tough, they got tougher still for women. Infanticide was practised throughout the islands in periods of famine, and it was girls who were sacrificed, never boys.

Power Struggle
The island clans were not averse to squabbling, and by the time the European conquest of the islands got under way in the 15th century, the islands were divided into some 25 fiefdoms (La Palma alone boasted an astonishing 12 cantons).

1821	1850–1890	1923	1927
The Canaries are declared a province of Spain, with Santa Cruz de Tenerife as the capital; Las Palmas de Gran Canaria demands that the province be split in two.	The continuing lack of employment and food leads to emigration figures peaking, with up to 40,000 islanders emigrating to Venezuela and elsewhere in Latin America.	General Miguel Primo de Rivera rises to power in Spain via a military coup and improves the infrastructure in the Canaries, including roads and water supplies.	Madrid finally decides to split the Canaries into two provinces: Tenerife, La Gomera, La Palma and El Hierro to the west; Fuerteventura, Gran Canaria and Lanzarote in the east.

local economy was rescued only by the growing export demand for wine, particularly in Britain, which was produced mainly in Tenerife.

Poorer islands, especially Lanzarote and Fuerteventura, remained backwaters, their impoverished inhabitants making a living from smuggling and piracy off the Moroccan coast – the latter activity part of a tit-for-tat game played out with the Moroccans for centuries.

Spain's control of the islands did not go completely unchallenged. The most spectacular success went to Admiral Robert Blake, one of Oliver Cromwell's three 'generals at sea'. In 1657, Blake annihilated a Spanish treasure fleet (at the cost of only one ship) at Santa Cruz de Tenerife.

British harassment culminated in 1797 with Admiral Horatio Nelson's attack on Santa Cruz. Sent there to intercept yet another treasure shipment, he not only failed to storm the town but lost his right arm in the fighting.

The island of La Gomera was the last place Christopher Columbus touched dry land before setting sail to the New World.

Island Rivalries

Within the Canary Islands, a bitter feud developed between Gran Canaria and Tenerife over supremacy of the archipelago.

When the Canaries were declared a province of Spain in 1821, Santa Cruz de Tenerife was made the capital. Bickering between the two main islands remained heated and Las Palmas frequently demanded that the province be split in two. The idea was briefly, but unsuccessfully, put into practice in the 1840s.

In 1927 Madrid finally decided to split the Canaries into two provinces: Tenerife, La Gomera, La Palma and El Hierro in the west; Fuerteventura, Gran Canaria and Lanzarote in the east.

Franco's Spain

In the 1930s, as the left and the right in mainland Spain became increasingly militant, fears of a coup grew. In March 1936 the government decided to 'transfer' General Franco, a veteran of Spain's wars in Morocco and beloved of the tough Spanish Foreign Legion, to the Canary Islands.

Suspicions that he was involved in a plot to overthrow the government were well founded; when the pro-coup garrisons of Melilla (Spanish North Africa) rose prematurely on 17 July, Franco was ready. Having seized control of the islands virtually without a struggle (the pro-Republican commander of the Las Palmas garrison died in mysterious circumstances on 14 July), Franco flew to Morocco on 19 July. Although there was virtually no fighting on the islands, the nationalists wasted no time in rounding up anyone vaguely suspected of harbouring republican sympathies.

The post-war economic misery of mainland Spain was shared by the islands, and many Canarios opted to emigrate. In the 1950s the

Capturing the spirit and excitement surrounding Admiral Nelson, *1797: Nelson's Year of Destiny*, by Colin White, covers the battle of Cape St Vincent and the fateful attack on Santa Cruz de Tenerife where Nelson lost his arm.

1936	1940s	1950s	1960s
In March the government decides to transfer General Franco, a veteran of Spain's wars in Morocco and sympathetic to the ruthless Spanish Foreign Legion, to the Canary Islands.	The damaging effect of the Spanish Civil War on the Canary Islands is considerable, with rationing, food shortages and overall poverty. The black market thrives.	The post-war fallout continues with economic misery throughout Spain and the Canaries. Once again, this is a time of mass emigration, including 16,000 Canarios who head for Venezuela.	Fortunes are reversed as jobs are created in response to the onset of tourism to the islands, particularly from the UK and Germany. Immigration concurrently increases.

situation was so desperate that 16,000 migrated clandestinely, mainly to Venezuela, even though by then that country had closed its doors to further immigration. One-third of those who attempted to flee perished in the ocean crossings.

Tourism, 'Nationalism' & Current Events

When Franco decided to open up Spain's doors to northern European tourists, the Canaries benefited as much as the mainland. Millions of holidaymakers now pour into the islands year-round.

Always a fringe phenomenon, Canaries nationalism started to resurface in opposition to Franco. MPAIC (Movimiento para la Autodeterminación e Independencia del Archipiélago Canario), founded in 1963 by Antonio Cubillo to promote secession from Spain, embarked on a terrorist campaign in the late 1970s. Dodging Spanish authorities, Cubillo fled to Algeria in the 1960s, but in 1985 he was allowed to return to Spain.

In 1978 a new constitution was passed in Madrid with devolution as one of its central pillars. Thus the Canary Islands became a *comunidad autónoma* (autonomous region) in August 1982, yet they remained divided into two provinces.

The main force in Canary Islands politics since its first regional election victory in 1995 has been the Coalición Canaria (CC). Although not bent on independence from Spain (which would be unlikely), the CC nevertheless puts the interests of the islands before national considerations. The Partido Socialista Obrero Español (PSOE) gained the most seats in the 2007 autonomous elections, but a ruling coalition government was formed by the nationalist CC and the conservative Partido Popular (PP).

Immigration from Africa and other parts of the world has changed the Canaries' population landscape drastically over the past decade and has forced the islands to reassess their relationship with the African continent. Over the past 15 years the islands have made cooperation with Africa a major priority, investing around €17 million in education, health and infrastructure in Africa, especially in transport and communication links with the continent.

The past few years have also seen a struggle between intense development and concerted efforts to preserve the islands' natural resources and beauty. Political groups, islanders and ecologists are in constant discussions about the best way to combine the archipelago's dependence on tourism – and the perceived need for more hotels, ports and golf courses – with the pressing need to conserve water resources, combat marine pollution and prevent development from infringing on the flora and fauna that have made the islands a nature lover's paradise.

Cuba was a particularly welcoming destination for many Canarios fleeing the effects of the Civil War and there remain strong links between the Canary Islands and Cuba, at both governmental and personal levels.

1982 / **1995** / **2007**

The new constitution that is introduced in Madrid in 1978 impacts the Canary Islands by deeming that they become a *comunidad autónima* (autonomous region) in August of this year.

The first regional elections take place throughout the archipelago, with the result being the formation of the Coalición Canaria (CC), which works in conjunction with the Spanish government.

The world's largest telescope starts monitoring the stars at La Palma's Observatorio del Roque de los Muchachos, one of the top astronomical sites in the northern hemisphere.

» Observatory at La Palma

Island Cuisine

Like mainland Spain, social eating and drinking is central to the lifestyle here. Locals will think nothing of travelling several kilometres to some new talked-about restaurant or tapas bar, especially at Sunday lunchtime, a traditional time for dining out here, along with the extended family, of course.

Typical Canary cuisine is all about using simple fresh ingredients and doing as little as possible to them: grilled fish, served with a zesty herb sauce; boiled potatoes with crinkly, salted skin; juicy grilled kid; green salads served with buttery locally grown avocado; and scrambled eggs with wild asparagus. The islands' traditional dishes are those made with ingredients produced on the islands and, although restaurants can now get any and every kind of exotic ingredient flown in, there is still no beating unfussy homestyle cooking. Ask a restaurant for their *plato del día* (daily special) or *pescado del día* (catch of the day); these dishes are almost sure to be culinary highlights.

Through the years, traditional Canary dishes have rubbed shoulders with mainland Spanish cuisine and even South American specialities, giving way to unique Canary spins on recipes from elsewhere. And, of course, these days you'll find everything from Chinese to Italian to pub fare in the big resorts. The very best dining experiences, however, are usually to be had away from the tourist swarms and in the cosy, farmhouse restaurants that dot the islands' interiors.

Staples & Specialities

The traditional staple or *pan de los Canarios* (bread of the Canaries) is *gofio,* a uniquely Canario product and, it must be said, a bit of an acquired taste. A roasted mixture of wheat, maize or barley, *gofio* is an integral part of the traditional Canary diet. It is mixed in varying proportions, and used as a breakfast food or combined with almonds and figs to make sweets. If you are really keen, you can seek out *gofio* ice cream or even *gofio* liquor. You can find it at supermarkets or buy directly from the few remaining mills.

The most-often-spotted Canarian contribution to the dinner table is the *mojo* (spicy salsa sauce made from coriander, basil or red chilli peppers). This sauce has endless variants and is used to flavour everything from chicken legs to cheese. You'll soon find you're addicted to one or other of them.

Papas arrugadas (wrinkly potatoes) are perhaps the next-best-known dish and they really come to life when dipped in one of the *mojos*.

Of the many soups you'll find, one typically Canarian variant is *potaje de berros* (watercress soup). Another is the hearty *rancho canario,* a kind of broth with thick noodles and the odd chunk of meat and potato.

The On the Road chapters have more information about local specialities.

At Christmas, *turrón* is an island-wide favourite. It's a uniquely Spanish kind of nougat, with a recipe that dates back to the 14th century, and is based on honey, almonds and sugar.

TURRÓN

Market-Fresh Ingredients

Other basic foods long common across the islands are bananas and tomatoes, but nowadays the markets are filled with a wide range of fruit and vegetables and you should definitely visit one during your trip. They are a real treat for all the senses with in-season produce such as plump dark figs, cut open to show their scarlet flesh, bundles of fragrant parsley and mint, glossy dark aubergines, bunches of brilliant-orange carrots, huge golden-yellow papayas and ropes of plump white garlic bulbs.

Beef, pork and lamb are also widely available (more often than not imported), but the traditional *cabra* (goat) and *cabrito* (kid) remain a staple animal protein. Most local cheeses also come from goat's milk and are, justifiably, famous, particularly in Fuerteventura, where the delicious Majorero is a must for any cheese aficionado and best sourced, also, at the market.

Papas arrugadas are made by boiling potatoes in heavily salted water, which makes the salt stick to the skin. The variety used is papas antiguas (old potatoes), descended from the first varieties imported from the Americas in the 15th century. Will you ever be able to replicate the recipe back home? Tricky, as the potatoes are only grown here – mainly in Tenerife.

Latin & Spanish Influences

Canarian cuisine owes a lot to the New World; it was from South America that elementary items such as potatoes, tomatoes and corn were introduced. From there also came more exotic delights such as avocados and papayas, while some mangoes arrived from Asia; look out for all three in the valleys and on supermarket shelves.

Some of the classic mainland Spanish dishes are also widely available, including paella (saffron rice cooked with chicken and rabbit or with seafood – at its best with good seafood), tortilla (omelette), gazpacho (a cold, tomato-based soup usually available in summer only), various *sopas* (soups) and *pinchos morunos* (kebabs).

Traditional Sweet Treats & Desserts

Canarios have a real sweet tooth. Some of the better-known sticky sweets are *bienmesabe* (a kind of thick, sticky goo made of almonds and honey – deadly sweet!), *frangollo* (a mix of cornmeal, milk and honey), *tirijaras* (a type of confectionery), *bizcochos lustrados* (sponge cake) and *turrón de melaza* (molasses nougat).

Don't miss the *quesadillas* from El Hierro – this cheesy cinnamon pastry (sometimes also made with aniseed) has been baked since the Middle Ages. *Morcillas dulces* (sweet blood sausages), made with grapes, raisins and almonds, are a rather odd concoction; perhaps the closest comparison is the Christmas mince pie.

Dining Times & Habits

Breakfast *(desayuno)* is usually a no-nonsense affair, with juice, coffee or tea, cereal or *gofio,* and toast with ham or cheese. *Churrerías* serve deliciously unhealthy deep-fried spiral-shaped *churros* (doughnuts), often accompanied by a cup of thick hot chocolate.

If you are a bacon-and-eggs breakfast person, head for one of the English-owned bars. Most hotels also have a hot and cold breakfast buffet.

MENÚ DEL DÍA

The traveller's friend in the Canary Islands, as in mainland Spain, is the *menú del día*, a set meal available at most restaurants for lunch and occasionally in the evening too. Generally, you get a starter (salad, soup or pasta) or side dish followed by a meat, fish or seafood main and a simple dessert, which can include local specialities or Spanish favourites such as *flan* (crème caramel), *helado* (ice cream) or a piece of fruit. Drinks, (possibly including a generous half-bottle of house wine) and coffee may or may not be included.

The Canary Islands may seem like paradise to some, but they can be more like purgatory for vegetarians, and worse still for vegans, who may be made to feel as if they have come from another planet. This is meat-eating country, so you will find your choices (unless you self-cater) a little limited. Salads are a staple, and you will come across various side dishes such as *champiñones* (mushrooms, usually lightly fried in olive oil and garlic). Other possibilities include *berenjenas* (aubergines), *menestra* (a hearty vegetable stew), *espárragos* (asparagus), *lentejas* (lentils) and other vegetables that are sometimes cooked as side dishes. Restaurants that cater particularly well for vegetarians are noted in this book with a 🖉.

The serious eating starts with lunch (*la comida* or, less commonly, *el almuerzo*). While Canarios tend to eat at home with the family, there is plenty of action in the restaurants too, starting at about 1pm and continuing until 4pm. In many restaurants, a set-price *menú del día* is served at lunchtime.

Dinner is served late at home, generally from around 9pm, while restaurants will normally open up at 8pm and serve until 11pm or later, especially in the tourist resorts. At-home dinners tend to be light for locals, but on weekends and special occasions they eat out with gusto.

Snacks are an important part of the Spanish culinary heritage. You can usually pick up a quick bite to eat to tide you over until the main meal times swing around. Standard snacks *(meriendas)* include tapas and *bocadillos*. Typically, this will be a rather dry affair with a slice of *jamón* (ham) and/or *queso* (cheese), or a wedge of *tortilla española* (potato omelette).

Drinks

Cafe culture is a part of life here, and the distinction between cafes and bars is negligible; coffee and alcohol are almost always available in both. Bars take several different forms, including *cervecerías* (beer bars, a vague equivalent of the pub), *tabernas* (taverns) and bodegas (old-style wine bars).

Coffee

The Canary Islanders like coffee strong and bitter, then made drinkable with thick sweetened condensed milk. It takes some getting used to. Coffee choices include the following:

» *Café con leche* About 50% coffee, 50% hot milk.

» *Sombra* The same, but heavier on the milk.

» *Café solo* A short black coffee (or espresso).

» *Cortado* An espresso with a splash of milk.

» *Cortado de leche y leche* Espresso made with condensed and normal milk.

» *Barraquito* A larger cup of *cortado* coffee.

» *Café con hielo* Glass of ice and hot cup of coffee to be poured over the ice.

Wine

The local winemaking industry is relatively modest, but you can come across some good drops. Wine comes in *blanco* (white), *tinto* (red) or *rosado* (rosé). Prices vary considerably. In general, you get what you pay for and can pick up a really good tipple for about €6.

One of the most common wines across the islands is the *malvasía* (Malmsey wine, also produced in Madeira, Portugal). It is generally sweet *(dulce),* although you can find the odd dry *(seco)* version. It is particularly common on La Palma.

If you like wine and you like exercise, consider Lanzarote's annual Wine Run, which takes place every June with a choice of 21km (for runners) and 10km (for walkers) and includes an opportunity to taste wine at six bodegas along the way.

Tenerife is the principal source of wine, and the red Tacoronte Acentejo was the first Canarian wine to earn the grade of DO (*denominación de origen;* an appellation certifying high standards and regional origin). This term is one of many employed to regulate and judge wine and grape quality. Other productive vineyards are in the Icod de los Vinos, Güímar and Tacoronte areas of Tenerife. In Lanzarote, the vine has come back into vogue since the early 1980s, and in late 1993 the island's *malvasías* were awarded a DO.

The New Spain – Vegetarian & Vegan Restaurants, by Jean Claude Juston, should be a bible for vegetarian and vegan visitors. It's available from L'Atelier (www.ivu.org/atelier).

Beer

The most common way to order a beer *(cerveza)* is to ask for a *caña,* which is a small draught beer (*cerveza de barril* or *cerveza de presión*). La Dorada, brewed in Santa Cruz de Tenerife, is a very smooth number. Tropical, which is produced on Gran Canaria and is a little lighter, is a worthy runner-up and the preferred tipple of the eastern isles.

Spirits

Apart from the mainland Spanish imports, which include the grape-based *aguardiente* (similar to schnapps or grappa), *coñac* (brandy) and a whole host of other *licores* (liqueurs), you could try some local firewater if you come across it. One to try is *mistela* from La Gomera, a mixture of wine, sugar, rum and sometimes honey – a potent taste!

Canarian Arts & Culture

Although the Canary Islands are Spanish, their architecture, art and overall culture is subtly distinctive from that of the mainland, with more than a glimmer of Latin American influence. Overall, the Canarios are a warm and friendly people, deeply devoted to tradition, the family – and to having fun. Fiestas here are wonderfully exuberant affairs: try and attend one if you can.

The Arts

Architecture

Any pre-Hispanic architecture you think you spot on the islands is either a reconstruction, heavily restored – or a theme park. The Guanches lived mainly in caves, and virtually nothing of the rudimentary houses they built remains today. Although people often talk about 'typical Canarian architecture', there have been so many different influences over the centuries, it is hard to specify exactly what this is. It is not uncommon, either, for a building to reflect more than one architectural style.

Colonial Period

The colonial-period architecture is a good example of this potpourri of influences, including elements from the Spanish, Portuguese, French, Flemish, Italian and English architectural schools. By the time the conquest of the islands was completed at the end of the 15th century, the Gothic and Mudéjar (a distinctive Islamic-style architecture) influences already belonged more to the past than the present. The interior of the Catedral de Santa Ana in Las Palmas is nevertheless a fine example of what some art historians have denominated Atlantic Gothic. Only a few scraps of the fascinating Mudéjar influence made it to the islands, most in evidence in magnificent wooden ceilings known as *artesonado*.

You can get the merest whiff of *plateresque* (meaning silversmith-like, so called because it was reminiscent of intricate metalwork) energy at the Catedral de Santa Ana in Las Palmas and the Iglesia de Nuestra Señora de la Concepción in La Laguna – the latter a veritable reference work of styles from Gothic through Mudéjar to *plateresque*. Baroque, the trademark of the 17th century, left several traces across the archipelago and is best preserved in the parish church of Betancuria, Fuerteventura.

Some of the most distinctive aspects of architecture during this period are the internal courtyards and beautiful carved wooden balconies. Las Palmas de Gran Canaria's historic Vegueta barrio has some excellent examples.

Best Mudéjar Artesonado

» **Iglesia de Nuestra Señora de la Concepción**, La Laguna, Tenerife

» **Iglesia de Santa Catalina**, Tacoronte, Tenerife

» **Iglesia del Salvador**, Santa Cruz de la Palma

» **Iglesia de Santa María**, Buenaventura, Fuerteventura

» **Iglesia de Nuestra Señora de Rega**, Pájara, Fuerteventura

Modern Architecture

Modernism makes an appearance along the Calle Mayor de Triana and in the private houses of the Triana district of Las Palmas de Gran Canaria.

But modern Canary architecture's greatest genius is, without doubt, Lanzarote native, the late César Manrique. His ecologically sensitive creations, often using volcanic stones and other Canary materials, are found throughout the islands, but especially on Lanzarote. His designs are so compelling that some people base an entire trip around visiting them all. For details, see p101.

The icon of contemporary Canary architecture is Santiago Calatrava's 'wave', the multifunction Auditorio de Tenerife dominating the waterfront of Santa Cruz de Tenerife with its unmistakable profile of a wave crashing onto shore. Las Palmas de Gran Canaria is another architectural hot spot; interesting architectural spaces include the interior of the Atlantic Modern Art Centre by Sáenz de Oiza, the Auditorio Alfredo Kraus by Óscar Tusquets, and the Woermann Tower by Iñaki Ábalos and Juan Herreros.

César Manrique Architecture

» **Jameos del Agua**, Malpaís de la Corona, Lanzarote

» **Parque Marítimo**, Santa Cruz de Tenerife

» **Fundación César Manrique**, Tahiche, Lanzarote

» **Mirador del Río**, Northwest, Lanzarote

Painting & Sculpture

For such a relatively small land mass, the Canary Islands have a considerable number of art museums, open-air sculptures and galleries. An appreciation for quality art also seems to have spilt over into the general populace, with restaurants and hotels often preferring to hang original artwork by local painters rather than those same old Picasso prints.

The Guanches

The art tradition dates back to the Guanches and there are some fine examples of their cave drawings at various sites, including the Cueva Pintada in Gáldar, Gran Canaria. Normally geometric in design, the ancient Guanche drawings have served to inspire some of the most famous artists, including Manolo Millares (1926–72), a native of Las Palmas de Gran Canaria, as well as the more accessible souvenir T-shirt and ceramic designs. The best-loved sculpture from these times is the *Ídolo de Tara* from Gran Canaria; a curvy feminine figure and Guanche idol which you can, again, see stamped on textiles and in pottery replicas.

Top Contemporary Sculptors

» Eduardo Gregorio

» Plácido Fleitas

» Manolo Millares

» César Manrique

» Juan Bordes

17th- to 19th-Century Artists

Gaspar de Quevedo from Tenerife was the first major painter to emerge from the Canary Islands in the 17th century. Quevedo was succeeded in the 18th century by Cristóbal Hernández de Quintana (1659–1725), whose paintings still decorate the Catedral in La Laguna in Tenerife. More important was Juan de Miranda (1723–1805), among whose outstanding works is *La Adoración de los Pastores* (The Adoration of the Shepherds) in the Iglesia de Nuestra Señora de la Concepción in Santa Cruz de Tenerife.

MARTÍN CHIRINO

Martín Chirino is widely considered to be one of the most significant Spanish sculptors of the 20th century. Born in Las Palmas de Gran Canaria in 1925, as a young man he spent time in Africa, including Morocco and Senegal, and this influence can be seen, especially in some of his earlier pieces. Chirino's giant, mainly bronze, sculptures are on view throughout the islands. They include *Espiral* (1999) in Santa Cruz de Tenerife; *El Pensador* (2002), gracing the grounds of the University of Las Palmas de Gran Canaria; and *Raíz* (1967), which can be viewed outside the Palacio de Congresos de Las Palmas.

In the 19th century, Valentín Sanz Carta (1849–98) was among the first Canarios to produce landscapes. Others of his ilk included Lorenzo Pastor and Lillier y Thruillé, whose work can be seen in the Museo de Bellas Artes in Santa Cruz de Tenerife.

The Canaries' main exponent of impressionism was Manuel González Méndez (1843–1909), whose *La Verdad Venciendo el Error* (Truth Overcoming Error) hangs in the *ayuntamiento* (town hall) of Santa Cruz de Tenerife.

20th-Century Artists

The Cuban-Canario José Aguiar García (1895–1976), born of Gomero parents, has works spread across the islands; the *Friso Isleño* (Island Frieze) hangs in the casino in Santa Cruz de Tenerife.

All the great currents of European art filtered through to the Canary Islands. Of the so-called Coloristas, names worth mentioning include Francesco Miranda Bonnin (1911–63) and Jesús Arencibia (1991–93), who created the impressive large mural in the Iglesia de San Antonio Abad in Las Palmas de Gran Canaria.

The first surrealist exhibition in Spain was held on 11 May 1935 in Santa Cruz de Tenerife. The greatest local exponent of surrealism, Tinerfeño Óscar Domínguez (1906–57), ended up in Paris in 1927 and was much influenced by Picasso. Others of the period include Cubist Antonio Padrón (1920–68), who has a superb museum displaying his work in his former Gran Canaria studio.

Leading the field of abstract artists is Manolo Millares (1926–72), while Alberto Manrique (1926–; no relation to César Manrique) from Gran Canaria enjoys altering perspective to dramatic, surreal effect. You can see a permanent exhibition of his work at the Centro de Arte Canario in La Oliva, Fuerteventura.

Canary Islands' Crafts

There is a deep-rooted tradition of craftwork here with different islands specialising in particular crafts. Fine lacework and embroidered tablecloths, napkins and table linen can be found all over the archipelago, with skills being handed down through the generations. Be wary of Chinese imports being passed off as locally made, particularly at the street markets. One way to identify the real item (aside from the obvious quality) is the cost. The original embroidery does not come cheap, reflecting the skill and time taken in the creation. Prices are dropping, however, as there is less demand for these items today.

Simple, usually striped and brightly coloured, woven carpets and rugs have a more dateless quality, and are still made painstakingly with a handloom. Other popular items to weigh down your hand luggage are woven baskets, Guanche-style pottery, ceramic pots and straw hats of all sizes and shapes.

Music

The symbol of the Canarios' musical heritage is the *timple,* a ukulele-style instrument of obscure origin, thought to have been introduced to the islands by Berber slaves in the 15th century. It's a small, wooden, five-stringed instrument with a rounded back (it is said the original Berber version was made of a turtle shell) and a sharp tone.

Whenever you see local traditional fiestas, the *timple* will be there accompanying such dances as the *isa* and *folía* or, if you're lucky, the *tajaraste* – about the only dance said to have been passed down from the ancient Guanches and still popular in La Gomera.

Traditional Crafts

» **La Gomera & Tenerife** Guanche-style pottery, basketware

» **Lanzarote & Gran Canaria** *Timples* (small string instruments)

» **El Hierro, La Palma & La Gomera** Woven rugs

» **Tenerife** Vilaflor lacework

Top Spanish actor Javier Bardem was born in Las Palmas de Gran Canaria. He originally set out to be a painter and studied art at the prestigious Escuela de Arte y Oficios in Madrid. Bardem started his acting life as an extra, which led to a full-time acting career (and marriage to Penelope Cruz).

Culture

Regional Identity

It's hard to sum up the peoples and traditions of seven islands. Mannerisms, expressions, food, architecture and music vary significantly from island to island and rivalries (especially between heavyweights Tenerife and Gran Canaria) are strong. Yet among all seven islands is a fierce pride in being Canarian, and the belief that their unique history and culture set them apart from the rest of Spain. While most of the Canary Island locals have the classic Mediterranean looks of the Spaniards – dark hair and eyes and an olive complexion – you might find that they don't think of themselves as all that Spanish.

Soon after the 1982 electoral victory of the socialists at national level, the Canary Islands were declared a *comunidad autónoma,* one of 17 autonomous regions across Spain. And a few vocal Canarios would like to see their islands become completely autonomous – keep an eye peeled for splashes of graffiti declaring 'Spaniards Go Home'.

The archipelago's division into two provinces, Tenerife and Gran Canaria, remains intact, as does the rivalry between the two provinces – so much so that the regional government has offices in both provincial capitals, which alternate as lead city of the region every four years.

Top Canarian Authors & Poets

» **Benito Pérez Galdós** Historic author

» **Tomás Morales** Historic modernist poet

» **Yolanda Soler Onís** Contemporary poet

» **José Luis Correa** Contemporary novelist

Lifestyle

The greatest lifestyle change that has come to the Canary Islands has been as a result of the tourism industry. In a matter of decades a primarily agricultural society became a society largely dependent on the service industry. Traditional lifestyles on small *fincas* (farms) or in fishing villages have been supplanted by employment in the tourism sector.

As the islands close the gap between their traditional, rural lifestyles and the fast-paced, modern lifestyle of the rest of Spain, some problems are inevitable. The cost of living has skyrocketed, forcing those who have kept traditional agriculture jobs to supplement their income with positions in the tourism industry. Education is another issue; since the small islands have no universities, young people have to study in Tenerife or Gran Canaria and this can deplete a family's already over-stretched budget. After school, many college-educated islanders end up leaving the island of their birth to look for better jobs on Tenerife, Gran Canaria or the mainland. By necessity, many Canarian families are separated.

Nevertheless, family remains at the heart of Canary culture. Big island celebrations are always celebrated with family, and islanders come from as far away as the Americas to reunite with family and friends. Most religious and cultural celebrations are also family-focused. Although families now are smaller than they used to be – one or two children is the norm – they're still an important social unit. As elsewhere in Europe, couples are waiting longer to get married (the average age is

The most famous shoe designer in the world, Manolo Blahnik, was born in 1943 in Santa Cruz de Tenerife. The son of a Czech father and Spanish mother, he spent his childhood among banana plants – an unlikely beginning for a world-famous fashion designer if there ever was one!

LOS SABANDEÑOS

The Canaries' best-loved folk group, Los Sabandeños, has been singing and strumming since 1966, when these Tinerfeños banded together in an effort to recover and popularise Canary culture across the islands. It's impossible to quantify the effects this group of nearly 25 men (including a few new recruits) has had on the islands. Suffice to say, they have a statue in their honour in Punta de Hidalgo, Tenerife and (at last count) seven streets, throughout the islands, named after them. Their CDs of light, melodic music are widely available; look for the latest release *Mass Sabandeño* (2009).

31 for women and 34 for men), although not necessarily later to have children (the average age is 30), proving that Canary society is not as traditional as it once was.

Sport

The Canary Islands are a sport-friendly destination, as they have a balmy, sunny climate, plenty of coastline and a laid-back, outdoor lifestyle that rewards activity. As part of Spain, there are no prizes for guessing the top sport here: football (soccer). Although there is a regional football team for the Canary Islands, they are not affiliated with FIFA, UEFA or CAF, because the islands are represented internationally by the Spanish national football team. The team only plays friendly matches.

Far more unusual is *lucha canaria* (Canarian wrestling), which is said to date back to the Guanches, a particularly robust and warlike crowd who loved a trial of strength: jumping over ravines, diving into oceans from dizzying heights...and this distinctive style of wrestling. One member of each team faces off his adversary in the ring and, after a formal greeting and other signs of goodwill, they set about trying to dump each other into the dust. No part of the body except the soles of the feet may touch the ground, and whoever fails first in this department loses. Size and weight are not the determining factors (although these boys tend to be as beefy as rugby front-row forwards), but rather the skill with which the combatants grapple and manoeuvre their opponents into a position from which they can be toppled.

If you want to find out if any matches are due to be held locally, ask at the nearest tourist office.

Multiculturalism

Nowadays the Canary Islands, for so long a region of net emigration, admit more people than they export. Workers in the hotel, restaurant and construction industries, and migrants from northern Europe seeking a place in the near-perpetual sun, all bolster the islands' population figures. With nearly 204,000 tourist beds in hotels, apartments and houses across the islands, there is a steady influx of tourists from across the world, mainly Europe, some of whom also decide to stay and make a life here.

A newer phenomenon are the immigrants from the Americas, many of them family members of Canarios who emigrated to Venezuela or other South American countries who are now returning to the islands of their ancestors.

Thousands of Africans try to make the journey to Europe each year as illegal migrants and, as the closest EU country to the African continent, Spain is on the frontline, in particular, the Canary Islands. Although some do succeed and are granted asylum, others end up in detention centres which, until recently, had been criticised for being overcrowded and in poor condition. Prejudice is hard to gage, but some tourists of African origin have reported discrimination, mainly in shops and restaurants and particularly in the southern resorts of Tenerife.

Religion

The Catholic church plays an important role in people's lives. Most Canarios are baptised and confirmed, have church weddings and funerals and attend church for important feast days – although fewer than half regularly turn up for Sunday Mass. Many of the colourful and often wild fiestas that take place throughout the year have some religious context or origin.

CANARIAN ARTS & CULTURE CULTURE

Naming Names: People of the islands

» **Gran Canaria**
Grancanarios or Canariones

» **Tenerife**
Tinerfeños

» **Lanzarote**
Conejeros

» **Fuerteventura**
Majoreros

» **La Gomera**
Gomeros

» **La Palma**
Palmeros

» **El Hierro**
Herreños

Nearly two-thirds of the archipelago's average of 10 million annual tourists are German or British, so it should be no surprise that these are also the largest expat communities.

Life on a Volcano

Many people think of the Canary Islands as consisting of little but flat, featureless sun-baked semi-desert, and while there are areas where this image rings true anyone who knows the islands well will speak in excited tones about the sheer variety of landscapes, climates and flora and fauna contained within this unique archipelago.

Volcanic Landscape

Formation of the Islands

La Palma is the steepest island in the world, relative to its height and overall area.

The seven islands and six islets that make up the Canary Islands archipelago are little more than the tallest tips of a vast volcanic mountain range that lies below the Atlantic Ocean. Just babies in geological terms, the islands were thrown up 30 million years ago when tectonic plates collided, crumpling the land into mammoth mountains both on land, as in the case of Morocco's Atlas range, and on the ocean floor, as in the case of the Cape Verde islands, the Azores and the Canaries. These Atlantic islands are collectively referred to as Macronesia. After the initial creation, a series of volcanic eruptions put the final touches on the islands' forms.

The Islands Today

The seven main islands have a total area of 7447 sq km. Their size may not be great, but packed into them is just about every imaginable kind of landscape, from the long, sandy beaches of Fuerteventura and dunes of Gran Canaria to the majestic Atlantic cliffs of Tenerife and

---

CUMBRE VIEJA & THE MEGATSUNAMI

On the island of La Palma – yes, that's right, the one very close to the beach you're lying on – is the Cumbre Vieja (Old Ridge). In 1949 a series of volcanic eruptions here caused a fissure about 2.5km long to open up, which sent the western side of the Cumbre Vieja slipping downwards, and westwards, by 2m.

Experts believe that it's only a matter of time before Cumbre Vieja erupts again and when it does some people fear that it could send up to 1.5 trillion metric tons of rock cascading down into the Atlantic. If this were to happen then it would generate a tsunami with an initial height of 600m, which would race across the Atlantic at around 1000km an hour. The north African coast would be hit within an hour, the English coast within 3½ hours and the eastern seaboard of the US within six hours. By this time the tsunami waves would be around 30m to 60m high (though on reaching shallower water they could grow to a several hundred metres) and the waves would travel around 25km inland, inundating the Caribbean and devastating Boston, New York and Miami.

How likely is this to happen? Well, that's where the arguments really start, but some say that it could be imminent.

Just time for another cocktail then?

The best-known native animals in the Canaries today are the giant lizards, which still hang on in a number of places (see p205). Impressive though these are they're nothing on what used to scamper around the hills here. Hailing from Tenerife, *Gallotia goliath* never shared the islands with humans, which is just as well as fossilised remains show that this monster measured a good metre in length. Today skeletons and casts of them can be seen in Tenerife's Museo de la Naturaleza y el Hombre.

Living alongside these lizards was a creature straight out of a nightmare. The Tenerife Giant Rat was around a metre long and weighed around a kilo when fully grown. It was actually still present when the Guanches first arrived on Tenerife but in a familiar tale people, and possibly domestic cats, quickly put an end to this monster. Gran Canaria had its own type of giant rat but this was a comparative minnow at just 25cm in length.

It's also thought a type of giant tortoise once lived on the islands.

mist-enveloped woods of La Gomera. The easternmost islands have an almost Saharan desertscape, while corners of La Palma and La Gomera are downright lush. The highest mountain in Spain is 3718m Pico del Teide, which dominates the entire island of Tenerife.

El Teide & the Others

El Teide, that huge pyramid peak that stands at the very centre of life on Tenerife, is at 3718m both the highest mountain in Spain and the third-largest volcano in the world. Teide is what's known as a shield volcano; it's huge and rises in a broad, gently angled cone to a summit that holds a steep-walled, flat-based crater. Although seemingly quiet, Teide is by no means finished.

Wisps of hot air can sometimes be seen around Teide's peak. Where the lava is fairly fluid, steam pressure can build up to the point of ejecting lava and ash or both in an eruption through the narrow vent. The vent can simply be blown off if there is sufficient pressure.

Other volcanoes on the island sometimes literally blow their top. Massive explosions can cause the whole summit to cave in, blasting away an enormous crater. The result is known as a caldera, within which it is not unusual for new cones to emerge, creating volcanoes within volcanoes. There are several impressive calderas on Gran Canaria, most notably Caldera de Bandama. Oddly enough, massive Caldera de Taburiente on La Palma does not belong to this group of geological phenomena, although it was long thought to.

These days in the Canary Islands, you can best get a feel for the rumblings below the surface on Lanzarote, where the Montañas del Fuego still bubble with vigour, although the last eruptions took place way back in 1824. Of the remaining islands, not an eruptive burp has been heard from Fuerteventura, Gran Canaria, La Gomera or El Hierro for centuries; Tenerife's most recent display was a fairly innocuous affair in 1909; and it was La Palma that hosted the most recent spectacle – a fiery outburst by Volcán Teneguía in 1971.

Wild Things
Canaries, Whales & Other Animals

There is wildlife out there, but it tends to be small and shy and largely undetected by the untrained eye. Lizards and birds are the biggest things you'll see – in some cases they are quite big indeed, like the giant lizard of El Hierro. There are around 200 species of birds on the islands, though many are imports from Africa and Europe. Five endemics are found

The Volcanoes of the Canary Islands by Vivente Araña and Juan Carracedo is a series of three volumes about – what else? – Canary Island volcanoes. Lovely photos and informative text.

Nature Trek (www.nature trek.co.uk) is a British-based wildlife-watching tour company that runs an eight-day tour in search of the native wildlife and plants of the Canary Islands.

DRAGON TREES: A LONG, SHADY PAST

Among the more curious trees you will see in the Canary Islands is the *drago* (dragon tree; *Dracaena draco*), which can reach 18m in height and live for centuries.

Having survived the last ice age, it looks different – even a touch prehistoric. Its shape resembles a giant posy of flowers, its trunk and branches being the stems, which break into bunches of long, narrow, silvery-green leaves higher up. As the plant (technically it is not a tree, though it's always referred to as one) grows, it becomes more and more top-heavy. To stabilise itself, the *drago* ingeniously grows roots on the outside of its trunk, eventually creating a second, wider trunk.

What makes the *drago* stranger still is its red sap or resin – known, of course, as 'dragon's blood' – which was traditionally used in medicine.

The plant once played an important role in Canary Island life, for it was beneath the ancient branches of a *drago* that the Guanche Council of Nobles would gather to administer justice.

The *drago* is one of a family of up to 40 species *(Dracaena)* that survived the ice age in tropical and subtropical zones of the Old World, and is one of the last representatives of Tertiary-era flora.

in the Canaries: Bolle's Pigeon, Laurel Pigeon, Blue Chaffinch, Canary Islands Chiff-Chaff and Canary Islands Chat. And yes, before you ask, this is where canaries come from but the wild cousins are of a much duller colour than the popular cage birds.

If it's big animals you want you need to turn to the ocean. The stretch of water between Tenerife and La Gomera is a traditional feeding ground for as many as 26 species of whales, and others pass through during migration. The most common are pilot whales, sperm whales and bottlenose dolphins.

Whale watching is big business around here, and 800,000 people a year head out on boats to get a look. A law regulates observation of sea mammals, prohibiting boats from getting closer than 60m to an animal and limiting the number of boats following pods at any one time. The law also tries to curb practices such as using sonar and other devices to attract whales' attention. Four small patrol boats attempt to keep a watchful eye on these activities. If you decide to take a whale-watching tour, join up with a reputable company.

Aside from the majestic marine mammals, there are many other life forms busy under the ocean. The waters around the Canary Islands host 350 species of fish. You can see them up close either by going scuba diving or eating a fish dinner. See the Outdoor Activities chapter and the activities sections of individual island chapters for more information.

Wild Books

» *Whales and Dolphins of the Canary Islands* (Volker Boehlke)

» *National Parks and Flora of the Canary Islands* (Otermin Ediciones)

» *Wild Spain: The Animals, Plants and Landscapes* (Teresa Farino)

» *A Field Guide to the Birds of the Atlantic Islands* (Tony Clarke)

Plants

The islands' rich volcanic soil, varied rainfall and dramatic changes in altitude support a surprising diversity of plant life, both indigenous and introduced. The Canary Islands are home to about 2000 species, about half of them endemic to the islands. The only brake on what might otherwise be a still-more-florid display in this largely subtropical environment is the shortage of water. Even so, botanists will have a field day here, and there are numerous botanical gardens scattered about where you can observe a whole range of local flora.

Possibly the most important floral eco-system in the Canaries is La Gomera's Parque Nacional de Garajonay, host to one of the world's last remaining Tertiary-era forests and declared a Unesco World Heritage site. Known as *laurisilva,* the beautiful forest here is made up of laurels, holly, linden and giant heather, clad in lichen and moss and often swathed in swirling mist.

Up in the great volcanic basin of the Parque Nacional del Teide on Tenerife, the star botanical attraction is the flamboyant *tajinaste rojo,* or Teide viper's bugloss *(Echium wildpretii),* which can grow to more than 3m high. Every other spring, it sprouts an extraordinary conical spike of striking red blooms like a great red poker. After its brief, spectacular moment of glory, all that remains is a thin, desiccated, spear-shaped skeleton, like a well-picked-over fish. Leave well alone; each fishbone has thousands of tiny strands that are as itchy as horsehair.

Environmental Issues

The Problems

As in mainland Spain, the 1960s saw the first waves of mass sea-and-sun tourism crash over the tranquil shores of the Canary Islands. The government of the day anticipated filling up the state coffers with easy tourist dollars, and local entrepreneurs enthusiastically leapt aboard the gravy train. Few, however, gave a thought to what impact the tourists and the mushrooming coastal resorts might have on the environment.

The near-unregulated building and expansion of resorts well into the 1980s has created some monumental eyesores, particularly on the southern side of Tenerife and Gran Canaria. Great scabs of holiday villas, hotels and condominiums have spread across much of these two islands' southern coasts. And the problem is not restricted to the resorts – hasty cement extensions to towns and villages mean that parts of the islands' interiors are being increasingly spoiled by property developers and speculators.

The massive influx of visitors to the islands over recent decades has brought or exacerbated other problems. Littering of beaches, dunes and other areas of natural beauty, both by outsiders and locals, remains a burning issue. Occasionally, ecological societies organise massive rubbish clean ups along beaches and the like – worthy gestures but also damning evidence of the extent to which the problem persists.

One of the islands' greatest and most persistent problems is water, or rather the lack of. Limited rainfall and the lack of natural springs have always restricted agriculture, and water is a commodity still in short supply. Desalination appears the only solution for the Canaries; pretty much all potable water on Lanzarote and Fuerteventura is desalinated sea water.

In summer, the corollary of the perennial water problem is the forest fire. With almost clockwork regularity, hundreds of hectares of forest are ravaged every summer on all the islands except the already-bare Lanzarote and Fuerteventura.

If you're interested in getting involved with marine conservation, in particular the protection of whales, get in touch with the Atlantic Whale Foundation (www .whalenation .org), a group that organises educational trips, volunteer opportunities and conservation campaigns on Tenerife. The website is a mine of information.

LIFE ON A VOLCANO ENVIRONMENTAL ISSUES

ENVIRONMENTAL ORGANISATIONS

The islands are swarming with environmental action groups, some more active than others. Most are members of Ben Magec – Ecologistas en Acción (Ben Magec – Ecologists in Action; www.benmagec.org). A few of the myriad individual groups you'll find on the islands are listed below (all websites in Spanish only).

Asociación Tinerfeña de Amigos de la Naturaleza (www.atan.org; Tenerife)
El Guincho (www.benmagec.org/elguincho; Lanzarote)
Guanil (www.ecologistasenaccion.org; Fuerteventura)
Tagaragunche (www.tagaragunche.com; La Gomera)

The Arguments

For the islands' administrators, it's a conundrum. Tourism has come to represent an essential pillar of the Canaries' economy, which quite simply it cannot do without. They argue that profits from the tourist trade are ploughed back into the community. However, this is still fairly haphazard and there have long been calls for more regional planning – and, every year more insistently, for a total moratorium on yet more tourism development. Short-term moratoriums are at times established on an island-by-island basis. Some of the damage done over the years, especially to the coastline, is irreversible.

One of the hottest issues of recent years is the proposed port of Granadilla, a huge commercial port slated to be built in southeastern Tenerife. For more on this, see p148.

The basic issue is prosperity (or perceived prosperity) versus preservation, and it's repeated across the islands. In La Palma, politicians have proposed building five new golf courses, some on protected land, while ecologists say the golf courses would unnecessarily destroy natural resources. On Gran Canaria, a new shopping centre in Gáldar is causing concern, while around Lanzarote and Fuerteventura the buzz about possible offshore petroleum deposits is stirring the environmentalists.

One island that's taken steps towards conservation is El Hierro, where, in 2007, the government unveiled a plan to become the world's first island able to meet all its energy needs with renewable sources (wind, water and solar) alone.

For the latest on what's riling ecologists on the islands, check into www.atan.org, which contains a treasure-trove of passionate articles denouncing poor ecological practices on Tenerife.

Survival Guide

Directory A–Z

Customs Regulations

Although the Canary Islands are part of Spain, for customs purposes they are not considered part of the EU. For this reason, allowances are much less generous than for goods bought within EU countries. You are allowed to bring in or take out, duty free a maximum of the following items:

» 2L of still wine
» 1L of spirits (or 2L of fortified wine)
» 60mL of perfume, 250mL of *eau de toilette*
» 200 cigarettes
» €175 worth of other goods and gifts

Activities

The Canaries are a great destination for some fun in the sun and there is a diverse range of activities offered for young and old. For more details, see the Outdoor Activities chapter (p24).

Business Hours

Reviews in this guidebook won't list business hours unless they differ from the following standards. These standard opening hours are for high season only; hours tend to decrease outside that time.

Banks: 8.30am-2pm Mon-Fri

Bars: 7pm-midnight

Post offices: 8.30am-8.30pm Mon-Fri, 9.30am-1pm Sat (large cities); 8.30am-2.30pm Mon-Fri, 9.30am-1pm Sat (elsewhere)

Restaurants: meals served 1-4pm & 8pm-late

Shops: 10am-2pm & 5-9pm Mon-Fri, 10am-2pm Sat

Supermarkets: 9am-9pm Mon-Sat

Climate

Las Palmas de Gran Canaria

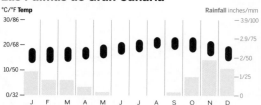

Puerto del Rosario

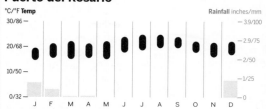

Santa Cruz de Tenerife

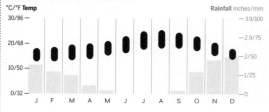

Discount Cards

To receive any discount, photo ID is essential.

Seniors Reduced prices for people over 60 or 65 (depending on place) at various museums and attractions and occasionally on transport.

Students Discounts (usually half the normal fee) for students. Not accepted everywhere.

Electricity

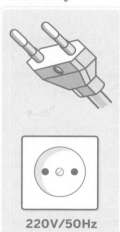

220V/50Hz

Embassies & Consulates

The following countries all have their main diplomatic representation in Madrid but also have consular representation in Las Palmas de Gran Canaria.

France (✆928 29 23 71; www.ambafrance-es.org; Calle Néstor de la Torre 12)

Netherlands (✆928 36 22 51; www.embajadapaisesbajos .es; Calle León y Castillo 244)

UK (✆928 26 25 08; www .ukinspain.com; Calle Luis Morote 6, 3rd fl)

USA (✆928 27 12 59; www.embuta.es; Calle Martínez de Escobar 3)

Countries that have consular representation in Santa Cruz de Tenerife include:

France (✆922 23 27 10; www .ambafrance-es.org; Calle José María de Villa 1)

Ireland (✆922 24 56 71; www .embassyofireland.es; Calle Castillo 8, 4th fl)

Netherlands (✆922 27 17 21; www.embajadapaisesbajos.es; Calle Villalba Hervás 5, 3rd fl)

UK (✆922 28 68 63; www .ukinspain.com; Plaza General Weyler 8, 1st fl)

Food & Drink

Throughout this guidebook, the order of restaurant listings follow the author's preference, and each place to eat is accompanied by one of the following pricing symbols. Prices are per main dish per person.

» €   under €7
» €€   €7 to €12
» €€€   over €12

Sitting inside rather than on the outdoor terrace can often save you 10% to 20% of the bill. See p256 for information on tipping. For more information on food and drinks, see the Island Cuisine chapter (p237).

Gay & Lesbian Travellers

Gay and lesbian marriages are both legal in Spain and hence on the Canary Islands. The Playa del Inglés and the Maspalomas dunes, on the southern end of Gran Canaria, is where the bulk of Europe's gay crowd heads when holidaying in the Canaries, and the nightlife here bumps and grinds year-round. By day, nudist beaches are popular spots to hang out.

Spanish people generally adopt a live-and-let-live attitude to sexuality, so you shouldn't have any hassles in the Canary Islands. That said, some small rural towns may not quite know how to deal with overt displays of affection between same-sex couples.

Useful websites:
Altihay (www.altihay.org, in Spanish) Fuerteventura-

PRACTICALITIES

» **Currency**: euro

» **Weights & measures**: metric

» **Local newspapers & magazines**: include *Diario de Avisos*, *La Gaceta de Canarias*, *Canarias 7*, *La Provincia* and the English-language *Island Connections*. You can also get Spanish newspapers *El País* and *El Mundo* and the foreign *International Herald Tribune*, *Hello!* and all the English and German tabloids.

» **Radio**: Radio Nacional de España has four stations. Local FM stations abound on the islands and the BBC World Service (www.bbc.co.uk/worldservice) can be found mainly on 6195kHz, 9410kHz, 12095kHz and 15485kHz.

» **TV**: the Canaries receives the mainland's big TV channels (TVE1, La 2, Antena 3, Tele 5) and has a few local stations that are of very limited interest.

» **Smoking**: On 2 January 2011 Spain's tough new antismoking law took effect, prohibiting smoking in all bars and restaurants, as well as on TV broadcasts, near hospitals or in school playgrounds.

HEALTH

Availability of Health Care

Spain has an excellent health-care system that extends to the Canary Islands. If you need an ambulance, call ☑112 (the pan-European emergency telephone number which can be called for urgent medical assistance). An alternative medical emergency number is ☑061. Alternatively, go straight to the *urgencias* (casualty) section of the nearest hospital.

Farmacias (pharmacies) offer valuable advice and sell over-the-counter medication. Throughout the Canaries, a system of *farmacias de guardia* (duty pharmacies) operates so that each district has one open all the time. When a pharmacy is closed, it posts the name of the nearest open one on the door. The standard of dental care is usually good; however, it is sensible to have a dental-check up before a long trip.

Health Insurance

For EU citizens, the European Health Insurance Card (EHIC), which you apply for online, by phone or by post, covers most medical care. It doesn't cover non-emergencies or emergency repatriation home.

Citizens from other countries should find out whether there is a reciprocal arrangement for free medical care between their country and Spain. If you need health insurance, strongly consider a policy that covers the worst possible scenario, such as an accident requiring an emergency flight home. Find out in advance if your insurance plan will make direct payments to providers or reimburse you later for overseas health expenditures.

Altitude Sickness

If you are hiking at altitude (such as at El Teide in Tenerife), altitude sickness may be a risk. Lack of oxygen at high altitudes affects most people to some extent. Symptoms of Acute Mountain Sickness (AMS) usually develop during the first 24 hours at altitude, but may be delayed up to three weeks. Mild symptoms include headache, lethargy, dizziness, difficulty sleeping and loss of appetite. AMS may become more severe without warning and can be fatal. Severe symptoms include breathlessness, a dry irritating cough, severe headache and lack of balance.

Treat mild symptoms by resting at the same altitude until you recover, usually for a day or two. Paracetamol or aspirin can be taken for headaches. If symptoms worsen immediate descent is necessary: even 500m can help.

Heat Exhaustion

Heat exhaustion occurs following excessive fluid loss with inadequate replacement of fluids and salt. Symptoms include headache, dizziness and tiredness. Dehydration is already happening by the time you feel thirsty – aim to drink sufficient water to produce pale, diluted urine. To treat heat exhaustion, replace fluids through water and/or fruit juice and cool the body with cold water and fans.

Required Vaccinations

No jabs are required to travel to Spain. The World Health Organization (WHO), however, recommends that all travellers should be covered for diphtheria, tetanus, measles, mumps, rubella and polio, regardless of their destination. Since most vaccines don't provide immunity until at least two weeks after they're given, visit a physician at least six weeks before departure.

Water

Tap water is generally safe to drink throughout the Canary Islands. If you are in any doubt, ask *¿Es potable el agua (de grifo)?* (Is the (tap) water drinkable?). Do not drink from lakes as it may contain bacteria or viruses that can cause diarrhoea or vomiting.

based gay association offering support and advice.
Gamá (www.colectivogama .com, in Spanish) Gay and lesbian association covering the entire archipelago.
Pink Canaries (www .pinkcanaries.com, in Spanish) Gay and lesbian association based in Tenerife, covering clubs, restaurants and gay-friendly accommodation.

Insurance

A travel-insurance policy to cover theft, loss and medical problems and cancellation or delays to your travel arrangements is a good idea. Paying for your ticket with a credit card can often provide limited travel-accident insurance and you may be able to reclaim the payment if the operator doesn't deliver. Worldwide travel insurance is available at www.lonely planet.com/travel_services. You can buy, extend and claim online anytime – even if you're already on the road.

Internet Access

Wi-fi Increasingly available at most hotels and in some cafes, restaurants and airports; generally, but not always, free. Connection speed often varies from room to room in hotels, so always ask when you check in. Hotels offering wi-fi are indicated throughout this book with an icon 🛜. If they, instead, have a public-access computer terminal, the icon is @.
Internet cafes Good cyber-cafes that last the distance are increasingly hard to find: ask at the local tourist office. Prices per hour range from €1.50 to €3.

Language Courses

Tenerife is particularly noted for its Spanish language courses; the following

organisations have a reputable name:
Canarias Cultural (www .canarias-cultural.com) Santa Cruz de Tenerife.
Don Quijote (www.donquijote .org) Puerto de la Cruz, Tenerife.
Galfir (www.galfir.com) La Laguna, Tenerife.
Study Abroad International (www.study abroadinternational.com) Las Palmas de Gran Canaria.

Legal Matters

Should you be arrested, you will be allotted the free services of an *abogado de oficio* (duty solicitor), who may speak only Spanish. You are also entitled to make a phone call. If you use this call to contact your embassy or consulate, it will probably be able to do no more than refer you to a lawyer who speaks your language. If you end up in court, the authorities are obliged to provide a translator if you have to testify.

In theory, you are supposed to have your national ID card or passport with you at all times. If asked for it by the police, you are supposed to be able to produce it on the spot. In practice it is rarely an issue and many people choose to leave passports in hotel safes.

There are three main types of *policía:* the Policía Local, the Policía Nacional and the Guardia Civil. But, should you need to contact the police, don't agonise over which kind to approach: any of them will do, but you may find that the Policía Local is the most helpful. The Canary Islands government provides a toll-free telephone number (📞112), which ensures that any emergency situation can be attended to by the nearest police available.

Money

The most convenient way to bring your money is in the form of a debit or credit card, with some extra cash for use in case of an emergency. You'll find information on exchange rates and costs on pp14-15.
ATMs The Canary Islands has a surfeit of banks, and pretty much every one has a multilingual *cajeros automáticos* (ATM). Remember that there is usually a charge of between 1.5% and 2% on ATM cash withdrawals abroad.
Cash Even if you're using a credit card you'll make a lot of your purchases with cash, so you need to carry some all the time. Small restaurants and shops may not accept cards.
Credit Cards All major *tarjetas de crédito* (credit cards) and debit cards are widely accepted. They can be used for many purchases (including at petrol stations and larger supermarkets, which sometimes ask to see some form of ID) and in hotels and restaurants (although smaller establishments tend to accept cash only).
Moneychangers You'll find exchange facilities at most air and sea ports on the islands. In resorts and cities that attract swarms of foreigners, you'll find them easily – they're usually indicated by the word *cambio* (exchange). Most of the time, they offer longer opening hours and quicker service than banks, but worse exchange rates. Wherever you change money, ask from the outset about commission, the terms of which differ from place to place, and confirm that exchange rates are as posted. A typical commission is 3%. Places that advertise 'no commission' usually make

up the difference by offering poorer exchange rates.

Tipping Menu prices include a service charge. Most people leave some small change if they're satisfied; 5% is normally fine and 10% extremely generous. Porters will generally be happy with €1. Taxi drivers don't have to be tipped but a little rounding up won't go amiss.

Travellers Cheques Increasingly overlooked by card-wielding travellers, travellers cheques are a dying breed. They should not, however, be written off entirely as they're an excellent form of backup, especially as you can claim a refund if they're stolen, providing you've kept a separate record of their numbers. Amex, Visa and Travelex cheques are the easiest to cash, particularly if in US dollars, British pounds or euros. Increasingly, banks are charging hefty commissions, though, even on cheques denominated in euros. Whatever currency they are in, travellers cheques can be difficult to exchange in smaller towns. Always take your passport as identification when cashing travellers cheques. For lost or stolen cheques, call:

Amex (✆800 91 49 12);
MasterCard (✆800 87 08 66);
Travelex (✆800 87 20 50); or
Visa (✆800 87 41 55).

Public Holidays

There are at least 14 official holidays a year in the Canary Islands. When a holiday falls close to a weekend, locals like to make a *puente* (bridge) – meaning they also take the intervening day off. On occasion, when a couple of holidays fall close to the same weekend, the *puente* becomes an *acueducto* (aqueduct)!

Following are the major national holidays, observed throughout the islands and the rest of Spain:

Año Nuevo (New Year's Day) 1 January

Día de los Reyes Magos (Three Kings Day) 6 January

Viernes Santo (Good Friday) March/April

Fiesta del Trabajo (Labour Day) 1 May

La Asunción de la Virgen (Feast of the Assumption) 15 August

Día de la Hispanidad (National Day) 12 October

Todos los Santos (All Saint's Day) 1 November. Gets particular attention on Tenerife.

La Inmaculada Concepción (Feast of the Immaculate Conception) 8 December

Navidad (Christmas) 25 December

In addition, the regional government sets a further five holidays, while local councils allocate another two. Common holidays include the following:

Martes de Carnival (Carnival Tuesday) February/March

Día de San Juan (St John's Day) 19 March

Jueves Santo (Maundy Thursday) March/April

Día de las Islas Canarias (Canary Islands Day) 30 May

Corpus Christi (the Thursday after the eighth Sunday after Easter Sunday) June.

Día de Santiago Apóstol (Feast of St James the Apostle, Spain's patron saint) 25 July. In Santa Cruz de Tenerife the day also marks the commemoration of the defence of the city against Horatio Nelson.

Día del Pino (Pine Tree Day) 8 September. This is particularly important on Gran Canaria.

Día de la Constitución (Constitution Day) 6 December

Telephone

Pay Phones

Public telephones are less prevalent these days, but the distinctive blue boxes can still be spotted throughout the islands; they accept coins, phonecards (*tarjetas telefónicas*) and, in some cases, various credit cards. Expect high prices from hotel-lobby payphones.

Mobile Phones

If you have a GSM, dual- or tri-band cellular mobile (cell) phone you can buy SIM cards and prepaid time.

All the Spanish phone companies (including Orange, Vodofone and Movistar) offer prepaid accounts for mobiles. You can then top up the cards in their shops or outlets, such as supermarkets and tobacconists.

The Canaries uses GSM 900/1800, which is compatible with the rest of Europe and Australia but not with the North American GSM 1900 or the system used in Japan. From those countries, you will need to travel with a tri-band or quadric-band phone.

On 1 July 2010 the EU's new Roaming Regulation came into force. It reduced roaming charges and set in place measures designed to prevent travellers from running up massive bills. Check with your mobile provider for more information.

Phone Codes

» **Mobile phone numbers** start with 6

» **International access code** ✆00

» **Canary Islands country code** ✆34 (same as Spain)

» **Island area codes** Gran Canaria, Lanzarote and Fuerteventura ✆928; Tenerife, La Gomera, La Palma and El Hierro ✆922

» **National toll-free number** ✆900

Phonecards

You can buy phonecards at tobacco stands, newsstands and at the *locutorios* (private call centres). In any case, there is an endless variety of phonecards, each with its own pricing scheme. The best card for you will depend on where you plan to call.

Time

The Canary Islands are on Greenwich Mean Time (GMT/UTC), plus an hour in summer for daylight-saving time. The islands keep the same time as the UK, Ireland and Portugal and are always an hour behind mainland Spain and most of Europe. Daylight-saving (summer) time starts on the last Sunday in March, when clocks are put forward one hour. Clocks are put back an hour on the last Sunday in October.

Australia During the Australian winter (Spanish summer), subtract nine hours from Australian Eastern Standard Time to get Canary Islands' time; during the Australian summer, subtract 10 hours.

Morocco Neighbouring Morocco is on GMT/UTC year-round – so in summer it is an hour behind the Canary Islands even though it's further east.

US Canary Islands' time is US Eastern Time plus five hours and US Pacific Time plus eight hours.

Although the 24-hour clock is used in most situations, you'll find people generally use the 12-hour clock in everyday conversations.

Toilets

Public toilets are not common and rarely inviting. The easiest option is to wander into a bar or cafe and use its facilities. The polite thing to do is to have a coffee or the

like before or after, but you're unlikely to raise too many eyebrows if you don't. This said, some curmudgeonly places in popular tourist areas post notices saying that their toilets are for customers only.

The cautious carry some toilet paper with them when out and about as many toilets lack it. If there's a bin beside the loo, put paper and so on in it – it's probably there because the local sewage system has trouble coping.

Tourist Information

All major towns in the Canary Islands have a tourist office, and while you may have to wait patiently and politely to be attended to, you can eventually get very good maps and information about the area. Though the Canary government offers region-wide and island-specific information on its excellent website www.turismode canarias.com, the tourist offices themselves are run by the *cabildos* (governments) of each island.

The major airports also have tourist offices which are a good source of information and can also assist with last-minute accommodation bookings.

Travellers with Disabilities

Sadly, the Canary Islands are not geared towards smooth travel for disabled people. Most restaurants, shops and tourist sights are not equipped to handle wheelchairs, although the more expensive accommodation options will have rooms with appropriate facilities. Transport is tricky, although you should be able to organise a specially modified hire car from one of the international hire companies (with

advance warning). In fact, advance warning is always a good idea; start with your travel agent and see what it can offer in terms of information and assistance. In the archipelago's cities, such as Las Palmas and Santa Cruz, some buildings (eg museums or government offices) have Braille in the lifts, and some specially textured floors before stairs, but not much else. Few concessions are made in the public infrastructure for deaf people.

Mobility Equipment Hire

Mobility Abroad (www .mobilityabroad.com) A long-standing company with outlets in Gran Canaria, Lanzarote and Tenerife. **Orange Badge** (☑922 79 73 55; www.orangebadge.com, Avenida Amsterdam, Los Cristianos, Tenerife) Wheelchair and mobility scooter hire in Tenerife.

Organisations

Accessible Travel & Leisure (☑01452-729739; www.accessibletravel.co.uk; Avionics House, Naas Lane, Quedgeley, Gloucester GL2 2SN) Claims to be the biggest UK travel agent dealing with travel for the disabled, and encourages the disabled to travel independently. **Society for Accessible Travel & Hospitality** (☑212 447 7284; www.sath.org; 347 Fifth Ave, Ste 605, New York, NY 10016) Although largely concentrated on the USA, this organisation can provide general information.

Visas

Spain is one of the 25 member countries of the Schengen Convention, under which 22 EU countries (all but Bulgaria, Cyprus, Ireland, Romania and the UK) plus Iceland, Norway and Switzerland have abolished checks at common borders.

The visa situation for entering Spain is as follows:

Citizens or residents of EU & Schengen countries No visa required.

Citizens or residents of Australia, Canada, Israel, Japan, NZ and the US No visa required for tourist visits of up to 90 days.

Other countries Check with a Spanish embassy or consulate.

To work or study in Spain A special visa may be required – contact a Spanish embassy or consulate before travel.

Extensions & Residence

Schengen visas cannot be extended. You can apply for no more than two visas in any 12-month period and they are not renewable once in the Canary Islands. Nationals of EU countries, Iceland, Norway and Switzerland can enter and leave the archipelago at will and don't need to apply for a *tarjeta de residencia* (residence card), although they are supposed to apply for residence papers.

People of other nationalities who want to stay in Spain longer than 90 days have to get a residence card, and for them it can be a drawn-out process, starting with an appropriate visa issued by a Spanish consulate in their country of residence. Start the process well in advance.

Volunteering

If you're interested in getting involved with marine conservation, in particular the protection of whales, get in touch with the **Atlantic Whale Foundation** (www .whalenation.org), a group that organises educational trips, volunteer opportunities and conservation campaigns on Tenerife. The website is a mine of information.

Women Travellers

Harassment is much less frequent than the stereotypes of Spain would have you believe, and the country has one of the developed world's lowest incidences of reported rape. Any unpleasantness you might encounter is more likely to come from drunken northern-European yobs in the big resorts than from the locals.

In towns you may get the occasional unwelcome stare, catcall or unnecessary comment, to which the best (and most galling) response is indifference. Don't get paranoid about what's being called out; the *piropo* – a harmless, mildly flirty compliment – is deeply ingrained in Spanish society and, if well delivered, even considered gallant.

Topless bathing and skimpy clothes are generally OK at the coastal resorts, but otherwise a little more modesty is the norm. Quite a few local young women feel no compunction about dressing to kill, but equally feel absolutely no obligation to respond to any male interest this arouses.

Work

EU, Norway and Iceland nationals are allowed to work anywhere in Spain (including the Canary Islands) without a visa, but if they plan to stay more than three months they are supposed to apply within the first month for a residence card. Virtually everyone else is supposed to obtain (from a Spanish consulate in their country of residence) a work permit and, if they plan to stay more than 90 days, a residence visa. While jobs (especially in tourist resorts) aren't that hard to come by, the procedures necessary to get your paperwork in order can be difficult and time-consuming.

Transport

GETTING THERE & AWAY

Getting to the Canary Islands is a cinch. Low-cost carriers are plentiful from all over Europe, particularly from Germany, the UK and Spain. Flights, tours and rail tickets can be booked online at www.lonelyplanet.com /travel_services.

Entering the Canary Islands

Citizens of the European Union (EU) member states and Switzerland can travel to the Canary Islands with just their national identity card. Nationals of the UK have to carry a full passport (UK visitor passports are not acceptable), and all other nationalities must have a full valid passport.

Check that your passport's expiry date is at least six months away, or you may not be granted a visa, should you need one.

By law you are supposed to have your identity card or passport with you at all times in the Canaries, in case the police ask to see it. In practice, this is unlikely to cause trouble. You might want to carry a photocopy of your documentation instead of the real thing. You will need to flash one of these documents (the original, not the photocopy) for registration when you take a hotel room.

As unfortunate as it is, white Europeans will encounter far less hassle at immigration than black Europeans or Africans. In general, though, you are likely to find the whole deal of flying into a Canary Islands airport remarkably lackadaisical.

Air

All of Spain's airports share the user-friendly website and flight information telephone number of **Aena** (☎902 40 47 04; www.aena.es), the Spanish national airport authority.

All seven Canary islands have airports. Tenerife, Gran Canaria, Lanzarote, Tenerife and, increasingly, La Palma absorb nearly all the direct international flights and those from mainland Spain, while the others are principally for interisland hops.

The following main airports handle international flights:

Tenerife Norte (Los Rodeos) Handles just about all interisland flights and most of those to the Spanish mainland.

Tenerife Sur (Reina Sofía) Handles the remaining scheduled flights, and virtually all charter flights to the island.

Gran Canaria Located 16km south of Las Palmas.

Guasimeta (Lanzarote) Located 6km southwest of the capital, Arrecife.

Dozens of airlines, many of which you'll never have heard of, fly into the Canary Islands; however, there are no non-stop flights from North America to the archipelago.

The following international airlines fly into and out of the Canary Islands.

Aer Lingus (www.aerlingus .com)

Air Berlin (www.airberlin .com)

Air Europa (www.aireuropa .com)

Binter Canarias (www .binternet.com)

British Airways (www .ba.com)

Condor (www.condor.com)

Easyjet (www.easyjet.com)

Iberia (www.iberia.com)

Martinair (www.martinair .com)

Monarch (www.monarch -airlines.com)

Ryan Air (www.ryanair.com)

Spanair (www.spanair.com)

Thomson Fly (www.thomson .co.uk)

Transavia Airlines (www .transavia.com)

Vueling (www.vueling.com)

Sea

Just about everyone flies to the Canaries. The only other alternative (apart from a very long swim) is to take a ferry from mainland Spain.

Acciona Trasmediterránea (☎902 45 46 45; www.tras mediterranea.es) Runs a weekly ferry service between Cádiz on the Spanish mainland and Santa Cruz de Tenerife (47 hours), with stops at Lanzarote (30 hours) and Las Palmas de Gran Canaria (39 hours).
Naviera Armas (☎902 45 65 00; www.navieraarmas .com) Runs a weekly service between Huelva on the Spanish mainland and Las Palmas de Gran Canaria (28 hours) and Santa Cruz de Tenerife (32 hours).

GETTING AROUND

Air

Now that all seven islands have airports, flying between them is an easy and popular option, and it can save serious time if you intend to do some island hopping.
Air Europa (☎902 40 15 01; www.aireuropa.com) Flies to Tenerife (Norte and Sur), Gran Canaria and Lanzarote.
Binter Canarias (☎902 39 13 92; www.bintercanarias.com) Flights to all islands.
Islas Airways (☎902 47 74 78; www.islasairways.com) Flights to all islands except La Gomera.
Spanair (☎902 13 14 15; www.spanair.com) Flies to Tenerife (Norte and Sur), Gran Canaria, Lanzarote and Fuerteventura.

Bicycle

Biking around the islands is an extremely pleasant way to see the sights, but don't necessarily expect drivers to accommodate you (or have much grasp of what it's like to be a cyclist tackling a hairpin bend uphill). Sadly, bicycle lanes in the urban environment are minimal, although beachside boulevards are increasingly incorporating space for bike riding.

If you plan to bring your own bike on a flight, check whether there are any costs associated with bringing your bike and whether you'll need to disassemble and pack your bike for the journey.

Taking your bike on ferries is pretty straightforward, and the good news is it's either free or very cheap.

Bicycle Hire

You can rent mountain bikes and city bikes at various resorts and in the more tourist-orientated areas of the islands. Expect to pay a minimum of €10 per day, with a standard deposit of around €50. Rental rates will include a helmet and some basic equipment.

Las Palmas de Gran Canaria offers free bicycle hire with several pick-up and drop-off locations throughout the city. See www.biciambiental.org/ for more information.

Boat

The islands are connected by ferries, 'fast ferries' and jetfoils. There are three main companies:
Acciona Trasmediterránea (☎902 45 46 45; www.tras mediterranea.com)
Fred Olsen (☎902 10 01 07; www.fredolsen.es)
Naviera Armas (☎902 45 65 00; www.navieraarmas.com)

See individual island chapters for detailed route information.

Do bear in mind that times and prices – and even routes – can and do change. This isn't so important on major routes, where there's plenty of choice, but it can mean a big delay if you're planning to travel a route that has only a couple of boats per day, or even per week. See the colour map at the front of the book for interisland ferry routes.

Bus

A bus in the Canary Islands is called a *guagua*, pronounced 'wa-wa'. If you've bounced around Latin America, you'll be familiar with the term. Still, if you ask about *autobuses*, you'll be understood.

Every island has its own interurban service. One way or another, they can get you to most of the main locations but, in many cases, there are few runs each day.

CLIMATE CHANGE & TRAVEL

Every form of transport that relies on carbon-based fuel generates CO_2, the main cause of human-induced climate change. Modern travel is dependent on aeroplanes, which might use less fuel per kilometre per person than most cars but travel much greater distances. The altitude at which aircraft emit gases (including CO_2) and particles also contributes to their climate change impact. Many websites offer 'carbon calculators' that allow people to estimate the carbon emissions generated by their journey and, for those who wish to do so, to offset the impact of the greenhouse gases emitted with contributions to portfolios of climate-friendly initiatives throughout the world. Lonely Planet offsets the carbon footprint of all staff and author travel.

APPROXIMATE DURATIONS FOR MAIN FERRY ROUTES

FROM	TO	DURATION
Lanzarote (Arrecife)	Las Palmas de Gran Canaria	8hr
Lanzarote (Playa Blanca)	Corralejo (Fuerteventura)	20min
Las Palmas (Gran Canaria)	Morro Jable (Fuerteventura)	3hr
Las Palmas (Gran Canaria)	Santa Cruz de Tenerife	2hr, 30min
Agaete (Gran Canaria)	Santa Cruz de Tenerife	1hr
Los Cristianos (Tenerife)	San Sebastián de la Gomera	45min
Santa Cruz de La Palma	Las Palmas de Gran Canaria	13hr, 30min

The larger islands of Tenerife and Gran Canaria have an impressive public-transport system covering the whole island. Frequency, however, varies enormously, from a regular service between major towns to a couple of runs per day for transporting workers and school children to/from the capital.

Check the timetable carefully before you travel at the weekend. Even on the larger islands' major runs, a frequent weekday service can trickle off to just a few departures on Saturday and one, or none, on Sunday.

In the larger towns and cities, buses leave from an *estación de guaguas* (bus station). In villages and small towns, they usually terminate on a particular street or plaza. You buy your ticket on the bus. Bus companies include the following:

Arrecife Bus (☑928 81 15 22; www.arrecifebus.com) Frequent service around Arrecife and Lanzarote's tourist areas; services to elsewhere are minimal or nonexistent.

Global (☑902 38 11 10; www.globalsu.net) Provides Gran Canaria with a network of routes, although the service to many rural areas is pretty thin.

Servicio Insular de Guagua (☑922 55 07 29) El Hierro's bus service has reasonable coverage throughout the island.

Servicio Regular Gomera (☑922 14 11 01; www.gomera-island.com/turismo/ingles/guaguas.htm) La Gomera's limited service.

Tiadhe (☑928 85 09 51, 928 85 21 62; www.tiadhe.com) Provides a limited service, with 17 lines operating around Fuerteventura.

TITSA (Transportes Interurbanos de Tenerife SA; ☑922 53 13 00; www.titsa.com) Runs a spider's web of services all over Tenerife.

Transportes Insular La Palma (☑922 41 19 24; www.transporteslapalma.com) Services La Palma with good overall coverage.

Bus Passes

On some of the islands you can buy a Bono Bus card which usually costs €12 or €30. It's sold at bus stations and shops such as newsagents. Insert the card into the machine on the bus, tell the driver where you are going, and the fare will be deducted from the card. You get about 30% off standard fares with the cards, so they are a good investment if you intend to use the buses a lot.

Costs

Fares, especially if you invest in a Bono Bus card, are reasonable. Destinations within each island are calculated pro rata according to distance, so ticket fares vary from €1 to €10 or more.

Car & Motorcycle

In general, renting a car in the Canaries is highly recommended. Bus services tend to be patchy and exploring inland, particularly in Tenerife and Gran Canaria, is only really possible with your own wheels.

Bringing Your Own Vehicle

Unless you're intending to settle on the islands, there's no advantage whatsoever in bringing your own vehicle. Transport costs on the ferry from Cádiz in mainland Spain are high and car-hire rates on the islands are significantly cheaper than in most EU countries. If you're one of the very rare visitors to bring your own vehicle, you will need registration papers and an International Insurance Certificate (or a Green Card). Your insurance company will issue this.

Driving Licences

Although those with a non-EU licence should also have an International Driving Permit, you will find that national licences from countries like Australia, Canada, New Zealand and the USA are usually accepted.

A licence is required for any vehicle over 50cc.

Gasoline (petrol) is much cheaper in the Canary Islands than elsewhere in Spain because it's not taxed as heavily. *Sin plomo* (lead-free) and *diesel* (diesel) petrol are available everywhere with generally two grades on offer for each.

Prices vary slightly between service stations and fluctuate according to oil tariffs, OPEC (Organisation of the Petroleum Exporting Countries) arm twisting and tax policy. You can pay with major credit cards at most service stations.

Hire

All the big international car-rental companies are represented in the Canary Islands and there are also plenty of local operators. To rent a car you need to have a driving licence, be aged 21 or over, and, for the major companies at least, have a credit or debit card. Smaller firms can sometimes live without this last requirement.

If you intend to stay on one island for any length of time, it might be worth booking a car in advance, for example in a fly/drive deal. Car-hire companies include the following:

Avis (☎902 18 08 54; www .avis.es)

Cabrera Medina (☎928 84 62 76; www.cabreramedina .com) Local company that covers all the islands.

Cicar (☎900 20 23 03, UK 0800 960 367, Germany 0800 182 1816; www.cicar.com) Local company that covers all the islands.

Europcar/BC Betacar (☎913 43 45 12; www.europ car.es)

Hertz (☎913 72 93 00; www .hertz.es)

Generally, you can't take a hire car from one island to another without the company's explicit permission. An exception for most companies is the Fuerteventura–Lanzarote sea crossing – most have no problem with you taking your car from one to the other and, in some cases, you can hire on one island and drop the car off on the other.

Insurance

Third-party motor insurance is a minimum requirement in the Canary Islands (and throughout Europe). Be careful to understand what your liabilities and excess are, and what waivers you are entitled to in case of accident or damage to the hired vehicle. Other incidentals (some optional) include collision damage waiver, extra passenger cover and 5% General Indirect Tax to the Canary Islands (IGIC). A European breakdown-assistance policy such as the AA Five Star Service or RAC Eurocover Motoring Assistance can be a good investment. You can ask your insurer for a European Accident Statement form, which can simplify matters in the event of an accident. Note that driving on a dirt road will generally render your policy null and void.

Road Rules

The blood-alcohol limit is 0.05% and random breath-testing is carried out. If you are found to be over the limit you can be fined and deprived of your licence within 24 hours. Nonresident foreigners will be required to pay up on the spot (at 30% of the full fine). Pleading

linguistic ignorance will not help – your traffic cop will produce a list of infringements and fines in as many languages as you like. If you don't pay, or don't have a local resident to act as guarantor for you, your vehicle could be impounded.

Legal driving age for cars 18

Legal driving age for motorcycles & scooters 16 (80cc and over) or 14 (50cc and under); a licence is required.

Motorcyclists Must use headlights at all times and wear a helmet if riding a bike of 125cc or more.

Roundabouts (traffic circles) Vehicles already in the circle have the right of way.

Side of the road Drive on the right.

Speed limits In built-up areas: 50km/h which increases to 100km/h on major roads and up to 120km/h on *autovias* (highways).

Hitching

Hitching is never entirely safe in any country in the world, and we don't recommend it. Travellers who decide to hitch should understand that they are taking a small, but potentially dangerous, risk. People who do choose to hitch will be safer if they travel in pairs and let someone know where they are planning to go.

Hitching is illegal on *auto-vias*. Choose a spot where cars can safely stop before slipways or use minor roads. The going can be slow on the latter and traffic is often light.

Language

WANT MORE?
For in-depth language information and handy phrases, check out Lonely Planet's *Spanish Phrasebook*. You'll find it at **shop .lonelyplanet.com**, or you can buy Lonely Planet's iPhone phrasebooks at the Apple App Store.

The language of the Canary Islands is Spanish (*español*), which many Spanish people refer to as Castilian (*castellano*) to distinguish it from the other tongues spoken in Spain – Catalan (*català*), Galician (*galego*), and Basque (*euskara*).

Spanish pronunciation is straightforward as there's a clear and consistent relationship between what's written and how it's pronounced. In addition, most Spanish sounds are pronounced the same as their English counterparts. The kh in our pronunciation guides is a guttural sound (like the 'ch' in the Scottish *loch*), ny is pronounced as the 'ni' in 'onion', and r is strongly rolled. Those familiar with Spanish might notice the Andalusian or even Latin American lilt of the Canarian accent – 'lli' is pronounced as y and the 'lisp' you might expect with 'z' and 'c' before vowels sounds more like s while the letter 's' itself is hardly pronounced at all – it sounds more like an 'h'– for example, Las Palmas sounds more like Lah Palmah. If you follow our coloured pronunciation guides (with the stressed syllables in italics) you'll be understood just fine.

Spanish nouns and the adjectives that go with them are marked for gender – feminine nouns generally end with -a and masculine ones with -o. Where necessary, both forms are given for the words and phrases in this chapter, separated by a slash and with the masculine form first, eg *perdido/a* (m/f).

When talking to people familiar to you or younger than you, use the informal form of 'you', *tú*, rather than the polite form *Usted*. The polite form is used in the phrases provided in this chapter; where both options are given, they are indicated by the abbreviations 'pol' and 'inf'.

BASICS

Hello.	*Hola.*	o·la
Goodbye.	*Adiós.*	a·dyos
How are you?	*¿Qué tal?*	ke tal
Fine, thanks.	*Bien, gracias.*	byen gra·syas
Excuse me.	*Perdón.*	per·don
Sorry.	*Lo siento.*	lo syen·to
Yes./No.	*Sí./No.*	see/no
Please.	*Por favor.*	por fa·vor
Thank you.	*Gracias.*	gra·syas
You're welcome.	*De nada.*	de na·da

My name is ...
Me llamo ...   me ya·mo ...

What's your name?
¿Cómo se llama Usted?   ko·mo se ya·ma oo·ste (pol)
¿Cómo te llamas?   ko·mo te ya·mas (inf)

Do you speak (English)?
¿Habla (inglés)?   a·bla (een·gles) (pol)
¿Hablas (inglés)?   a·blas (een·gles) (inf)

I (don't) understand.
Yo (no) entiendo.   yo (no) en·tyen·do

ACCOMMODATION

I'd like to book a room.
Quisiera reservar una habitación.   kee·sye·ra re·ser·var oo·na a·bee·ta·syon

How much is it per night/person?
¿Cuánto cuesta por noche/persona?   kwan·to kwes·ta por no·che/per·so·na

Does it include breakfast?
¿Incluye el desayuno?   een·kloo·ye el de·sa·yoo·no

I'd like a ... room.	Quisiera una habitación ...	kee·sye·ra oo·na a·bee·ta·syon ...
single	individual	een·dee·vee·dwal
double	doble	do·ble
campsite	terreno de cámping	te·re·no de kam·peeng
hotel	hotel	o·tel
guesthouse	pensión	pen·syon
youth hostel	albergue juvenil	al·ber·ge khoo·ve·neel
air-con	aire acondicionado	ai·re a·kon·dee·syo·na·do
bathroom	baño	ba·nyo
bed	cama	ka·ma
window	ventana	ven·ta·na

DIRECTIONS

Where's ...?
¿Dónde está ...?   don·de es·ta ...

What's the address?
¿Cuál es la dirección?   kwal es la dee·rek·syon

Could you please write it down?
¿Puede escribirlo, por favor?   pwe·de es·kree·beer·lo por fa·vor

Can you show me (on the map)?
¿Me lo puede indicar (en el mapa)?   me lo pwe·de een·dee·kar (en el ma·pa)

at the corner	en la esquina	en la es·kee·na
at the traffic lights	en el semáforo	en el se·ma·fo·ro
behind ...	detrás de ...	de·tras de ...
far away	lejos	le·khos
in front of ...	enfrente de ...	en·fren·te de ...
left	izquierda	ees·kyer·da
near	cerca	ser·ka
next to ...	al lado de ...	al la·do de ...
opposite ...	frente a ...	fren·te a ...
right	derecha	de·re·cha
straight ahead	todo recto	to·do rek·to

EATING & DRINKING

What would you recommend?
¿Qué recomienda?   ke re·ko·myen·da

What's in that dish?
¿Que lleva ese plato?   ke ye·va e·se pla·to

I don't eat ...
No como ...   no ko·mo ...

That was delicious!
¡Estaba buenísimo!   es·ta·ba bwe·nee·see·mo

KEY PATTERNS

To get by in Spanish, mix and match these simple patterns with words of your choice:

When's (the next flight)?
¿Cuándo sale (el próximo vuelo)?   kwan·do sa·le (el prok·see·mo vwe·lo)

Where's (the station)?
¿Dónde está (la estación)?   don·de es·ta (la es·ta·syon)

Where can I (buy a ticket)?
¿Dónde puedo (comprar un billete)?   don·de pwe·do (kom·prar oon bee·ye·te)

Do you have (a map)?
¿Tiene (un mapa)?   tye·ne (oon ma·pa)

Is there (a toilet)?
¿Hay (servicios)?   ai (ser·vee·syos)

I'd like (a coffee).
Quisiera (un café).   kee·sye·ra (oon ka·fe)

I'd like (to hire a car).
Quisiera (alquilar un coche).   kee·sye·ra (al·kee·lar oon ko·che)

Can I (enter)?
¿Se puede (entrar)?   se pwe·de (en·trar)

Could you please (help me)?
¿Puede (ayudarme), por favor?   pwe·de (a·yoo·dar·me) por fa·vor

Do I have to (get a visa)?
¿Necesito (obtener un visado)?   ne·se·see·to (ob·te·ner oon vee·sa·do)

Please bring the bill.
Por favor nos trae la cuenta.   por fa·vor nos tra·e la kwen·ta

Cheers!
¡Salud!   sa·loo

I'd like to book a table for ...	Quisiera reservar una mesa para ...	kee·sye·ra re·ser·var oo·na me·sa pa·ra ...
(eight) o'clock	las (ocho)	las (o·cho)
(two) people	(dos) personas	(dos) per·so·nas

Key Words

appetisers	aperitivos	a·pe·ree·tee·vos
bar	bar	bar
bottle	botella	bo·te·ya
bowl	bol	bol
breakfast	desayuno	de·sa·yoo·no
cafe	café	ka·fe

Signs

Abierto	Open
Cerrado	Closed
Entrada	Entrance
Hombres	Men
Mujeres	Women
Prohibido	Prohibited
Salida	Exit
Servicios/Aseos	Toilets

children's menu	menú infantil	me·noo een·fan·teel
(too) cold	(muy) frío	(mooy) free·o
dinner	cena	se·na
food	comida	ko·mee·da
fork	tenedor	te·ne·dor
glass	vaso	va·so
highchair	trona	tro·na
hot (warm)	caliente	ka·lyen·te
knife	cuchillo	koo·chee·yo
lunch	comida	ko·mee·da
main course	segundo plato	se·goon·do pla·to
market	mercado	mer·ka·do
menu (in English)	menú (en inglés)	oon me·noo (en een·gles)
plate	plato	pla·to
restaurant	restaurante	res·tow·ran·te
spoon	cuchara	koo·cha·ra
supermarket	supermercado	soo·per·mer·ka·do
with/without	con/sin	kon/seen
vegetarian food	comida vegetariana	ko·mee·da ve·khe·ta·rya·na

Meat & Fish

beef	carne de vaca	kar·ne de va·ka
chicken	pollo	po·yo
duck	pato	pa·to
fish	pescado	pes·ka·do
lamb	cordero	kor·de·ro
pork	cerdo	ser·do
turkey	pavo	pa·vo
veal	ternera	ter·ne·ra

Fruit & Vegetables

apple	manzana	man·sa·na
apricot	albaricoque	al·ba·ree·ko·ke
artichoke	alcachofa	al·ka·cho·fa
asparagus	espárragos	es·pa·ra·gos
banana	plátano	pla·ta·no
beans	judías	khoo·dee·as
beetroot	remolacha	re·mo·la·cha
cabbage	col	kol
carrot	zanahoria	sa·na·o·rya
celery	apio	a·pyo
cherry	cereza	se·re·sa
corn	maíz	ma·ees
cucumber	pepino	pe·pee·no
fruit	fruta	froo·ta
grape	uvas	oo·vas
lemon	limón	lee·mon
lentils	lentejas	len·te·khas
lettuce	lechuga	le·choo·ga
mushroom	champiñón	cham·pee·nyon
nuts	nueces	nwe·ses
onion	cebolla	se·bo·ya
orange	naranja	na·ran·kha
peach	melocotón	me·lo·ko·ton
peas	guisantes	gee·san·tes
(red/green) pepper	pimiento (rojo/verde)	pee·myen·to (ro·kho/ver·de)
pineapple	piña	pee·nya
plum	ciruela	seer·we·la
potato	patata	pa·ta·ta
pumpkin	calabaza	ka·la·ba·sa
spinach	espinacas	es·pee·na·kas
strawberry	fresa	fre·sa
tomato	tomate	to·ma·te
vegetable	verdura	ver·doo·ra
watermelon	sandía	san·dee·a

Other

bread	pan	pan
butter	mantequilla	man·te·kee·ya
cheese	queso	ke·so
egg	huevo	we·vo
honey	miel	myel
jam	mermelada	mer·me·la·da
oil	aceite	a·sey·te
pasta	pasta	pas·ta
pepper	pimienta	pee·myen·ta
rice	arroz	a·ros
salt	sal	sal
sugar	azúcar	a·soo·kar
vinegar	vinagre	vee·na·gre

Drinks

beer	cerveza	ser·ve·sa
coffee	café	ka·fe
(orange) juice	zumo (de naranja)	soo·mo (de na·ran·kha)
milk	leche	le·che
tea	té	te
(mineral) water	agua (mineral)	a·gwa (mee·ne·ral)
(red) wine	vino (tinto)	vee·no (teen·to)
(white) wine	vino (blanco)	vee·no (blan·ko)

EMERGENCIES

Help!	¡Socorro!	so·ko·ro
Go away!	¡Vete!	ve·te
Call ...!	¡Llame a ...!	ya·me a ...
a doctor	un médico	oon me·dee·ko
the police	la policía	la po·lee·see·a

I'm lost.
Estoy perdido/a.   es·toy per·dee·do/a (m/f)

I had an accident.
He tenido un accidente.   e te·nee·do oon ak·see·den·te

I'm ill.
Estoy enfermo/a.   es·toy en·fer·mo/a (m/f)

It hurts here.
Me duele aquí.   me dwe·le a·kee

I'm allergic to (antibiotics).
Soy alérgico/a a (los antibióticos).   soy a·ler·khee·ko/a a (los an·tee·byo·tee·kos) (m/f)

SHOPPING & SERVICES

I'd like to buy ...
Quisiera comprar ...   kee·sye·ra kom·prar ...

I'm just looking.
Sólo estoy mirando.   so·lo es·toy mee·ran·do

May I look at it?
¿Puedo verlo?   pwe·do ver·lo

I don't like it.
No me gusta.   no me goos·ta

Question Words		
How?	¿Cómo?	ko·mo
What?	¿Qué?	ke
When?	¿Cuándo?	kwan·do
Where?	¿Dónde?	don·de
Who?	¿Quién?	kyen
Why?	¿Por qué?	por ke

How much is it?
¿Cuánto cuesta?   kwan·to kwes·ta

That's too expensive.
Es muy caro.   es mooy ka·ro

Can you lower the price?
¿Podría bajar un poco el precio?   po·dree·a ba·khar oon po·ko el pre·syo

There's a mistake in the bill.
Hay un error en la cuenta.   ai oon e·ror en la kwen·ta

ATM	cajero automático	ka·khe·ro ow·to·ma·tee·ko
credit card	tarjeta de crédito	tar·khe·ta de kre·dee·to
internet cafe	cibercafé	see·ber·ka·fe
post office	correos	ko·re·os
tourist office	oficina de turismo	o·fee·see·na de too·rees·mo

TIME & DATES

What time is it?	¿Qué hora es?	ke o·ra es
It's (10) o'clock.	Son (las diez).	son (las dyes)
Half past (one).	Es (la una) y media.	es (la oo·na) ee me·dya
morning	mañana	ma·nya·na
afternoon	tarde	tar·de
evening	noche	no·che
yesterday	ayer	a·yer
today	hoy	oy
tomorrow	mañana	ma·nya·na
Monday	lunes	loo·nes
Tuesday	martes	mar·tes
Wednesday	miércoles	myer·ko·les
Thursday	jueves	khwe·bes
Friday	viernes	vyer·nes
Saturday	sábado	sa·ba·do
Sunday	domingo	do·meen·go
January	enero	e·ne·ro
February	febrero	fe·bre·ro
March	marzo	mar·so
April	abril	a·breel
May	mayo	ma·yo
June	junio	khoo·nyo
July	julio	khoo·lyo
August	agosto	a·gos·to
September	septiembre	sep·tyem·bre
October	octubre	ok·too·bre
November	noviembre	no·vyem·bre
December	diciembre	dee·syem·bre

Numbers

1	*uno*	*oo·no*
2	*dos*	dos
3	*tres*	tres
4	*cuatro*	*kwa·*tro
5	*cinco*	*seen·*ko
6	*seis*	seys
7	*siete*	*sye·*te
8	*ocho*	*o·*cho
9	*nueve*	*nwe·*ve
10	*diez*	dyes
20	*veinte*	*veyn·*te
30	*treinta*	*treyn·*ta
40	*cuarenta*	kwa·*ren·*ta
50	*cincuenta*	seen·*kwen·*ta
60	*sesenta*	se·*sen·*ta
70	*setenta*	se·*ten·*ta
80	*ochenta*	o·*chen·*ta
90	*noventa*	no·*ven·*ta
100	*cien*	syen
1000	*mil*	meel

TRANSPORT

Public Transport

boat	*barco*	*bar·*ko
bus	*autobús*	ow·to·*boos*
plane	*avión*	a·*vyon*
train	*tren*	tren
tram	*tranvía*	tran·*vee·*a
first	*primer*	pree·*mer*
last	*último*	*ool·*tee·mo
next	*próximo*	*prok·*see·mo

I want to go to ...
Quisiera ir a ...   kee·*sye·*ra eer a ...

Does it stop at (Vilaflor)?
¿Para en (Vilaflor)?   *pa·*ra en (vee·la·*flor*)

What stop is this?
¿Cuál es esta parada?   kwal es *es·*ta pa·*ra·*da

What time does it arrive/leave?
¿A qué hora llega/sale?   a ke o·ra *ye·*ga/*sa·*le

Please tell me when we get to (Arico Nuevo).
¿Puede avisarme   *pwe·*de a·vee·*sar·*me
cuando lleguemos   *kwan·*do ye·*ge·*mos
a (Arico Nuevo)?   a (a·*ree·*ko *nwe·*vo)

I want to get off here.
Quiero bajarme aquí.   *kye·*ro ba·*khar·*me a·*kee*

a ... ticket	*un billete de ...*	oon bee·*ye·*te de ...
1st-class	*primera clase*	pree·*me·*ra *kla·*se
2nd-class	*segunda clase*	se·*goon·*da *kla·*se
one-way	*ida*	*ee·*da
return	*ida y vuelta*	*ee·*da ee *vwel·*ta
aisle seat	*asiento de pasillo*	a·*syen·*to de pa·*see·*yo
cancelled	*cancelado*	kan·se·*la·*do
delayed	*retrasado*	re·tra·*sa·*do
platform	*plataforma*	pla·ta·*for·*ma
ticket office	*taquilla*	ta·*kee·*ya
timetable	*horario*	o·*ra·*ryo
train station	*estación de trenes*	es·ta·*syon* de *tre·*nes
window seat	*asiento junto a la ventana*	a·*syen·*to *khoon·*to a la ven·*ta·*na

Driving & Cycling

I'd like to hire a ...	*Quisiera alquilar ...*	kee·*sye·*ra al·*kee·*lar ...
4WD	*un todo-terreno*	oon to·do·te·*re·*no
bicycle	*una bicicleta*	*oo·*na bee·see·*kle·*ta
car	*un coche*	oon *ko·*che
motorcycle	*una moto*	*oo·*na *mo·*to
child seat	*asiento de seguridad para niños*	a·*syen·*to de se·goo·ree·*da* pa·ra *nee·*nyos
diesel	*gasóleo*	ga·*so·*lyo
helmet	*casco*	*kas·*ko
mechanic	*mecánico*	me·*ka·*nee·ko
petrol/gas	*gasolina*	ga·so·*lee·*na
service station	*gasolinera*	ga·so·lee·*ne·*ra

Is this the road to ...?
¿Se va a (La Laguna)   se va a (la la·*goo·*na)
por esta carretera?   por *es·*ta ka·re·*te·*ra

(How long) Can I park here?
¿(Por cuánto tiempo)   (por *kwan·*to *tyem·*po)
Puedo aparcar aquí?   *pwe·*do a·par·*kar* a·*kee*

The car has broken down (at Masca).
El coche se ha averiado   el *ko·*che se a·ve·*rya·*do
(en Masca).   (en *mas·*ka)

I have a flat tyre.
Tengo un pinchazo.   *ten·*go oon peen·*cha·*so

I've run out of petrol.
Me he quedado sin   me e ke·*da·*do seen
gasolina.   ga·so·*lee·*na

GLOSSARY

aljibe – water system
artesonado – coffered ceiling
autovía – motorway
ayuntamiento – town hall

barranco – ravine or gorge
barrio – district, quarter (of a town or city)
Bimbaches – indigenous Herreños
bocadillo – sandwich made with baguette bread
bodega – traditional wine bar, or a wine cellar
bote – local variety of shuttle boat developed to service offshore vessels
buceo – scuba diving

cabildo insular – island government
cabra – goat
cabrito – kid (goat)
caldera – cauldron
calle – street
cambio – exchange
cañadas – flatlands
Carnaval – festival celebrating the beginning of Lent, 40 days before Easter
casa rural – a village or country house or farmstead with rooms to let
caserío – traditional farmhouse or hamlet
catedral – cathedral
centro comercial – shopping centre, usually with restaurants, bars and other facilities for tourists
chiringuito – kiosk
churros – fried dough
comida – lunch
Corpus Christi – festival in honour of the Eucharist, held eight weeks after Easter
cruz – cross
cueva – cave

denominación de origen – appellation certifying a high standard and regional origin of wines and certain foods
desayuno – breakfast
drago – dragon tree

ermita – chapel
estación – terminal, station
estación de guaguas – bus terminal/station
estación marítima – ferry terminal

faro – lighthouse
feria – fair
fiesta – festival, public holiday or party
finca – farm

gofio – ground, roasted grain used in place of bread in Canarian cuisine
Gomeros – people from La Gomera
gran – great
guagua – bus
guanarteme – island chief
Guanches – the original inhabitants of the Canaries

Herreños – people from El Hierro
horario – timetable
hostal – commercial establishment providing accommodation in the one- to three-star range; not to be confused with youth hostels (of which there is only one throughout the islands)
hoteles – one- to five-star hotel

IGIC – Impuesto General Indirecto Canario (local version of value-added tax)
iglesia – church

jamón – cured ham

lagarto – lizard
laurisilva – laurel
librería – bookshop
lucha canaria – Canarian wrestling

malpaís – volcanic badlands
malvasía – Malmsey wine
marcha – action, nightlife, 'the scene'
mencey – Guanche king

menú del día – set menu
mercado – market
mesón – old-fashioned restaurant or tavern
mirador – lookout point
mojo – Canarian sauce made with either red chilli peppers, coriander or basil
montaña – mountain
Mudéjar – Islamic-style architecture
muelle – wharf or pier
municipio – town council
museo – museum, gallery

norte – north

Palmeros – people from La Palma
papas arrugadas – wrinkly potatoes
parador – chain of state-owned upmarket hotels
parque nacional – national park
paseo marítimo – seaside promenade
pensión – guesthouse (one- or two-star)
piscina – swimming pool
plateresque – silversmith-like
playa – beach
pozo – well
pueblo – village
puerto – port

ración – large tapas
romería – festive pilgrimage or procession

sabina – juniper
Semana Santa – Holy Week, the week leading up to Easter
señorío – island government deputising for the Spanish crown
s/n – *sin numero* (without number); sometimes seen in street addresses
sur – south

taberna – tavern
tapas – bar snacks originally served on a saucer or lid (*tapa*)

taquilla – box office
tasca – pub, bar
terraza – terrace; outdoor cafe tables
thalassotherapy – warm sea-water treatment

designed to remove stress and physical aches
timple – type of ukulele and the musical symbol of the Canary Islands
Tinerfeños – people from Tenerife

valle – valley
vega – plain, flatlands
volcán – volcano

zumería – juice bar

behind the scenes

SEND US YOUR FEEDBACK

We love to hear from travellers – your comments keep us on our toes and help make our books better. Our well-travelled team reads every word on what you loved or loathed about this book. Although we cannot reply individually to postal submissions, we always guarantee that your feedback goes straight to the appropriate authors, in time for the next edition. Each person who sends us information is thanked in the next edition – and the most useful submissions are rewarded with a free book.

Visit **lonelyplanet.com/contact** to submit your updates and suggestions or to ask for help. Our award-winning website also features inspirational travel stories, news and discussions.

Note: We may edit, reproduce and incorporate your comments in Lonely Planet products such as guidebooks, websites and digital products, so let us know if you don't want your comments reproduced or your name acknowledged. For a copy of our privacy policy visit lonelyplanet.com/privacy.

OUR READERS

Many thanks to the travellers who used the last edition and wrote to us with helpful hints, useful advice and interesting anecdotes:

A Vanessa Ambrosius **B** Dylan Bell, Gerard Berney, Hrvoje Bobinac, Borut Bratuž **C** Margaret Cabrera, Michael Chu, Ian Coldicott, Alastair Cuthbertson **D** Wouter De Sutter **E** Giuseppe Esposito, Lynn Emmerson **G** Jordana Garbati, Spartaco Giolito, Nikolai Grandy, Sandra Grant **H** Daniel Hammerer, Hans Hirschberger, Bärbel Horat **J** Jill and Bill Jackson Joern **K** David Kornhall, Mary Kuhn, Adriana Caznoch Kürten **M** Jose Miguel Martinez, Labiano Marielaura Mozzetti, Gabriele Muellenberg **N** Alice Nishimoto **O** Etain O'Carroll, Kathleen Orth **P** Leo Paton, Mark Polson, Annette Plesner **R** Petr Rabusic, Keith Refault, Michael Rice, Philipp Ringgenberg, Lily Rowe **S** Faith Stern **T** Louise Taffel-Andureau **V** Arie van Oosterwijk **W** Heike Wieland, David Wilson **Z** Ariana Znaor, Tomas Zilinsky

AUTHOR THANKS

Josephine Quintero

A special *gracias* goes to Saro Arenciba from the Las Palmas de Gran Canaria tourist office, to Roger Bradley for his invaluable hiking advice, to Tila and Michelle from Lanzarote-based Eco Resorts, to Robin Chapman for sharing a bottle of wine at the end of a long day and to Kirsty Jones for her inspirational stories about kiteboarding in the Canaries. Thanks also to Dora Whitaker for being an ever-supportive CE and to Stuart Butler, my stellar co-author.

Stuart Butler

Thank you to all the tourist-office staff who helped me out with advice and tips. I'd especially like to thank the staff of the Senderos de Abono (Tenerife) and Ibo Alfaro (La Gomera) hotels for their help (and baby-sitting skills). Thank you also to Peter and Jill Standing for the fantastic hike up Teide. Finally, thanks as always to my wife Heather and baby son Jake for being the best travel companions I could ever have.

ACKNOWLEDGMENTS

Climate map data adapted from Peel MC, Finlayson BL & McMahon TA (2007) 'Updated World Map of the Köppen-Geiger Climate Classification', *Hydrology and Earth System Sciences*, 11, 1633–44.

Cover photograph: Cactus garden, Lanzarote, Camille Moirenc/Corbis. Many of the images in this guide are available for licensing from Lonely Planet Images: www.lonelyplanet images.com.

This Book

This 5th edition of *Canary Islands* was researched and written by Josephine Quintero and Stuart Butler. Josephine, Miles Roddis, Sarah Andrews and Sally O'Brien have all made significant contributions to previous editions. Damien Simonis wrote the 1st edition. This guidebook was commissioned in Lonely Planet's London office, laid out by Cambridge Publishing Management, UK, and produced by the following:

Commissioning Editors Suki Gear, Dora Whitaker

Coordinating Editors Catherine Burch, Andrea Dobbin

Coordinating Cartographer Jacqueline Nguyen

Coordinating Layout Designer Julie Crane

Managing Editors Annelies Mertens, Tasmin Waby McNaughtan, Helen Christinis

Senior Editor Susan Paterson

Managing Cartographers Adrian Persoglia, Amanda Sierp

Managing Layout Designer Jane Hart

Assisting Editors Kathryn Glendenning, Ceinwen Sinclair, Fionnuala Twomey

Cover Research Aude Vauconsant

Internal Image Research Sabrina Dalbesio

Indexer Amanda Jones

Language Content Branislava Vladisavljevic

Thanks to Ryan Evans, Nora Gregory, Daniel Moore, Naomi Parker, Trent Paton, Averil Robertson, Sally Schafer, Gerard Walker

BEHIND THE SCENES

NOTES

index